LYNCHBURG
and
ITS NEIGHBORS

DEDICATED TO THE MEMORY
OF
ROBERT DAVIS YANCEY
BORN SEPTEMBER 15, 1855
DIED JANUARY 3, 1931

Robert Davis Yancey

LYNCHBURG
AND
IT'S NEIGHBORS

By
ROSA FAULKNER YANCEY

Southern Historical Press, Inc.
Greenville, South Carolina

This volume was reproduced from
An 1935 edition located in the
Publisher's private Library

All rights reserved. No part of this publication may be reproduced,
stored in a retrieval system, transmitted in any form, posted
on to the web in any form or by any means without
the prior written permission of the publisher.

Please direct all correspondence and orders to:

www.southernhistoricalpress.com
or
**SOUTHERN HISTORICAL PRESS, Inc.
PO BOX 1267
Greenville, SC   29601
southernhistoricalpress@gmail.com**

Originally published: Richmond, VA 1935
ISBN #978-1-63914-007-7
All rights Reserved.
Printed in the United States of America

CONTENTS

BOOK ONE

CHAPTER		PAGE
I.	Early Days	7
II.	When Tobacco Was King	16
III.	Neighbors	22
IV.	The Water System	32
V.	The Re-establishment of the Colonial Church	36
VI.	Preachers and People	44
VII.	Master and Slave	49
VIII.	Lynchburg in the 1830's	57
IX.	War	66
X.	Battle of Lynchburg	77
XI.	A Few Distinguished Military Records	95
XII.	After Surrender	129
XIII.	Reconstruction	135
XIV.	Recollections and Comment	150
XV.	After the War	163
XVI.	Lynchburg Awakens to New Interests	165
XVII.	Rebuilding	168
XVIII.	The Press	174
XIX.	Public Institutions	181
XX.	An Epic of American Industry	202
XXI.	Lynchburg Poets and Writers	211
XXII.	Negro Songs and Hymns—Other Old Songs and Ballads	230

BOOK TWO

XXIII.	Some Lynchburg Families and Genealogies	241
	Index	450

INTRODUCTION

This work is presented to the public with a feeling of regret that so many people who should have been recorded here have been omitted. It was not our desire that any person who has helped to make Lynchburg history should have been left out of this book, but in many cases data was unavailable, or too inaccessable to be reached. Among the families alluded to are the Almond, Baber, Beasley, Bocock, Bohannon, Breathed, Button, Clift, Cochran, Cohn, Crump, Doyle, Dunn, Engledove, Estes, Folkes, Goggin, Goode, Harris, Hickey, Hickson, Holt, Hughes, Lawson, Lecky, Lemmon, Mays, Moses, O'Brien, Oglesby, Poston, Quinn, Rucker, Sackett, Sneed, Spence, Thaxton, Urquhart, Vaughan, Venable, Waldron, Wall, White, Witt, Woodson, Shelton, Casey and Mallan families, and others equally as important.

There are others to whom we would pay a tribute, inadequate though it be. There were five men killed long ago by a falling wall in the fire that destroyed an entire square on Main Street, May 30th, 1883. The heroes of this disaster were Halsey Gouldman, J. A. Vaughan, J. T. Clement, Captain W. R. Moore and Felix Delbelvre, who were buried in the burning ruins. There were another five men in later years, buried under a falling wall which they were pulling down at the western corner of Fifth and Church Streets. There was Joseph Woodward, a man in his early thirties, who wrecked his automobile, accepting death thereby, rather than run over a little child who had suddenly crossed the street in front of him. And there were those unknown men of that latest and most deplorable of all Lynchburg disasters, those nineteen men who died last Spring when the Transient Bureau on Church and Twelfth Streets was burned down. Let these also be put down in this book of memory.

CHAPTER I

EARLY DAYS

IN OCTOBER, 1786, the Virginia Assembly granted John Lynch the right to set aside forty-five acres of the land he had recently purchased from Edmund Winston, lying contiguous to Lynch's Ferry in the County of Campbell, for the purpose of establishing a town. The trustees in whom the land was vested were John Clarke, Adam Clement, Charles Lynch, John Calloway, Achilles Douglass, William Martin, Jesse Burton, Joseph Stratton, Micajah Moorman, and Charles Brooks, Gentlemen. They were empowered, or any six of them, to lay off the land in lots of one-half acre each, with convenient streets, and it was stipulated by Mr. Lynch that the town was to be named Lynchburg. The lots were to be sold at public auction for the benefit of John Lynch, and he very shrewdly reserved the right to retain one square containing two acres in whatever part of the new town he chose to select; he reserved, also, those lots on which he had already erected buildings. Each purchaser was to bind himself to build within three years from the day of sale a dwelling house at least fifteen feet square, with a brick or stone chimney.

Ever since the Revolutionary War the order of the day had been the building of towns. Under the colonial government the life of the people had centred around the parishes into which the counties were subdivided. Much business of a purely secular and civil nature was placed in ecclesiastic hands, such as educational matters, regulation of sanitation, legal care of the poor, and numerous other duties which we have come to consider as under jurisdiction of the state. With the overthrow of the Church of England these old systems were entirely disorganized, and towns were springing up around every courthouse, crossroads, ford and ferry to take the place of the abandoned parish life. Many a landowner saw an opportunity to reap profit, either for himself or his neighborhood, by procuring from the Virginia Assembly a grant for the right to build a town on his land.

For some years John Lynch had been owner of a ferry across the Fluvanna River to Amherst. At first it had been operated from a part of the property which had come to him from his father, Charles Lynch, but later he had bought land from Judge Edmund Winston, and had moved the ferry near to the old ford on James River. In the words of Christopher Anthony, the place was a howling wilderness before the town was built, and although the land had been acquired by Lynch for little more than the fees and expenses of location, yet in his own lifetime he saw it advance in value so that it constituted the source of a great fortune for himself and his descendants. He was not so successful in his next venture in this line. In 1791 he laid out another town on the opposite side of the river on his Amherst land, under the name of Madison, but better known as Scuffletown to the older Lynchburg citizens.

It has been the custom to speak of Lynch as our greatest benefactor, an entirely misplaced sense of obligation, for rather did he owe gratitude to our ancestors for enriching him by buying land which was unsuitable for town lots as it had doubtless proved for farming. Nowhere could have been found a more unlikely place to build a town. Taxes which might have been spent to a far better purpose if a more suitable site had been chosen, for many generations have gone to leveling and filling up the gorges and chasms which cut through the streets in the natural progress of water running down hill to the river. By this transaction in town building, however, we did gain a scene of surpassing beauty; a noble panorama which changes with every street as it rises in terraces above the river.

The first of the Lynch name to come to Virginia was Charles Lynch, the father of John Lynch. He was a native of Ireland, and being penniless when he arrived in this country, he served out his passage as an indentured servant on the plantation of Christopher Clark, a wealthy Quaker gentleman of New Kent

The Quaker Memorial Church, Lynchburg, Va.

County. At that time the Clark plantation was in New Kent, later it was in Hanover, which was cut from New Kent in 1720, and is now in Louisa, which was formed from part of Hanover in 1742. The will of Christopher Clark is now a matter of record in Louisa County. Charles Lynch married Sarah Clark, daughter of Christopher Clark, in 1733. There was no disgrace attached to indentured service, which many early emigrants were forced to make in order to pay their passage to this country, otherwise Christopher Clark, a wealthy and prominent planter, would not have consented to this marriage.

Charles Lynch patented a large tract of land near Candler's mountain and there established a home called Chestnut Hill. Sarah Clark Lynch became the founder of the Quaker Church in this vicinity, and donated the land where the old stone Quaker Meeting House was built with its burial ground which still stands on the Salem Turnpike. At one time the roof had fallen in and only the walls of the building were left, but it was restored and re-established as a place of worship some years ago by the Presbyterian Church. Sarah, being left a widow, married Major John Ward. She had no children by this marriage. Her son, John Lynch, who founded Lynchburg, was born in 1740. He married Mary Bowles. The descendants of the Lynch family are to be found in the pages devoted to genealogy, among whom the most distinguished was General James Griffin Dearing, a gallant soldier of the Confederacy, whose record is given elsewhere in this book.

John Lynch lived in the old Ferry House. On the other side of the river a small and peaceful tribe of Indians had a village, near which the town of Madison was laid out. I do not believe it is too great a strain on the imagination to suggest that some of that excellent handling of tobacco which caused the development of Lynchburg from a mere village to a place of importance as one of the largest tobacco markets in the world may have been due to these Indian neighbors. It is natural to suppose that they knew a great deal about tobacco, and that they gave their friends among the early settlers the benefit of their knowledge.

The land on which Lynchburg now stands was once a part of Albemarle County. It was given by Albemarle to Bedford in January, 1755, Reign of George II, "from which day all that part of the County of Albemarle on the south side of James River that lies above the head of Falling River, and from thence a direct course to the mouth of Stonewall Creek on James River; and all that part of the County of Lunenburg that lies to the westward of a line to be run from the mouth of Falling River north, 20 degrees east, to intersect the line of Prince Edward County, shall be added to and deemed part of the County of Bedford." (See Hening's Statutes, Vol. VI, page 441). This was done for the convenience of the people living in these parts. Bedford was already a very large county, before we were added, so large that it extended to the Ohio River. In the year 1781 Campbell County was made from Bedford.

In Howe's History of Virginia it is stated that the Ferry House was the only building here at the time the town was incorporated, but that could hardly have been the case, since John Lynch reserved for his own use those lots on which he had already erected buildings. This being true, there must have been buildings of some sort in the town at the very beginning, although it does appear that the business life of the town was confined at this period to the Madison side of the river. Howe's History makes no mention whatever of the church on the hill, which we have absolute evidence was standing there when the town was planned. It was a house of worship built as a part of the Established Church as early as 1765. It was a frame building, and the grounds around it were used as a churchyard. After the forfeiture of all Church of England property to the state, the place was turned into a school. In 1802 the building was destroyed by fire, and a few years later Mr. Lynch gave the Methodist Cemetery to the city. In 1808 he deeded the city the cemetery, and the land for the courthouse and the jail.

LYNCHBURG AND ITS NEIGHBORS

Until 1805 court was held at the corner of Church and Eleventh Streets, where the Hill City Lodge of Masons now have their hall. On this site there was a building in which court was presided over by Judge Creed Taylor. Mrs. Cabell describes him in her book as wearing short knee breeches, fastened with buckled garters with his hair done in a queue. As his health declined, and old age grew upon him, the bar found it very hard to deal with him. His fretfulness was almost unbearable, and he was unable to conduct himself with common civility. There was one Lynchburger, however, who remembered him in her old age with great respect. This was Mrs. George D. Davis, who died at her home on Clay Street (where Senator Glass now has his town house), August 20th, 1905. Mrs. Davis was the daughter of the late John Wills, a well-known lawyer of this city, an architect of unusual merit, and clerk of the court as well. Mrs. Davis was eighty-six years old at her death and well remembered Chancellor Creed Taylor, who died in 1835 when she was sixteen years old. He was always entertained at her father's home when he came to Lynchburg to hold court. When, in 1827, Mr. Wills built his home, he had a room set aside for the Chancellor's special use and for seventy-eight years this room was known as Chancellor Taylor's room.

Our first Courthouse was built in 1812 on the site of the present Courthouse. A jail was built about ten years later, which is standing today, the stone portion of the jail being the original building. Mrs. Royal on her visit here described it as the best jail in Virginia, and the equal of any in the country, but the most optimistic citizen could hardly make that boast at the present time. The present Courthouse building was erected in 1852 on land deeded the city by John Lynch in 1808. It replaced the first Courthouse, built in 1812 on the same site, which was pulled down to make room for the new building designed by W. S. Ellison. Expert opinion declares it to be a fine example of Graeco-Roman style, and one does not need to be an expert to feel that it is good to look at, a jewel set on a hill. Ellison was also architect of old Saint Paul's Church on Church Street. The bell and clock which were on the first Saint Paul's Church were discarded when the new building was put up, so the city fathers rescued these and put them on the Courthouse. While the Courthouse was in construction, one of the walls fell, and had to be replaced.

Courthouse, built in 1852.

The deed in which Lynch and his wife gave the acre of land for the burying ground mentions names and places which are of interest to us now. The earliest Deed Book contains many family names that are still with us today, such as Hancock, Kyle, Diuguid, Patteson, Norvell, Owen, Cabell, Davis, Thurman, Irvine, Ford, Fox, Graham, Wiatt, Perkins, Stewart, Roane, Taliaferro, Schoolfield, Warwick, Sullivan, Humphreys, Timberlake, Mallory, Saunders, Gilliam, Cocke, Hubbard, Farmer, Sneed, Winston, Moseley, Langhorne, Lewis, and many others.

In the deed the land given for a burying ground is described as lying and being on a hill on the west side of the main road leading from the upper end of Lynchburg towards New London, and near the forks of the road leading towards Edmund Tait's mill, and southwest of Andrew Smiley's tanyard. It is stated that this lot shall be held forever for the purpose of a burying ground, or the building of a house for public worship, and for none other purpose. If not used for this purpose, it shall be returned to the heirs of Lynch. Witnesses to this deed are Samuel Irvine, James Benagh and Thomas Claytor.

As the reader will perceive, from this gift was made the Methodist Graveyard, and thus the dead who had been interred on Court Street in the old churchyard were removed by relatives and friends to this new resting place. But in many cases there was no one to remove them, and they were left, as was shown when Court Street became a popular residential section, about the year 1880. In digging the foundations for the houses between Tenth and Eleventh Streets many bones of the dead were uncovered, and among these was the skeleton of some forgotten giant who had walked this way, for it was the mortal framework of a man who must have measured seven feet in life. It is said that a prominent citizen who was having the foundation of his home made on this particular spot was forced to build elsewhere, for his wife refused to live where this giant's bones had reposed for so many years.

James Benagh, one of the witnesses of the Lynch deed was clerk of the court here and lived on the property on Clay Street which is now owned by Senator Carter Glass. Mrs. Alice Harris, the widow of Mr. W. H. H. Harris is a descendant of Mr. Benagh.

On the eastern corner of Eighth and Church Streets is standing a battered old frame house built by Mr. Thomas Claytor about 1790. It contains some fine old hand-made mantels and wainscoting, and was one of our fashionable dwellings in earlier days, but for generations it has served as an office building. It was once Dr. Thomas Craddock's dental office, later Dr. Dennis succeeded him, and there practiced dentistry until recently. This same old house marked the progress of the popular tomato from the front porch to the kitchen of the inhabitants of Lynchburg. Mrs. Owen lived in this house, and taught school here in the early part of the last century. She and her husband, Mr. Owen Owen, came from Augusta County in 1790, their oldest child, William, being then three years old. Among their children and grandchildren are numbered many whom Lynchburg has always delighted to honor, in this number being ex-Senator Robert Latham Owen, of Oklahoma. When Mrs. Owen lived here, Thomas Jefferson was spending several months of each year on his fine estate, Poplar Forest, which he had inherited from his wife. While there, he frequently rode to Lynchburg. One summer day he came riding as usual through town, and as he passed Mrs. Owen's house he noticed a tomato plant bearing a ripe tomato in a flower pot on the front porch, with Mrs. Owen's little daughter, Jane, standing by it. The great Thomas reined in his horse.

"Why don't you eat that tomato?" he asked.

"Its poisonous," said the child.

He dismounted, pulled the tomato off the vine, and ate it himself, then rode away.*

There were two or three Indian villages in the vicinity of the Ferry during this time, one village on Judge Winston's property

---

*Through researches made by Miss Georgia Morgan (mentioned in the Genealogical Section of this book as a distinguished artist) in the Deed Books at Rustburg, it has lately been discovered that the house pulled down in the last few months, which occupied the corner at Eighth and Church Streets, was built by Mr. Miller in 1790, and not by Thomas Claytor, as has been supposed. The original purchaser of this lot was Mr. Thackston, who bought it from the trustees who had laid out the city. The date of this sale is 1786, the lot known as lot 15 in the original plat of the town. Mr. Miller sold it again in 1790, having meanwhile built upon it the house which is described in the deed as "the mansion house." It is mentioned that some person, whose name is unknown, is buried on this lot. In Dr. Asbury Christian's book, Lynchburg and Its People, in a footnote on page 84, appears the anecdote concerning Thomas Jefferson and the tomato, or love-apple, as tomatoes were then called, which occurred when Mrs. Owen was teaching school in this building. The exact location of this school is given on page 74 of the same book. This house will soon be rebuilt in Riverside Park, and used as a museum for Lynchburg antiquities.

[14]

near White Rock Hill, and one, already mentioned, on the opposite side of the river close to Madison. They were peaceful Indians, belonging to the Monagan tribe. Virginia Indians were of the Algonquin branch, and were Powhattans, a companion tribe to the Manhattans of New York. They gave no trouble to our early settlers, not even to those benighted travellers camping on the river banks, who, as often happened, found on reaching the Ferry, that the river had grown into a widespread and dangerous torrent, impossible to cross.

Samuel Irvine owned the Indian Queen Tavern, but Charles Hoyle had been running it for a number of years. In 1806 the lease was recorded for another period, ten years, as stated in the Court record, at a yearly rental of $400.00. It was a three-story brick building situated on lot number 19 in the original plat of the town, and was leased with the sign, bell, porch, benches and other appurtenances. The stables and gardens were on the opposite side of the street. The Indian Queen was probably Lynchburg's earliest hostelry worthy of the name, and must have presented a lively picture, with the sign of the Indian Queen swinging in front, and spacious gardens and grounds, stables and stableyards, with horses, dogs, carts and carriages. Mrs. Cabell, who wrote a book on Lynchburg, published about ninety years ago, tells us that Hoyle was a native of Ireland, and had belonged to the Irish gentry before he emigrated to this country with his wife, son, daughter and nephew. His wife was an amiable and refined lady, and Lynchburg people became much attached to this couple. Mr. Hoyle was long remembered in Lynchburg as maintaining the very highest standard as a tavern or hotel keeper. He finally retired after making a fortune here. His place was conducted in a style superior to any in Virginia. "The excellence of the table, the perfect order of the establishment, the handsome, antique furniture" (antique in 1800!), "the fine pictures, the kindly bearing of host and hostess, all these assisted in making such a public house as we can never see in this age of steam and telegraph," so writes Mrs. Cabell.

CHAPTER II

WHEN TOBACCO WAS KING

IT WAS in Madison, or Scuffletown, or Madison Heights, as we now call this locality, that the first tobacco market in this immediate section was situated. Before the first warehouse was built on the Lynchburg side of the river, and long before the building of either town, Madison was the centre of a dark leaf tobacco trade. The Madison warehouse stood on the hill above the road leading to the Ford; it was owned by John Lynch, and it is believed that the village was named for this warehouse. Here the tobacco hogsheads were lowered by ropes over the river bluff into boats which came up the James to freight them to the seaboard.

The first warehouse built in Lynchburg, the Spring Warehouse, built in 1791 at Twelfth and Commerce Streets was named for a fine spring, one of the favorite places to get water in those early days before there was a water system. A part of this warehouse is still standing and being used by the H. E. DeWitt lumber yard. About seventy-five years ago the wagon and carriage manufactory of Mr. John Bailey occupied this same old Spring warehouse. The Horseford Road, that short road, the length of only two squares from the old Ford to Main Street, runs between this property and the site of an old stone building recently torn down, which is said in several books and papers to have been the first tobacco factory in the town.

Other warehouses were soon built, as business increased, four being erected between 1800 and 1805. The Blackwater Warehouse was located at the foot of Cabell Street, on the present site of the Southern Railroad freight station. Liberty Warehouse was built next at Seventh and Commerce Streets. Part of this is still standing, being used as a garage. The wagon entrance to Liberty Warehouse was from Main Street. Lynch's Warehouse, at Ninth and Commerce Streets, came next. Most of this has been razed to make place for modern construction. The last of the four built during this period was Martin's Warehouse, at Tenth and Commerce, which is still in constant use. It is now 127 years old. The sixth warehouse was begun in 1806 by Mr. William Davis, Sr., called "Friend Davis." A permit was secured for a tobacco inspection centre on this site in October, 1806, and the work was begun then but not finished until 1808 or 1809. This was Friend's Warehouse, the remains of which have only been lately torn down to make way for the new Post Office building. About 1810 Planter's Warehouse was built on Main Street, between Fifth and Sixth, where the Paramount Theatre now stands.

Lynchburg's First Tobacco Factory
(on Elm Avenue, near Horse Ford Road)

In those days Lynchburg was the greatest dark leaf tobacco market in the world, and the city attained its success not only by reason of the excellence of its tobacco, but from the cleverness of the early merchants in inventing methods of improving the crude product. During colonial days it had been the custom to burn all inferior tobacco in the warehouses, and this rule of dealing in only the very highest grade was strictly adhered to by our old tobacco dealers. In other markets tobacco was sold in the hogshead by sample, but here the hogshead was opened up on the warehouse floor, so that the buyer might inspect each leaf before making his purchase. A unique figure of that time was Colonel Augustine Leftwich, born in Bedford in 1794, who came here when he was eighteen, and made a large fortune in tobacco. He belonged to a family of great distinction, both here and in England. He would stroll to his factory on a summer morning like an Indian nabob, clad in spotless white linen, a Negro slave walking behind him and holding a great green umbrella over his head. His cousin, Dr. James Saunders, likewise a native of Bedford, wrote Mr. Rives, his brother-in-law, in July, 1836, that in a brief sojourn down the Mississippi River he had sold $20,000 worth of tobacco.

Among those who made a great fortune in tobacco were Mr. Labby and his partner, Mr. Jesse Hare. Mr. Labby belonged to a French family whose original name was L'Abbé. These old names, Labby and Hare, are historic in the annals of Lynchburg, and partly because of the enterprise and ability of their owners Lynchburg became the greatest tobacco market in the world. The business was not restricted to certain streets; it was all through the town. There was a large stone factory at the corner of Eleventh and Clay Streets, owned by the Langhornes; Mr. Ammon Hancock's factory was on Fifth Street between Church and Main, and Mr. John M. Otey's factory was on Twelfth Street. On the corner of Fifth and Clay was the factory of Mr. Seth Halsey. The factories were everywhere, and though strangers might object to the powerful odor, the native-born were never heard to complain. It is said that every town has its distinctive smell, and just as the whole of New Orleans is permeated with the aroma of burnt coffee, it is certain that Lynchburg reeked of tobacco from one end to the other. I know of no locality that did not have its factories except Diamond Hill, and that section was probably free of them because it was inaccessible to wagons by reason of the wide ravines that isolated it from the other part of town.

The handling of tobacco called for plenty of space; a vacant lot was needed for the wagons to unload, and a place to sun the tobacco on fair days. Some of the factories were made flat and low, with a wide roof on which the weed could be spread out to be sunned. I remember especially the Langhorne factory on the corner of Eleventh and Clay, a long, low, rock building, to the roof of which the Negro hands would come, singing lustily as they brought the tobacco in wide, shallow hampers of woven white oak splits. The annual crop grown in the surrounding counties, of which Lynchburg was the natural market, finally reached the amount of seventy-five million pounds. That enormous yearly crop of leaf tobacco was distributed from our warehouses for export trade, and manufactured in our factories into plug, twist and smoking tobacco under innumerable brands. This gave occupation, directly and indirectly, to the greater portion of the people in town. The buyer might inspect every leaf before making his purchase, and thus was avoided all risks of dispute and controversy. So did Lynchburg acquire the well deserved name of furnishing the very best tobacco that could be found anywhere. The manner of selling tobacco was the old auction system, which has always been in use here.

After the War Between the States the high quality of Lynchburg's tobacco was no longer maintained, and many a large fortune was made by using her good name to sell a degraded article. For the old type of tobacconist was dying out, and so in the minority from age and misfortune that he was no longer in a position to uphold the standard of the market. So Lynchburg tobacco lost its high reputation, except in the case of one or two manufacturers who individually determined to keep their tobacco up to that high standard of excellence set for it by past generations.

In the early days tobacco was being brought in to town continually. When the roads were dry enough it came loaded on wagons, the wagons mostly covered with canvas or oil-cloth, were of the same type as the covered wagons that carried some of our brethren across the plains, westward. Sometimes the "Devil's Weed," as it was called, was protected with old bed-quilts or hand-woven counterpanes that collectors of the antique would fight for in this day. Often the roads were so bad that the heavily loaded wagons would get mired, and for months the only method of selling the crop was to roll it to market in the hogsheads, or bring it in bateaux.

The manner of preparing a hogshead to be rolled to market was unique. Through the centre of each cask, after it was headed, was driven a long wooden spike. A part of this projected to serve as an axle tree. A split sapling was fitted for shafts, and extended to the rear, the ends being connected with a hickory withe. A few slabs were nailed to the front of the cask to form a footboard, or box in which were kept the provisions for the journey. This was all that was necessary unless the rolling was to cover a long distance, say fifty or more miles. In this case it was not deemed safe to trust merely to the hoops of the hogshead, although they were strong and numerous, and stout felloes were attached to each end for re-enforcement. Either horses, mules or oxen were hitched to the hogsheads, and so they were rolled along the roads to their destination.

There were men especially engaged in this work, called tobacco rollers, a rough set generally. They travelled in parties, assisting each other on the way. Sometimes they were one or two weeks making these trips and returning. Their provisions were a middling or two of meat, a bag of meal, a frying pan, a hoe, an axe, and a blanket for shelter at night, with corn and fodder for the animals. When the sun went down they would kindle a fire in the woods by the roadside, bake a hoecake on the hoe, fry a rasher of bacon, feed their team, and roll up in the blanket to sleep by the fire near to the hogshead. This primitive mode of tobacco transportation was in use for many years.

But no story of the epic of tobacco trade on the James River can ever be written without mention of the bateau. "A bateau was forty or fifty feet long, about two feet deep, and four to five feet wide. Each bateau was managed by three strong slaves, who took great pride in their skilful poling. They were furnished with sixty pounds of meat and two bushels of meal for the trip, and they helped themselves to the tobacco, corn and potatoes of the cargo going down, and to the salt, sugar, molasses and whiskey of the upgoing cargo. Fresh fish were abundant. Eggs and milk could be traded for or bought along the way. Fleets of bateaux," wrote Dr. Bagby, "used to be moored on the river bank, near the depot of the Virginia and Tennessee Railroad. Picturesque craft, which were thrown into disuse when the packet boat came in. For a long time one of them used to be in the mouth of Blackwater, near the toll bridge. The Negro bateauman gloried in his calling. The job was truly a man's job, demanding skill, courage and strength to a high degree. A plank ran along the gunwale to afford him footing, his long pole was shod with iron. Two men, one on each side, poled the boat, while a third Negro used a great oar for a rudder." They would come down in a fleet that started from the headwaters of the James, and the whole river resounded with their mighty singing, each boat taking up the refrain, and the bluffs giving back the echo of their favorite song, the chanty of the James:

"I'm gwine long down
Ter Lynchburg town
Ter kerry my 'backer down dar."

CHAPTER III
NEIGHBORS

WE HAD in those days some very interesting people living around Lynchburg. They came to the town on business and pleasure, and were entertained right royally, either at the Indian Queen or in our hospitable homes. Even the servants in those times ate food fit for Lucullus, that prince of epicures. The woods close at hand were full of the choicest game, which could be easily snared or trapped, and even shad, before the river was dammed, came up as far as Lynchburg. An old colored servant, Aunt Rhody Tyler, told me that her master, in the early days, would send his servants every spring with wagons and seines to get shad out of the river, and these would be salted down like roe herring to feed the slaves until spring came again and the shad bush bloomed in the woods to remind old master that the shad were running in the river again.

The most interesting neighbor in those days was Thomas Jefferson. He frequently rode into town from his estate at Poplar Forest, where he spent some months of each year, and the kindliness and respect our good people felt for him was in no wise abated by the fact that in his old age he was very poor, though it hardly seems suitable to apply that term to one so rich in spiritual and intellectual gifts. He was quite busy at this time, being anxious to complete the home he was building for Francis Eppes, his grandson. The urge to carry out his noble dreams in architecture lasted him even unto death, and old age and cramped means could not rob him of these dreams. He built in the woods of Bedford County what has justly been called a Greek temple, and it bears testimony today that the sureness of his sense of beauty lasted him to the end.

Jefferson in his later life seems to have felt a great attachment to this property in Bedford County. It had come to him from his wife, who inherited the estate from her father, John Wayles.

Poplar Forest, Bedford County.

Two views of "Poplar Forest," the Bedford County home of Thomas Jefferson. This place is three miles from old New London, where Patrick Henry made his famous speech in the Johnny Hook case. Here Jefferson retired with his family after his escape from Tarleton's troops at "Monticello." The place is an octagonal brick house modeled on the same plan as "Monticello," though not so large. "Poplar Forest" commands a beautiful view of the Blue Ridge Mountains. This place and Forest Depot both get their name from "The Forest," home of Jefferson's wife, which was the scene of their marriage. Jefferson wrote his celebrated book "Notes on Virginia" while living at "Poplar Forest."

Courtesy of Mr. C. S. Hutter.

LYNCHBURG AND ITS NEIGHBORS

Jefferson called the place Poplar Forest, by which name it is still known, and gave the name of The Forest to this entire section of the county, naming it after The Forest, his wife's home in Charles City County where they were married. It well deserved the name at that time for it was then miles and miles of woodland of virgin growth. After his retirement from the Presidential office Jefferson was besieged at Monticello by a continual stream of visitors. As many as fifty visitors a day, so his daughter, Mrs. Randolph, writes, frequently required to be fed and housed for the night, as well as the horses which had brought them. On this account Poplar Forest was a place of grateful retreat, where he found privacy and quiet to read and write, as he loved to do. He became much attached to the neighbors and to the neighborhood, and sent his grandson, Francis Eppes, to near-by New London Academy. Evidently he wished Francis Eppes to become identified with this section of Virginia, and for this reason built him the beautiful home, Poplar Forest, he, until its completion, resided in a wooden structure on the place which was torn down in later years. After all his labor, and struggle to get the place built, for with the handicap of old age and poverty he literally ran a race with death in order to complete the plan, the grandson only lived there a short time.

Francis Eppes married the daughter of Thomas Eston Randolph, an Englishman, reputed to be a merchant prince, who while visiting Mr. Thomas Randolph, of Tuckahoe, courted and married his daughter, Jane. After marrying Jane, of Tuckahoe, Thomas Eston Randolph lost his money, and lived for a time at New London, removing later to Lynchburg, and then to Florida. After this Eppes ran for the Legislature from Bedford County and was defeated. He was deeply mortified at his defeat, and as his wife had never liked living at Poplar Forest they moved to Florida to be with her people.

Poplar Forest is now the summer home of Mr. C. S. Hutter, who has a very interesting table, the top of which is a plan of the interior of Poplar Forest, designed by Jefferson and made by his directions.

In the Jones' Library of Lynchburg are a few relics of Thomas Jefferson given by Mrs. Eldridge, who was Miss Frances Brown Steptoe before her marriage to Major Eldridge, an officer of the Federal Army. She was the daughter of Dr. Steptoe, of Bedford, and the granddaughter of the famous clerk of the court, Jemmy Steptoe, and his wife, Frances Calloway Steptoe. She was also the half sister of Colonel Edward S. Steptoe, a distinguished soldier of the Mexican War, whose wife was Roxana Claytor. Her father, Dr. Steptoe, lived in the old brick house on the right-hand side of the road going from Forest to New London. The house was bought from the Steptoe estate by Wm. Tudor Yancey, whose father, Major Joel Yancey, had also been a neighbor and friend of Jefferson's, and whose son, Robert Yancey, inherited the house and used it for a summer home.

Seven miles from Lynchburg an even nearer neighbor than Jefferson was Colonel William J. Lewis, of Mount Athos, who commanded a corps of mountain riflemen at the siege of Yorktown in 1781. His home, which was burned many years ago, must have been a very imposing structure. It was built on top of the mountain in the year 1796, with a beautiful garden surrounding it, and a glorious view. The house on the mountain always went by the name of Mount Athos. The plantation, laid out at the foot of the mountain in a bend of the river, was one of the most princely estates in Eastern Virginia and was called Buffalo Lick Plantation. Colonel William J. Lewis was born in 1766, and died in 1828. He was the son of Colonel William Lewis and Anne Montgomery Lewis, and the nephew of General Andrew Lewis. He married Elizabeth Cabell, of Nelson County, but left no children. Colonel Lewis was a very talented and cultured man, and a great student of history. Having large means, he lived a most delightful life in his home on top of the mountain overlooking the James River. He served in Congress one term, 1815-17, and was defeated by one vote for Governor of

Virginia, governors at that time being elected by the Legislature. Having no children he left his beautiful home to his niece, Ann Trent, daughter of his sister, Elizabeth Montgomery Lewis, born 1777 at Sweet Springs, the home of her father, Colonel William Lewis, and married to Colonel John Trent, of Cumberland County.

Ann Trent was one of three children, Eliza Trent, Ann Trent, and John Trent, M.D. She married Judge John Robertson, of Richmond, said to be a very unique character. A lineal descendant of Pocahontas, he was gifted, brilliant and eccentric. He was a member of Congress, and for many years was judge of the Chancery Court of Richmond. All his vacations were spent at Mount Athos. After the War Between the States he would never accept the oath of allegiance. He died in 1870, being over eighty. One of his sons was named Bolling, and one Powhatan.

In that day the Calloways were perhaps the greatest family in this part of Virginia. Sir William Calloway, as he was always known, was the founder of the family in this state. He had five sons and two daughters, who lived to maturity, serving the country in war and peace. All of the sons figured prominently as officers of militia in the French and Indian War. Colonel Richard Calloway, after serving from sergeant to colonel in this war, went to Kentucky with Daniel Boone, and was a member of Kentucky's first Legislature, which met under a tree. He and John Todd were the first representatives from Kentucky to the House of Burgesses in Virginia, in 1777, and in 1779 Richard Calloway and Evan Shelby were commissioned by the House of Burgesses to make a road over the Cumberland Mountains, and to establish a ferry at Boonsboro. Calloway County, Kentucky, is named for Colonel Richard Calloway. His daughters, Elizabeth and Frances Calloway, with Jemima Boone, the daughter of Daniel Boone, were captured by Indians July 14th, 1776, and carried down the Ohio River, but were retaken by Daniel Boone the next day. James Fenimore Cooper wrote of this incident in his book, The Last of the Mohicans.

Another son, William Calloway, born in 1714, patented 15,000 acres of land in Lunenburg, Brunswick, Bedford and Halifax Counties. In 1761 William Calloway, gentleman, made a free gift of one hundred acres of land adjoining the Courthouse to the County of Bedford, to be settled as a town and to be called New London. In the French and Indian War, 1755-61, Richard Calloway gained his title as colonel. His oldest son, James, who was born December 21st, 1736, and died 1809, was a man of great wealth and influence, and a friend of Washington. He owned lead mines and iron furnaces, and was detailed from active service by Washington to make iron for military use. His second son, John, was a colonel in the Revolution, whose home still stands near Lynchburg at Evington, and is the residence of Mrs. Thomas Langhorne, a lineal descendant. Colonel William Calloway, another son, was also a gallant soldier of the Revolution. This family furnished to the Revolutionary War two indispensable materials, men and iron. Near Lynchburg and just two miles west of Concord still stands the old Oxford Furnace, from which James Calloway supplied arms and munitions to Washington and near by are the iron mines. This furnace was operated until 1875. It is now owned by Mr. D. W. Myers, of this city, and on it are located valuable deposits of manganese. It can be seen from this short account that the Calloways owned estates as great or greater than many a European principality, and in five wars they gave of their best to their country.

A well-known character and neighbor was Jamie or Jemmie Steptoe, already mentioned as clerk of Bedford Court. The Courthouse was then at New London, which was the Lunenburg Courthouse until Bedford was made from Lunenburg in 1753. One of Mr. Steptoe's daughters married Harry Langhorne, of Lynchburg, the great-grandfather of Lady Astor, and of Mrs. Charles Dana Gibson. Mr. Steptoe's wife was Frances, the daughter of Colonel James Calloway, whose sister, Elizabeth

Prentiss Calloway, became the second wife of Mr. Charles Johnston, the uncle of General Joseph E. Johnston. Mr. Johnston's first wife was Letitia Pickett. From the Richmond Dispatch of November, 1905, in an article signed L. M. B., of Bedford City, the following remarkable anecdotes are narrated:

"Soon after the Revolution Mr. Charles Johnston was sent from Virginia to Ohio on some law business. The country was full of Indians, and near a place called Sandusky he was captured by the Indians and held prisoner for a year. He told his children in after years that the Indians spared his life because he made them such good pan cakes. After being a prisoner for a year he was tied to a tree to be burned. The fagots were lighted, when an old Frenchman named Dr. Shuget came up in his peddler's cart, and seeing what was going on he begged the Indians to release the man in exchange for some of his goods. After a little parley Mr. Johnston was released, and Dr. Shuget brought him back to Virginia. Soon after this Mr. Johnston was sent on government business to Paris. The ship on which he sailed also carried Lafayette to France after his visit to General Washington. While on the ship Mr. Johnston entertained Lafayette and his staff with the narrative of his capture and imprisonment among the Indians. The General was so interested that he requested Mr. Johnston to write the account out for the Paris papers, which he did, and the adventure was printed in them at that time. Years after this, when Lafayette again visited Virginia, he inquired for Mr. Charles Johnston. He was told that he lived at Botetourt Springs, Virginia (now Hollins Institute), and learning that his road to North Carolina, where he was going to visit General Nathaniel Green, would take him near Botetourt County, he determined to visit Mr. Johnston. Soon after this General Lafayette and his staff arrived at Mr. Johnston's home, and who should ride up a little later to join them there, most unexpectedly, but Dr. Shuget."

This story was told by L. M. B., of Bedford, as having been narrated to her by Mrs. Cunningham, of Richmond, the daughter of Mr. Johnston, who was thirteen years old at the time of Lafayette's visit. She also recalled that Lafayette said he did not believe that Marshall Ney ever came to America. This account of Mr. Johnston is of particular interest to the people of Lynchburg because he built the house in our suburbs so well known as Sandusky. He named it for the region in Ohio near which he had his adventure with the Indians. It was near this same place in Ohio that Colonel William Crawford, in June, 1782, was tortured by the Indians for days and then burnt at the stake, having undertaken at the urgent request of Washington and William Irvine, to lead an expedition against the Wyandot and Delaware Indians. Crawford, a Virginian and a Revolutionary soldier of great distinction, had retired to his plantation to enjoy a peaceful life for the rest of his days when he was persuaded to go on the expedition. The Sandusky estate has been in the hands of the Hutter family for many generations. It was bought by them after Mr. Johnston's removal to Botetourt Springs and is closely identified in the minds of Lynchburg people with Colonel Risque Hutter, a brave officer of the Confederacy, who lived there with his lovely wife. The place has now passed into the hands of their sons.

Another hero and neighbor of those times, General Andrew Lewis, was taken sick in what proved to be his last illness at Williamsburg, where he was acting in the Council of State. Realizing that he was ill, he started for his home in Botetourt, now Roanoke County. But on reaching Bedford he was so much worse that he discontinued his journey, and he breathed his last in a dwelling located not far from old Mount Zion Church, which is in the valley of Goose Creek. He was within half a day's ride from his own home, where he was buried, but later he was removed to the cemetery west of Salem, where the Federal Government has erected a handsome monument of granite over his grave.

An old Indian trail led from the southwest, coming through the Blue Ridge at Buford's Gap into Goose Creek Valley. It tra-

(1) "Shady Grove," home of Spottswood Henry, son of Patrick Henry, in Campbell County.
Courtesy of Kiah T. Ford Company, Realtors.

(2) Otter Burn, home of Benjamin Donald, in Bedford.

(3) Distant view of "Winton," home of Patrick Henry's mother, Sarah Winston, in Amherst County.
Courtesy of Kiah T. Ford Company, Realtors.

versed the valley northward, and recrossed the Blue Ridge at the head of the valley into Augusta County, now Rockbridge County. Many Indian relics and skeletons have been discovered in this neighborhood.

At the time of the Revolution and directly afterward New London was the centre of a delightful neighborhood, and there are all through Bedford County even today many lovely old homes and the representatives of many fine old Virginia names. The old town of New London was founded about 1750 and at the time of the Revolution was quite a flourishing place. There was at that time a United States Armory at New London which was later moved to Harper's Ferry, and under the old district system the Superior Court was held in the town. "The New London Academy," wrote Joseph Martin, whose Gazetteer was published in 1834, "is situated a mile west of the town. At this institution a student may be prepared to enter any of the colleges or universities with credit. * * * The buildings consist of a handsome and commodious academy, a president's house, and a large brick church well enclosed. * * * Five or six Scotch merchants, who were largely engaged in business about the commencement of the Revolution, refused to take the oath of allegiance, broke up their establishments and left the country. These circumstances, combining with the establishment of Lynchburg so near it on James River, have given a shock to the prosperity of the town from which it cannot recover."

But even today there hangs an atmosphere around the almost abandoned town of New London—the tall boxwood around the inn, the old road up the hill bordered with mock orange trees, the tumble-down houses—there is something about these old places that speaks with a very eloquent voice.

The Radford Family, near The Forest, as Jefferson called it, has always been closely identified with Lynchburg as have many Bedford County families. The founder of the Radford family in this part of Virginia was Colonel William Radford, who, with his kinsman, Major Joel Yancey, bought a large tract of land from Thomas Jefferson. This estate reached from Forest to Clay's Crossing, and is one of the most beautiful stretches of land in this part of Virginia. Not only is the view of the mountains surpassingly beautiful, but the lovely, rolling fields of the foothills form a perfect landscape. One has only to drive on the public highway from Clay's to Forest to be impressed with the remarkable beauty of this land which was once owned by Jefferson. Colonel Radford built his home and called it Woodburn. It is now owned by Mr. Alex Mitchell. Major Yancey built a brick house in a grove of oaks near the road, and named it Rothsay. It is on this plantation that Major Yancey is buried. The house was burned some years ago, but was rebuilt on the same site and out of the same brick by Mr. Locksley Radford, who now lives there, his father, Colonel Carlton Radford, having bought it over seventy-five years ago.

Colonel William Radford equipped a number of privateers in Revolutionary times, being aided in this patriotic enterprise by Governor Floyd. In an engagement with a British fleet Radford and Floyd were both captured and confined in the Tower of London, but with the help of English friends they made their escape to France, where they were kindly received, and assisted to return to America by Marie Antoinette. Colonel Radford married Elizabeth Moseley, whose father was a major in the Revolutionary forces.

The ancestors of Dr. Perroneau Brown, son of the late Mr. Thompson Brown, had to fight for possession of their grant of land at Ivy Cliff near New London. Before the Revolution, when the Brown family came from Botetourt to Bedford, they were attacked by Indians, whom they repulsed only after killing several.

Eagle Eyrie, the official name given by the Highway Department to the gap in Locke's Mountain, is but the original name which Nicholas Davies, its first owner, gave to the hunting lodge he maintained there. He was a native of Wales, and came to Virginia with a large grant to land in this section made him by

George III. This was a huge tract containing 31,000 acres, and the grant was dated in 1771. Mr. Davies' first wife was Judith Randolph, of Tuckahoe. Judith's Creek was named for her, and runs near the site of the lodge. Mr. Davies also built an inn at the top of the mountain, and placed in charge an innkeeper named Ogden, into whose hands the property finally passed by purchase. The mountain was named for the Locke family, who bought it some years later, and who sold it to the late Dr. C. E. Busey, who built a home there.

CHAPTER IV

THE WATER SYSTEM

AT FIRST Lynchburg enjoyed what George Bagby called "spring and gourd days"; nor did the need of a public water system weigh heavily upon our people when there were plenty of little darkies to run to the spring whenever a fresh drink was desired. There were bold springs in almost every street of the town, and wells in nearly every back lot. No doubt each householder boasted of the superior quality of his own particular well, or the spring which boiled up under the spreading oak in his back yard. Few had any idea of the dangers of polluted water. I have seen the remains of two long rows of Negro cabins, "the quarters," as they were called, built on each side of the pathway leading downhill to the spring which supplied water for one of the most beautiful homes in Virginia. Seeing this, it is easy to understand why epidemics of typhoid so frequently visited our plantations, for the world was then as ignorant of bacteria as it had been in the days of King James, when so many at Jamestown paid the penalty of their ignorance. The people were satisfied with the purity of their springs, and as the town grew it was only the danger of fire which finally aroused them to the necessity of improving their water supply.

The first step to provide protection against this menace was made in 1799, when the Lynchburg Fire Company obtained leave from the town trustees to sink wells and erect pumps on Main Street, for the convenience and safety of the citizens. This right, however, was only used to a very limited extent, although several pumps were placed on the sidewalk of Main Street, where they remained for many years.

In 1811 the Council granted to John Lynch the privilege of conveying water in wooden pipes through the streets from the springs on his farm at the head of Horseford Branch. The pipes were made by boring augur holes in logs of wood, the sections

First Lynchburg Water Pipes--bored hole in trunk of trees---dug up lately by city.

of logs being fastened together by iron bands. Some of these crude pipes have been unearthed in late years and it was found that the iron bands were made in Scotland. The water was conducted by gravity to the lower streets and Lynch was authorized to charge the citizens for its use, but the town reserved unlimited rights in cases of extinguishing fires. The better to avail themselves of this privilege, the city fathers in 1813 had a small reservoir built on Ninth Street, between Main and Court. This structure must have been near to the place where the old Fireman's Fountain once stood, which is now the site of the memorial to our soldiers who fell in the World War. The reservoir was twelve feet square and ten feet deep, and was kept full of water to meet the need of fire emergency. Four fire plugs were put up at the same time, from which the town's little fire engine could be supplied.

This arrangement never proved satisfactory. The reservoir leaked badly, and consequently the street around it was almost impassable. In 1817 John Lynch sold out his interest in this primitive water system to James Wade. Although it was a nuisance in many ways, it was still some help to the volunteer companies in cases of fire, and so continued in use until 1828, when Mr. John Victor, a native of Fredericksburg who had moved to Lynchburg began to agitate the question of our serious condition in regard to city water. It was his idea to settle this matter in a big way, not only for his own generation, but for generations to come, and he placed before the people of Lynchburg the necessity of borrowing enough money to construct a suitable reservoir. To Mr. Victor, who was made Chairman of the Water Committee, is due the credit for the reservoir now on Clay Street. It was necessary, in order to meet the needs of a town so full of hills, to have a double forcing pump which could raise the water to an elevation of 253 feet above the level of the river. Albert Stein, an engineer of distinction, had charge of the work, which exceeded anything in this line ever before attempted in the

United States. It cost the town $50,000 and was the first debt ever raised by the City of Lynchburg.

On Saturday, August 23rd, 1828, the cornerstone of the reservoir was laid. At 9 o'clock in the morning, at the First Presbyterian Church, which then stood on the lower end of Main Street, between Twelfth and Thirteenth, the procession was formed in the following order: The Military; The Reverend Clergy; The Engineer; The Members of the Common Council, led by the Water Committee; The Judge of the General Court for the Circuit and the Mayor of the Town; The Recorder and Aldermen; The Masonic Fraternity; Citizens.

When the procession, under the direction of the marshalls of the day, Major James B. Risque, Colonel Maurice H. Langhorne, Captain R. R. Phelps, Samuel I. Wiatt and A. M. Gilliam reached the ground, the artillery and rifle companies formed a hollow square, within which were the Masons. The adjacent banks were thronged with spectators. The impressive ceremonies commenced with a prayer by the Rev. W. S. Reid, followed by solemn music. The Rev. F. G. Smith then implored of the Supreme Architect of the Universe a blessing on the undertaking and the Masonic Fraternity proceeded to lay the cornerstone. The plate bears the following inscription:

"This stone, the foundation of a work executed by order of the Common Council of Lynchburg for supplying the town with water, was laid under the direction of John Victor, John Thurman, John Early, David G. Murrell, and Samuel Claytor by the Rt. Rev. Howson S. White, D.D., Grand Master, and the Worshipful Maurice H. Garland, Master of Marshall Lodge No. 39 of Free and Accepted Masons, on the 23rd of August, A. M. 2828 A. D. 1828, in presence of Mayor, Recorder, Aldermen and Common Councilmen of said town; the members of said Lodge; the Artillery and Rifle Companies, commanded by Captains J. E. Norvell and Jas. W. Pegram, and numerous citizens, Albon McDaniel, Esq., Mayor, John Thurman, Esq., President of the Council, Albert Stein, Engineer."

Mr. John Victor, Chairman of the Water Works, delivered an address, after which the military fired a salute, and the gratified beholders returned to their homes, inspired by Mr. Victor's words: "Let us join hands, nothing doubting that we, too, can accomplish what others have so often done."

At that early day there was a man in Lynchburg named Samuel Miller. Probably he was present on this great occasion for the town. Even then he was busy laying the foundation of his own fortune, which was to be one of the greatest fortunes in Virginia, and later by his generosity was added another chapter to the history of the water system of Lynchburg.

CHAPTER V

RE-ESTABLISHMENT OF THE COLONIAL CHURCH

ALTHOUGH the Quakers had established a colony of their own, which they called South River Meeting, as early as the year 1757, the oldest building on the site of Lynchburg of which we have any real record was a Church of England built as a house of worship in colonial times, as early, certainly, as the year 1768, and possibly earlier. It was situated in a grove of oaks on the southwestern side of what is now Court Street, and beginning about the middle of the square between Ninth and Tenth, ranged through Tenth to the corner of Eleventh and Court, where the John Wyatt School stands today. In the rear it extended back as far as Madison, where there used to be a strong, bold spring of fine water, which the city has now closed, and from which the congregation procured drink for man and beast. The church contained the pews of Judge Edmund Winston and Major Scott. Judge Winston married the widow of Patrick Henry.

The Church of England in America suffered complete disorganization after the Revolutionary War. In Lynchburg the story of the Episcopal Church was that of all other Virginia towns. The old church on Court Street had been served in its later years by the Rev. Charles Clay, who was in charge of the parish in Bedford, of which this section was a part at that time. Parson Clay, as he was known, lived on the place owned until recently by Mr. duVal Radford. Clay was a minister of the Established Church before the Revolution, and was from Saint Anne's Parish, Albemarle, a man of learning, and particularly distinguished for the accuracy and extent of his classical knowledge. He and Thomas Jefferson met each other by accident, and from this casual meeting a friendly intimacy grew between the two men, as the Clay homestead was only about six miles above Poplar

Forest. The Parson's son, General Odin Clay, who was born in 1801, remembered many interesting conversations between these two friends. He also remembered, during his early days, his father's relative, Henry Clay, a tall, slender youth, arriving at their home alone and on horseback. After a few days' visit Henry Clay resumed his journey to the wilderness which was then Kentucky where he was to make such a great name for himself.

Parson Clay and Jefferson exchanged many letters in which the former President aired his views upon religion. In one of his letters he mentioned a pair of spectacles he had given the Parson, with an extensive set of glasses warranted to suit his eyesight from youth to old age. Parson Clay's journeys were all made on horseback, and for the most part his services were held in private homes. The Episcopal churches being abandoned and prayerbooks being scarce, he carried a leather bag containing cards which were printed on both sides with abbreviated forms of the service. It was his custom to distribute these among his congregation, thereby enabling them to make the proper responses. He died in 1819 and was buried on his plantation. A great cairn of rocks marks his grave, at his request thrown there by his sons: one stone for each time they had disobeyed him.

Parson Clay did not live to see the Episcopal Church revived, but he must have seen signs before he died that new life was beginning to stir. On September 14th, 1822, a meeting for reorganization was held in the Franklin Hotel, which stood at the corner of what was then Second Street and Sixth Alley, where Guggenheimer's store used to be, on the corner of Main and Eleventh Streets. Bishop Cobbs was made the secretary of this meeting. In the year of Bishop Cobbs' birth, 1795, there was not a single Episcopal church or chapel in this diocese. When he was an infant his mother took him to Charlottesville on horseback, a distance of sixty miles, to be baptized. He was born at Rose Hill, near Goodes, in Bedford County, close to the Peaks of Otter, and frequently he would say he was a better man for having been born within sight of those Peaks. His high opinion of them was shared by John Marshall, who came with his body servant once a year to sleep on the summit and to see the sun set and rise again. Cardinal Gibbon, also, made a long journey for that same privilege, and Father McGurk joined him here. Bishop Cobbs was the father of the Episcopal Church in all this section of Virginia. Bishop Otey was also a native of Bedford. He and Bishop Cobbs were lifelong friends, one being the first Bishop of Tennessee, and the other the first Bishop of Alabama. Bishop Otey was one of the instructors of Matthew Fontaine Maury, and a great source of inspiration to "the pathfinder of the seas." In Lynchburg many of those who had been reared in the doctrines of the English Church, having no church in which to worship on Sunday, receive Communion, marry, baptize their children, and to bury their dead had joined what was then called the non-Conformists. In a rural community the Church answers a great social need of the people, and some had become Quakers, and others Methodists, Baptists or Presbyterians. Thus as they had helped, with great earnestness and industry to build up the church of their adoption, many decided to stay where they were. So the little organization for the Episcopal Church, the first in Virginia made above Tidewater, though entertained with great hospitality and kindness, must have been disappointed to see how many Lynchburg people had taken other vows. Still they met with generous response. Mrs. George Cabell gave a lot at the south corner of Sixth and Seventh Streets for the church. Mrs. Cabell was Sarah Winston, the daughter of Judge Edmund Winston, who had held a pew in the old church on Court Street. She also gave $300 of the $2,804 raised for the building. Among the other subscribers were Elijah Fletcher, Chiswell Dabney, Thomas T. Bouldin, David Kyle and Rev. John Early, who afterwards became a Bishop of the Methodist Church, and Marshall Lodge No. 39 of Masons.

Rev. Franklin Genet Smith, a native of New England, who had opened a school in the Masonic Hall, and who had in

September, 1824, assumed charge of the little congregation, was the first rector of the re-established church. Mrs. Cabell wrote of him: "A man of great worth, exercising at all times that charity which beareth all things and is not easily provoked." He remained in charge until 1837, when he resigned to engage in educational work further south. He married Sarah Davis, the daughter of Mr. Henry Davis. During his ministry here a Sunday school was organized, and a pipe organ installed at the cost of $1,000, which was the first organ in the community. The first person buried from this church was Sarah Winston Cabell, who gave the land on which it was built.

Mr. Smith was succeeded by the Rev. Thomas Atkinson, who came from Norfolk, staid until 1843, and was one of the ablest and most beloved ministers who ever held this parish. Ten years after he left Lynchburg he was made Bishop of North Carolina. When the War Between the States came on he upheld the position that Secession did not separate the Southern Diocese from the Protestant Episcopal Church of the United States. However, a different idea prevailed, and the Protestant Episcopal Church in the Confederate States of America was formed. This was never recognized in the North, the names of the Southern Dioceses were kept on the rolls of the parent organization, and when the War was over they were received back as if they had never been absent. A letter from Bishop Hopkins, of Vermont, the presiding Bishop, was addressed to each of the Southern Bishops under date of July 12th, 1865, assuring them all of a cordial welcome to the General Convention, appropriately held that year in Philadelphia, the City of Brotherly Love. The promise was abundantly made good, and under the leadership of Bishop Atkinson the Southern Bishops returned into the open arms of Mother Church.

In the summer of 1843 the Rev. William H. Kinckle, who had been in charge of a church in Cumberland County, was called to succeed Dr. Atkinson, and until his death on the 2nd of March, 1867, in the forty-ninth year of his age, he served his congregation with rare ability and faithfulness. A tablet to his memory was placed on the wall of the old church, and is now in the Sunday school room of the building on Clay Street. It is inscribed: "A faithful soldier of the Cross; he wears the Crown." During Mr. Kinckle's tenure of rectorship a new church building was erected on the site of the first one. The cornerstone was laid June 10th, 1850, and the first services were held on Easter Sunday, 1851. The architect of the building was W. S. Ellison, who also designed the Courthouse, and both buildings proved him to have been a man of talent and culture. The church, though small, was an excellent example of Gothic architecture, and the Courthouse is an unusually fine type of Graeco-Roman style. A portion of the church is still standing on Church Street, where its wall was used in making an apartment house. There was a bell of great sweetness in its tower, which has been transferred to Randolph-Macon Woman's College. During the War Between the States the vestry passed a resolution offering this bell to the government at Richmond in case the Confederacy had need of the metal, but it was never used by the Confederate Government. The bell taken from the first Saint Paul's Church was placed in the Courthouse, and continues to ring out the hours for the city. The clock which also once adorned this same church is the one now used for a town clock on the Courthouse. In Saint Paul's Church a beautiful window was placed to the memory of Rosanna Claytor Steptoe, the widow of Colonel Edward S. Steptoe, already mentioned. She was a lady of large means, and in 1857 had paid off the debt on the church.

During Mr. Kinckle's term at Saint Paul's Grace Memorial Church, so named after he died, and in his memory, was built to accommodate the Diamond Hill neighborhood. This church was built on land donated for the purpose by Mr. Jellis. The land for the rectory was given by Mrs. William Tudor Yancey and was situated about the middle portion of the square on Grace Street where she lived, which city block was a wedding present to her from her father, Henry Davis. It was here that Dr. John Janney Lloyd, and his wife, Ella Hubard Lloyd, remained for fifteen years, and gave to the church and the community at large a very blessed and beautiful service. Grace Church has now been torn down, the ground on which it stood made into a little park, and only memories of it are left, but these memories are very dear to many now living. The congregation is scattered; some to Saint Paul's and some to that other Grace Church built on Fort Hill out of the green rock of old Epiphany Church.

Dr. Henderson Suter came to Saint Paul's after Mr. Kinckle's death. He was a man of deep piety, and fine cultivation of mind. He remained at Saint Paul's from July 1st, 1867, until October 1st, 1869, when he was called to Christ Church in Alexandria, where he served with distinction for many years. In 1870 came Mr. Theodore M. Carson, a native of Winchester, and it was under his leadership that Epiphany Church was built for the benefit of the neighborhood near Miller Park. Mr. Edward S. Gregory was placed in charge at Epiphany Church. He was called the "Poet Priest," and until his death a few years later gave a devoted service. After this the Rev. Mr. Cary Breckenridge Wilmer, a brilliant and accomplished man and a nephew of Bishop Wilmer, was rector at Epiphany Church.

It was during Mr. Carson's ministry that the present stately and beautiful house of worship was built by Saint Paul's congregation. The first sermon preached in the church was on the Sunday before Christmas, 1895, with the Rev. Mr. Lacy assisting in the service. Mr. Carson's sermon was beautiful and eloquent. He was a man of fine presence, and great dignity of character, with a peculiar gift for suitable and fitting words for the occasion. After thirty-three years of labor in behalf of Saint Paul's he, too, was gathered to his fathers. He had grown steadily in the estimation of his people, a good man, full of years and honor. Among those who came to his house after his death was Father McGurk, priest of the Church of the

Holy Cross across the way, and his neighbor for many years. For a long, long time he knelt by his side and prayed.

With Mr. Carson's death we come to comparatively modern times, and a great many of us can remember what has happened since then, but these men I have recalled form a link between the present day and those old, rollicking, fox-hunting priests sent us by the Church of England. It would have been hard to find a more disreputable class of men than some of those Virginia parsons of the eighteenth century. It is said the earlier ones who came over in the seventeenth century were much better men, but later the Church fell on evil days. No doubt that is why the non-Conformists found such a fruitful field in Virginia. That worldly spirit which pervaded the Church of England in the eighteenth century was only too faithfully reflected in the colonial establishment. Many of our Virginia parsons associated themselves with the most dissolute of the laity; they diced, swore, and drank; they backed their favorite birds at the county cock-pits and were as subservient to the great land-owners as ever a cockney was to a lord. There is one good fighting tale about a parson in the Tidewater who was anything but subservient. He fell out with the vestry, who had great power in those days, as they belonged to the privileged and ruling class. In their quarrel they went from words to blows and the parson, who was a man of notable strength, by himself thrashed the whole vestry. On the next Sunday he added insult to injury by preaching from the following text, which he had gone to some pains to cull from Nehemiah: "And I contended with them, and cursed them, and smote certain of them, and plucked off their hair."

Of course, there were exceptions among those eighteenth century parsons, for some of them were good men. But in the days when the Church was restored in Virginia those noble Churchmen stand forth in contrast like true men of God, for they were giants in faith and accomplishment.

When the Episcopal Church was restored in Virginia it had

a hard road to travel, and was very poor. Most of its rich and prominent members had turned Non-Conformist. One of the Wallers had become a Baptist evangelist. The Langhornes were now Methodist and Presbyterian and the Rodes family were Presbyterian. John Camm had been supreme head of the Church of England in Virginia, where the rector of Bruton Church was ruler in all clerical matters since American bishops were not allowed by the English Church. Now, in less than fifty years, his descendents were numbered among the Presbyterians and the Methodists.

CHAPTER VI

PREACHERS AND PEOPLE

AT ONE TIME one of the loveliest homes in Lynchburg was the Saunders home on Court Street. It still stands at the top of the steps leading up Ninth Street to the Courthouse, to the right, and across from the Presbyterian Church. Here Dr. James Saunders and his family lived for many years. The beautiful objects which this noted home contained, the furniture, silver, china and pictures, would form a notable collection for any of the great museums of today. Dr. Saunders, a surgeon in the War of 1812, was a prominent figure in the state. He was a delegate to the Convention of 1829-30, and of 50-51. He made a large fortune in tobacco, and married Anne Rives, whose niece is Amelia Rives, the Princess Troubetskoy. Mrs. Anne Rives Saunders became a noted figure in the Methodist Church, which in the early days was very close to John Wesley in its teachings.

There were many interesting people in this Church, and many preachers of rare ability and eloquence. Among these will be recalled the elder Dr. Williams E. Edwards, a tiny little man, so small that he had to remove the Bible from its accustomed place on the marble altar of the old Methodist Church, for he could not see over it. He spoke with a ringing fervor and with an inspired beauty of thought and language. A unique little figure, with clean shaven upper lip, and small white goatee, he was always dressed with immaculate neatness in a Prince Albert suit and a beaver hat. He spent his last years in Lynchburg, and towards the end Dr. George Carter was sent to assist him.

Dr. Carter had been a brilliant and dashing Confederate soldier, and was a speaker of great force and power. His reasoned sermons were in complete contrast to the old time eloquence of Dr. Edwards. Dr. Carter had had a checkered career. He was a native of Virginia, and had been a professor, a college president, a preacher, a lawyer, an orator, and a colonel in the Confederate Army; but he had fallen sadly from grace. After having shed his blood in the Confederate cause he joined the carpet-baggers. When he grew old he turned again to the Church, which received him back into the fold, and his first charge was given him at Court Street Methodist Church, being sent to help Dr. Edwards in a period of probation. During the shady period of his life he had fought many duels, in one of which he had lost an eye. He was a tall man, and very large. Old ladies remembered him with regret as having been a gallant and handsome figure, but in his later days he had become a sad and battered wreck, an argument in himself for a good life. The beautiful dignity of Dr. Edwards by the side of Dr. Carter produced an impression of an ancient saint and an ancient satyr, of Christianity and Paganism in old age, side by side.

In the Methodist Church Mr. Edward S. Brown and Mr. E. C. Glass taught a Sunday school class for men. The Sunday school was very largely attended, and there was great enthusiasm in the work. Miss Lucy Brown, the granddaughter of Bishop Early, whose portrait hung above the altar in the old church, taught the infant class. When she became the wife of Mr. John Wesley Childs the class was taken by Miss Cornelia Brown. The old church had beautiful Corinthian columns on each side of the altar. When it was taken down to be superseded by the present church these columns were salvaged by Mrs. Thomas D. Christian, and used in her front porch on Washington Street. The Adams family of Daniel's Hill was prominent in this church, all three brothers, Mr. Holcombe Adams, Mr. duVal Adams, and Captain Richard Adams being members. Colonel James Watts and his family and Mr. John W. Carroll's family also attended, and for years Mr. John P. Pettyjohn has been a tower of strength to this church.

There are many now gone whose activity and usefulness as members of the Court Street Church are remembered; among them were Colonel Forsberg and Mrs. Forsberg, who lived for years in that historic building which, having served as a Masonic Hall, was rolled on wheels up to Fifth Street, between Church and Main, and there converted into a picturesque and charming home. Valued members of this congregation were Mr. and Mrs. Edward S. Brown and their talented daughters, and Mr. Winston Ivey, their son-in-law. The Seay, the Jennings, the Gregory, the Jones, and the Williams families, all closely connected and kin, were of this congregation. Miss Ellie Seay was organist there for years, and her sister, Mrs. Tipton Jennings was also a prominent member. Ruth Jennings, the daughter of Mr. Tipton Jennings, who married Mr. Lawton, of South Carolina, became a strong figure in the United Daughters of the Confederacy. Of this church also was Marcella Jones, known to the youth of Lynchburg as "Miss Marce," who for years has been engaged in instructing the younger generation. Her humor, her charm and wisdom, have been no small asset in the development of Lynchburg people. Of this congregation many today recall that fine, soldierly figure, Mr. William Gregory. After the death of his wife he devoted the rest of his life with singular fidelity to his little daughters. The Confederate soldier and the Virginia gentleman to the end of his days, he left to his children and his grandchildren a proud heritage.

In all of Lynchburg there was no kinder or more generous man than Mr. James T. Williams. Particularly was his kindness realized by young men from the country who came to town seeking their fortunes, for he helped them make their way with rare goodness. Many of our citizens remember his home on Federal Street, at the corner of Ninth, the place once owned by Mr. John Speed. Here Mr. Williams had a beautiful terraced garden, where summer houses, gay flowers, and strutting peacocks contrived to make a veritable fairy land for childish eyes.

Another wonderful garden on Federal Street belonged to Mrs. Rosanna Claytor Steptoe, widow of that distinguished soldier of the Mexican War, Colonel Edward S. Steptoe, already mentioned for her generosity to Saint Paul's Church. She lived in

The Lecky House, built 1810; "Hope Dawn," built 1810, near Boonesboro, Lynchburg, Va.
Courtesy of Kiah T. Ford Company, Realtors.

the large house on the corner of Sixth and Federal Streets which is now the residence of Mrs. R. A. Owen. Her garden extended a whole square, up to Fifth, where her lilies and larkspur bloomed on the high wall overlooking Fifth Street. Many noted homes were on Federal Street. Near Mrs. Steptoe's house, and across the street, was the residence of Colonel Augustine Leftwich. Up on the hill beyond Mr. Williams' house, where the school building now stands, was the former residence of Mr. Chas. L. Mosby, one of the most brilliant of all Virginia lawyers. The next residence was the home of Judge Daniel A. Wilson. Here his daughter, Miss Lucy Wilson, taught school for many years after the War Between the States. Opposite Judge Wilson lived Mr. Thomas Holcombe, a member of a distinguished family, who owned the school at Bellevue which Mr. Abbot later bought. The residence now owned by Mr. Claiborne Gooch, on the corner of Federal and Eleventh, then belonged to Mr. John M. Otey, who, with Mr. Daniel Warwick, owned that entire square.

Many of the finest homes in Lynchburg were built by members of the Murrell family. They owned the place which later passed into the hands of Mrs. Steptoe, and which has been described above. They built the handsome brick residence now occupied by Mr. Harper, which was also at one time the Halsey residence. They built the fine old mansion which for so many years was associated in the minds of Lynchburg people with General Munford. This typical ante-bellum residence was exchanged by the Murrell family for a very fine place called Glen Alton, which General Munford had inherited from his first wife. Glen Alton, which has since been burned down, was in Bedford County and one of the most noted homes in this section of Virginia. The present residence of Mr. William Hickson on Madison Street, which for a brief season was the home of Colonel Huger and his wife, who before her marriage was Miss Julia Treble, was likewise built by one of the Murrells.

About fifty years ago one of our papers contained the following recollections of Court Street: "It is a curious fact that in the death of Dr. Robert S. Payne almost the last of our old citizens whose families have adorned Court Street society within the last thirty years have been removed from amongst us. There were once his next door neighbors Bishop John Early and his excellent wife, then John M. Warwick and wife; next Dr. James Saunders, Anderson H. Armistead and wife, Mrs. Susan B. Adams, Alexander Liggat and wife, Whitmel P. Tunstall, James L. C. Taylor, Edwin Mathews, Dr. Henry Latham and wife, Henry D. Flood, Henry Dunnington and wife, Benj. E. Scruggs, Col. Abram F. Biggers and Capt. A. F. Biggers, Wm. T. Towns and wife, A. B. Rucker, James L. Brown and wife, Mrs. Caroline M. F. Morgan, Wm. T. Booker, Mr. and Mrs. Amos Botsford, Col. Robert L. Owen, Robinson and Thomas L. Stabler, Sr., Peter L. Dudley and Joseph B. Nowlin. This long list of once prominent and leading citizens on a single street have all gone down, one after the other, to the silent tomb within the last generation. After a close survey of the whole field, the writer of this can call to mind only one single member of all the old family regime on Court Street (a noble Christian woman), who still survives her comrades and friends, waiting for the reaper to come with his resistless scythe, to pass her over the river to rest, with her husband and departed companions, under the shade of the trees.

But while it is sad to remember that all these heads of families have been, in the course of nature, gathered to their fathers in a single generation, it is still pleasing to the mind and gratifying to the pride of our people to observe how rapidly Court Street has grown in the last decade in population, in wealth, and in adornment, and with what strides it is springing into one of the most beautiful and desirable streets in our beautiful City of Hills."

CHAPTER VII
MASTER AND SLAVE

IN ITS issue of December 8th, 1923, Collier's Weekly printed these words in an article, said to have been written by a Southern man: "I grew up to dislike Negroes generally, just as almost everybody in the South does, for no particular reason except that a nigger is a nigger." Southern people must have read this with astonishment. By the side of that statement may be placed this item, which a little later was published in The News of Lynchburg:

A Home in the Virginia Mountains, Built About 1808

"Bland Massie was buried Friday at two o'clock in his family burying ground at Tyro, his home in Nelson County. Rev. Frank Messick, rector of Grace Episcopal Church at Massie's Mills, of which Mr. Massie was a member, conducted the service, and Mr. Massie's colored friends sang 'Good Night' at the grave."

This account of Bland Massie's funeral is typical of the Southern gentleman. Mr. Massie was born in 1858. His people were large slave owners and large land owners. They owned most of the land in that part of Nelson County where he lived and died. So after the War, when he was growing up, he might be said to have suffered all the reverses incidental to the freeing of slaves, and if there was hatred for the Negro in Virginia he should have felt it. The Negro question had plunged him from a position of affluence into those struggles with disaster which followed the War. Yet that scene at his grave can not be said to indicate hatred.

The mountains surround Nelson County as a hedge surrounds a garden, though there is no hedge of royal blue which grows so high that it seems to touch the sky itself. It is like that around the little church at Massie's Mills. Close by Tye River a mountain stream full of speckled trout leaps its way over rocks and ridges. It is a scene of heart-breaking beauty. And it was there that those melodious voices of Bland Massie's colored friends swelled out until they filled that lonely, lovely space between the mountains and climbed the tall peaks up into the blue sky in farewell to young marster, and to old marster; a long farewell to the old perishing order which soon will be as extinct as the wood duck.

It seems impossible that a Southern man could have expressed such a sentiment towards the Negro as that quoted from Collier's. The fact is undeniable that the white people in the South have a deep-rooted attachment for the colored race. In times past, colored people themselves had a simple but effective rule by which they classified the white people of the South. To them white people either belonged to families who had owned slaves or to families who did not. Strange as it may seem, to an outsider indeed the veriest paradox of a situation, there has always been a bitter antipathy between the Negro and not the man who

Old Slave Cabin on the Quick Place in Amherst County.

Courtesy of Kiah T. Ford Company, Realtors.

owned slaves, but the man who did not own slaves. To the Negro the people who did not own slaves before the War were "po' white folks," and always would be, no matter how rich they had grown since the War. However poor the old slave owner and his descendants had become, they would always be what the Negro called "the top of the pot." The reason this enmity was returned by the non-slave-owning element of the population was because the Negro had been a very serious rival to the white laboring man, mechanic and artisan in his efforts to gain a livelihood in the South. The Negro had his own primitive way of showing his scorn for those who were not able to buy slaves; he did not hesitate to make himself as obnoxious as he dared be towards those he considered natural-born enemies. In spite of the changes which have taken place in the last decade there is still something of this same feeling left, and no thoughtful person can deny the fundamental justice of it. The sense of responsibility that the old slave owner continued to feel towards his emancipated servants helped to push him down into deeper poverty than that in which the War had left him. He knew that the slaves were not able to stand alone, and he realized an obligation to the Negroes which would not allow him to turn them adrift. The former slave-owner was now poorer than his neighbor who had never owned slaves, and was further encumbered by his sense of duty to share his little mite with his old servants, and out of his poor means to continue to clothe and house those who were not able to do this for themselves. These were no small burdens to the Southern aristocrat in his efforts to forge ahead after the War. Since the land has changed hands, there is no doubt the colored people miss these good old friends. They used to talk about how "rebbish" old Master and old Miss were, but in these days they speak of them with regret and affection.

Some years ago Major Halsey wrote this article which he has kindly allowed me to use here:

LYNCHBURG AND ITS NEIGHBORS

Justice

I was in the Confederate Army from Manassas to Appomattox, and what I have to say about the Negro is that our homes and families were left almost, and in many cases entirely in their care, and if in the whole South there was a single instance of abuse of this confidence during that period, I never knew or heard of it. With the same blood in their veins, the present generation must be as true blue as our dear old colored mammies and uncles of that day, and this being so you can depend on them now all right. My old cook, a servant of the family, was captured in a charge we made upon the enemy. He was late coming into our camp that night, and I said to him, "Joe, where have you been?" and he said, "They captured me this morning when you charge them, and one of their officers asked me where I belonged, and I said, 'To them over there,' nodding to our Confederate side; he then asked me where I wanted to go, and I told him, 'Over there,' when he said to me, 'Then, damn you, go!' And I went." This is the bond which existed between the whites and the blacks in the South, in those days, and if the test comes you will find the same exists now. Keep your eyes open for the misguided of both races. It wont hurt the true of either.

S. P. HALSEY.

We have gone through many phases with the Negro; we have seen them led astray by misguided leaders, white and black, for they are an emotional race, easily swayed by momentary feeling; but in most cases they have not gone too far before reason and sanity have regained control over their minds and hearts.

One great charm about the old Virginia life was its entire lack of pretense. We lived to ourselves in a delightful way, each plantation being a little principality in itself, its owner a veritable lord of his own domain; but we were an unpretentious people, and consequently unselfconscious. Nothing has been more absurdly exaggerated than the tales of the Virginia planter's grandeur. There were some very fine old homes, and numbers of them are standing yet, but many have fallen into ruins or have been burned. Frequently an outsider is disappointed when he at last sees some of these much talked of old homes. The descriptions he has heard have no doubt aroused visions of lordly mansions, when the reality is a very nobly designed and well-built brick house of possibly eight rooms with "office" buildings for overflow guests outside, or maybe just a rambling old frame house. These oft-told splendors of the Edgewoods and Otterviews and Sailor's Rests may well bring a smile to the lips of the outsider when he looks upon them as they really are, but never to a Virginian who knows the large welcome, and the princely hospitality extended within those gates. Though simplicity reigned in these houses, the greatest cabinet makers of England were none too good to furnish them. The Virginia ladies had a very nice taste in beds and bureaus, in sofas and tables, in china and in silver, and no man would go further than a Virginian to please his wife. And she herself loved to please him. One of his chief weaknesses was a love of good food, and she saw to it that he ate like a king. Under the discriminating eyes of these Southern mistresses their Negro cooks developed a culinary art which has probably never been excelled. Their meals were prepared from an assortment of recipes handed down in families from generation to generation, and gathered from strangely different sources. Some were brought from the great, flag-paved kitchens of old England, others can be traced back to the native villages of Africa, or to the camp-fires of the Powhatan tribe of Indians, and thus there were such distinctive things on Southern tables as brunswick stew, beaten biscuit, corn pudding, corn fritters, batterbread, with roe herring, fried chicken and Virginia ham. The Virginia people were a simple people, without any desire for display and ostentation, and your pompous fellow, full of pride and vain-glory, is no true son of Virginia. For instance, in those days fox-hunting was a fine sport, and the natural pastime of the Virginia gentry. But do not imagine the old Virginia gentleman tricked out in a pink coat and riding as if he were in a circus ring. He and his neighbors had inherited the love of fox-hunting from their ancestors, who had brought with them from the mother country this habit and its customs at a period when it was practised in a very different style from the present way. In those days they started their fox at daybreak, and pottered along after slow hounds for hours and hours, and they got a fox, and a fine day's outing. If a rail fence stood in their way, they pulled it down, unless it was a mighty low one, and there was none of the glitter and affectation of this modern steeple-chasing: they went out, not to show off fine hunting clothes or feats in riding, like a country boy at a tournament, but to get a fox in an honest-to-God fox-hunt.

As to the way they lived in their own homes, a further authority is an extract from a letter written by Mrs. Carrington, a kinswoman of the Washingtons, which very clearly shows that, when not entertaining distinguished company, George Washington and his wife, Martha, lived a simple and industrious life. Mrs. Edward Carrington, whose maiden name was Elizabeth Jaquelin Ambler, was born March 11th, 1765, and died February 15th, 1842. She was married first to William Brent, who did not live long, and her second husband was Colonel Edward Carrington. She left no children. Colonel Carrington was a great favorite with Washington and Generals Green, Marion and Sumpter also thought most higly of him for services he had rendered them in the Southern Campaign. Colonel and Mrs. Carrington visited Mount Vernon not long before Washington's death, and of this visit she writes to her sister, Mrs. Fisher.

She speaks of the hearty welcome they received from the General and his lady, Martha, and though their usual hour for retiring was nine, on this occasion they sat up until twelve while Colonel Carrington and his host were lost in old scenes, and discussing old campaigns with Pulaski, Kosciusko and others. Mrs. Washington also spoke of her old days, her public life of levees and receiving company, but she called them her lost days. Her bedroom is described as being more of a sittingroom and workroom, where she directed the servants, and where General Washington sat before the fire and read. Many of us will recognize this picture of old Virginia life. In the words of Mrs. Carrington: "Let us repair to the old lady's room, which is precisely in the style of our good old aunt's; that is to say, nicely fixed for all sorts of work. On one side sits the chambermaid with her knitting; on the other a little colored pet, learning to sew. An old, decent woman is there, with her table and shears, cutting out the Negroes' winter clothes, while the good old lady directs them all, incessantly knitting herself. She points out to me several pairs of nice colored stockings and gloves she has just finished, and presents me with a pair half done, which she begs I will finish and wear for her sake. It is wonderful after a life spent as these good people have necessarily spent theirs, to see them in retirement assume those domestic habits that prevail in our country.

If the wife of General Washington, having her own and his wealth at command, should thus choose to live, how much more would the wives and mothers of Virginia with moderate fortunes and numerous children. How often have I seen, added to the above-mentioned scenes of the chamber, the instruction of several sons and daughters also going on, the churn, the reel, and other domestic operations, all in progress at the same time, and the mistress, too, lying on a sick bed. There are still such to be found, though I fear that the march of refinement is carrying many beyond such good old ways."

It is quite possible that the march may not always be towards refinement, for to this typical scene of Southern life we may add the fact that the Southern women had almost entirely in their hands the evangelization of thousands of a heathen race. That this duty was well performed by them is borne out by the fine type of Christian character which most of us remember in our old "Mammies" and "Uncles," and by the fact that a Negro who hadn't "got religion" was unheard of. In caring for the sick and disabled Negroes, in teaching good manners, cooking, sewing, spinning and weaving and other handicrafts to a savage and primitive people the Southern women gave the world a constructive work in social service. Superintending the instruction and administering the welfare of large numbers of these people was an executive work such as few women of today have an opportunity of accomplishing. The life was a culture in itself and it bred a people with a high sense of responsibility towards the laborer. If "Ole Master's" fortunes suffered from drought, flood or pestilence, and he came upon lean years, there was no thought of turning his dependents out to shift for themselves "until business picked up." The slaves were fed and clothed and housed, and their sick were cared for regardless of the tight pinch in which "Ole Master" found himself. This spirit of "Noblesse Oblige," which has been so sadly lacking in our country during the present depression, was the real tie between the Negro and his Master. It was a very human tie, and a genuine affection and gratitude was the bond that kept our old servants faithful during those bitter years of the War.

CHAPTER VIII
LYNCHBURG IN THE 1830's

IT HAS been said that a great drought in 1755 was largely responsible for bringing on the Revolutionary War. The tobacco crop was an utter failure that year, and as tobacco was the general currency of the colony the people could not pay the clergy, and so started a row which gathered and grew until it had spread throughout all the colonies. Tobacco must have played no small part in bringing about the War Between the States. The New England people were naturally very much disgruntled by the manner of life of the Southerners. There they were, God's chosen, working and sweating on their poor and stony ground for a bare subsistence, and here were the Southern planters raking in the shekels from tobacco and cotton, and nothing to do but sit in the shade and drink mint juleps with plenty of darkies to wait on them. To the Puritan mind it just wasn't right for any one to be so comfortable. There was Richmond with its fast clipper ships, its tea trade with the East, and its South American and Cuban trade, holding auctions twice a month, selling its goods all over the country and becoming a great port. Even little Lynchburg was now the greatest tobacco market in the world, and the richest city for its size in the country. Harriet Beecher Stowe's venomous book became a bestseller because it fitted right into the mood of the North. The South could not enjoy all this luxury without the Negro, so the Negro must be freed, and the Abolitionist began to work himself into a frenzy over slavery.

Lynchburg deserved her success, for her tobacconists had done as much for the tobacco trade as the tobacco trade had done for them. Lynchburg tobacconists took the crude weed, which was being used mostly in the primitive state just as it had been used by the Indians, and they worked it into various forms for the convenience of the public. Mr. Labby and Mr. Hare discovered a formula for treating tobacco with licorice, a thing never before done, which rendered it far more palatable. Mr. Maurice Moore made further improvements in its manufacture which were of great value to the trade. At one time Mr. Moore had the largest tobacco business in the world, and his favorite brand, Killickinick, was the most widely known brand of tobacco in the world. This name, Killickinick, which he selected, is one of the most appropriate of all names for a brand of tobacco, for Killickinick is an Indian word of Algonquin origin meaning a mixture for smoking. Mr. Moore invented the first machinery ever used for pulverizing tobacco. Until this time the dried leaf was broken up by each individual for immediate use in his pipe, as the occasion demanded, but by Mr. Moore's invention the tobacco was pulverized to a suitable consistency for smoking, and then packed into wooden boxes, about the size of our coffee can of today. He prepared his tobacco with extreme care, and by a special treatment originating with him, he greatly improved the flavor, depriving it of its rankness and imparting to it a mild and mellow quality hitherto unknown. This was done by spreading the tobacco on the factory floor and sprinkling it with water. When the mass became heated and began to smoke he would have his factory hands toss it from one side of the floor to the other, until it had been properly ripened to that well-flavored condition which smokers find desirable. Mr. Moore's life was a notable example of the true American who finds intelligence, industry and integrity the only capital needed for building a fortune. He came to Lynchburg from Fluvanna County at the age of seventeen, and when he reached this town he had two dollars and a half in his pocket. At the end of thirty-six years he retired from business, having made all the money he wanted. During that period his factory had been burnt out twice, and so he was twice compelled to start at the beginning. In spite of these two disasters, which would have meant ruin to a lesser man, and in spite of a very frail and delicate constitution, he had become one of the most important figures in the tobacco business of the world. He was the pioneer manufacturer of smoking tobacco in the United States, the first manufacturer in the world to make smoking tobacco, and in 1861 his was the world's largest tobacco business.

Mr. Moore's success was somewhat equalled by that of Mr. John Wesley Carroll, who also came to Lynchburg seeking his fortune and built up a vast trade in the manufacture of granulated smoking tobacco. His famous brand, Lone Jack, received world-wide recognition. On the little yellow cotton bags in which it was packed was pictured the likeness of a man smoking a pipe, a brand which made a large fortune for its owner because of its unvarying excellence.

There were many peculiar customs in regard to the sale of tobacco, some of which have been completely forgotten. When "the breaks were on," which expression meant that a sale of tobacco was to be held in the warehouse, a man would go up and down the street winding a horn. In later years a bell was rung to notify those interested, and even today a bell for this purpose is now hanging in Pace's Warehouse. This warehouse will soon be torn down to make room for a new City Market.

The advent of the packet boat put an end to the custom of bringing tobacco to market in bateaux, or rolling it in packed hogsheads, as previously described in this book. George Washington himself staked out the James River and Kanawha Canal. The original proposition was a plan to connect this system with the Ohio River, by running the boats through West Virginia on the Kanawha, which empties into the Ohio, and thus establishing a water course from the Atlantic to the Gulf of Mexico. But the work was never completed any further than Buchanan. However, on December 2nd, 1839, it had been finished from Richmond to Lynchburg, and on the third of December the first packet boat arrived in the Lynchburg waters.

Before describing the festivities occasioned by the arrival of the packet boat, let us pause and take a look at the town. From the earliest days of its history the wild beauty of our country had been remarked on. One of the first travellers this way, who left a record of the town, was Mrs. Ann Royal, and although she wrote of our people with a pen dipped in gall, she could find nothing but admiration for the scene in which we dwell. In her Black Book, which describes a tour made through the South, published in 1830, she speaks of leaving Charlottesville before day "on a Monday, for Lynchburg on James River near the Blue Ridge, a place of considerable trade, and one I had long wished to see." Travelling by stage coach, she reached Lynchburg about 8:30 in the evening, having stopped at Amherst for dinner at a house kept by one Powell. The journey carried them through a scene of surpassing beauty, as she said, the Blue Ridge Mountains overtopped by the Peaks of Otter seemed to move on in concert with them as they traveled.

The next day disclosed one of the richest pictures of scenery and activity, doubtless to be found in Virginia. "In point of scenery," she declared, "it is far beyond Richmond, and very little behind it in business, and the scenery the most rich and varied in the same bounds of which any town in the Union can boast. Situated on James River, the land on which it stands ascends from the water's edge, at first gradual, then more abrupt, and finally terminates on an elevated plain, or table land. From this summit you have a view unequalled for grandeur or beauty. A smooth, broad river rolls at your feet, and against the opposite shore, which rises in an abrupt, high bluff, with huge rocks of terrific wildness, terminating in smooth, conic hills, beyond which are seen farms and houses. Again, up the river, the wildest hills and ledges of rocks run close to the river's edge, and beyond are the Blue Ridge. The banks of the river are lined with towering trees; the enormous sycamores, with their outstretched branches; to this we may add freight boats" (bateaux) "moored, ready for use, skimming wild duck, farms and pleasure grounds, falling gardens, rolling carts, rattling stages, thundering wagons, and a busy multitude. The long warehouses, the gay shops, and the elegant buildings present a most life-

Early Means of Transportation.

Courtesy of Mrs. Blencowe.

stirring scene. The rough, the smooth, the sublime, the beautiful thickly mingle and combine here every phrase of the picturesque and fanciful; certainly the most finished picture of spontaneous as well as studied beauty to be met with perhaps in the world, appealing most powerfully to the feelings—never such a number of images drawn within so narrow a compass." This writer, however, tells us that our town was cursed with priestcraft and missionaries, which seems paradoxical in view of the fact that she also says: "The ladies of Lynchburg are very handsome, but spoil themselves by laying on ten times as many curls upon their heads as the fashion requires. * * * These are the handsomest females I met in Virginia."

The year of Mrs. Royal's visit to Lynchburg was the year that the new water system was installed, and of this also she gives a long account in her book. The population she states was "6,000; established by Legislature in 1786, incorporated in 1805. At that time there were 15 lawyers, 18 physicians, 11 stores, 41 grocery stores, 3 auction stores, 3 confectionery stores, 1 brass foundry, 3 hat stores, 2 Bible societies, 3 rope walks, 6 tailor shops, 3 chair factories, 3 cabinet warehouses, 2 printing offices (each publishing a semi-weekly paper), 2 Methodist churches, 1 Reformed Methodist church (very splendid), a Masonic Hall, a Courthouse with a large bell attached to it, a stone jail, 18 dry goods stores, 3 apothecary shops, 5 millinery stores, 3 tin and coppersmith stores, 3 shoe stores, 2 book stores, 1 tract society, 5 saddler's shops, 7 shoemaker's shops, 3 coach-maker's shops, 1 gunsmith's shop, 2 banks, 1 Presbyterian church, 2 Baptist churches, and 1 Episcopal church (a very fine building) that has a large organ.

The jail was supposed to be the best in Virginia, and equal to any in the United States. There are 7 tobacco warehouses, which annually inspect from 15,000 to 18,000 hogsheads, each weighing 1,500 pounds. This is the largest tobacco inspection in the United States. They export annually from 20,000 to 30,000 barrels of flour. The produce is conveyed in bateaux from here to Richmond, upon an average of 9,000 pounds, varying according to the height of the river. There are about 500 bateaux employed between this and Richmond, which keeps about 1,500 hands employed. There are two large manufacturing mills. The Messrs. Langhorne are now erecting one on a much larger scale in the upper county; they purchased their water-power from the Corporation here. The town owns besides 1 carding machine, 1 powder magazine, 1 toll bridge across James River 225 yards wide. The merchants of Lynchburg purchase 10,000 head of hogs annually, principally in droves from the states of Kentucky and Ohio." Mrs. Royal also mentions the good turnpike road to Salem.

In an old Lynchburg Virginian on Thursday, September 1st, 1831, are found various items which draw an interesting picture of the busy little town at this time. The Langhorne Mills referred to by Mrs. Royall advertise that they had been in readiness for wheat since July 20th; "those mills are situated on the bank of Blackwater Creek, just above the toll bridge. The creek being navigable will admit of boats receiving and delivering their loads at the door of the mills." (The owners of these mills were Maurice Langhorne and Harry S. Langhorne, Lady Astor's great-grandfather.) "The Lynchburg Mills, owned by John and C. E. Lynch, are also announcing their readiness to receive wheat, and they notify the public and the farmers that they are erecting a lumber house on Main Street near the Union Hotel for the reception of wheat, which will obviate the inconvenience and sometimes difficulty of getting to the mill.

Flour is selling at $4.50 per barrel, wheat at 87 and ½ cts. per bushel, whiskey at 41 to 42 cts. per gallon. Freight down the River per hundred 16 to 18 cts. Freight up the River, 25 to 30 cts.

On Friday Evening, in front of the Market House, C. & D. B. Phelps will sell three or four Negroes at auction.

Garland Tate and Seth Woodruff advertise for 150 likely

Negroes of both sexes. Particularly do they wish 2 blacksmiths, 2 bricklayers, and 2 or more good coopers.

On Bank Square Turner and Kerr are this day opening 1 case handsome Dumstable Bonnets, 10 pieces Nankeen crape, 10 pieces Pongee, 30 pieces beautiful figured Swiss Muslin. Also Italian Leutstring, Changeable silk, and gauze crepe Lisse shawls.

Dinkle & Rumbough advertise 50 cases of fur hats of superior quality, at their old hatter's stand on Bank Square. Philo Lacy advertises boots and shoes at the store he has taken on Bank Square a little below Dr. Duval's. The Races over the Rocky Mount Course will commence on Thursday, Sept. 22nd. Benjamin Schoolfield gives notice to the public of his petition to the next Virginia Legislature for leave to build a toll-bridge over James River near Lynchburg, from his land in Amherst County to the land of Judge William Daniel on the opposite shore. Kyle and Borland advertise Prints, Cambric, Muslins, Jaconet, Belt Ribbons, Swiss Crepes and Collars, Black Prunella, German and British Oznaburgs, shell tuck combs, and 30 boxes of the best genuine hair Puffs.

Piedmont Stage Coach leaves Washington at noon on Tuesday, Thursday and Saturday. Distance from Washington to Salem, Va., 253 miles, time 3 and ½ days, fare 17.25. There were many lotteries advertised: The Dismal Swamp Lottery was one of them.

Church Street was called School Street because of its numerous schools. Rev. W. S. Reid and his brother, John Reid, kept a school here, also Mr. John Carey, Mr. Franklin Genet Smith, Mr. Rawson, Mrs. Victor, Miss Maria Victor, and Mrs. Loyd. J. & S. Cole and Robert O. Burton advertise the opening of their schools for the fall session. Mr. Smith opens on the 12th of September for young ladies, and Mrs. Tompkins, he mentions, will continue to give lessons in music, and will receive young ladies in her family as boarders. Mr. Vincent, now employed at Hampden-Sidney College as a teacher of French, is engaged to give lessons in this school. Terms for the session of five months, including fuel, stationary and all other charges, were $15, payable in advance."

Such then was the scene of Mrs. Royal's visit about 1830. Another important visitor came to Lynchburg in 1839. It was the first packet boat, which arrived in these waters December 3rd. There were now six thousand three hundred and ninety-five people here, and all of this number who could possibly get there were down on the river bank waiting for the boat to come in; every citizen of the town, every man, woman and child, white or black, rich or poor, was hanging on the banks of the James. Those of us who had ancestors here at that time know exactly where those ancestors were on that day. The Mayor, the Council, the Clergy, the volunteer companies with bands, all were there, and there they remained, for it was about four o'clock of the short winter afternoon when the winding of the boat horn announced that the packet boat was near. Again and again it was heard, each time sounding nearer, until around the curve the horses could be seen coming up the tow-path as fast as they could trot, and then the boat appeared to the wildly cheering populace.

The guns began to fire, the bands began to play, while the boat came in and docked at Renwick's Warehouse, on the place where the building of the George D. Witt Shoe Company stands today. Mr. Charles L. Mosby now stepped on board, and was introduced as the speaker of the occasion. He first presented a stand of colors to the helmsman, and then began to make his speech. Near its close, in a burst of eloquence, he made a sweeping gesture, and so losing his balance he fell into the water. As he came out, dripping wet, a fellow townsman shouted: "Neighbor, you've quit the Presbyterians and jined the Baptists!"

Before the spring of 1840 the line of boats were well established between Lynchburg and Richmond. The John Marshall, the Joseph C. Cabell and the Captain Huntley, fare eight dollars, were leaving on Monday, Wednesday and Friday of each

The Old Packet Boat "Marshall," on which the remains of "Stonewall" Jackson were conveyed to Lexington, Va., via Lynchburg. For many years this old boat rested on the banks of James River just above Orange Bridge, in the corporate limits of Lynchburg.

week, at 7:30 A. M. The line was finally finished as far as Buchanan, but no effort was made to carry out Washington's original plan for connecting the system with the Ohio River, for the day of railroads was at hand. However, until 1880 these boats were in operation, for although slow they offered a charming mode of traveling, and were said to have been like a delightful house party where one met all one's friends, had plenty of time to talk to them, and to hear all they had to say in return. The food on these boats was very fine, and although the inconvenience of sleeping, washing, and dressing, must have been considerable, travelling on a packet boat was on the whole a very agreeable experience.

One of the last packet boats to be used on the canal was the "John Marshall," which carried the body of Stonewall Jackson from Richmond to Lexington to be buried on May 13th, 1863. When its working days were over the old boat was drawn ashore just above the Orange Bridge and there it rested for many years. An old man and his wife lived for a long time under the decaying roof of this last packet boat. About twenty years ago, during an unusually high flood of the James River, the old boat washed away and it was a very pathetic sight to see the poor old couple trudging off down the railroad tracks with their mattress on their shoulders.

CHAPTER IX
WAR

THE people of the South were fully acquainted with the causes which led them into war; there were many causes, and all of them did not hinge upon slavery. As early as 1826 Lynchburg had her Colonization Society, which was instrumental in sending out many Negroes as colonists to Liberia. General Jackson, as we know, had only one slave, and him he bought at the slave's request. Certainly Jackson did not fight for slavery. Slavery, of course, was an opportune argument for the North and an easy brand with which to fire men's emotions, just as in later days Weyler's cruelty fired men to battle, and German "inhumanity" was fine propaganda for the Allies, so slavery became in the hands of zealous political leaders. Many thoughtful people today deplore the entire defeat of States Rights, and dread the too-great power delegated to the Government at Washington. George Bagby describes an incident in his life at Camp Lee, the instruction camp situated at Richmond, where he was learning the art of war before the first Battle of Manassas. "The company next to ours was from Campbell County, and composed almost wholly of illiterate countrymen. Hearing an animated conversation going on towards their camp-fire one night, I drew nigh and listened. The causes that led to the War were being discussed, and the principal speaker, a sergeant, gave an account of the formation of our government that would have done credit to a constitutional lawyer. On inquiry I learned that the sergeant was by trade a plasterer, and what he knew about the government he had learned from stump speakers. He was a pretty fair specimen of the average Confederate soldier, who knew what he was about when he entered into the War."

In Lynchburg the Home Guard was the first military organization produced by the alarms which preceded the War Between the States. Samuel Garland, a young lawyer and a graduate of the Virginia Military Institute, had been deeply stirred by the feeling displayed in the North against the South at the time of John Brown's Raid, and with the assistance of several young men of the town he formed the company on November 8th, 1859.

When the call to arms reached Lynchburg it found ready volunteers. Describing the beginning of that famous regiment, the Second Virginia Cavalry, are these words of General Thomas T. Munford: "The Second Virginia Cavalry was the first mounted regiment organized, and the only regiment thoroughly organized in the Virginia State Troops until after the first Battle of Manassas. It was mustered into service by Colonel Jubal A. Early at Lynchburg, May 18th, 1861, Colonel E. Kirby Smith commanding that post. Colonel R. C. W. Radford commanding a company of Rangers, whose rendezvous was Forest Depot, Bedford County, Virginia, tendered the services of his company in response to the call of the Governor of Virginia for troops to repel invasion, and in reply received from Governor Letcher a Colonel's commission, with a Lieutenant-Colonel's Commission for his first Lieutenant, Thomas T. Munford, with authority to raise a regiment of mounted men. Steps were immediately taken to perfect the organization, his old company electing Winston Radford, elder brother of the Colonel, Captain by acclamation. Colonel Radford established his headquarters at Lynchburg, and in a few weeks had accepted three companies from Bedford, one from Franklin, one from Botetourt, one from Amherst, one from Campbell, one from the city of Lynchburg, and one from Albemarle. Colonel Radford, having served eight years in the regular army, a graduate of the United States Military Academy at West Point, was familiar with all the details of this work, and surmounted a thousand difficulties in the way of supplies for the ordinance and quartermaster departments. Selecting the present Fair Grounds" (now Miller Park), "then a beautiful grove one mile west of the city, the companies were put under rigorous discipline and drill as fast as they arrived, and soon realized the fact that this was a serious business. They were supplied with double-barrelled shot-guns, and a few old-fashioned sabres used by Virginia troops during the Revolutionary War" (thus they used the same arms with which our men under Washington had fought the British).

"Troops from the South were daily pouring in on every train, and generally all armed. You rarely met a fellow without his Bowie knife, varying from six to eighteen inches in length, sticking out of his belt, balanced on the other side by one or two Colt's revolvers, according to the weight of his knife. But, alas! how few knew what they would meet. How few of these generous-hearted original volunteers were living after the War to recount those early and gay scenes, and to recall the pleasures and fancied hardships of this rigorous camp of instruction. How terrible it seemed to them not to be allowed by the Colonel to leave camp without his written permission, to be required to mount a horse on his left side, when he had been accustomed to get up either on the right or the left side ever since he had learned to ride, to hold the reins in his left hand when a man was right-handed, and had always held the reins in his right hand. Accustomed to arms and horses all their lives, each man furnished both at his own expense. I hazard nothing in saying that it was composed of the best material, and as splendid a regiment as ever took the field. Colonel Radford was supported by at least one graduate of the Virginia Military Institute in every company, a squadron whose military training added so much to perfect the training of the Army of Northern Virginia.

"During the six weeks at the camp of instruction thousands of our people, wives, children, parents, sweethearts and friends visited the brave soldier boys. Many were the joys and sorrows at parting, many the tears that fell, and the prayers that were offered for these joyous, dashing lads who were going to leave their mountain homes, to meet the Yankees, many for the first time, and the last time."

This was the first Regiment of Cavalry to be organized in Virginia, but it surrendered its rightfully deserved number as a courtesy to General J. E. B. Stuart, and was called the Second Virginia. Before this the Lynchburg Home Guard had been fully armed and equipped, except for a flag, and on the 30th of March, 1860, a stand of colors was presented them by the ladies of the town. Of this company Samuel Garland, Jr., was elected Captain, with Kirkwood Otey, Marcellus N. Moorman, John G. Meem, Jr., and Samuel M. Simpson as Lieutenants, ranking in the order mentioned here.

At the Battle of Manassas the Lynchburg companies were under the command of Longstreet in the Eleventh Regiment, and evinced, as reported, "the most soldierly spirit." The Second Virginia Cavalry, though under fire all day was not actively engaged until, when the enemy was in full retreat, they were ordered to intercept them between the Stone Bridge and Centreville. The regiment, one thousand strong, drew sabres and with a loud rebel yell dashed through a cornfield and a body of woodland on to the turnpike. There the enemy turned to make a stand, and they met battle with a heavy volley which emptied many saddles. Without stopping the Lynchburg men charged the batteries facing them and captured the men and guns. The retreat soon became a complete rout, the Northern troops throwing away guns, knapsacks, haversacks, overcoats and, in short, everything that could impede their flight back to the safety of Washington. Our regiment pursued them far into the night until they were obliged to turn back in order to get rid of the many prisoners they had taken. Never before has the history of warfare recorded such a stampede of an army.

"After this ignominious rout of 'the grandest army of the planet' the Eleventh Regiment was detailed to guard the captured material. Amongst the spoils so lavishly scattered by the Federals in their panic we found a large quantity of handcuffs which were intended for those whom bigotry could accuse of nothing but defence of their State when it was invaved. This mode of spreading liberty is, we believe, unprecedented."

Among those brave men who fell at Manassas was Captain Winston Radford, a gallant gentleman. The regiment, both officers and men, showed the spirit of true soldiers.

After the Battle of Fredericksburg, General Stuart, torn by the thought of the suffering brought on the town, sent a circular letter among the soldiers asking for a donation for the people of the town. The response was immediate and generous; in a few hours he had in his tent $2,100 given by the men of the Second Virginia, as scarce as money was at that time.

Used to an easy going Southern way of living, life in the army was trying to most of them. "Reveille was a misery," wrote Bagby about his own experiences in camp life. "I was three and thirty years old, a born invalid, whose habit had been to rise late, bathe leisurely, and eat breakfast after everybody else was done. To get up at dawn, to the sound of fife and drum, to wash my face in a hurry in a tin basin, wipe on a wet towel, and go forth with a suffocated skin and a sense of uncleanliness to be quadrilled by a fat little cadet, young enough to be my son, of the Virginia Military Institute, that, indeed, was misery. How I hated that little cadet! He was always so wideawake, so clean, so interested in the drill; his coat tails were so short and sharp, and his hands looked so big in white gloves. He made me sick."

At the Battle of Manassas Garland had in his command five well-organized companies, known at first as Garland's Battalion, though the name was afterwards changed to the Eleventh Virginia Regiment. Bagby in his writings described the discontent felt among the men when Garland was put in command, as many preferred Maurice S. Langhorne, Captain of Company A. The men said Garland was too much of a scholar to be a good soldier. But Samuel Garland, refined and scholarly gentleman though he was, showed such conspicuous courage in action, and so marked a capacity for warfare, that when he fell at Boonsboro in the second year of the War he was counted one of the most promising young officers of the whole army. "Lynchburg," so Bagby maintained, "had reason to be proud of two such men as Garland and Rodes, my old school-mate, a Lynchburger by birth, but in command of Alabama troops. In him Beauregard had special confidence, giving him the front as McDowell approached. Rodes was killed in the Valley in 1864, a General of Division, full of promise, a man of ability, a first-rate soldier."

Lynchburg, with only ten thousand citizens, acquitted herself nobly by the number of companies she sent out:

The Rifle Grays, Captain Maurice S. Langhorne.
The Lynchburg Rifles, Captain J. E. Blankinship.
The Jefferson Davis Rifles, Captain J. Risque Hutter.
Lee Battery, Captain Pierce B. Anderson.
Beauregard Rifles, afterwards Moorman's Battery, Captain Marcellus N. Moorman.
Latham's Battery, Captain H. Grey Latham.
Davidson's Battery, Captain Geo. S. Davidson.
Heavy Artillery, Captain Samuel D. Preston.
Lee's Body Guard, Captain, A. H. Pettigrew.
Kirkpatrick's Battery, Captain Thos. J. Kirkpatrick.

The captains of the companies of the Second Virginia Cavalry were:

Company A, Captain William R. Terry, Bedford County.
Company B, John S. Langhorne, Lynchburg.
Company C, Andrew Lewis Pitzer, Botetourt.
Company D, G. W. B. Hale, Franklin County.
Company E, Captain Edgar Whitehead, Amherst County.
Company F, Captain James Wilson, Bedford County.
Company G, Captain R. C. W. Radford, Bedford County.

Company H, Captain Joel W. Flood, Appomattox County.
Company I, J. D. Alexander, Campbell County.
Company K, Eugene Davis, Albemarle County.

On the 19th of June, when orders came to move on to Manassas, the soldiers met with ovations all along the line of march. At every town ladies were waiting for them, and all along the roadside, "with flowers, ice-water, baskets of lunch, given with smiles and tears. The gallant mountain lads moved steadily on to the front, never allowing the bugler to pass a gate without sounding his bugle with 'Dixie,' or 'The Girl I Left Behind Me'."

Captain H. Grey Latham was a great favorite in camp. He always wore a red shirt. Before leaving for the front his little boy, only two years old, and dressed in full Rifle Gray uniform, was brought to see him, and became the toast of the hour among the soldiers.

But on the whole the news brought to our people by friends recently come from Washington was not encouraging. They spoke of the stout-built, magnificently equipped men pouring by the thousands upon thousands down Pennsylvania Avenue. Beside these our men compared poorly in bodily weight and substance, and even more poorly in arms, dress and equipment. But the first Battle of Manassas was close at hand to prove their quality, which for four long years rose superior to every advantage of the Northern Army, and which only death and starvation could subdue. The following quotation is from a letter written by a color-bearer of the Second Virginia Cavalry to his sister:

"Dear X⸺

As we move away from here pretty soon, and there is no telling where we will go to, I only write you a few lines tonight to ask you to please fix up that long talked of box, and send it to Mr. G⸺ at Richmond, from where I can get it very easy. I expect we will move from here about the first of next week. I want you to send me five or six hams, some chines and sausages, and one of those half firkins of butter and one of lard; for goodness sake, get the butter, as we cannot get a particle here except for $2.50 per pound. You can also send turkies, chickens, etc. I want you to fix up a *buster,* as we will starve if we don't get something from home, as the Gov. is issuing nothing except flour and pickled pork which isn't fit for a dog to eat. We have nothing to do here now but cuss the Yankees and quarrel with the Quarter Masters and Commissaries for starving man and beast; our horses are dying every day for want of food. W―――― went to Richmond today to try to get us some clothing from the Gov. Bureau, as we heard they had gotten in a large stock of cloth for officers' uniforms, though I expect the Qu. Masters and their clerks have gotten it all by this time; when I went to Richmond the other day I did not think there was as much gold braid in the world as I saw those chaps supporting on their sleeves. I would meet a fellow and I would think him a Maj. Gen. and on inquiry would find out to be a post Quarter Master Sergeant. No news here at all. We are all very well, and hoping for the War to end in the Spring. My love to all, and write me soon. I remain your aff. brother ――――――――."

"Hartwell Church, Hd. Qu. 2nd Va. Cavalry.

Dear X――――

Your sweet and very acceptable letters were received yesterday on my return to camp. We have just gotten back from a three day's raid over the River in the enemies lines. We started out from camp on Tuesday morning the 24th of Feb., the snow about eighteen inches deep. That night we stopped in a piece of woods about twenty miles from camp, the most cheerless place that you ever saw, but we soon cleared away the snow, laid down some fence rails, and some pine tops on the top of them, built large fires and spent a very comfortable night. The next morning we started at eight o'clock and marched about ten miles when we came to the first picket of the enemy. Gen.

Lee" (Fitz Lee) "sent forward a Lieutenant and about 20 men from the 1st Regiment, who succeeded in capturing the whole picket with the exception of two; in about fifteen minutes we saw the Yankees swarming out of a piece of woods, and forming a line of battle. The First was ordered to charge them, and did so very handsomely, driving the Yankees before them like sheep. Pretty soon we saw another Regiment, and the General ordered ours up to charge them; we went in with a loud yell, though just as we got fairly started Col. Munford saw another Regiment coming up on our flank as if trying to cut us off, so he cut off all of the Regiment except the 1st Squadron and went at them, who no sooner saw him coming than they put to flight. I was with the Squadron that was charging the first Regiment that we saw; we pitched ahead thinking that the whole Regiment was coming, but lo and behold! this one Squadron of about 60 men was chasing a Yankee Regiment of about 400. We ran them about five miles, when I ran upon an infantry picket, who poured a volley into us, and receiving orders from Gen. Lee we withdrew. As soon as the Yankees saw us falling back, they commenced forming and following us, though at a very respectful distance. When we reached the main body, both Regiments were formed, and the Third thrown forward, and sharpshooters in front of them, when we commenced retiring. After falling back about a mile the Yankees, (having gathered their scattered Regiments) came up to charge us and capture the whole concern; but as soon as they commenced charging Gen. Lee ordered the Third to charge, who rushed forward and drove the Yankees back about a mile; we then withdrew without further molestation to where we had camped the previous night, and the next day returned to camp. We killed several, and brought back 150 prisoners, representatives of 9 different Regiments, and we only had 3 very small ones. I killed one, or mortally wounded him with my pistol; I was not more than five steps from him, and when I shot I saw him throw up his hands and bellow like a calf; I also took sev-

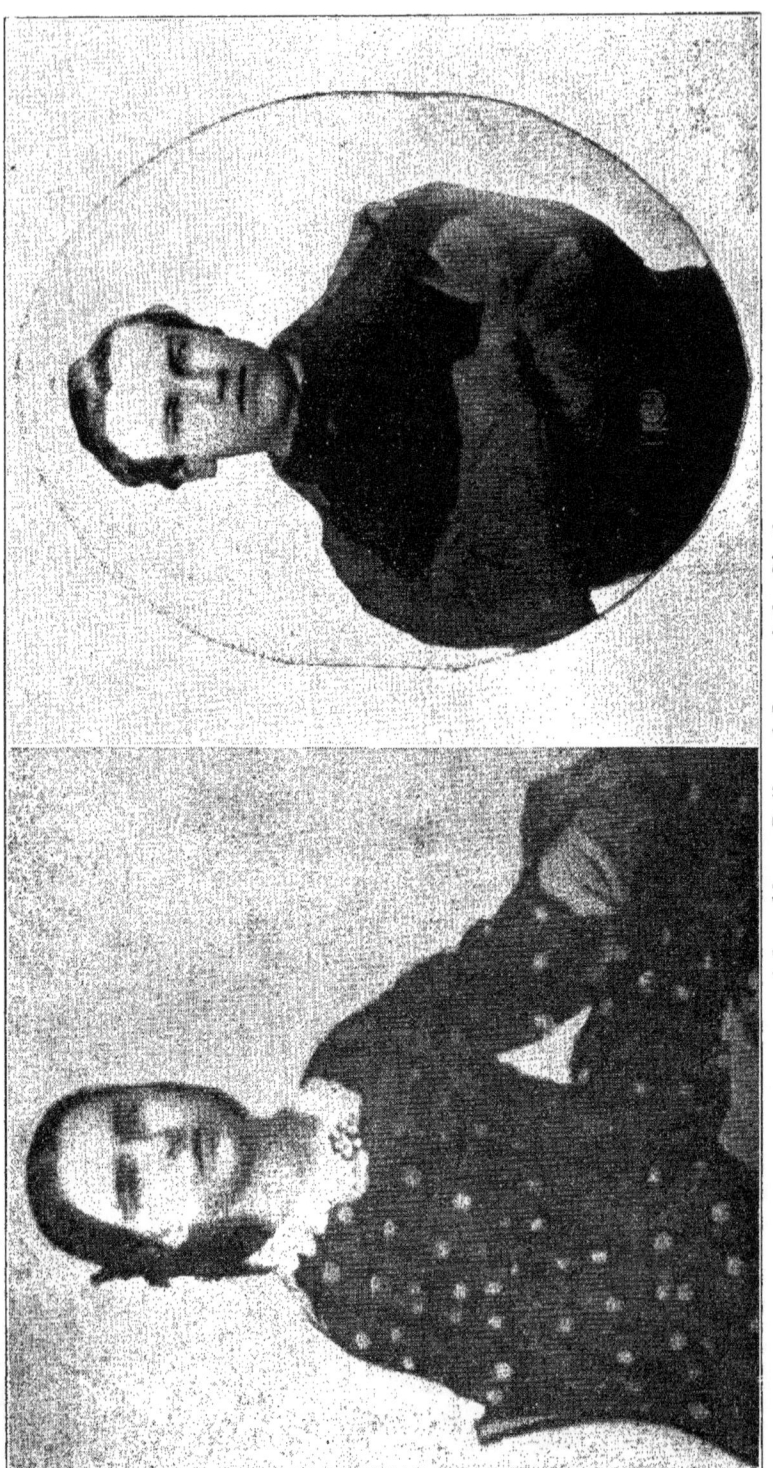

A Lynchburg Belle and Beau of the Sixties.

eral prisoners, although it is very much against my principles to do such a thing. I have no tiding of the box yet that you wrote of; am sorry you forgot the *hams* and *sausage meat;* for goodness sake send them down by Whitten when he comes, for we are truly in a state of starvation here, having nothing at all to eat but the rations we buy from the Commissary, and they are very scant, consisting of beef and flour. Lee has gotten up a Company from the different Regiments of musicians, which he calls Lee's Minstrels, who give concerts at the G. H. for the edifications of the Brigadiers. I went to hear them the other night and found it to be quite good; they were all blacked up like Negroes, and gave us some pretty good music. This is the poorest place you ever saw, nothing in the world but mud, nothing to eat for man or beast. We depend entirely on the R. R. for our supplies. We get nothing but corn for our horses, and frequently the cars miss coming and we get nothing in the world for them for two or three days at a time; they are dying off very fast; Col. Munford lost his fine horse while he was at home. I am sorry to hear that M_____ has been so unwell; I hope she has recovered ere this. I have made an application for furlough, though doubt whether I get it. It seems remarkable how some men manage to get home so often, and others never can. I thought at one time there was some probability of the War ending, though since this recent act of the Lincoln Congress I see no probability of it. There is nothing new here, so I close, hoping to hear from you again soon. My love to all.

I remain your affectionate Brother,

_____."

I have heard men say there is no joy like the joy of battle. "It is well war is so terrible," said Lee at Fredericksburg, "we should grow too fond of it." Major Waller M. Boyd, of Nelson County, was in Pickett's Division at the Battle of Gettysburg and is said to have been the first to get over the top of Cemetery Ridge. He was only nineteen, and the very lowest officer of the command, but when he reached the top, where he was seized by Yankee soldiers, he was a major by the rigid process of elimination, for all those of intervening rank had been killed. He had no arms when captured, only a sword hilt in his hand from which the blade was broken clean away. I have heard him say there never was such glory as he felt in that charge. After the War, he used to entertain his children by singing "Benny Havens," a song he learned from the young lieutenants fresh from West Point while we was in a Yankee prison. Once they told him they were going to hang him at sunrise, but for some reason they changed their minds, for he lived to a ripe old age. He planted great orchards on his Nelson County farm, which he had inherited from his mother, Judith Massie Boyd, and for many years he supplied Queen Victoria with Albemarle Pippins.

CHAPTER X

BATTLE OF LYNCHBURG

LYNCHBURG was of great strategic value to the Confederate cause during the War Between the States. It was the depot for most of the commissary and quartermaster stores which could be gathered from the country which lay along the route of the Virginia and Tennessee Railroad. It was the key of the inside line of communications by which the Confederate troops were moved without the attention of the enemy from the northern to the eastern lines of defence. It was also the storage place for most of the medical supplies of the Confederacy, and its many hospitals were the refuge of the sick and wounded from both the eastern and northern lines of battle. The Confederates were on the alert to guard a post so valuable to them, but they could not spare the troops necessary to garrison it properly. They were, therefore, forced to trust to the natural advantages of the town for defence against the enemy, and to the ease with which forces could be hurried to its support. During the first three years of the War a good many raids were made on the railroad line west of Lynchburg for the purpose of destroying Lee's communications with the South and the Southwest. Much damage was done by destroying depots and bridges, but no attack was made on the town, which sat quietly surrounded by the fortifications of nature. Either the Federal forces were unaware of its importance, or else they were afraid it might prove too difficult to capture.

It was not until June, 1864, that General Grant wrote General David Hunter that the complete destruction of the Central Railway (now the Chesapeake and Ohio) and the Canal on the James River were of great importance to the Federal cause, and that Hunter was to proceed to Lynchburg and commence there with the campaign. "It would be of great value to us to get possession of Lynchburg for a single day," wrote Grant. To this day General David Hunter is as much hated in Virginia as

LYNCHBURG AND ITS NEIGHBORS

General Butler is in Louisiana, and with good cause, for he with his kinsman and staff officer, David Hunter Strother, went through the Valley and descended upon Lynchburg as though possessed of the devil.

David Strother, a Virginian, early in his career in the Federal Army, was attached to the Topographical Corps. He had visited at many of the homes of his kinsmen in Virginia and on hunting and fishing excursions among them had obtained a knowledge of the land which served him now.

"Hunter's delay in advancing from Staunton had been most remarkable," General Early wrote, in his Memoir of the Last Year of the War, "and can be accounted for only by the fact that indulgence in petty acts of malignity and outrage upon private citizens was more congenial to his nature than bold operations in the field. He had defeated Jones' small force at Piedmont, about ten miles from Staunton, on the 5th, and had united with Crook on the 8th, yet he did not arrive in front of Lynchburg until near night on the 17th. The route from Staunton to Lynchburg by which he moved, which was by Lexington, Buchanan, the Peaks of Otter and Liberty, is about one hundred miles in distance. It is true McCausland had delayed his progress by keeping constantly in his front, but an energetic advance would have brushed away McCausland's small force, and Lynchburg, with all its manufacturing establishments and stores, would have fallen before assistance arrived."

He writes further: "At Lexington he had burned the Military Institute with all its contents, including its library and scientific apparatus; and Washington College had been plundered and the statue of Washington stolen. The residence of ex-Governor Letcher at that place had been burned by orders, and but a few minutes given Mrs. Letcher and her family to leave the house. In the same county a most excellent Christian gentleman, a Mr. Creigh, had been hung, because on a former occasion he had killed a straggling and marauding Federal soldier while in act of insulting and outraging the ladies of his family. These are but some of the outrages committed by Hunter, or his orders, and I will not insult the memory of the ancient barbarians of the North by calling them acts of Vandalism. If those old barbarians were savage and cruel, they at least had the manliness and daring of rude soldiers, with occasional traits of magnanimity. Hunter's deeds were those of a malignant and cowardly fanatic, who was better qualified to make war upon helpless women and children than upon armed soldiers. The time consumed in the perpetration of these deeds was the salvation of Lynchburg, with its stores, foundries and factories, which were so necessary to our army at Richmond."

"The scenes on Hunter's route from Lynchburg had been truly heart-rending," Early further describes. Let us say here that Early was no sentimentalist, but as grim a warrior as war ever produced. Nevertheless, General Early was a man and a soldier, and as he hurried along in the wake of Hunter he must have felt like one who follows in the trail of a foul beast. "Houses had been burned, and helpless women and children left without shelter. The country had been stripped of provisions, and many families left without a morsel to eat. Furniture and bedding had been cut to pieces, and old men, and women and children robbed of all the clothing they had except that on their backs. Ladies' trunks had been rifled, and their dresses torn to pieces in mere wantonness. Even the Negro girls had lost their little finery. We now had renewed evidences of the outrages committed by Hunter's orders in burning and plundering private houses. We saw the ruins of a number of houses to which the torch had been applied by his orders. * * * On this day we passed through Newtown where several houses, including that of a Methodist minister, had been burned by Hunter's orders, because a part of Mosby's command had attacked a train of supplies for Sigel's force at this place. The original order was to burn the whole town, but the officer sent to execute it had revolted at the cruel mandate of his superior, and another had been sent who but partially executed it, after having forced the people to take an oath of allegiance to the United States to save their houses. Mosby's battalion, though called 'guerillas' by the enemy, was a regular organization in the Confederate Army, and was merely serving on detached duty under General Lee's orders. The attack on the train was an act of legitimate warfare, and the order to burn Newtown, and the burning of the houses mentioned were most wanton cruel, unjustifiable and cowardly."

These descriptions given by General Early show what mortal terror must have been upon the people when the news reached them that Hunter was on his way down the Valley to sack Lynchburg, for they well knew that except by a miracle the Confederate troops could not get here in time to save the city. It was at this time that Mr. Ivey, who had been wounded some time before, and incapacitated for further war service, got up in the dead of night and went out in the woods with an old Negro servant to bury his bank's money. It was at this time that Mr. Sam Miller was busy hiding away from the Yankees his great fortune which in later years was to do so much good for Lynchburg and for Virginia. While this was going on every soldier that was in the hospitals, or being nursed in private homes, who could stand on his legs, or mount a horse, was joining that anxious band of old men and little boys who had gathered together to die in defence of their town. Among these brave wounded men was General Francis T. Nichols, who with only one arm and one leg left, took command of the post, and commenced organizing the sick, wounded and crippled, the old men and little boys, into an army of occupation. With these he determined to hold the town against the force of Major-General Hunter, which numbered 25,000 fresh, well-equipped men, high in spirits, because they had just completed a conquest at Piedmont over General Jones' small detachment, after Jones himself was killed, and his men disorganized. Staunton had fallen an easy prey to them, and with a great fanfare of trumpets they were marching down upon Lynchburg.

Major-General Robert E. Rodes

LYNCHBURG AND ITS NEIGHBORS

The town had already sent every able-bodied man she had to fight with Lee; and now it seemed there were left none to protect her, for what could the little band Nichols had in command hope to do against 25,000? With brave but despairing hearts the women must have realized this. So worn they were, every cent they owned was invested in Confederate bonds, most of them had sold their jewels to buy proper food for the wounded soldiers who crowded the city; sick, suffering boys of the far South, and distant parts of Virginia, homesick and sad. Food was so scant they could barely produce enough to stay the hunger of their own children and servants. So coarse had their fare become that they could hardly bear the sight of it, for the best was saved to provide boxes to send to the camps, and to furnish the hospitals. All their sheets and table-linen had been torn up for bandages, all their time was given up to nursing the sick, and to sewing and knitting for the fighting men. No longer were their servants employed in beautifying their homes, and in making life easy for their mistresses, for they were kept busy spinning and weaving cotton cloth and woolen blankets. Life for those in Lynchburg had become a grim, hand-to-hand struggle with death and despair, and though they had not had actual battle in the town, yet they had suffered every other disaster that war can bring. Every day brought news which desolated some household, every hour some woman's heart was wrung with anguish. Only their homes remained and their sorrow can be imagined as they awaited Hunter's approach.

The Lynchburg soldiers, fully aware of the desperate situation of their homes, were straining every nerve to reach the town. It is not surprising that there were hot words between Rodes and Early when Rodes found out that General Ramseur's division was to be sent ahead of him. There were not enough cars to accommodate both divisions. Early ordered Rodes to follow along the road in the rear to take the train on its return trip, and would not hear to Rodes' demand to go first in defense of his native town, where his wife and child and his old father were living. At sunrise on the morning of the 17th of June, Early, who had reached Charlottesville, started with his corps for Lynchburg, some by rail, and the rest by wagon train, or marching along the track. But the motive power was so poor that the train did not reach Lynchburg until the afternoon of that day, and the rest of his army did not arrive until almost nightfall on the 18th, too late to take part in the engagement. When Early left Charlottesville General Hunter was already at Liberty (now Bedford) only twenty-five miles from Lynchburg and going strong. Early had marched eighty miles in four days.

A very potent factor in the delay of Hunter's progress from Staunton to Lynchburg was General McCausland, who, with a small body of cavalry, had been operating in the Southwest, and was now ordered across the country to meet Hunter. Near Staunton he was joined by Colonel William E. Peters with a small brigade, which gave McCausland a force of about 1,600 men. Ably supported by Colonel Peters (the father of Dr. Don Peters, and the uncle of Major Stephen Halsey), General McCausland began to harry Hunter. Hanging on his front lines and engaging his advance columns, yet always drawing back when the main column appeared, McCausland kept up constant skirmishing, which delayed Hunter at every step. Near Buchanan McCausland set the enemy back a whole day by an act of great bravery in which he destroyed the bridge over James River. First he sent his men over the bridge, and when Hunter came up to cross they opened fire, checking the advance of his troops. McCausland already had hay, saturated with oil, piled upon the bridge, and he himself with Captain St. Clair of his command remained on the north side to light the fire, for he was anxious that all of his men should get safely across. When the enemy drew very close he lighted the hay and at that same moment Captain St. Clair ran up the river bank on the opposite side. In their effort to kill St. Clair the enemy did not see General McCausland, who escaped in a small boat under the burning bridge, and was not even under their fire until he, too, reached the opposite side and was climbing the river bank. The story of the bravery shown by our men on this march against Hunter forms a notable chapter in the annals of Southern heroism. Among the bravest was Major Stephen Halsey, who distinguished himself time and again under the command of his uncle, Colonel William E. Peters. After the War, Colonel Peters was for many years Professor of Latin at the University of Virginia.

Meanwhile, in the midst of its alarm, some comfort had reached the town of Lynchburg. General Breckenridge had arrived on the night of the 16th with his bloody, battle-torn little command. They were only bronzed, bare-footed, dirty men, but the streets were lined with women, waving handkerchiefs and cheering as they moved out to a line on the hills west of the city, for the news had already been received that Hunter had crossed the saddle between the two Peaks of Otter and was heading this way.

General Breckenridge had already been badly injured by the fall of his horse, killed under him near Cold Harbor. He had moved from Rockfish Gap to Lynchburg by forced march when he heard of Hunter's advance, but after reaching his goal he was compelled to go to bed. General D. H. Hill happened to be in the town, and at Breckenridge's request took command of what troops were at hand. Most of these troops were without shoes or hats, but they went at a double-quick up Main Street to Fifth, looking, as an eye-witness said, like long, lean grayhounds. As they swung up Fifth Street a young girl, Miss Sally Scruggs, who was standing on a wall on the corner of Church and Fifth, took off a broad-brimmed straw hat, gayly decorated, which she had just made for herself, and threw it to a redheaded soldier who had neither shoes nor hat. He caught the bonnet and tying it over his shock of red hair, he raised his musket to present arms, and marching on, the whole brigade cheered as long as it was in sight.

LYNCHBURG AND ITS NEIGHBORS

Lines of defence had been already thrown up to protect the city before General Early arrived. Imboden with his small remnant of cavalry, and McCausland with his two little brigades, were occupying a position close to the old Quaker Meeting House on the Salem Turnpike. They held Hunter in check, but as the main body of the enemy advanced they were being slowly driven back when Early's troops arrived to re-enforce them. At once men were set to work throwing up new breastworks in order to save the city injury from shells, and only a few shells did fall in the town, in the neighborhood of the present Catholic church on Clay Street, a place then known as Meem's garden. During the night of the 17th a yard engine with boxcars attached was run up and down the Southside Railroad to make the enemy believe that re-enforcements were rapidly arriving. When General Early reached the town the people were well aware that those few troops and slight fortifications out on the Turnpike would not long be able to hold Hunter's forces, 25,000 strong. When at last they heard Tinsley's bugle call, and saw old Jube in his white hat leading a part of "Stonewall" Jackson's old brigade at a double-quick through the streets, their cheers broke out in wild joy. That day heard Tinsley's last bugle call! Bugler for the Stonewall Brigade, he met a soldier's death in the rescue of Lynchburg.

On the 18th Early acted on the defensive, waiting to do battle when the rest of his troops arrived, and perfecting arrangements for attacking Hunter at daybreak on the 19th. Much to the surprise of our troops, and of his own as well, it seems, Hunter never waited for that attack. Sometime during the night of the 18th, after the rest of Early's troops had come in, it was discovered that Hunter was retreating. With the arrival of Early's troops he evidently considered it too great a hazard to try to carry out General Grant's instructions to hold Lynchburg if only for one day. He went through Buford's Gap, and took possession of the crest of the Blue Ridge, finally arriving at Salem and so on to Lewisburg and West Virginia. That was Grant's last effort to capture Lynchburg.

As mentioned before, General Jubal A. Early commanded the old Stonewall Brigade, which was all that was now left of "Stonewall" Jackson's own men. Bare-footed, bronzed, lean as greyhounds, and trained in privation and in daring by the hand of that great leader, they were seasoned veterans, and if Hunter knew whom he faced he had reason to be afraid. Graven on the memory of these men was the destruction of their homes in the Valley. Fresh in their hearts was a picture of the desolation of the women and children of Louisa County, who had flocked to the road to beg them for something to eat, grasping eagerly at the bits of cold corn bread that the soldiers could spare them from their haversacks as they hurried on to the aid of Lynchburg. As these lean veterans came into town, General Francis Nichols, our post commander, who was later Governor of Louisiana, one-armed and one-legged, rode out on the line where his little troop of defenders was carrying on. They were slowly falling back before Hunter's skirmishers while Lieutenant Carter Berkeley, with his few guns near the toll gate, was doing his best to rally them. General Nichols brought the news that Early and his men had arrived; soon Tinsley appeared, trotting up the road sounding the advance, and behind him was Ramseur's Division. Then through the smoke came the vision of Old Jube's broad, white slouch hat with its black feather! He rode among them, and shaking his fist at the enemy cried out: "No buttermilk rangers after you now, damn you!" You could have heard the cheers and rebel yells almost to the Peaks of Otter that day. In that moment, when Hunter looked through his field glasses and saw those mighty sons of battle, it is probable that then and there he knew in his heart it was time to go.

"Some description," wrote Captain Blackford, "of Hampton's great cavalry battle at Trevillian's Depot would strictly be a part of any history of the siege and Battle of Lynchburg, for had he failed Lynchburg would necessarily have fallen into the hands

LYNCHBURG AND ITS NEIGHBORS

of the enemy. * * * It was one of the most brilliant and successful engagements in which our war troops were involved during the War, and one which shed well-deserved renown, not only on General Wade Hampton, who commanded, but on every officer and man under him. Conspicuous for their gallantry and valuable service in that battle was the Second Virginia Cavalry, under our distinguished fellow citizen, General T. T. Munford. This great regiment was made up of companies from Lynchburg and the surrounding counties, and was therefore one of whose record we all have a right to be proud. On the day of that fight it was especially distinguished for its daring courage and for its achievements. It was in front of the charging column which broke Custer's line, and captured four out of the five caissons lost by Sheridan on that day. It captured Custer's headquarters, his sash, and private wagons and papers. The wagon was used by General Munford until it was captured a few days before Appomattox." When it is recalled that Custer and Sheridan were considered two particular stars in the Northern Army, and that our men by this time were grim, dirty, barefooted wretches, with no equipment at all except what they captured, the realization comes clear that they still had a great will to fight, and to save their homes from Sheridan, whom Grant had ordered to join Hunter to complete the destruction of Lynchburg.

We have already mentioned Lieutenant Carter Berkeley, who had charge of the two guns in Breckenridge's command, which he handled with great skill. When Berkeley arrived in Lynchburg with his guns it was thought that the Yankees were already in sight. He started up Ninth Street, but seeing how steep was Courthouse hill he went up Church Street to Eighth, and thinking this was the nearest way to the enemy he attempted to get his guns up by this route. Putting several men at each wheel, he urged the tired horses at the steep hill, but they could not make it. Some of Imboden's cavalry happened to be coming along, who gave their assistance, and soon had the guns up on

LYNCHBURG AND ITS NEIGHBORS

Court Street, and from there they easily moved on at a gallop to the line of battle. Berkeley, who was a native of Staunton, made a great name as an artillery man. He practised medicine in Lynchburg after the War. The Botetourt Artillery under Captain Douthat, with six guns and about one hundred men, also deserve special mention. Before coming to Lynchburg Captain Douthat had saved Tye River Bridge from destruction by Hunter, and yet reached here in time to give important service. Two of his guns were stationed on the Forest Road near the old Soap Stone Quarry to protect the railroad bridge over Ivy Creek. The other four were on this side of the Forest Road supporting the brigade under Colonel Forsberg. One of the gunners of this battery was Mr. A. H. Plecker, photographer in Lynchburg for many years after the War. He was offered a commission, but refused it, thinking he could do a greater service as gunner.

In delaying Hunter's march on Lynchburg, one of McCausland's most important feats was the sharp attack made on Hunter at New London on the 16th. Colonel William E. Peters and his nephew, Major Stephen P. Halsey, figured prominently in this engagement at New London. Major Halsey narrowly escaped with his life, for he was struck by balls twice, though not injured. The last time, near the Quaker Meeting House, the bullet was deflected by his belt buckle, which was broken in two pieces. At that time also Major John W. Daniel, just recovering from desperate wounds, followed with the other cripples from the hospital, that intrepid one-armed and one-legged commander, General Francis T. Nichols.

A paper written by Judge Don P. Halsey, and published April 13th, 1924, in the Lynchburg News, and Captain Blackford's Campaign and Battle of Lynchburg, have furnished much material for this chapter. Hunter made his headquarters at Sandusky, the place we have described as being originally built by Mr. Charles Johnston, uncle of the Confederate general, Joseph E. Johnston. Sandusky at the time of the War was owned by Major Hutter. McKinley and Hayes, two men who afterwards became Presidents of the United States, were both with Hunter's troops at the time he occupied Sandusky, McKinley being a major and Hayes a colonel in the Federal Army.

As we have already mentioned, many soldiers who were not Lynchburg men, being in this neighborhood, and hearing of the dire need of the town, came to its defence. General D. H. Hill, assisted by General Harry T. Hays, of Louisiana, one of our convalescents, had established breastworks on College Hill. Colonel James Watts and Captain E. E. Bouldin, of Charlotte, were both engaged in delaying Hunter, and Major Robert C. Saunders, of Campbell, was doing scout duty. Mike Connell, eighty years old, served in line for us that day, as did also E. C. Hamner and W. C. Folkes, who were at that time fifteen-year-old boys. Captain Stephen Adams had a line of battle established on the place he later bought for his home. Some V. M. I. cadets came, too, and succeeded in capturing part of the clothes Hunter's men had stolen from their trunks in Lexington.

Showing the spirit of gratitude among the people of Lynchburg, and the intense feeling against Hunter, is a letter written many years later by an honored citizen, Mr. Alexander Thurman, and printed in The News.

"To the Editor of The News:

As War and Peace conferences seem to be the principal topics of the day, and nearly the entire world engaged in this inexpensive and exhilirating pastime, I thought I would add my mite with some of the reminiscences of what occurred sixty years ago, should you deem it interesting enough to give to your readers.

In 1864, General Grant, then in command of the Union Armies, conceived the idea of capturing Lynchburg, which at that time was a depot of supplies, and was also manufacturing war munitions to some extent. For this purpose in June he directed Generals Hunter and Sheridan to do this work. General Hunter, a renegade Virginian, with 20,000 troops, proceeded down the Valley, his line of march marked by the destruction of the Virginia Military Institute and many private homes, as well as other acts of Vandalism, was to approach Lynchburg from the west; General Sheridan, with 12,000 picked cavalry was to advance from the east by way of Charlottesville.

That you may have an idea who and what General Hunter was, I here insert a copy of a letter written by Mrs. H. B. Lee, of Shepherdstown, Virginia, one of his victims, which was given to me by her son, Colonel Lee, of Clarke County, a neighbor of mine when I was a resident of that county a few years ago.

'Shepherdstown, Va., July 20th, 1864.
General Hunter:

Yesterday your underling, Captain Martindale of the First New York Veteran Cavalry, executed your infamous order and burned my home. You have had the satisfaction ere this of receiving from him the information that your orders were fulfilled to the letter; the dwelling and every other outbuilding, seven in number, with the contents, being burned. I, therefore, a helpless woman whom you have cruelly wronged, address you, a Major General of the United States Army, and demand why this was done. What was my offense?

My husband was absent, an exile. He has never been a politician, or in any way engaged in the struggle now going on, his age preventing. This fact David Strother, your chief of staff, could have told you. The house was built by my father, a Revolutionary soldier who served the whole seven years for your independence. There was I born; there the sacred dead repose; it was my house and my home, and there has your niece, who lived among us all this horrid war up to the present moment, met with all kindness at my hands. Was it for this that you turned me, my young daughter and little son, out into the world without a shelter? Or was it because my husband is a grandson of the Revolutionary patriot and rebel, Richard Henry Lee, and the kinsman of the noblest of Christian warriors, the greatest of generals, Robert E. Lee? Heavens blessing be upon his head forever! You and your Government have failed to conquer, subdue or match him, and disappointed rage and malice find vent upon the helpless and inoffensive. Hyena-like you have torn my heart to pieces, for all hallowed memories clustered around that homestead, and demon-like you have done it without even the pretext of revenge, for I never saw or harmed you.

Your office is not, like a brave man and a soldier, to lead your men to fight in the ranks of war, but your work has been to separate yourself from all danger, and with your incendiary band steal unawares upon helpless women and children to insult and destroy. Two fair homes did you, yesterday, ruthlessly lay in ashes, giving not a moment's warning to the startled inmates of your wicked purposes, turning mothers and children out of doors, your very name execrated by your own men for the cruel work you gave them to do.

In the case of Mr. A. R. Boteler both father and mother were far away. Any heart but that of Captain Martindale (and yours) would have been touched by that little circle comprising a widowed daughter just risen from her bed of illness, her three fatherless babes, the eldest not five years old, and her heroic sister. I repeat, any man would have been touched at that sight. But Captain Martindale—one might as well hope to find mercy and feeling in the heart of a wolf bent on its prey of young lambs as to search for such qualities in his bosom. You have chosen well your man for such deeds, doubtless you will promote him. A Colonel of the Federal Army has stated that you deprived forty of your officers of their command because they refused to carry out your malignant mischief. All honor to their names for this, at least. They are men; they have human hearts, and blush for such a commander. I ask, who that does not wish infamy and disgrace attached to him forever would serve under you? Your name will stand on history's page as *the hunter* to destroy defenceless villages, and refined and beautiful homes; to torture afresh the agonized hearts of suffering widows; *the hunter* of Africa's poor sons and daughters, to lure them on to ruin, and death of soul and body; *the hunter* with the relentless heart of a wild beast, the face of a fiend, and the form of a man. O! Earth, behold the monster!

Can I say, God, forgive you? No prayer can be offered for you. Were it possible for human lips to raise your name heavenward, angels would thrust the foul thing back again, and demons claim their own. The curse of thousands, the scorn of the manly and upright, and the hatred of the true and honorable will follow you and yours through all time, and brand your name, Infamy! Infamy!

Again I demand, Why have you burned my house? Answer, as you must answer the Searcher of all hearts. Why have you added this cruel, wicked deed to your many crimes?

HENRIETTA B. LEE'."

The Lynchburg troops engaged in the Battle of Lynchburg were General Jubal A. Early, commanding the army; General Robert E. Rodes, commanding a division; Major S. P. Halsey, Major M. N. Moorman, Colonel M. S. Langhorne, who happened to be at home recovering from wounds, and the Lee Battery under Captain W. W. Hardwick. General Sheridan, in his advance from the east to join Hunter at Lynchburg, never got nearer than 75 miles of the city. General Wade Hampton, who had succeeded General Stuart, met Sheridan in a fierce two-days' combat at Trevillian's Station in Louisa County on the Chesapeake and Ohio Railroad with 5,000 cavalry, and so completely routed Sheridan that he sought protection under the Federal gunboat on the Pamunkey River in Eastern Virginia. The Lynchburg troops serving in this engagement were General T. T. Munford, Colonel Richard Burks, Shoemaker's Battery and the Wise Troop, known in the army as Company B, Second Virginia Cavalry.

To say that the citizens of Lynchburg were wild with joy at their deliverance expresses it but mildly—their gratitude was unbounded. A handsome sword and silver spurs were a present to the gallant General McCausland, who with his heroic band had harrassed and retarded the advance of Hunter the entire length of his march. Nothing was too good for the soldiers, and the whole town was turned over to them. The women, though they had but limited supplies for themselves, vied with each other in catering to the comfort and welfare of the scantily clad and emaciated but thoroughly animated Confederate soldier. The City Council held a meeting on June 24th, 1864, at which the following resolutions were unanimously passed:

"Resolved: That the thanks of the City are due, and are hereby tendered to Lieutenant General Jubal A. Early and Major General J. C. Breckenridge, and the officers and soldiers under their command, for their timely and efficient services in driving the enemy from our borders.

And to Brigadier General F. T. Nichols, commander of the post, for his untiring and successful efforts to meet, with the local forces, the advancing foe.

And to Major General D. H. Hill, and Brigadier General H. T. Hays, for their co-operation in organizing the local forces, and constructing the lines of defence.

And to Lieutenant Colonels Richard E. Burks and E. J. Hoge, though themselves on crutches, who generously volunteered and were placed in command of the convalescents.

And the cadets of the Virginia Military Institute, a noble band of youthful heroes, for their promptness in the hour of danger.

And to Brigadier General McCausland, and the officers and soldiers under his command, for their gallantry in opposing for ten days the march of a greatly superior force, thereby retarding the advance of the enemy on our city until a proper force could be organized for its defence.

And to Major Generals Wade Hampton and Fitzhugh Lee, and the officers and soldiers under their command, for the defeat of Sheridan, thereby preventing a junction of the enemy forces at this place.

Resolved that the authorities and the citizens gratefully acknowledge our obligations to the defenders of Lynchburg; they will ever find seats around each fireside, and plates at every board, and old and young will greet them at the threshold, and bid them welcome, thrice welcome to our homes and hearths.

A copy teste. JAMES O. WILLIAMS, *Clerk*."

Let no one suppose in reading this record of the Battle of Lynchburg we have nothing but hatred for the armies of the invaders of our homes. There was indeed a division of opinion as to States' Rights among the early statesmen of Virginia who framed the Constitution of the United States, and it is well known that Parick Henry opposed them and the Constitution on the grounds that it delegated too much authority to the central government. On the other hand, there were many in the North who were firm believers in States' Rights. We have already mentioned in this brief sketch several Northern men who, having made their homes here, cast their lot with us to defend the cause upheld by the South. There is no one living in the South today who does not know of deeds of generosity and consideration extended to old men and women and little children left defenseless in their homes during the War, and of deeds of friendship shared on the battlefield between fighting men who had been former college chums. It is men like Hunter and David Strother Sheridan and Butler that have made hideous the memory of those years in the South.

There is a lady, who lived near Fredericksburg, who said that at one time during the War a Yankee colonel made her home his headquarters. Her family put the best foot foremost in trying to conceal their poverty and actual want while the Northern soldiers occupied their home. But their last remaining cow, which furnished milk for the children, and their mule, which was all their faithful servants had left to plow the crops, died of starvation while they were there. This lady was only a little girl at the time but that she could never forget her utter despair when one day, after the Yankees had left, she found her mother in the garden weeping because there was no food left for her children and the dependent Negroes. Two days later a large army wagon appeared full of provisions for the family, and two Federal soldiers brought up the rear leading a fine cow and a pair of strong mules sent as a present from the Yankee colonel.

After the Battle of Lynchburg, all available vehicles in the town were sent out to the battlefield to gather up the wounded. Among them went a little boy with the driver, in his mother's carriage, as he used to tell in later years. He carried a supply of bandages, and other first-aid equipment. His father's home, as were most of the other homes in town, was filled with wounded soldiers. As he passed along the Turnpike that day, he saw a young Yankee soldier lying dead in a turnip field by the side of the road. One arm was thrown over his head, and a turnip was still in his mouth which he had been eating when he was killed—a pathetic picture etched on that boy's memory which remained with him all his life.

Many pictures exist in our minds of the terrible futility and waste of war; and only the brief glimpses of compassion, of unselfishness, of individual kindness, and of undying courage in the face of disaster which have come down to us, can atone for so much sorrow and destruction and keep alive our faith in the human race.

CHAPTER XI

A FEW DISTINGUISHED MILITARY RECORDS

General Munford

THOMAS TAYLOR MUNFORD was born in Richmond, Virginia, in 1831. He was the son of Colonel George Wythe Munford, who was for twenty-five years Secretary of the Commonwealth. Thomas Munford graduated in 1852 from Virginia Military Institute. Although born in Richmond, he can justly be claimed by Lynchburg, as he spent most of his life here. He married Miss Etta Tayloe, of Bedford, whose father gave her a very handsome estate as a wedding present. Their home was one of the notable places in this part of Virginia, and in its frescoed ballroom was celebrated many a great occasion. Here General Munford settled down as a planter until the War. He had several children, among whom were George, William, and Emma, a daughter, who married Mr. Boyd, an Episcopal clergyman. After the death of Etta Tayloe Munford General Munford married her cousin, Miss Emma Tayloe, and their children were Thornton, Clare, and Glen. It was after his second marriage that he traded his estate, Glen Alton, left him by his first wife, to the Murrell family for their home on Harrison Street in Lynchburg. In later years the Glen Alton home was burned down. General Munford became engaged in several business ventures which were started in Lynchburg about this time.

General Munford entered the service of the Confederate cause May 8th, 1861, as lientenant-colonel of the Thirtieth Virginia Mounted Infantry, subsequently known as the Second Virginia Cavalry, though it was really the first. At Manassas he commanded what actually was a brigade. In the spring of 1862 he was attached to Ewell's command, and then joined Jackson in the Valley. He succeeded Ashby when that officer fell, being personally named by General Robert E. Lee. He led Jackson's advance in the Chickahominy campaign, and joined Stuart in the Manassas campaign, where he received two sabre wounds. He was a brigade commander in the Maryland campaign, and later commanded a division. After Chancellorsville he commanded the brigade of Fitzhugh Lee, under whom he took part in the Gettysburg campaign. He was with General Early in the Valley, and in November, 1864, was promoted to brigadier-general and given command of Fitzhugh Lee's Division. He made a gallant fight at Five Forks, and on the Confederate retreat from Richmond, and at Appomattox he commanded the cavalry on the Confederate right. After the surrender of General Lee he endeavored to rally the scattered Confederate bands with a view to making a junction with General Johnston in the South. Failing in this he disbanded in April. After the War he divided his time between his home in Lynchburg and Union Town, Alabama.

I do not think anyone who once saw General Munford can ever forget him. He was one of the handsomest men of his day. Even in old age, with snow white hair, piercing black eyes, fine features, and an erect and soldierly figure, his appearance carried nobly the traditions of a great name, and to the limit of his ability he added lustre and honor to a high cause.

General Garland

Samuel Garland, Jr., was the only child of Maurice H. and Caroline M. Garland. He was born in Lynchburg December 16, 1830. His father was the junior member of the law firm of S. and M. Garland. Mr. Maurice Garland was a popular and prominent citizen, but he died when his son was quite young. His mother was the daughter of Spottswood Garland and Lucinda (Rose) Garland. Thus on his maternal side, he was descended from Robert Rose, a man of great usefulness and prominence in the early history of Virginia.

LYNCHBURG AND ITS NEIGHBORS

At the age of fifteen Samuel Garland entered the Virginia Military Institute; after graduating there he matriculated at the University of Virginia in 1848, where he studied law for two years. Having received the degree of Bachelor of Law, he began the practise of his profession in Lynchburg before he was twenty-one.

In 1856 he married Eliza Campbell Meem, youngest daughter of John Gaw Meem, a merchant here. Garland's career as a lawyer was marked with success. He gave lectures on Law of Nature and Nations at the then recently established Lynchburg College. As said before, he was among the first to see the handwriting on the wall, and to realize the necessity of preparation for approaching war. To this end he organized the Home Guard of Lynchburg, of which company he was unanimously chosen captain.

In 1861, after the actual outbreak of the War, having been ordered to Richmond, he was promoted to the rank of major. A little later, as the regular organization of the army progressed, he was placed in command of the Third Virginia Regiment, and given a colonel's commission. Meanwhile, his wife became ill in Lynchburg, and died on June 12th, 1861. In August his son and namesake died.

After the Battle of Williamsburg, in which Samuel Garland received a painful wound, he was made a brigadier-general. He was then given command of four North Carolina regiments, forming a part of A. P. Hill's Division. This command was heavily engaged at Seven Pines, Gaines Mill and Second Manassas, and was the first to cross the river in the campaign of Maryland.

Just before the Battle of Sharpsburg General Garland was ordered to hold the mountain pass called Boonsborough Gap. On the night of September 13th he bivouacked on the western side of the mountain, but early on the morning of the 14th his brigade was attacked by an overwhelming force, in front and on the flank, and his men were thrown into confusion. Well knowing the importance of checking the advance of the enemy at this point, Garland put himself at the head of his force in order to rally the men, thus exposing himself to the hottest fire of the enemy. He fell, shot through the body. "I am killed. Send for the senior colonel and tell him to take command," he said.

Thus he died at the age of thirty-one, in his twelfth battle, a gallant young soldier. Almost the entire force of McClellan had been pushed forward to strike Garland at Boonsborough Gap, which was being held by this one brigade.

GENERAL DEARING

James Dearing was born in Campbell County, Virginia, April 25th, 1840. He was the son of Captain James Griffin Dearing and his wife, who was before her marriage Mary Ann Lynch, daughter of Anselm Lynch. James Dearing was a great grandson of Charles Henry Lynch. He was graduated at Hanover Academy, near Richmond, Virginia, and was appointed to the United States Military Academy at West Point, but in 1861, when Virginia passed the ordinance of Secession, he resigned to join the Confederate Army. He was successively lieutenant of the Washington Artillery of New Orleans, captain of Latham's Battery, major and commander of Denny's Artillery Battalion, and colonel of a cavalry regiment from North Carolina. He was promoted to the rank of brigadier-general for gallantry at the Battle of Plymouth. He participated in the principal engagements between the Army of Northern Virginia and the Army of the Potomac. On the retreat of the Confederate forces from Petersburg to Appomattox Courthouse, he was mortally wounded near Farmville in a singular encounter with Brigadier-General Theodore Read of the Federal Army. On April 5th, the two generals, at the head of their forces, on opposite sides of the Appomattox River, fought a duel with pistols at High Bridge, near Farmville. General Read was shot dead, and General Dearing, fatally wounded, was brought to Lynchburg to the old City Hotel, which had been turned into the Ladies' Hospital. There his brief and brilliant career came to an end on April 22nd. It was said that General Read and General Dearing had been classmates at West Point, and that on that day when they met on High Bridge they fought out an old grudge they had held against each other from the days of their boyhood.

General Dearing was a strikingly handsome man, standing six feet two inches in his stockings. He was in his twenty-fifth year, his birthday was April 25th, three days after his death. He married Roxana Birchett, and a daughter, Mary Lucretia, was born to them August 27th, 1864. She married Judge Frank P. Christian.

General Rodes

Robert Emmet Rodes was born March 29th, 1829. His father was General David Rodes, a native of Albemarle County, but long a resident of Lynchburg, and his mother was Martha Yancey Rodes, a daughter of Major Joel Yancey of the War of 1812, who was a friend and neighbor of Thomas Jefferson in Bedford County. Robert Rodes entered the Virginia Military Institute in July, 1845, and graduated with distinction in 1848. He was at once appointed an assistant professor, a position which he held for two years. During this period he acquired some experience in civil engineering on the North River Canal, near Lexington, and decided to adopt engineering as his profession.

For some years he was engaged in railroad construction, first in Virginia, then further South, where his ability received especial recognition. He was made chief engineer of the U. E. and S. W. Railroad in Alabama, which he managed with great skill and energy, until the commencement of the War Between the States. Just before the War he was elected Professor of Applied Mechanics in the Virginia Military Institute, a position which he nominally held until the day of his death. He was married September 10th, 1857, to Miss Virginia Hortense Woodruff, of Tuscaloosa, Alabama.

When the War came he raised a volunteer company called the Warrior Guard, which in January, 1861, he conducted to Fort Morgan. Returning to Tuscaloosa he devoted himself to perfecting the drill of his men, and in getting the business of the railroad in such a condition that it could dispense with his services. In May his company was ordered to Montgomery, where the Fifth Alabama Regiment was organized, and he was elected its colonel. The regiment proceeded to Pensacola, but in June his strong desire to join the Virginia army was gratified by an order to proceed to Manassas, where he was attached to Ewell's Brigade of Van Dorn's Division. From this time his regiment was actively employed, though chiefly on the outposts. As is well known, the failure to receive orders prevented Ewell, who was then at Union Mills, from participating to any extent in the first Battle of Manassas.

In October Rodes, whose zeal and ability had attracted notice, was made brigadier-general, took command of a brigade composed of the Fifth, Sixth and Twelfth Alabama, the Twelfth Mississippi Regiments, and Thomas H. Carter's Battery of light artillery. With these he accompanied General Johnson to the Peninsula in April, 1862, where Page's Battery of heavy artillery was united with his command.

On May 31st, at the Battle of Seven Pines, General Rodes in a brilliant attack upon the enemy captured their line of works, including a formidable redoubt defended by nine Napoleon guns, which he turned against them. So bloody was this battle that nearly eleven hundred men were lost, including most of the field officers. Rodes himself was badly wounded, but would not leave the field until the close of the day's operations. It was a month before his wound healed sufficiently for him to again join his command. At the first Battle of Cold Harbor he succeeded in carrying the crest of the hill in his front, bristling with cannon, which were all captured by him. But the bodily exertion was too much for him: his recent wound reopened, accompanied by a high fever. He was carried to Richmond on the night of the 29th, and his brigade was gallantly led at White Oak Swamp and Malvern Hill by Colonel (subsequently Lieutenant-General) John B. Gordon, who commanded the Sixth Alabama Regiment.

Rodes was not able to join his brigade until the 6th of September, near Frederick, Maryland, where Jackson was then operating against Pope. On the 14th of September was fought the Battle of South Mountain or Boonsborough Gap. Here General McClellan, having found a lost dispatch, became acquainted with General Lee's designs, and pushed forward with almost his entire force to strike him near Boonsborough, while Jackson was away on his expedition against Harper's Ferry. The Gap in the mountains was defended by one brigade of Hill's Division, commanded by General Samuel Garland, likewise a native of Lynchburg, and a graduate of the Virginia Military Institute, who fell early in the action. The rest of the division was brought rapidly forward when the advance of the enemy was known, and was formed in front of the crest of the mountain. Rodes' Brigade alone occupied the east side of the turnpike, and for hours held the enemy at bay unaided, until Longstreet's troops arrived from Hagerstown, and moved on to his assistance. The pressure of the Federal advance was so tremendous that the Confederate troops were forced to give back, fighting behind trees and rocks, while being slowly forced over the top of the mountain. No decisive result was reached in this engagement. At the Battle of Sharpsburg a few days later, Rodes was wounded again. Gordon was shot in five places, and his brigade was ripped to pieces.

January 16th, 1863, General D. H. Hill being transferred to North Carolina, Rodes assumed command of the division, consisting of Rodes' Alabama Brigade, Ramseur's and Iverson's North Carolina Brigades, and Dole's and Colquitt's Georgia Brigades. After the Battle of Chancellorsville the Georgia Brigade was exchanged for Daniel's North Carolina Brigade. On April 29th, the enemy being reported as crossing the river, the division was ordered to Hamilton's Crossing, and on

May 1st, in the van of the Second Corps, commenced that extraordinary flank movement which will ever remain the crowning glory of General Jackson's military career. During the greater portion of that day and the next, Jackson rode with Rodes at the head of the column. At a point on the route near Catherine's Furnace, where a road entered at right angles from the direction of the enemy, General Jackson directed Rodes to leave a regiment to protect the artillery which followed. This regiment, from Colquitt's Brigade, was placed in a railroad cut, and was almost taken by Sickles, who would have captured the whole train but for the splendid conduct of Colonel J. Thompson Brown, who drove them off with his guns alone.

Late in the afternoon of the 2nd of May, line of battle was formed in the woods on the left, which was on the north side of the old Orange Courthouse and Fredericksburg Turnpike. Rodes' Division occupied the first line; Edward Johnson's Division, temporarily commanded by Brigadier-General Colston, the second, and A. P. Hill, the third line. About 6 P. M. the advance was sounded, and almost instantly the enemy was struck and hurled back in the wildest confusion and dismay. So rapid and unexpected was the attack that Federal soldiers were shot down in the pens, slaughtering cattle for supper, and two staff officers of General Rodes, leaping from their saddles for a moment to drink a cup of coffee which had been abandoned found it too hot to be swallowed. The rout, second only to that of Manassas, was pressed back to the heights of Chancellorsville; cannon, flags, and plunder of all sorts being left behind. Hooker's left was completely demolished.

Night had settled down, and the divisions of Rodes and Johnson, now being mingled in great confusion, were halted, and General A. P. Hill, who had not fired a shot, was ordered to come up to take their place. During this movement, General Jackson rode forward with his staff to reconnoitre. On his return his party were mistaken in the darkness for a body of the enemy's cavalry and he was fired on by his own troops.

LYNCHBURG AND ITS NEIGHBORS

Few men have ever shown to greater moral advantage than did General Rodes in the events that took place that night after Jackson was wounded, although his fame as a soldier suffered undoubted loss. When Jackson fell at Chancellorsville General A. P. Hill was also temporarily disabled, and thus the command devolved on General Rodes. Although only a brigadier-general, he was the ranking officer present, and so entitled to receive Jackson's command. Already his gallantry at Chancellorsville had won highest praise from Jackson, who on his deathbed recommended his immediate promotion to major-general, to take effect from May 2nd, the day he had won it. The Second Corps had just gained a splendid victory, which was attributed largely to Rodes and his command, and Rodes was looking forward to a no less glorious morrow, when the fruits of success would be laid at the feet of his wounded commander, Jackson, who was also his warm friend. Rodes was making his dispositions for a renewal of the attack at daylight when Major-General J. E. B. Stuart, in command of the cavalry, rode up and claimed the command on the ground of seniority. The reason Rodes yielded to his demand is told in his own words in his report of the battle:

"I was informed that Lieutenant-General Jackson was wounded, and also received a message from Major-General Hill that he, likewise, was disabled, and that the command of the corps devolved on me. Without loss of time I communicated with Brigadier-Generals Heth and Colston, commanding respectively the divisions of A. P. Hill and Trimble and made the necessary arrangements for a renewal of the attack in the morning, it being agreed that the troops were not in a condition to resume operations that night. Just at this time (about twelve o'clock) the enemy made an attack on our right, but being feeble in its character, and promptly met, it lasted but a short time. Very soon after Major-General J. E. B. Stuart, who had been sent for by Major A. S. Pendleton, assistant adjutant-general of Lieutenant-General Jackson, arrived on the ground and assumed command.

I deem it proper to state that I yielded the command to Stuart, not because I thought him entitled to it, belonging as he does to a different arm of the service, nor because I was unwilling to assume the responsibility of carrying on the attack, as I had already made the necessary arrangements, and they remained unchanged, but because from the manner in which I had been informed that he had been sent for, I inferred that General Jackson or General Hill had instructed Major Pendleton to place him in command, and for the still stronger reason that I feared that the information that the command had devolved on me, unknown except to my own immediate troops, would in their shaken condition be likely to increase the demoralization of the corps. General Stuart's name was well and very favorably known to the army, and would tend, I hoped, to re-establish confidence. I yielded because I was satisfied the good of the service demanded it."

On the 6th of May the corps, now consisting of Early's, Johnson's and Rodes' Divisions, under command of General Ewell, moved to the Valley, where Rodes was detached. After engagements at Brandy Station and Front Royal, Rodes continued on to Gettysburg. He captured Berryville on the 12th, with several hundred prisoners; he captured Martinsburg on the 14th, with a few cannon and large supplies. On the 15th he crossed the Potomac at Williamsport, his division being the first to touch the soil of Maryland.

After a few days' delay at Hagerstown, where the Confederate troops were always received with great joy and hospitality, Rodes proceeded on the 23rd to Greencastle, Pennsylvania, and thence by Chambersburg to Carlisle, where he arrived on the 27th, and established his quarters in the United States Cavalry barracks. In this entire march through the enemy's country the most scrupulous care was taken by him that his troop should commit no depredations. All supplies were procured through the quartermaster and commissary departments, and even the fences were protected with a care never exhibited in Virginia. At Carlisle the Confederate flag was raised to the masthead of the barracks amid patriotic speeches from General Rodes, Trimble and others.

At one time in this campaign the city of Harrisburg lay at their feet, unprotected. Rodes could easily have captured it, but he had orders to go to Cashtown, so he rode on with regret, leaving the barracks as he had found them. They were subsequently burned.

On reaching Gettysburg Rodes found Heth's Division of A. P. Hill's Corps heavily engaged with the advanced Federal column. Forming in line, he dashed to the rescue. Daniel's Brigade in full charge came up and also helped drive the enemy back. Iverson's Brigade had suffered greatly. Riding along the line, so wrote Major Green Peyton, he saw what he took to be a regiment lying down in a sunken road. It proved to be a whole line of Iverson's men who had fallen dead "in a line as straight as a dress parade." Early's Division arrived from York at the crucial moment, striking the exposed right flank of the Federals, while at the same moment Rodes made a forward movement with his whole command. Their combined efforts forced the Federal troops to give away in every direction and they rushed in great disorder through the town of Gettysburg to the heights beyond, leaving five thousand prisoners in the hands of General Ewell. General Lee was an eye-witness to this charge, and he sent Rodes a message, in which he called him "a gallant, efficient and energetic officer," and said also, "I am proud of your division."

The shattered remnant of Iverson's Brigade, which had been so shot to pieces, was rallied and reorganized by a young staff officer, who still pressed forward, and "made a dashing and effective charge, just in time to be of considerable service," as General Rodes described it. He also said in his report that "the conduct of this officer and his men was such as to entitle them to the admiration of brave men, and the gratitude of a good people." The officer thus commended was likewise a Lynchburger, Major Don Peters Halsey, the brother of Major Stephen Halsey, the brother-in-law of Major John W. Daniel and the father of Judge Don P. Halsey, of Lynchburg.

During the days that followed in the Battle of Gettysburg, Rodes' troops occupied the town. They were not seriously engaged in the fighting after the victory of the first day, which was largely due to their brilliant charge.

In the retreat from Gettysburg, when the Potomac was crossed, the Rodes' Division forded a mile above Williamsport in a drenching rain; mud was knee-deep, and the water of the river rose to their armpits. The weary troops finally reached Orange Courthouse, coming from Front Royal, through Manassas Gap, where they repulsed a demonstration from the enemy, by Thornton's Gap and Madison Courthouse. At Orange life was made very pleasant for them by the kindness of the community and the hospitality of the ladies; splendid reviews were held under the eyes of General Lee, and it was a season of rest and recreation for officer and soldier.

On October 8th, Lee started on a flank movement against Meade. Rodes moved back the way he had come, towards Madison Courthouse. He struck the Federal Cavalry near Jeffersonton, driving them in confusion across the Rappahannock at Warrenton Springs. The object of Rodes' activities in this locality was to keep Meade from crossing the river to make a flank attack upon Lee. Many times he defeated the Federal general in this purpose. Once Meade came across at Germanna, but met with so determined a front at Mine Run that he finally abandoned the enterprise, and on the night of October 30th he went back over the Rapidan.

In the days after Gettysburg the Confederates were fighting with their backs to the wall. Rodes' Division was destined to take a large part in the events which preceded Appomattox. It was engaged in more than forty actions, and its marches mounted up to more than two thousand miles. It commenced the campaign in May, 1864, with 6,987 in its ranks. In the fall of that same year it had lost and killed, wounded and missing, 6,408. Included in this number was one major-general, 4 brigadier-generals, 52 field and staff officers, and 363 company officers. It is believed that only seven hundred of this division were left to surrender at Appomattox the following May.

In the disastrous Battle of the Wildnerness the division did great work, a notable part of which was taken by Ramseur's Brigade. At that point, where the Federal Army penetrated the Confederate line, inch by inch Ramseur's men drove them back into their captured salient. All who saw this considered it a great piece of generalship. It was Rodes' responsibility to withdraw the troops from the front to a new line of entrenchment in the rear, which General Gordon was actually preparing for them at about 2 A. M. on the 13th, under the ceaseless fire of the enemy. The exposed and exhausted troops had been in ceaseless combat for twenty-four hours. In order to give them relief it was necessary to withdraw them to the interior line over ground cut into a hundred trenches, and covered with dead and dying men. To add to the difficulty, the rain poured in torrents, and the darkness was impenetrable. The coolness, judgment and skill with which the operations of this most trying day were managed by General Rodes were the subject of universal commendation.

From May 4th, when winter quarters were abandoned, until the 22nd, when the division reached Hanover Junction, neither commander nor men had seen wagon or tent, so incessant was the fighting. June 13th was the date that General Early, under whom the corps was now serving, was ordered to intercept Hunter on his march to take Lynchburg, when Early and General Rodes had such hot words about General Ramseur's Division preceding Rodes to his native town. On July 4th Rodes occupied Harper's Ferry, and captured badly needed commissary and ordnance military stores in abundance. Crossing the Potomac he assisted in the defeat of General Lew Wallace at the Battle of Monocacy on the 9th. On the 11th his division struck the fortifications at Washington City. Throwing forward his skirmish line, which was soon warmly engaged, he deployed his troops, and felt the works at several points. They were found to be very strong and apparently well defended. He was decided in the opinion that they could not capture Washington with the means they had. This opinion has been clearly vindicated by General Early.

From the time he recrossed the Potomac, on the 14th, where he had engaged in several brushes with the enemy, the scene of his actions was mostly confined to the Valley of Virginia. On the 18th the enemy threw a large force across the Shenandoah River, near Castleman's Ferry, close to the place where the division was camped. They were promptly met by Rodes and driven back with great slaughter, large numbers of them being drowned in trying to cross the river. Very little has been said or known of this engagement which, for the numbers engaged, was the most severe and bloody of the Valley campaign.

The army moved back on the 21st to Fisher's Hill, whence on the 24th it was launched against Crook at Kernstown, routing him completely. Notwithstanding the severe march of the morning, Rodes pursued the flying troops to Stevenson's Depot, six miles beyond Winchester. From this period to August 17th, the history of Rodes' command consists of a series of marches and countermarches: one day in Maryland, the next in Virginia, he was perpetually engaged with Averill's Cavalry, with the occasional exercise of destroying the Baltimore and Ohio Railroad. Some idea may be formed of the active life of this division when it is stated that during the summer campaign it was in camp six times at Fisher's Hill, and that Rodes pitched his tent nine different times in identically the same spot at Bunker Hill.

On August 17th General Early, having been re-enforced by Anderson, moved forward from Fisher's Hill against the enemy, now under command of Sheridan, who fell back before the Confederates towards Harper's Ferry. Rodes was slightly engaged at Winchester on that day, and quite actively engaged with the cavalry on the 21st near Charlestown. On the 24th Sheridan sent his cavalry around toward Early's rear, to cut his communications. Rodes encountered them near Kearneysville, and drove them across the Potomac. On this occasion he lost an esteemed friend and aide, Lieutenant Arrington, whose thigh was broken by a rifle ball, an injury which subsequently caused his death.

The following month he was mostly engaged with Averill's Cavalry, which was uncommonly active and bold. On the 18th he was at Stevenson's Depot, six miles beyond Winchester on the Martinsburg Road. On the morning of the 19th Sheridan was announced to be advancing, and Rodes' Division was hurried towards Winchester to support Ramseur, who had met the shock of the Federal troops alone. When he arrived upon the field Gordon's Division had been forced to give ground before the enemy, who were pushing forward to capture Colonel Braxton's eight guns that gallantly stood their ground in the open field. Rodes' own Alabama Brigade, under General Battle, was in advance of his column. Deploying at once in rear of the artillery it swept forward, carrying everything before it. General Ramseur is reported to have said that this splendid charge saved his army that morning. Gordon's men rallied at once. The rest of Rodes' Division formed on Battle's right. The whole line moved forward, the enemy giving way before it. At that instant, in the full flush of success, cheering his men on to victory, Rodes was struck in the head by a musket ball and fell from his horse. From that moment fortune seemed to desert the army of the Valley. The sun of Winchester set in gloom and defeat and never rose again to victory.

General Rodes' body was brought to Lynchburg, where his father, General David Rodes was living. He was buried in the Presbyterian Cemetery near the gate, where his body lies today, by the side of his brother, Virginius Rodes, who died January 16th, 1878.

Major Green Peyton, to whom I am indebted for this sketch of General Rodes, wrote these words in his memory: "Those who knew him best deemed him worthy of high command. For myself I can speak of the man not less than the soldier. I shared his blanket, and I believe his heart. Upright, truthful, just, stern in the discharge of his duty, and in exacting it from others, but soft and genial in his hours of ease and relaxation, he was universally beloved. He left a son about a year old, and a daughter was born to his wife some months after his death. It is not my province to speak of the immeasurable loss which they sustained in the death of this tender husband and father, but even their grief was scarcely greater than that of him who pens this hasty and inadequate tribute to his memory."

General Early

Jubal Anderson Early was born in Franklin County, Virginia, November 3rd, 1816. He died in Lynchburg March 2, 1894. He was graduated from the United States Military Academy in 1837. In 1838, when first lieutenant of artillery, he resigned from the army and returned to Franklin County to engage in the practice of law. He was a member of the House of Delegates in 1841-42, and Commonwealth's Attorney of Franklin County from 1842 to 1852, except during that period from 1847-48, when he served in the Mexican War as major of volunteers.

In 1861, as a member of the Virginia Convention, he opposed Secession, but when Secession came he went with his State. He commanded a brigade at Manassas, as colonel of the Twenty-fourth Virginia Regiment, and was promoted to brigadier-general. His public service was important and distinguished, as a veteran of three wars. In the War Between the States he fought about fifty battles and skirmishes. The list is long: Bull Run, Manassas, Yorktown, Williamsburg, Malvern Hill, Cedar Mountain, Groveton, Fauquier Springs, Bristoe, Second Ma-

LYNCHBURG AND ITS NEIGHBORS

nasses, Ox Hill (or Chantilly), Harper's Ferry, Sharpsburg, Fredericksburg, Chancellorsville (or Second Fredericksburg), Salem Church, Winchester, Gettysburg, Second Bristoe, Rappahannock, Mine Run, the Wilderness, Spottsylvania, the Po, Bethesda, Lynchburg, Monocracy, Washington Parkers Ford, Shepherdstown, Kernstown, Winchester again (or Opequon), Fishers Hill, Cedar Creek and Waynesboro, and lesser affairs, such as Auburn, Somerville Ford, Fairfield and Port Republic. Some of these names stand for several days of battle.

Perhaps there was no officer or soldier in the Army of Northern Virginia who was oftener under fire than General Early. He served Lee, he served Jackson, and both of them had perfect confidence in him. He was successively colonel, brigadier-general, major-general and lieutenant-general. His promotions were received because of his ability, and he commanded with equal success a regiment, a brigade, a division, a corps, and an army. It was his brigade which at the first Battle of Manassas broke the east front of resistance offered by the enemy. In his narrative of the War, General Joseph E. Johnston says of Colonel Early: "He reached the position intended just when the Federal Army was apparently about to assume the offensive and assailed its exposed front. The attack was conducted with too much skill and courage to be for a moment doubtful. The Federal right was at once thrown into confusion. A general advance of the Confederate line, directed by General Beauregard, completed our success and won the battle." It was for this operation that Early won his first step and was made a brigadier-general.

General Early was no figure of romance, but a stern warrior of the Jackson, Forrest and Rodes type. When, at the Battle of Lynchburg, he reached the town, he was just in time to save it from Hunter. He shook his fist over the rampart at the enemy, and he yelled at them: "No buttermilk rangers after you now, damn you!" He spoke the truth; no buttermilk ranger was Early, as Hunter well knew. With this knowledge he scrambled over the top of the mountains like the devil himself was after him.

General Early was the subject of much unjust criticism. People forgot that he fought under a "paling star." It is true he had succeeded to "Stonewall" Jackson's command, but the command had been cut in pieces time and time again. When he went into the Valley to engage Sheridan there was no food left anywhere for man or beast. Sheridan, acting in accordance with his well-known motto of compelling even the crow to carry his own rations, had left the fruitful Shenandoah country a barren waste. Burning barns, had flamed on every farm, and troops of cavalry had driven the stolen herds down the turnpikes. Sheridan went even further than his threat, for he left the women of the Valley "nothing but eyes to weep with." They were starving men and starving horses who rode with Early; and many of his great captains sick, many wounded, many in prison, and many gone forever.

This is Early's tribute to his soldiers: "I believe that the world never produced a body of men superior in courage, patriotism and endurance to the private soldiers in the Confederate armies. I have repeatedly seen these soldiers submit with cheerfulness to privations and hardships which would appear to be almost incredible; and the wild cheers of our brave men (which were so different from the studied huzzahs of the Yankees) when their lines sent back opposing hosts of Federal troops, staggering, reeling and flying, have often thrilled every fibre of my heart. I have seen with my own eyes ragged, barefooted and hungry Confederate soldiers perform deeds which if performed in days of yore by mailed warriors in glittering armor would have inspired the harp of the minstrel and the pen of the poet."

"Through the vista of vanished years I seem to see them now," added Major John W. Daniel, "they go along the roads, and over the fields with almost shoeless feet, their slouch hats, their gray jackets, and their battle flags, all tattered and torn; but their steps proud and elastic and their high, expectant faces all eager

LYNCHBURG AND ITS NEIGHBORS

for the fray. Hark! there rings out o'er the rattling musketry and the thundering cannon their lofty cheer—yonder they are—we see them through the smoke drifts, now as they stand, defiant and dauntless amidst dead, dying, and falling comrades, weather-beaten and bronzed, sweat-begrimed, and powder-stained, half-starved, half-clothed—without reward, without complaint, asking for nothing but orders, fearing nothing but defeat, hoping nothing but victory. I believe them entitled to eternal glory and everlasting life."

After the War General Early adopted Lynchburg and took up his abode in his brother's house, near the corner of Main and Fifth Streets. The Early home was a fine colonial mansion of old brick; stone steps with iron hand railings led up to the front porch. The roof of the porch was upheld by large white Corinthian columns. The house stood a little way off Main Street, overlooking the bluff. The Elk's Home now occupies its former site. Here he could be seen daily, except in the coldest winter months, which he spent in New Orleans: an ancient, stooping figure, with a long white beard, a noble dome of a head, and the eye of an eagle, he always wore his neat gray uniform of a Confederate general. He never took the oath of allegiance to the United States Government. He was a bitter opponent of Secession, but having seceded he never went back. Always he was the old Reb, unreconstructed to the last, but in spite of the little matter of the oath, he voted the Democratic ticket in every election, and no judge at the polls dared dispute his right.

He grew old and cantankerous but our people loved him none the less. To his nieces, no doubt, he was very trying to live with. One fall he surprised them by inviting them to go with him to New Orleans to spend the winter. Miss Ruth and Miss Mollie hastened to prepare their wardrobes for the great event, and for weeks were engaged in buying new dresses and hats. The time came, and the General got ready for his departure, but he said no more about taking them. "Well girls," he said one day, "I'm pulling out for New Orleans tonight." "But

Uncle Jubal," Miss Ruth said, "have you bought our tickets? We are ready to go with you." "I've changed my mind. I'll be too busy this trip to be bothered with a passel of fussy women."

He spent some hours each day in the lobby of old Arlington Hotel, or on warms days sitting under the awning outside, where a row of split-bottom chairs used to stand on the pavement. There he would smoke a long clay pipe and talk. He also went every day to The Virginian office, to converse with Mr. McDonald and Mr. Wysor, the editors, or with Mrs. C. J. M. Jordan, or anyone else who happened to be around. He then took in The News office, to tell Mr. Glass and Mr. Button what he thought of their editorials, or any other matter in the newspapers. All subjects pertaining to the town came up for a rigid criticism interspersed with bitter comment on the Yankees. He was the mentor of Lynchburg affairs, and his acrid humor, his sharp tongue and unique oaths were the delight of the people. Once when Mr. Stockton Terry, owner of the Arlington Hotel, got after him about the violent language he had used at the hotel in a heated discussion of some sort the town rose up against Mr. Terry. People said that General Early was an old man, that he had saved Lynchburg, and that in this town he ought to be allowed to do and say anything he liked. And this is exactly what he did to the end of his days.

Many tales are told about him. Wentworth Mosby, clerk of the Arlington Hotel and Mr. Terry's nephew, was one day interviewed by an out-of-town woman who was getting up material for publication about the families of Confederate generals.

"Talk to General Early about his family. There he is over there," said Mr. Mosby, well knowing that General Early was a bachelor.

The woman went over to the General's place in the lobby and proceeded to question him about his military career. After he had very courteously told her what she asked she inquired of him further:

[114]

"Now tell me about your family, General. Have you any children?"

"None that I care to mention, Madam," he replied most politely.

Its own generals, Garland, Rodes and Dearing, being dead, Lynchburg took this old man to its heart, and loved him for his faults as well as his virtues. He owned a building on Main Street which the city had condemned as being unsafe. The work of pulling it down had started when he remembered he had left some papers in his office, so he went in to get them and was sitting at his desk examining these papers when the entire building collapsed. All business on Main Street stopped. From every direction men ran out of stores and offices to help the fire department and the military companies to dig the old General out of the debris, though they had no hope of finding him alive. After hours of intensive work, throwing out timbers, bricks and mortar they finally located him. He was practically uninjured. The room he was sitting in had dropped, floor and all, to a lower level and a few timbers had formed an archway of protection over the General. There he sat with his old campaign hat still on his head, and white with plaster he calmly waited for the people to get him out.

The Mayor of the town took charge of the excavation. When the General was finally located the old man looked up and called out to him:

"Hey, Bob, I didn't know you were up there, boy! I can direct these fellows for you. You go and get me a julep."

When he returned with the julep and lowered it down the General sank back in utter contentment and sipped his drink while all hands finished the job of excavation.

On March 2, 1894, General Early died, being in his seventy-eighth year. As he lay in state in his coffin, dressed in his gray uniform, one of his old followers came forward and reverently kissed his forehead. Saint Paul's Church was roped off and guarded to admit only a few, because it was feared that the foundations could not hold the great crowd of people. There over the body of General Early a touching eulogy was pronounced by Mr. Carson, the rector, who took for his text the words, "A Prince in Israel is Fallen." Old and wrinkled veterans, bearing a tattered battle flag, followed his hearse to the grave.

He was carried to Spring Hill Cemetery, and the entire town followed. His grave was made only a few yards from his old headquarters in the battle against Hunter. Here, where Tinsley of the Stonewall Brigade had sounded the advance thirty years before, a grizzled old bugler now sounded taps and the artillery and the corps of cadets from the Virginia Military Institute fired a last salute. So did Lynchburg see the last of "Old Jube" just as the sun was sinking behind the Peaks of Otter. Major John Warwick Daniel, with his gift for noble expression, repeated those words spoken by the Indians of Powhatan, their great king who was no more: "Our chief has passed beyond the mountains to the setting sun."

Major Don Peters Halsey

Don Peters Halsey, the second son of Mr. Seth Halsey and Mrs. Julia D. B. Halsey, was born September 15th, 1836, and spent his boyhood in and around Lynchburg. He went to school to the famous Peter Nelson, who taught in a little house still standing on Clay Street. After attending this and other schools in Lynchburg, he went to a boarding school kept by Mr. William Claytor at Liberty, now Bedford City. He next entered Emory and Henry College, graduating with distinction in 1855. In the fall of that year he began to teach ancient languages in Roanoke College, which chair he had been unanimously elected to fill, though at that time he was only nineteen years old. He soon decided that he was too young for the position, and determined to continue the cultivation of his own mind.

Having vacated the chair at Roanoke College late in the fall, his father, at the earnest insistence of his uncle, Professor William E. Peters, sent him to the University of Virginia. Entering in February, 1856, he remained until the close of the session, and graduated in Latin, Greek, French and Spanish; a truly remarkable achievement for so short a time. In the fall of the year 1856 he went to Europe and for four years pursued his studies in Germany, at Bonn, Berlin and Heidelberg, receiving diplomas in the various courses he had taken and the highest praise from his learned instructors. He studied science and philosophy as well as languages. At the University of Heidelberg he gave much attention to the law, particularly civil law, based upon the Roman law or Code of Justinian, as at that time he had determined to practice in Louisiana, where civil law instead of common law prevails. But he did not on this account neglect study of the common law, which most of the American states have received from the mother country. His knowledge of the history and principles of the great judicial system was profound. So it was that Don Peters Halsey became one of the most scholarly Virginians of his time, but he was destined to throw aside the cap and gown, and to win new laurels for himself with the sword.

Learning of the troubles of Secession confronting his native State, he came home, and there cast his lot with those who believed that these difficulties could be settled without bloodshed. At Holcombe Hall he made a speech memorable for its ability and earnestness, and he worked for the election of Union delegates to the State Convention, but when Virginia was swept on with the flood he went with his State. In May, 1861, he, with his two younger brothers, Alexander Lemuel Halsey, and Stephen Peters Halsey, rode out to Forest to the meeting held there in answer to Governor Letcher's call for troops. There at Forest the first cavalry regiment organized in the State was brought together under Colonel R. C. W. Radford. It was mustered in at Lynchburg May 25th, 1861, under the name of the Radford Rangers, later it was changed to the First Virginia Regiment, and finally to the Second Virginia Regiment of Cavalry. Don Peters Halsey was made a second lieutenant in Company G of this regiment. He participated in the Battle of Manassas, where the captain of the company, Winston Radford, was killed. In his report Colonel R. C. W. Radford spoke of Lieutenant Halsey as having distinguished himself in a most dashing charge. In the reorganization of the regiment following the casualties of battle, Halsey was promoted to a first lieutenancy. This rank he held until the following spring, when he became a volunteer aide-de-camp on General Longstreet's staff. His company, with four others of his regiment, under the command of Lieutenant-Colonel T. T. Munford, having belonged to General Longstreet's Brigade. After a short time, he was commissioned as an aide on General Garland's staff.

Don Peters Halsey's quality as a soldier far excelled any rank he ever gained. His gallantry, zeal and efficiency were not to be exceeded, and that these qualities were remarked upon by every officer under whom he served is shown by record after record in the official reports. He served in many of the heaviest battles fought: Manassas, Seven Pines, all through the Peninsula campaign, South Mountain, Sharpsburg, Chancellorsville, Gettysburg. In nearly every great battle he played his heroic part, as well as in many minor skirmishes and fights, which are no less a test of courage. He served on the staffs of Generals Garland, Iverson, R. D. Johnston, Ramseur and Wharton. At Seven Pines he displayed notable bravery, and there he received a wound from a minie ball which deprived him of the sight of his right eye. In the words of General Garland's report (War of the Rebellion Records, Vol. XI, pp. 945-6): "My aide-de-camp, Lieutenant Don P. Halsey, having attracted universal applause throughout my entire command by his handsome behaviour, was rallying a disordered regiment and leading it forward, with the colors in his hand, when he received a dangerous wound in the head, which will deprive me of his valuable services for a long time to come." His uncle, Colonel William E. Peters, in a letter to Major Halsey's son, Judge Don P. Halsey, refers to his gallantry at Seven Pines as follows: "I did not serve with him during the War, but he had the reputation of a soldier second to none. I remember one thing when I was on the field of the Battle of Seven Pines. The works of the enemy were assaulted by his brigade. The brigade recoiled from the assault, when he seized the brigade colors, rallied and led the brigade, and fell within a short distance of the enemy's works. It was reported that he had been killed. I went in search of his body, but he had been removed, desperately wounded, to a hospital in Richmond. I have always considered that your father was in a great measure responsible for carrying the enemy's works in this desperate battle." It would seem from this, and General Garland's report, that Lieutenant Halsey led not only his regiment, but the whole brigade in this splendid charge.

As soon as his wound healed he returned to active service. The sight of his right eye was hopelessly destroyed, but strange to say the appearance of it was not changed, and no one would have noticed this defect. In the fall of the same year, 1862, he took part in the Maryland campaign, and in the hot fighting which took place at Boonsborough, South Mountain and Sharpsburg. On September 14th, 1862, General Garland was killed at South Mountain, and when he fell, Captain Halsey was the first to reach his side and received his dying message: "I am killed. Send for the senior colonel." This was Colonel D. K. McRae, of the Fifth North Carolina, who promptly took command of the brigade. He also mentions Captain Halsey's usefulness. Captain Halsey was wounded again and was captured at Sharpsburg a day or so later, but his wound was not serious. He was exchanged in a short time, and returned to active service.

At the Battle of Chancelorsville he was mentioned in General Rodes' report as having been under fire, and Brigadier-General Alfred Iverson, on whose staff he was now serving, also praises his efficiency. Perhaps his greatest service was rendered at Gettysburg. On the first day of the battle, when the Second and Third Army Corps under General Ewell and General A. P. Hill attacked and routed the enemy, Iverson's Brigade, in which Halsey was still serving, while taking part in the attack of General Rodes' Division, through some mistake in orders on the part of the advancing troops, was exposed to a dreadful fire from the enemy. The brigade gallantly stood its ground until almost three entire regiments had fallen. The men had fought and died like heroes; five hundred who would not give an inch lay dead and wounded on a line as straight as a dress parade. In the midst of this terrible slaughter a few of the soldiers raised white handkerchiefs on their bayonets, but not a man ran to the rear. It was at this critical moment that Captain Halsey rallied the demoralized soldiers, and led them forward in a brilliant charge.

The accounts in the official reports show that Rodes' Division bore the brunt of the fighting, and was responsible for the victory on that occasion. All the officers engaged unanimously declared that Captain Halsey's action in rallying the disordered brigade was not only one of the greatest deeds of the War, but was most opportune and valuable in saving the entire movement from disaster. In his report General Ewell speaks of Captain Halsey first in mentioning those who distinguished themselves, praising him for his conspicuous gallantry and his great service in rallying the brigade which he led to its final attack. Rodes also speaks of Captain Halsey's rallying the men and guiding them onward in a dashing and effective charge just in time to be of service to the other generals in the attack.

When it is remembered that Captain Halsey at Seven Pines had seized the colors and rallied the frightened men to a desperate charge against the enemy, and when it is also remembered that on the first occasion he had been deprived of that most precious possession, the sight of one of his eyes, it would seem that along with the highest type of courage he possessed a sure understanding of the psychology of soldiers. In the thick of battle he could change them from defeated men into heroes! Aside from his high courage, his ability to inspire men to great adventure should have elevated him to a high command. Captain Halsey fought not for hope of high reward: for Virginia he gave his best, content that Virginia should have that gift from him.

In December, 1863, Colonel Thos. M. Garrett, of the Fifth North Carolina Regiment, in his report to Major-General Fitzhugh Lee, speaks of Halsey as displaying "his usual spirit and self-possession in the field," in the fighting which took place at Morton's Ford and Raccoon Ford. During the year 1864 he served on the staff of General R. D. Johnston, and was in the Valley campaign of General Jubal A. Early. After the Battle of Winchester, he was transferred to the staff of General Gabriel C. Wharton, who succeeded to General J. C. Breckenridge's Division when that officer entered the Cabinet of President Davis. At the Battle of Waynesborough, March 2nd, 1865, Captain Halsey had his horse shot from under him and was captured by Sheridan's troops. This time he was not exchanged but remained in prison at Fort Delaware until some time after the close of the War, as he was not released until June, 1865. It is believed that Captain Halsey was promoted to a major in 1864 or '65. General Johnston, General Wharton, and several of his superior officers were of this opinion, and he was addressed by his comrades as Major, but his family, having no official proof, have never claimed this honor for him.

Of the Battle of Waynesborough, the last battle in which he fought, General Wharton wrote in a letter to Captain Halsey's son, Judge Halsey, of Lynchburg:

"Your letter making some inquiries in regard to your gallant and honored father, and my personal friend, is received. Major Don P. Halsey was assigned to the Division I commanded when and after General J. C. Breckenridge assumed the duties of Secretary of War. This was the latter part of September, 1864. About the same time Major J. P. Smith was assigned as inspector-general. Major Halsey as adjutant-general served in this capacity until the unfortunate affair at Waynesborough, when General Early, thinking that Sheridan would take the same route to Lynchburg that Hunter had taken, viz: through Lexington, placed our troops on the west side of Waynesborough, with the river in our rear, effectually preventing any retreat. As we had only about 800 men to oppose 7,500 splendidly equipped cavalry, of course we had no show and fell an easy victim. Your gallant father had charge of my left wing, and held his position as long as possible. When forced back he reported to me that this old horse, that he so loved, was fatally shot, and when he rode up was about to fall. I told him to put old John (I think he called his horse) out of the way, and try to get to a place of safety, as the Yankees were getting all around us, and all would be killed or captured. I am sure your gallant father held a commission as major, as I remember the order assigning him major and adjutant-general, as did the order of Major Smith as inspector-general. I esteemed your father most highly as a brave and cool officer, and valued his advice. Our relations were most cordial and intimate."

After Halsey's return to Lynchburg, he began the practice of law. On the 4th of March, 1866, he was united in marriage to Miss Sarah Ann Warwick Daniel, the daughter of Judge William Daniel, Jr., and the granddaughter of Mr. John M. Warwick, from whose house the wedding took place. For a while he was in partnership with his wife's father and brother, Judge Daniel and John Warwick Daniel, afterwards Senator Daniel, under the firm name of Daniel, Halsey and Daniel. Later he moved to Richmond, where he lived for years and built up a fine practice, particularly with the German element of the town, because of his knowledge of the German language. But war had taken too heavy a toll of his strength, and the long marches, the hardships and privations of camp life, the sufferings and confinement of prison, all had weakened his resistance to disease. In 1880 he was compelled to give up his practice, and hoping to regain his health he retired to his farm in Nelson County on Tye River. But in spite of the outdoor life he lived at Fern Moss he grew worse. In 1882 he spent several weeks in Philadelphia under the treatment of Dr. Weir Mitchell, and came home much improved. Soon after, however, he caught a deep cold which developed into pneumonia and this he did not have the reserve

Major Stephen Halsey

force to combat. He died the 1st day of January, 1883, in the forty-seventh year of his age, and was buried in Spring Hill Cemetery in Lynchburg.

Captain Halsey was a tall man, fully six feet in height, of fine proportions and a soldierly carriage. He had a nobly intellectual face, and the courtly manners of the Virginia gentleman of his time. He was a very accomplished lawyer, accurate and painstaking, deeply learned in the law, and of a profound and logical cast of mind. Of high character as a man and a Christian, he was destined to shine in any walk of life. His home life was particularly happy, and his death was a very heavy blow to his wife and children. She in that same year suffered the further loss of her two young daughters. Their children were:

Caroline Daniel Halsey; born November 3rd, 1868; died August 18th, 1883.

Don Peters Halsey; born December 29th, 1870. Married Miss Mary Michaux Dickinson, of Hampden-Sidney, Virginia.

Julia Olive Halsey; born November 15th, 1873; died August 8th, 1883.

Seth Cabell Halsey; born July 4th, 1876.

John Warwick Daniel Halsey; born January 3rd, 1879; died December 10th, 1933.

Edwin Alexander Halsey; born September 4th, 1881.

Major Stephen Peters Halsey

Major Stephen P. Halsey began service in the War Between the States in Company G, Second Virginia Regiment of Cavalry, or the Radford Rangers. The regiment was known for a while as the First Virginia, a rank to which it was justly entitled, as it was the first regiment organized in Virginia. Formed at Forest by Colonel Richard Carlton Walker Radford, it was mustered in at Lynchburg on May 15th, 1861, at the old Fair Grounds, since changed to the City Park. It is difficult to gain any particulars of his own exploits from the Confederate soldier. He will not talk about himself as a hero, and Major Halsey is no exception to this rule. His comrades now living, and the records of the War reveal the story of his gallant service.

Major Stephen P. Halsey and his brothers, Don and Alex, were in the Second Virginia Cavalry for a year. Captain Alex Halsey was killed at the Battle of Smithfield, after two years of brave and devoted service. The brilliant record of Don Peters Halsey has already been given in this book. Major Stephen Halsey served throughout the entire War, from Manassas to Appomattox. General John S. Williams, his commanding officer, makes mention in his reports of the splendid quality of his service. Stephen's first commission, that of captain, was dated October 25th, 1862, and signed by Governor Letcher under the Act of the Virginia General Assembly, authorizing him to raise troops. When the Twenty-first Virginia Regiment of cavalry was formed Colonel William E. Peters was its commanding officer, and by the vote of all the officers in the regiment, Stephen Halsey was made its major. The commission as major was dated March 24th, 1864, but provided that he should rank as major from the 31st day of August, 1863, when he was only nineteen years old. This commission was signed by James A. Seddon, Secretary of War of the Confederacy, and with his commission as captain is still in Major Halsey's possession.

While with the Twenty-first Virginia Cavalry Major Halsey and his brother, Alex, served in Virginia, West Virginia, Tennessee, Kentucky, Maryland and Pennsylvania. Major Stephen Halsey was with Colonel Peters when the latter was threatened with court martial for his refusal to burn Chambersburg, an act which might well have been justified, in reprisal for the vandalism committed by the Federals in the South, but which Colonel Peters and the chivalrous officers and soldiers under him refused to commit.

Major Halsey's recollections of the War are full of very amusing and touching stories. After the Battle of Manassas, when the Northern soldiers were in retreat, Major Halsey's horse, wild with excitement, could not be restrained, but ran a long way after the fleeing Federals. The crowd that had flocked from Washington in carnival spirit and holiday dress, to see the Southern rebels beaten into subjection, were now a bedraggled crew and in their panic they blocked the road, running a mad race with their own army to get back to the protection of Uncle Sam. In the midst of all this confusion Major Halsey had some difficulty in quieting his horse, and when he finally turned back he met his body servant who had come to look for him, "Does you know me, Marse Stephen?" he asked him.

Once in West Virginia, in the natural gas section, Major Halsey said the soldiers, after a long march, came upon a scene that was strange and alarming to them. Close to the banks of the Sandy River, near Warfield, they saw great flames leaping straight up from the water. One of them cried out: "Major, this ain't no place for us to fight."

In Tennessee, after a hard day, they reached the top of a mountain, where Major Halsey had been ordered to camp for the night, and to charge the enemy at daybreak. They had no tents, and the snow was falling fast. This happened many times, and often when morning came the men would be lying entirely covered by snow. Many of them were barefooted, riding with metal stirrups in the freezing weather, with no protection for their feet except rags or old newspapers. Sometimes the Major's horse, which he loved like a brother, would be a solid sheet of ice from head to tail. These sparse anecdotes which could be gained from Major Halsey are well worth recording, as the recollections of an eye-witness invariably are. Always he pays his tribute to the soldier, the brave private of the Confederate Army, and the gay, humorous spirit of him which would not be downed.

Two towns in Virginia, Wytheville and Lynchburg, have to thank Major Halsey that they were not destroyed. Mr. Herman Agnew gave this account of the encounter near Wytheville: Near the town, on April 10th, 1864, as the vanguard of the regiment rode along, they saw the Federal soldiers moving towards Crockett's Gap on their way to attack the place. With the few men he had with him Major Halsey hastened forward, and disposed his men to the best advantage to make a stand. They did this most gallantly, until he could go back and bring up the regiment. Here a fight raged for about four hours, but finally the Northern soldiers were driven off, and Wytheville was saved from capture.

At the close of the War Major Halsey reached Lynchburg just in time to save the town from pillage and the story of this was often told by the older men in whose protection the town was left while the younger men were serving in the army. Right after the surrender, when the troops were returning to their homes, Major Halsey rode into Lynchburg, accompanid only by his body servant, having left the regiment behind at Sandy Hook. He entered the town by Horseford Road and when he reached Main and Ninth Streets he found a great mob gathered at the lower edge of what was then the market place. Mr. Thad Ferguson, an older citizen, had called a few men to his aid to quiet this uprising, which was composed of a gang of Yankee camp followers, unruly Negroes, and the riff-raff of the town who, demoralized by news of the surrender, were bent upon looting the stores and houses. The persuasions of the old men under Mr. Ferguson had no effect whatever upon the mob. It was by lawless mobs of this kind that Richmond and many other Southern towns were set on fire. As Major Halsey looked over the scene, Mr. Untermyer's store, which was the second from the northeast corner of Ninth and Main, about where Kresge's Dollar Store now is, burst into flames, and Mr. Ferguson, coming up to him, said in despair:

"Major, look, just look!"

Feeling that the entire town would soon be at the mercy of the rabble unless something was done, the Major drew his sword and rode into the rabble, slapping right and left with the broad side of it.

One man cried, "Get out of the way! He'll kill us!" while the Negro body servant, riding as close to his master as he could yelled back:

"You're damn right he will!"

In a few moments the mob had scattered. Major Halsey followed some of them down Ninth Street, to the place where Mr. Nathan Handy now conducts his business. There was a commissary there at that time, and a few barrels of flour were stored in the space formed by the lower and upper levels of Ninth and Jefferson Streets. A crowd had collected here, intent on breaking into the place and stealing these few stores. Major Halsey began shooting over their heads, and in a few moments he had them in some semblance of order. He instructed Mr. Ferguson, and the citizens with him, to fire into the mob, after giving them due notice, if they gave any further trouble, and thus to hold them in check while he went after the regiment. He then rode away to meet the cavalry and to hurry them on from Sandy Hook, but when they reached the city the crowd had dispersed and the streets were quiet.

Major Halsey was in the Battle of Lynchburg, as shown in the description of that engagement. He served then under his uncle, Colonel William E. Peters, and the scene of their activities was near New London, where our soldiers, greatly outnumbered, hung around Hunter's troops, annoying and delaying them in their advance on Lynchburg. On Ward's Road, as has already been related, Major Halsey, in a hot skirmish with the enemy, came near receiving a mortal wound, when the buckle of his sabre belt was shot in two pieces.

The Twenty-first Virginia Cavalry was at first a part of the brigade of General John S. Williams. After serving under him, Major Halsey was transferred to the command of Brigadier-General William E. Jones, one of the ablest cavalry officers in the army. Shortly before the Battle of Lynchburg, General Jones, while at Glade Spring, found that many of the horses his troops were riding were unfit for service. In order to circumvent

Hunter, whose advance towards Lynchburg was threatening, he dismounted his men, and sent them to Lynchburg, Charlottesville and Staunton by train.

At the unveiling of the monument to the Second Virginia Cavalry in Miller Park, Lynchburg, on October 1st, 1913, when Major Halsey, as Commander of the Garland-Rodes' Camp of Confederate Veterans presided as chairman, he said: "Lynchburg was saved on more than one occasion by the cavalry. At Trevillians by Hampton, Munford and others, and at New London by McCausland and his iron brigade. Here Hunter was delayed ten to twelve hours, giving General Early time to reach Lynchburg ahead of him. General W. E. Jones, with his dismounted cavalry, that is, those whose horses were unfit for the journey, hurried by train to intervene between Hunter and Lynchburg, and confronted him (Hunter) at Piedmont in the Valley of Virginia. There a severe conflict occurred, resulting in disaster to both parties, as Hunter was fatally delayed, and General Jones was fatally wounded and killed. General Jones was my old commander, and a veritable Jackson of Cavalry was General Jones. All honor and peace to his memory."

This chapter contains only a few records selected to illustrate the type of soldier that Lynchburg produced and who made their homes here. I have included Major John Warwick Daniel in another chapter because he also distinguished himself in other fields. In order to publish a complete account of the many officers and men whose brilliant records reflect honor upon the city this sketch of Lynchburg would have to be extended into many volumes. The memory of these men is well-beloved in Lynchburg and includes such distinguished records as those of General Holmes Smith, Colonel Maurice Langhorne, Colonel James Watts, Colonel Risque Hutter, Colonel Forsberg, the Otey brothers, Colonel John G. Meem, Major Winfree, Colonel Richard Burks, Major Thomas J. Kirkpatrick and others equally as illustrious, many of whose families are included in the Genealogical Section of this book.

CHAPTER XII
AFTER SURRENDER

CAPTAIN CHARLES MINOR BLACKFORD wrote this description of life in Virginia in those earliest days after the surrender: "My wife, Nannie and myself, staid at the University, living in one room, and with only three dollars and fifty cents in current money for two months. We made the money go very far. I bought two hams and a barrel of flour on credit, giving my bond at twelve months for $25 therefor, and with the money we bought some sugar and coffee, which we hoarded." Captain Blackford had gone to the University of Virginia the night of the evacuation of Richmond, travelling by way of the tow-path of the James River and Kanawha Canal. In three days he reached the University where Mrs. Blackford and their little girl, Nannie, were staying in a single room in one of the professor's houses. Two days after he reached them he heard of Lee's surrender at Appomattox. He had $3.50 in money. His house in Lynchburg was mortgaged for $4,000, which was much more than it was worth at that time, and he had his horse and a very scanty supply of clothing for himself and his family. "Strange as it may appear, the time passed pleasantly," he continues, "for all were trying to make the best of everything. There were a great many charming men and women there at the time, and a great many pretty girls, and quite a number of crippled soldiers who had entered college for a while. Vegetables and milk were given us daily by Mr. Colston and others, and we got along very well. I had managed through Mr. John M. Miller, of Lynchburg, to get some money for mother's use in Lynchburg; and though I had none myself I was quite happy, except as to how I was to secure bread and meat in the future, but my long experience as a soldier had taught me to let the future take care of itself to a philosophical degree.

This state of things could not last, and I determined to go back to Lynchburg on a prospecting tour. My horse had been making his own living grazing in the University grounds, but he had cast a shoe, and I had no money to have it replaced, and I left him until I could have him shod. At that time there was a gravel train which ran out from Lynchburg to Tye River where they were rebuilding the bridge. It started back at 4 o'clock. There was also a sort of handcar which left Covesville at 10 o'clock in the morning and connected with it. My intention was to reach Covesville in time to use it, though I did not have any money. I told my wife goodbye at 5 o'clock and struck out at a swinging gait without stopping a moment until I reached Covesville, where I found the car started at 9 o'clock, and had been gone some twenty minutes. I pushed on, determined to make the whole forty-two miles to Tye River before 4 o'clock, which I did, only stopping once at Miss Peggy Rives, where I spent ten cents, all I had, in eggs for myself and a Negro whom I overtook, and to whom I promised a ride over from Tye River on the cars if he would carry my coat, vest and watch, which he faithfully did, much to my relief. I reached Tye River at half past three o'clock, having made the forty-two miles, including the stop to boil and cook the eggs, in ten and one-half hours on a hot, summer day. I induced the conductor to permit my colored friend and myself to go over on the flats deadhead. It was my first ride over the road as a deadhead, yet strange to say I have never paid anything for travelling on it since. I was made a director of the road by Governor Pierpont the next year, and have been first, director, and then counsel for it ever since.

I got to town by sundown, and on the way up to my mother's" (Mrs. Blackford lived in a brick house on Clay Street, next to the one which is now owned by Mrs. Thomas Adams, formerly used as the Presbyterian Manse, and the home of Dr. Paxton) "I met Mr. William T. Booker, to whom I told my condition as to finances, and asked for a loan, only meaning to borrow five dollars. He drew out five twenty-dollar goldpieces and offered them to me. Seeing no chance for paying him back I took only twenty dollars, telling him I feared he would never see it again. While talking to him I saw Mr. Abell, a bank officer in Charlottesville, passing down street on horseback. I hailed him and found he was going over to a friend's in Amherst to spend the night, and the next day to Charlottesville. I gave him the twenty dollars, and he promised to give it to my wife, which he did.

I at once went to work, getting ready for any employment which might come. I got back into my old office, and had my books unpacked, and some furniture I had at mother's, and an old carpet put down, making quite a respectable appearance. I was the only lawyer in town who kept his office open, for there were no courts and no business. People on Main Street sat out on the sidewalk gossiping and smoking, and some with tables playing chess, backgammon and cards, and as the sun moved they moved from one side of the street to the other to get the shade. Some men were settling up their books and old matters, and occasionally a controversy would arise about Confederate Contracts, as they were called, and my services were invoked to settle them. I was very rusty in the law, of course, and stuck close to my office, trying by hard study to catch up.

I shall never forget my first case. Two gentlemen, who afterwards became very prominent business men in the city, and good clients of mine, walked into my office and startled me by saying they wanted me to decide a question in regard to a contract payable in Confederate money. I looked wise, heard them both, and gave my decision. They then asked my fee. I told them I charged them nothing as the matter was small. They said they must pay something, and each laid down a half dollar and walked off. I was amazed at my wealth, seized it, closed the office and went home to show the spoils of my bow to my wife, who had come home by way of Scottsville and the canal. With a part of it we bought our first herring and a slice of cheese. No one can tell how good a herring and a piece of cheese is until they have had none for four years.

Other small work came in of the same character, and in July

I made good laborer's wages by giving opinions and sitting as arbitrator. I was very earnest and very needy, and attended faithfully to small matters; very soon the courts were opened, large matters became plentiful, and I got my full share.

When I got home the Yankees were in full possession, and the town was under military law, but they did nothing to annoy us, and we got on with them very smoothly, for which we were very thankful to General Gregg, who was in command, and who acted with wisdom and consideration."

It was a very great thing in those days to be young, and to have hope, but all were not able to take Captain Blackford's optimistic view, either from temperament, from seeing so many misfortunes around them, or from ill-health and wounds. The business life of the town was completely paralyzed. Many of the older men had lost their sons in battle, and they themselves were unable to rebuild their fortunes under such adverse conditions. Many of the men who came back were drained of energy and resource. They had given all they had to the War, and they were beaten. The greater part of the disaster of war is that it leaves so many derelicts behind: those who are injured not by shot and shell but in some more subtle way, by which they, through no fault of their own, are forever deprived of being any more use in the world. By the very circumstances of the South's defeat there was a much larger class of these last than war generally leaves; for being an agricultural country, and in a large sense dependent on crops for which slave labor was a necessity, the whole life was now disrupted. Their plantations were grown up in bushes and the land gone to waste. A new order had indeed come. Many ladies belonging to the best families of Lynchburg hired themselves out to make little yellow bags as containers for smoking tobacco. Men went into the ever profitable whiskey business to support their families. The owner of one of the finest farms in Virginia, thousands of acres of rich land which he had no means of working, became a professional gambler rather than see his family starve. A man whose family had belonged to one of the greatest houses of England, in whose hall here stood suits of armor that his ancestors had worn in England's defence, was now glad to accept the post of engineer on a railroad train. These were among Virginia's greatest fighting men, and noblest families.

This description of Virginia, given by a Northern observer, is from Walt Whitman's War Note Book:

"Dilapidated, defenceless and trodden with war as Virginia is, wherever I moved across her surface I found myself roused to surprise and admiration. What capacity for products, improvements, human life, nourishment and expansion. Everywhere that I have been in the Old Dominion (the subtle mockery of that title now) such thoughts have filled me. The soil is yet far above the average of any of the Northern States; and how full of breadth is the scenery, everywhere with distant mountains, everywhere convenient rivers. Even yet prodigal in forest woods, and surely eligible for all the fruits, orchards and flowers. The skies and atmosphere are most luscious, as I feel certain from more than a year's residence in the State, and movements hither and yon. I should say very healthy as a general thing; then a rich and elastic quality by night and by day. The sun rejoices in his strength dazzling and burning, and yet to me never unpleasantly weakening. It is not the panting, tropical heat, but invigorates. The North tempers it. The nights are often unsurpassable. Last evening (February 8th, 1863) I saw the new moon, the old moon clear along with it; the sky and air so clear, such transparent hues of color, it seems to me I had never really seen the new moon before. It was the thinnest cut crescent possible. It hung delicate just above the sulky shadow of the Blue Mountains. Ah! if it might prove an omen and good prophecy to this unhappy State."

As Captain Blackford pointed out, the people of Lynchburg had no great cause for complaint right after the War, since the Negro population here did not exceed the white population, and there was no particular reason for apprehension under the military officials in command of the town. There were carpetbaggers, of course, whose activities Horace Greely describes in these words:

"They are fellows who crawled down South in the track of our armies, generally at a very safe distance in the rear; some of them on sutlers' wagons, some bearing cotton permits, some of them looking sharply to see what might turn up; and they remain there. They at once ingratiated themselves with the blacks, simple, credulous, ignorant men, very glad to welcome and to follow any whites who professed to be the champions of their rights. Some of them got elected senators, others representatives, some sheriffs, some judges and so on. And there they stand, right in the public eye, stealing and plundering, many of them with both arms around Negroes, and their hands in their rear pocket, seeing if they cannot pick a paltry dollar out of them."

These plunderers and tax-gatherers in many cases manipulated families out of their fine old homes and took possession themselves. But a full history of all this, as taken from the Government's own records, would fill many pages, and is only indicated in this history of our town and our neighbors in order to show the spirit of the times. The troubles of Virginia were nothing as compared to those of the people further South, and the reasons for this are explained in the following chapter.

CHAPTER XIII

RECONSTRUCTION

WHEN Reconstruction in the South is discussed the question most frequently asked, and most generally unanswered, is: Why did Virginia fare so much better than other Southern states at that time? The answer is that nine men appointed themselves a committee to adjust affairs between Virginia and the Federal Government. They performed for Virginia an unexcelled service in statesmanship when war had failed, and by their efforts our State and its people were spared those excesses visited by the fanatic leaders of the North and a corrupt political majority upon the conquered Southern states.

After Appomattox, there had been a lull in the storm that beat over the South. During this period Andrew Johnson was standing in the breach, and putting up that great fight for the South which, with singular ingratitude, the South has only in recent years acknowledged. As yet no great disaster had befallen Virginia, though much humiliation. When the Southern states were divided into five military districts, each district in command of a Federal general, Virginia's name was taken from her, and she was shorn of all reminders of her past glory. She was no longer a Commonwealth, no longer the Old Dominion, nor even Virginia; she was now known only as District Number One. The people knew that more and worse was coming, and were gathering their shattered and scattered political forces together to meet the impending storm.

Meanwhile, the Negroes were roaming about at will. They subsisted off the Freedmen's Bureau, and when desiring a change of diet, they broke into hen-roost and smoke-house. Soon after the Surrender several ladies of Lynchburg arranged a series of lectures with a view to relieving the monotony of life and boosting up the spirits of the people, but the Provost Marshall prohibited these lectures when he learned that the subject of them was to be Southern Chivalry. Some excitement and resentment was also provoked in Lynchburg when Mrs. Cornelia J. M. Jordan's book, called Corinth and Other Poems, was burned in the courthouse square, the entire edition being destroyed by order of General Alfred H. Terry, Commandant of District Number One. And yet Virginia was still producing useful men for the country. In this very generation of which we write there were born in Lynchburg three joint authors of that great and useful bill, the Federal Reserve Act: Mr. Samuel Untermyer, ex-Senator Robert Latham Owen and Senator Carter Glass.

Not until 1867 did the people of Virginia receive the first real cause for alarm. By General Order 65, issued September 12th, 1867, and later orders, it was provided that an election should be held in this State for the purpose of selecting delegates to a Convention to make a new Constitution for District Number One. The Hall of Delegates in the City of Richmond was designated as the meeting place for this Convention, and the time set for December 3rd, 1867. The election was duly held, and it was then that Virginians fully realized the class and character of men chosen to make their new constitution. Their worst fears were confirmed, for there was no discounting the fact that the very lowest element in the State had been given complete control of their lives and happiness.

The people who represented the best interests of the State then called a convention of their own, to rally their forces, and to discuss ways and means of averting the calamity threatened by this election. Eight hundred of Virginia's leading men responded to the call. Every section of the State was represented, and when they met in Richmond they laid aside all former party affiliations. Old Line Whig and Old Line Democrat forgot those differences for which they had once so bitterly fought each other, and now joined hands to save the State from Negro, carpet-bag and scalawag domination. They called themselves the "Conservative Party," and forming into a solid organization they decided in the face of desperate odds to put up the best fight possible. They even formed a ticket for the forthcoming election of a governor to succeed Governor Pierpont, though by every indication it appeared that not a single member of their convention would be allowed to vote. On this "Conservative" ticket Colonel Robert Enoch Withers was nominated for governor, General James A. Walker for lieutenant-governor, and John Lawrence Marye for attorney-general.

Meanwhile, the Constitutional Convention for District Number One, afterwards known as the Underwood Convention, was still in session. It sat from December 3rd, 1867, to April 17th, 1868, when it was adjourned. That portion of this new Constitution which was the hardest for the people of Virginia to accept was contained in two clauses, known as the Disfranchising Clause and the Test Oath Clause. By the passage of these acts no person would be permitted to vote or hold any office whatever who had ever held office of any kind under the State Government or the United States Government, and had subsequently rendered any aid, countenance, or encouragement whatever to the Confederate Government, or to any person engaged in the Confederate service. By these provisions every white man of any standing in the State of Virginia, with the possible exception of a few Union men, would be prohibited from voting or holding any office.

Three days after the Underwood Convention had adjourned, a signed statement, or address, as it was called, appeared in the pages of the Richmond Dispatch under date of April 20th, 1868. The daring of this openly signed and published address is perhaps without a parallel in the history of a conquered people:

"The Convention consisted of one hundred and five members, of whom some thirty-five were Conservatives, some sixty-five were Radicals, and the remainder doubtful. The Radicals were composed of twenty-four Negroes, fourteen native-born white Virginians, thirteen New Yorkers, one Pennsylvanian, one member from Ohio, one from Maine, one from Vermont, one from Connecticut, one from South Carolina, one from Maryland, one from the District of Columbia, two from England, one from Ireland, one from Scotland, one from Nova Scotia, and one from Canada. Of the fourteen white Virginians belonging to this party, some had voted for Secession, others had been in the Confederate service, others are old men whose sons had been in the Confederate army; hardly one had a Union record. A large proportion of the Northern men and foreigners were drifted here in some non-combatant capacity by the War.

The Convention organized by electing a New Yorker president. A native of Maryland was elected secretary. A Marylander was elected sergeant-at-arms. An Irishman, resident of Baltimore, was elected stenographer. The assistant clerk was from New York. Two Negroes were appointed door-keepers. A clergyman from New York was appointed chaplain. Even the boys appointed as pages, with one exception, were Negroes, or sons of Northern men, or foreigners; while the clerks of the twenty standing committees, with two or three exceptions, were also Northern men or Negroes."

The address concludes in the following words: "It is difficult to realize the situation which we have reached in the South. The mind is stupefied at the initiation of Negro domination. It is a waking nightmare, whose horrible shadow cannot be pierced by the struggling faculties, a spell that neither the senses nor the reason can dissolve. The only escape from such a fact is that which the stout and resolute always discover from the storms and the floods of an unpropitious fortune. Resolved to swim, they breast the tempestuous waves with heroic hearts and sinewy arms, unterrified and undiscouraged, confident that if but true to themselves they were not born to be drowned. In such a spirit should the white people of Virginia buffet with the rude surges that break over them in this moment of adversity; in such a spirit should they beat down the heaving bosom of the dark flood in which they struggle; in such a spirit should they wrestle with the swift and swollen current of this revolutionary period, which has submerged all the ancient landmarks, has subverted the foundations of the Federal Government, has swept away all the sentiment of constitutional liberty at the North, and is now raging like a howling waste of waters over the lately fair and lovely vistas of the South."

To some readers this may seem an extravagant statement, made by one with a flair for hyperbole. True it was expressed in the language of the time, but any book on Reconstruction in the South couched in the language of our present day shows that the facts are not exaggerated. In The Tragic Era are cold statements, fully substantiated, which are far more astounding than anything contained in the above address. The people recognized this message as a cry of despair, and of warning. The address was signed by the Conservative members of the lately adjourned Constitutional Convention: Men of Augusta and Amherst, of Wythe and Giles, of Botetourt and Rockbridge, and other Virginia counties which had managed to send Conservative delegates. Day after day for four months they had sat in that Underwood Convention, their hands tied while the rights of their State were being pillaged. But though their hands were tied their tongues were not, and every inch of the ground was fought by this helpless minority. Eustace Gibson, of Giles County, a man from the mountains, put up a memorable fight and poured out the acid of his irony upon the majority. So bitter were the darts of his wit that they found their mark even in this assemblage, which did all in its power to have him expelled, but failed to do so.

Virginia had pride in her Constitutional Conventions. Heretofore she had sent only of her very best to take part in framing her laws. In Williamsburg, on Monday, May 6th, 1776, a Convention met which made the first written Constitution for a free State in the annals of the world, and from this Convention went five delegates, chosen to represent the Colony in the General Congress on the 11th of the following August. Compare these men with your Hunnicutts and your Underwoods, for Virginia's five men were: George Wythe, Thomas Nelson, Richard Henry Lee, Thomas Jefferson and Francis Lightfoot Lee. Virginia was not over-fastidious in her scorn of the Underwood Convention, the records of this Convention themselves, the newspapers of the day, the memoirs of many gentlemen who lived through that time and left their written testimony, and all other evidence that can be gathered from authentic sources, shows that there is no exaggeration in the statement that "this was the most conglomerate and heterogeneous body of men ever assembled in the history of the world to frame a Constitution for a free and enlightened people. Made up of different nationalities and different races, carpet-baggers and Negroes, with a hopeless minority of reputable Virginians trying to stem the tide of the majority in the attempt to humiliate the people of the State, and to disgrace her name. The Hall of the Convention became a bedlam of chaotic confusion, perturbation and anarchy. It is a well-known fact that most of the members were constantly armed on the floor of the Convention, and that many of the majority on leaving the Hall engaged in brawls and street fights."

The Convention was named for Underwood, the presiding officer. James C. Underwood was a Northern man who had come to Virginia a few years before the War. He had opened a school in Fauquier County, but by his habit of continually denouncing slavery in this slave-holding community he made himself unpopular with both patrons and pupils, and his pupils finally left the school. At this failure in his venture, he went North again, but came back to Virginia after the War. Another member of the Convention was James W. Hunnicutt, delegate from Richmond City. He was a scalawag from South Carolina, who had once been a preacher, had run a religious paper, and had been a man of property and a slave-owner before the War. He had voted for Secession, and was a deserter from the Confederate Army. Later he became an out-and-out scalawag, hanging on to the Republicans, and stirring up no end of trouble among the colored people. Men of this type were familiar figures of every town in Virginia.

As already stated, the Underwood Convention, which was also called the Black and Tan Convention, adjourned April 17, 1868. Except for the address in the Richmond Dispatch already quoted no action against the Convention had been taken. At this critical time Alexander Hugh Holmes Stuart came forward with a constructive plan of action. Mr. Stuart was born in Staunton, Virginia, April 2nd, 1807. He came from one of those great Scotch-Irish families which settled in Augusta County in the early part of the Eighteenth Century. The Stuarts came to Augusta in 1738, when Archibald Stuart, their progenitor, having been engaged in one of the rebellions in Ireland, was compelled to fly to America for safety. For seven years he remained in hiding in Western Pennsylvania, but after this time, in consequence of some act of amnesty, he was able to send to Ireland for his wife and children. He removed to Augusta County, Virginia, then a wilderness, and acquired large landed estates and died in 1761, leaving four children: Thomas, Benjamin, Alexander, and a daughter, who married Benjamin Hall. This Benjamin Hall was the father of Judge John Hall, of North Carolina, and of Dr. Isaac Hall, an eminent physician of Petersburg.

Alexander Stuart left a number of children, among them Judge Archibald Stuart, of Staunton, who was the father of Alexander Hugh Holmes Stuart. Alexander Hugh Holmes Stuart served one term in Congress, and was Secretary of State under President Millard Fillmore. A great many of his speeches have been published, and his work, A Narrative of Virginia, was printed in 1869. General J. E. B. Stuart, cavalry leader of the Confederacy, was descended from another son of Alexander Stuart. Of such stock then was Alexander Hugh Holmes Stuart, who, when it became apparent that if the public was to get any relief from the Underwood Constitution they must take matters in their own hands, inaugurated what became known as the Committee of Nine. His first move was to write a letter to the Richmond Times signed Senex. In this letter he reviewed the political situation, and called attention to the disastrous results which the white people of the State would suffer if the Constitution with the test oath and disfranchising clauses were adopted. He proposed that a new Constitution should be formed in which should be embodied "the universal suffrage, likewise the universal amnesty proposition in its broadest terms, and Negro eligibility to boot." (Stuart, Restoration of Virginia, page 23). He proposed that this new Constitution should be submitted to the Congress of the United States as a substitute for the Underwood Constitution. After much difficulty, the editors of the Dispatch and the Whig were induced to publish the letter. The publication was made in both papers, December 25th, 1868. A storm of opposition was raised at Mr. Stuart's proposition of universal suffrage and universal amnesty. So little did the people realize the extreme peril of their situation that many of the most prominent men in the State denounced it in the bitterest terms.

Nevertheless, Mr. Stuart felt convinced that some plan of compromise must be carried out, and while disturbed at the way his proposition had been received, he refused to be turned aside from the true issue. He conferred with the leading men about him, and it was decided to send letters throughout the State, inviting the leading men in every section to meet in Richmond December 31st, 1868, to confer together and decide what measures should be adopted to save the State from the dangers of the Underwood Convention. Among those consulted in this crisis were Thomas J. Michie, Judge Hugh Sheffey, Nicholas K. Trout and Major H. M. Bell. On December 30th, 1868, Mr. Stuart, Mr. Michie, General Echols and Major Bell left for Richmond to attend the meeting which was to take place the next day.

"The meeting was well attended and assembled at noon December 31st at the Exchange Hotel. It was organized by electing Mr. Stuart chairman, and C. C. McRay secretary. The chairman explained the object for which the meeting had been called. After a good deal of discussion, it was determined that a committee of eight (of which Mr. Stuart was made chairman by the meeting) should be appointed to report suitable business for the consideration of the meeting. The chairman was authorized to appoint other members of the committee, and thereupon he named Messrs. George W. Bolling, of Petersburg; Thomas S. Flournoy, of Halifax; John L. Marye, Jr., of Fredericksburg; D. C. DeJarnett, of Caroline; Frank G. Ruffin, of Chesterfield; B. H. Magruder, of Albemarle, and James Johnston, of Bedford. The meeting then adjourned until the next day to receive the report of the committee. When it reassembled, which was the first day of January, the committee submitted its report, which declared:

"While the convictions of the undersigned and, as they believe, of the people of Virginia generally remain unchanged, that the Freedmen of the Southern states, in present uneducated condition, are not prepared for the intelligent exercise of the elective franchise and the performance of other duties connected with public affairs, and are therefore at this time unsafe depositaries of political power; yet in view of the verdict of public opinion in favor of their being allowed to exercise the right of suffrage as expressed in the recent elections, the undersigned are prepared to surrender their opposition to its incorporation into their fundamental law, as an offering on the altar of peace, and in the hope that union and harmony may be restored on the basis of universal suffrage and universal amnesty.

To give effect to this purpose, and to spare no effort to effect a speedy and permanent restoration of union and harmonious relations between the portions of our country which have for some years past been alienated, the undersigned will appoint a committee of nine from different parts of the State, and reflecting, as far as may be practicable, the public sentiment of the State, whose duty it shall be at an early date to proceed to Washington and be authorized to make known the views and purposes hereby declared to the Congress of the United States, and to take such other measures as they may think proper to aid in obtaining from that body such legislation concerning the organic law of Virginia as Congress, in its wisdom, may deem, expedient and best under all the circumstances. The delegation so to be constituted may fill vacancies, and are authorized to enlarge their number at their discretion."

After elaborate discussion of the report, it was adopted, and the meeting requested Mr. Stuart to serve as chairman of nine persons to visit Washington for the purpose indicated in the report. The chair was authorized to appoint a committee of three to recommend the names of eight other gentlemen who, with Mr. Stuart, should constitute the Committee of Nine. The chair named Messrs. John Echols, F. G. Ruffin, and James D. Johnston, who made their report recommending Messrs. John L. Marye, Jr., James F. Johnston, W. T. Sutherlin, Wyndham Robertson, W. L. Owen, John B. Baldwin, James Neeson and J. F. Slaughter, and they were unanimously elected.

As soon as the meeting adjourned, Mr. Stuart issued a summons to his associates on the Committee of Nine to assemble in Washington on January 8th, 1869. In the meantime he was active in many ways in advancing the movement. He wrote to Horace Greely, editor of the New York Tribune, with whom he had had a personal acquaintance many years before the War, informing him of the proceedings of the Richmond meeting, and of the appointment of the Committee of Nine to visit Washington with the hope of securing a compromise of the Underwood Constitution on the basis of universal suffrage and universal amnesty. He asked Greely if possible to meet the committee in Washington, and to give them his assistance in accomplishing their object. Horace Greely promptly replied by a letter addressed to Mr. Stuart, which stated that he could not be present at Washington, but would try to make himself felt in New York through the columns of the Tribune, and he enclosed an editorial on the subject which had just appeared in

LYNCHBURG AND ITS NEIGHBORS

his paper. Mr. Greeley begged Mr. Stuart to confer directly with General Grant, and advised him especially to call upon Senator Sumner. Greeley made good his promise, and his paper contained many leading editorials which produced a favorable effect upon members of Congress. Acting upon the suggestion of a letter received from John L. Marye, Jr., Mr. Stuart secured the active co-operation of George W. Bolling, of Petersburg, and through him of Gilbert C. Walker, of Norfolk, who both attended the meetings of the committee in Washington and rendered valuable service."

The proceedings of this committee were so vital to the future of the Virginia people, that they would seem to deserve a place in the history of Lynchburg. The first meeting of the committee was held in Washington, on January 8th, 1869. Every member was present; the proceedings were informal, and no record of them was kept. It was decided that the committee should meet daily * * * and that they should invite the co-operation of Bolling, Gilbert C. Walker, and his brother, Jonas Walker, and of all the citizens of Virginia who might be in Washington, in promoting the work of the committee. "It was agreed that they would call in a body on President Andrew Johnson to pay their respects, but as the close of his term was near at hand, and his relations with Congress were unfriendly, they did not see that anything could be gained for their cause in asking his aid. They decided to seek an interview with General Grant, the President-Elect, and to fully explain to him their grievances, invoking his aid. The members of the committee, and all others who would co-operate with them, were also without delay to seek conferences with the leaders of the two houses of Congress, and to ask their help.

Soon after the committee had reached Washington, two delegations from Richmond appeared there. One consisted of men of intelligence and education, Franklin Stearns among them, who had come, not with the purpose of opposition to the committee, but to look after the interests of the Conservative Republicans. The other delegation was headed by Governor H. H. Wells, and was composed of white and colored men who desired the Underwood Convention to go through without any change.

The committee, according to the plan agreed upon, appeared before the Reconstruction Committee of the House of Representatives, and the Judiciary Committee of the Senate, and explained the object of their mission. Mr. Stearns and Governor Wells, with their respective adherents, were also present at the hearings. The first meeting was before the Committee of the House. The chairman of the Committee of Nine opened the hearing, giving a brief account of the origin and the objects of their mission. The discussion on behalf of the committee was conducted by Colonel Baldwin. He was followed by Governor Wells, the Underwood supporter, who said he did not believe that loyal men would be safe from wrong and outrage if the white people of Virginia were all enfranchised. He believed the only way to protect them would be to adopt the Underwood Constitution as it was. He was satisfied that the adoption of the plan of the Committee of Nine would destroy the Republican Party. He was sure the people, whatever they might say then, would in a few years take away the rights of the Negro unless the Republican Party became strong enough to protect them, and the only way to secure strength to that party was to give it power to direct the restoration of the State. None but the Republican Party could secure justice to all and rebuild the State. There could be no justice, no education, no prosperity, save through the Republican Party. He declared that the new movement did not have the support of the Virginians; that he did not believe ten thousand white people in Virginia would support it; that if it was carried it would have to be carried by Republican votes, but the Republican Party would not vote for it. They were opposed to reconstructing Virginia in that way. They would be willing to see the whites enfranchised after a few years when it could be done safely, but not then." (Stuart, Restoration of Virginia, page 36).

Colonel Baldwin spoke eloquently in reply, and expressed his firm conviction that the people of the State of Virginia would support the plan which he advocated in good faith.

By request Mr. Franklin Stearns addressed the Reconstruction Committee. He endorsed the plan of the Committee of Nine and condemned the Underwood Constitution. He believed what the Committee of Nine proposed was the only chance of reviving prosperity in Virginia. The committee, through General Schofield, then arranged an interview with General Grant. He expressed his disapproval of the test oath and the disfranchising clause, and showed that he appreciated the injustice of the Underwood Constitution, but referred to the fact that he was only a military officer and there was nothing he could do. However, the distinct impression was retained that if the Senate did not act upon the pending bill before his inauguration, he would then take some action in the matter. At the second interview with Grant his attitude was even more favorable, and the committee felt this meeting was more satisfactory than the first. After ten days spent in efforts in Congress, they believed they had fulfilled their mission and returned home.

The committee headed by Alexander Hugh Holmes Stuart had thus aroused the attention of the whole country, not only in Virginia and the South, but the people in the North as well were made aware of the enormities of the Underwood Convention. They had secured as advocates of justice to Virginia, the New York Tribune, New York Times, Boston Advertiser, Chicago Tribune, and other leading organs of public opinion in the North and Northwest. They had arrested the endorsement of the Underwood Constitution by the Senate, and they had received satisfactory assurance from General Grant that, as soon as practicable after his inauguration as President, he would bring the subject to the attention of Congress, and endeavor to obtain substantial relief for Virginia.

General Grant was inaugurated March 4th, 1869. On April 7th he sent a message to Congress in reference to the restoration to the Union of the states which had been engaged in the so-termed Rebellion. In this message he referred to the Convention held in Richmond, and called the attention of Congress to the propriety of providing by law for the holding of an election in Virginia during the months of May or June, at which the question of the adoption of the Underwood Constitution should be submitted to the citizens of the State, and more important still, he recommended that a separate vote be taken on such parts as might be thought expedient.

On April 10th, 1869, Congress passed a law providing for the election, and also granting power to the President to submit to a separate vote such provisions of the Constitution as he might deem best. If the Constitution were ratified, the legislature of the State should be elected as provided for. With the withdrawal of the Conservative candidates from the field, and the consolidation of all the better classes in Virginia on the election of the Conservative Republican ticket, the entire plan was carried out with success. When all seemed plain sailing, General Canby, who was then district commanding general in Virginia, provided some excitement by announcing that no member of the Legislature would be permitted to serve until he had taken the iron-clad oath. A word from the President, however, shut him up on this subject. The Underwood Constitution was carried at the election, but the two obnoxious clauses were defeated at the polls and were stricken out.

If the Underwood Constitution had been ratified in full, according to the estimate of the Committee of Nine in their paper submitted to the Judiciary Committee of the Senate, ninety-five per cent of the adult white population of Virginia would have been deprived of the right of suffrage, ineligible to any office, and rendered incompetent to serve on any jury, civil or criminal.

It is strange to consider how casual has been the attention history has given to this consummate accomplishment in diplomacy made at the dictation and direction of Alexander Hugh Holmes Stuart. If any man doubts the greatness of this service to Virginia, let him consider the condition of the other Southern states during Reconstruction: Consider South Carolina, Louisiana, Georgia and Mississippi, and ponder the condition of things which brought into being the Ku Klux Clan. Let him read that powerful indictment against General Grant's administration contained in the book published by the United States Government on its investigation of the Ku Klux Clan. Let him then ask himself if it was because of the good will of General Grant that an exception was made in Virginia's case and she, to a large extent, was spared the horrors of Reconstruction. The only possible answer is that the Committee of Nine saved Virginia, and that no great man ever gave Virginia a higher service than did Alexander Hugh Holmes Stuart.

At the request of the Virginia Historical Society Mr. Stuart wrote a full account of the proceedings of the Committee of Nine, under the title of The Restoration of Virginia to the Union. It was published by the Virginia Historical Society, and from it the material for this chapter on Reconstruction in Virginia has been largely drawn, in many paragraphs using the exact words of Stuart's book.

CHAPTER XIV
RECOLLECTIONS AND COMMENT

HENRY CLAY had many ardent admirers in the neighhood of Lynchburg. He had Clay relatives in Bedford County, and his mother being a Hudson and his grandmother a Jennings, he also had numerous relatives and family connections in Lynchburg. There is an account of one of Clay's visits here written in the early annals of the town which tells how, as he came riding towards Lynchburg, every gentleman in town got on his horse and rode out the Salem Turnpike to the old Quaker Meeting House. There they waited to greet Henry Clay, and they fell in behind him and formed an escort to conduct him to the town.

Within the recollection of most Lynchburg people there lived among us one of Virginia's most illustrious sons: a brave man, a statesman and the last of Virginia's line of great orators. Perhaps no man in public life ever bore a nobler appearance than did John Warwick Daniel. That beautifully handsome face with its antique features and perfect brow was as remarkable as some great sculptor's highest achievement in marble, but lighted by deep blue eyes. Even his terrible lameness could not detract from his dignity and beauty.

Because I am only too well aware that we in the South are accused of idealizing our heroes, and because I am also conscious that a deep personal friendship may easily over-color an historical estimate of a man, I give here two appreciations of Senator John Warwick Daniel from entirely unprejudiced sources: from the memorial address delivered by Senator Lodge, of Massachusetts, and from an article published in the Saturday Evening Post shortly before Senator Daniel's death in June, 1910. Senator Lodge says:

"When, as a member of the House, I first saw him on the floor of the Senate, I was arrested by his appearance, and found

Senator John Warwick Daniel

a fascination in watching him. He was very striking in his looks, with a head and face which would have been remarked anywhere and in any assemblage of men * * * Senator Daniel had long passed youth, had gone beyond middle age, and yet he seemed to me still to have the expression of those who in the flush of young manhood sought the great prize of death in battle for the sake of beliefs to which their hearts clung, in pursuit of visions seen only by them. The touch of romance, the look of the dreamer, the passionate energy of the man of action, all seemed to meet in his aspect and in his eyes.

With a brilliant record as a soldier, not merely eminent at the bar, but as a writer on law of high authority, after much public service in his own State and in the House of Representatives, Senator Daniel came to this body with distinction already achieved, and with a high reputation in many fields already secured. He had as a gift of nature great eloquence of speech, and this gift had not only been enlarged by care and practice, but had been made weighty and serious by the studies he had pursued, and by the reflective and philosophical cast of his mind. * * * His style was of the old school. * * * It has passed out of fashion now. * * * Yet the school to which Senator Daniel belonged produced speakers who have never been surpassed in the annals of oratory * * * the heights in the great art of speech to which some of the men of that age attained remain today lonely and unscaled. Senator Daniel exhibited all the qualities of that earlier time in high degree. * * * He had in large measure the 'high seriousness' which Aristotle commends in the poet. * * * Except in the golden age of Athens I do not think that any community of equal size, only a few thousand in reality, has produced in an equally brief time as much ability as was produced by the Virginian planters at the period of the American Revolution. Washington and Marshall, Jefferson and Madison, Patrick Henry, the Lees and the Randolphs, Masons and Wythe. What a list it is of soldiers and statemen, of orators and lawyers! The responsibility of representing such a past and such a tradition is as great as the honor. Senator Daniel never forgot either the honor or the responsibility. Can more be said in his praise than that he worthily guarded the one and sustained the other? * * * Not only did he fitly and highly represent the great past, with all its memories and traditions, but he also represented the tragedy, as great as the history, which had fallen upon Virginia. To the cause in which she believed she had given her all, even a part of herself, and the maimed soldier with scars which commanded the admiration of the world finely typified his great State in her sorrows and her losses as in her glories and her pride."

From the Saturday Evening Post comes an estimate which is entirely different in tone but which says the same thing in a different way:

A Virginia Cavalier

"The Yankees must have thought John Warwick Daniel, of Virginia, a considerable menace to the success of their cause, for they kept plugging at him something scandalous during those iron days—as T. R. was wont to say when regretting he didn't get a chance to be a hero until those pewter days of 1898—those iron days from '61 to '65.

They got the dashing young Virginian, too, those Yankees; sifted a bullet into him at first Battle of Manassas, another at Boonsboro, Maryland, and landed him for fair at the Wilderness, on May 6th, 1864, when a ball shattered his hip and put him on crutches for the rest of his life. After that, the Yankees had somewhat the better of it until the end.

For various reasons it was not the good fortune of the Veracious Chronicler to see John Warwick Daniel during those iron days—taking phrase, that!—but if he was as good-looking as a young man as he is an old man it is no wonder the flower of the youth of Virginia let a shrill yip out of them and followed wheresoe'er he led. He looks like an Old Roman Warrior now, and he must have been a pippin as a Young Roman Warrior, with that eagle eye, that classic profile and that general pulchritudinous *tout ensemble,* as John Dalzell, the greatest French scholar in Congress, would say.

He was nineteen when the war broke out, and he entered the Confederate Army as a lieutenant at the first tap of the drum, being assigned to the Stonewall Brigade. After he was wounded at Boonsboro, he was promoted to be a major and made chief of General Jubal Early's staff, and there he served until they nailed him at the Wilderness. Virginia sent a lot of good soldiers to the front, but down there they still speak of Daniel as a sort of a conglomerated type of all that a Virginia soldier should be and mostly was.

Prodigal Nature didn't stop with Daniel by making him good-looking and a brave soldier. She gave him one of those melodious voices and fixed him up with a silver tongue. After he had finished fighting, he began talking, and it was soon discovered he could talk as well as he had fought. What was the result? An unnecessary and simple question. The result was—as it is now and ever has been, when a man flashes in the South with a melodious voice and a silver tongue—that John Warwick Daniel went into politics and into the law.

There are some thing which are immutable. That is one of them.

He was elected to the Virginia House of Delegates and served from 1869 to 1872. Then, in 1875, he went to the Virginia Senate and served until 1881. They made him the Democratic candidate for governor in 1881, but Cameron, the Readjuster, beat him, and in 1884 he came to the House of Representatives. In 1887 Mahone left the Senate and Daniel took his seat. He has been there ever since, his present term expiring in 1911, when it is probable he will be re-elected and go on and on for years and years.

Politics did not take all his time, for he developed into a profound lawyer. Two of his law-books, Daniel on Attachments and Daniel on Negotiable Instruments, are standards. He was lecturing on law at the Washington and Lee University, one day, when a student arose and said: 'I beg your pardon, Mr. Daniel, but may I ask a question?'

'Certainly.'

'Well, sir, I would like to know how many days of grace are allowed in this State?'

'Really,' said Daniel, 'I cannot recall at this moment, but if you will refer to my work on Negotiable Instruments you will readily ascertain. Now, young gentlemen, as I was saying——'

He is a kindly and companionable man, extremely felicitious as an after-dinner orator, an excellent story-teller and beloved by both sides of the Senate. He is on the big Finance and Appropriations committees.

And he is always a Virginian—the pink of politeness, a most courtly gentleman. He is obliged to use a crutch because of his wounded hip, but gets about spryly. His accent is pronouncedly Southern. Meeting Senator Frye, of Maine, in the Marble Room, one day, and desiring to see Senator Hoar, he asked: 'Senatuh, is Senatuh Ho' on the flo'?'

'No,' replied Frye, 'Senatuh Ho' is not on the flo'. He went out that do' at half-past fo'.'"

Memories of Mrs. John Janney Lloyd, whose husband was for so long the rector of Grace Memorial Church, brings to Lynchburg people the history of her father also: of his unique beginnings as an artist, and of his connection with Virginia's greatest statue, the Houdon statue of George Washington in the Capitol at Richmond. Mr. William J. Hubard was born in Warwick, England, in 1807. At the age of twelve he had already shown an unusual talent for painting, and when he was thirteen he had started on his career as a portrait painter. Very early in life he developed a pronounced ability for delineating any object in nature or art with a pair of common scissors, from which start he readily advanced to an astonishing skill in making silhouettes. He went to Ramsgate in September, 1822, where he attracted the attention of the Duchess of Kent, then at Townley House, and there he cut portraits of the whole household, among these being one of the little Princess Victoria, who was afterwards Queen of England. It is said that these portraits are still in the gallery, and attract attention as Master Hubard's earliest productions. In 1824 he came to America. He was the first professional profile cutter in America who did not use a mechanical device, and he met with a particularly warm reception in Boston. He was justly proud of his ability as a silhouettist, and varied his accomplishment in black and white by making painted profiles or tinted and lightly gilded silhouettes. He came to Virginia later on, where he spent the remaining years of his life. In 1834 his portraits, painted in Baltimore, were exhibited at the National Academy of Design. A portrait he painted of John C. Calhoun is in the Corcoran Art Gallery.

According to Mrs. Lloyd, who made her home here after the death of Dr. Lloyd, the part Jefferson played in the making of the Houdon statue of George Washington has been greatly magnified in late years. It was a well-known fact in earlier days that Jefferson and Washington were not friends, and it was not Jefferson, but Lafayette who persuaded Washington, greatly against his will, to consent to having the cast made for the statue. Underneath all the whitewash that has been applied to the great characters of former days, and the political situations in which they moved and had their being, we are forced to recognize the truth that Washington and Jefferson were personal and political enemies, and that Washington considered Jefferson a slick politician and a demagogue, and Jefferson thought Washington a ponderous old fellow with a third-rate mind. But Washington loved Lafayette.

Lafayette came back to America in 1784 and spent five months as the guest of the nation. His visit recalled to the mind of the Virginia House of Delegates that a resolution concerning him, which had never been carried out, had been passed by that body in 1781. It had been resolved in that year, and directed by the General Assembly, that a bust should be made of the Marquis de la Fayette out of the very best marble by a suitable sculptor, to be presented to him as a gift from the State of Virginia. But there the matter had died. In 1784 no bust had been made. On the 1st of December, 1784, changing the original act, another resolution was passed in the House of Delegates, purposing to have two busts made of Lafayette. One bust was to be presented, not to Lafayette himself, but to the City of Paris, and the other to remain in Virginia as a companion piece to the statue of George Washington, which the House had already resolved in June of that same year to have made. It was specified that these two works of art should be kept together in the same place in Richmond, and it was particularly required that the two busts and the statue should be of the finest marble and the best workmanship to be procured.

To Lafayette the best workmanship could mean only one artist, Houdon, the greatest sculptor of his day, and as Lafayette had the choice of a sculptor for his own bust, he recommended Houdon to Washington. But Washington was greatly opposed to the whole project. He was past middle age, and not being a Frenchman he had no illusions about his manly beauty. The making of a cast was a very uncomfortable procedure, but necessary in order to gain an exact likeness, and he did not take kindly to the idea of lying encased from head to foot in a plaster cast, breathing for a long time through reeds that might become displaced and leave him to smother. It was very close to being buried alive, and Washington did not covet the experience. Lafayette told him he owed it to his country to leave an accurate likness of himself, to which Washington quite truthfully replied that he felt that he had done enough for his country already. Finally Lafayette urged it as a personal favor to himself, and on these grounds and on these alone did Washington consent. So it was that Lafayette, on his return to France, was able to induce Houdon to come to Mount Vernon to make the cast.

It was many years later that Mr. Hubard, now become an artist and sculptor in Virginia, enters into this history of Washington's statue. A drunken man came along and chipped off three fingers of one of those august hands, which Lafayette had once said were the biggest hands he had ever seen on a man. This act of vandalism aroused the Assembly: Suppose some accident were to happen, completely destroying it, the only true likeness of Washington? Down in Williamsburg the fun-loving students had chopped off Governor Spottswood's nose. So the Assembly decided that something must be done to preserve for posterity a true knowledge of Washington's appearance. Therefore, they prepared the resolution of March 21st, 1851.

"Resolved by the General Assembly that for the purpose of guarding against the consequences of any mutilation or destruction of Houdon's statue of Washington, believed to be the only correct representation in marble of the Father of his Country, the governor of this Commonwealth be requested to cause casts in plaster to be taken from the said statue, and the same to be distributed among the several collegiate institutions of this Commonwealth."

It being necessary to mend the broken fingers, this commission was given to Mr. William J. Hubard, who, we are told, was the only sculptor in Virginia at that time. The Assembly was so pleased with Mr. Hubard's work that it was decided to entrust him with making the casts. Also, this second commission resulted in the construction of foundries on James River, where the bronze casts were molded successfully under Mr. Hubard's directions and thence distributed to several colleges. Among these bronze casts was one given the Virginia Military Institute, and another was presented to the Government at Washington. The one given the Virginia Military Institute was stolen by General Hunter during the War Between the States but was later returned. Mr. Hubard was given sole authority to reproduce these figures. Unfortunately in 1862 his activities came to an end from an accident in which the foundry was burned up, and in which Mr. Hubard lost his life. Many of his silhouettes are still in existence, and are highly valued by their owners and by collectors. They were particularly popular in New England, and are frequently mentioned in the antique magazines of this country, though the Northern admirers of his work seem to have lost all trace of Mr. Hubard after his first early sojourn among them.

Robert Latham Owen, ex-Senator from Oklahoma, was born in Lynchburg February 2nd, 1856. He was the son of Colonel Robert Latham Owen, and the great-grandson of Owen Owen and Jane Hughes Owen, mentioned before in this book as having come here from Augusta County in the early settlement of the town. Senator Owen's mother was Narcissa Chisholm Owen. She had a strong strain of Cherokee blood, and Robert L. Owen himself, a strikingly handsome man, bears a marked resemblance to the Indian. He studied law at Washington and Lee University, graduating in 1878, and began practice in 1880. Early in his career he left Virginia to make his home in the West, where he had inherited large properties. The Lynchburg people, who recognized his early promise, took leave of him with regret as he had endeared himself to this community by his rare qualities of mind and character.

From 1885 to 1889 Robert Latham Owen was Indian Agent for the Five Civilized Tribes. He organized the First National Bank of Muskogee, Oklahoma, and was its president from 1890 to 1900. He was deeply interested in banking, as he was also in real estate and in all public affairs, serving three terms, from 1907 to 1925, as United States Senator from Oklahoma. Senator Owen travelled extensively in Europe, and was a deep student of the financial systems of foreign lands, in preparation for the great work he had in view. With the aid of Mr. Samuel Untermyer he formulated the Federal Reserve Law which was passed in the Wilson Administration. Honorable Carter Glass, at that time a member of Congress was patron and floor manager of this Act in the House of Representatives. It is a noteworthy fact that by the combined efforts of these three Lynchburg men this great piece of legislation was incorporated into the laws of the country. President Wilson, in signing this Bill, used three pens, giving one to each of these men as a memento of the occasion.

Senator Owen was married to Miss Daisy Hester, December 31st, 1889. They have one child, Dorothea.

Samuel Untermyer, born June 6, 1858, in Lynchburg, Virginia, was the son of Isadore and Therese Untermyer. His father was a lieutenant in the Confederate Army, who died soon after the close of the War. The family then moved to New York, where Samuel Untermyer was reared. He was educated in the public schools, and at the college of the City of New York. Having completed the course at the College, he entered Columbia Law School, from which he received the degree of LL.B. in 1878. As he was not of age at that time, he could not be admitted to the bar until the following year, when he at once entered upon the practice of his profession. When he was a young man he was said to have tried more cases in a single year than any other member of the New York bar. By the time he was twenty-four he had represented many important interests in the city, acting as council for the local, State, and United States Brewers Associations. He was senior counsel in two very celebrated divorce cases, both of which were bitterly contested and the evidence for which was gathered from various places in Europe. Another very important case he had when he was still a very young man was the noted conspiracy case of Betz versus Bauer and Daily.

This was the beginning of a brilliant career as a lawyer. He defended Asa Bird Gardner when an attempt was made to remove him from the office of district attorney of New York County. He represented the Wertheimers, English art dealers, in a controversy with the Count and Countess de Castellane, in which he won twenty million francs for the creditors of the Castellane estate. In the struggle of James W. Alexander to oust James Hagen Hyde from control of the Equitable Life Assurance Society, Mr. Untermyer as counsel for Hyde, brought on the investigation of life insurance companies which led to the passage of reform laws in many states, and to the correction of many irregularities of management in insurance companies.

Another famous case which he won was the Dodge-Morse Controversy, which led to the disbarment and penitentiary sentence of Abram H. Hummel, a New York lawyer. Mrs. Dodge had secured a divorce from her husband, and had married Charles W. Morse, a banker. Abram Hummel and Mr. Dodge conspired to have the divorce set aside on the ground that he had never been served with process in the divorce suit. They succeeded in doing this and Morse was forced to secure an annulment of his marriage to Mrs. Dodge because of the illegality of the Dodge divorce. Mr. Untermyer, through court proceedings, secured a restoration of the divorce, reinstating Mrs. Dodge as the lawful wife of Morse, and Hummel was punished for the fraud he had perpetuated.

Mr. Untermyer has organized many great brewing, manufacturing, mining, industrial and railway corporations for which he is general counsel. He is director in a large number of corporations. As counsel for the leading copper and metal companies of the United States, he successfully carried through the merger of the Utah Copper Company with the Boston Consolidated and Nevada Consolidated Companies, representing a market value of over one hundred million dollars. For this he received the largest fee ever paid to an attorney in this country: seven hundred and seventy-five thousand dollars.

Although among the first to realize the great economic advantage of corporate combinations, Mr. Untermyer is a firm opponent of the abuses which arise from such combinations. His fearless attacks upon the misuse of these great powers in finance show that he carries the courage of his convictions. His exposure of the financial plan of the reorganization of the United States Shipbuilding Company caused the abandonment of the proposed plan, for which was substituted a scheme that saved millions of dollars to the bondholders. It is said that his candidacy for the United States Senate in 1911 was opposed by many large financiers because of his activity in such matters.

He has constantly upheld, regardless of his own personal ambition, the rights of minority stockholders, urging changes in the law for their protection. He has been active in putting forth plans for the enforcement of the Sherman law, and in seeking the enactment of more stringent laws for Federal regulation of trusts, reform in criminal laws, and legislation to curb the concentration of wealth through use of corporate funds. These and kindred subjects have been the themes of many public addresses delivered before the great political and legal clubs of the North and of articles published in the North American Review and other magazines.

Mr. Untermyer's activities can be only partly enumerated here for it would seem that in the short space of human life no one man could accomplish as much as Samuel Untermyer. Not least of the many services he has rendered this country was that work which, in combination with Senator Robert L. Owen and Carter Glass, resulted in the passage of the Federal Reserve Act. To these three men, all born in Lynchburg, belongs the honor of the authorship of this great piece of legislation, and through their efforts it was made a law.

Mr. Untermyer was married in 1880 to Miss Minnie Carl, of New York. He is now the senior member of the law firm of Guggenheimer, Untermyer and Marshall.

CHAPTER XV

AFTER THE WAR

ABOUT fifteen years after the War a new generation of young men had grown up in Lynchburg. These, added to the number who had left their homes in the country to seek their fortunes in town, and those who, coming from other towns had decided to make Lynchburg their home, formed a very brilliant and charming little coterie. Many had gone to college together. Some had hung up shingles directing the public up side steps or alleys where they had set up modest offices for the practice of their professions. They formed a small club, and for this purpose rented a room over a store on Main Street. This club was the forerunner of the Piedmont Club and was located between Tenth and Eleventh Streets, not far from the Norvell House, which had not yet been pulled down. Among its members were Dr. Dick Lemmon, Willie Dudley, Charlie Lumsden, Woodville Smith, Ned Hamner, Minor Lyle, Dr. Carter Wade, Armistead Long, Page Morris, Randolph Harrison, Bob Owen, Bob Yancey, Jim Langhorne, Dick Edmunds, Jim Edmunds, Frank Roane, Ross Murrell, Willie Chambers, Davis Christian, Willie Adams, Charlie Wiermann, Charlie Heald, Sam Withers, John Cobbs, Sam Wingfield, Will Owen, Estes Vaughan, Mike Davis, Ed Miller, Dan Mitchell, Walter Jones, Bransford Younger, Leonard Lyne, Elgin Biggers, Alfred Ravanel, and many others. Some of these young men lived in hotels, some had rooms over stores, and some in boarding houses. One group kept Bachelors' Hall in the home of Mr. Tudor Yancey, who with the approach of age had lately retired to his farm in Bedford County. This Bachelors' Hall became a very gay centre, where many delightful entertainments took place in that period just before the gay nineties.

The typical simple life of the Southern town after the War now prevailed at Lynchburg, and its life reflects the Southern

A Group of Young Members of the Lynchburg Bar. They are (seated) Robert Yancey, Randolph Harrison, Armistead Long, and James Edmunds. (Standing) Charles Wiermann, Charles Calhoun, and William Dudley.

scene of that time. The ladies organized their little circles and societies for various benevolent purposes. They gave charades and bazaars in old Holcombe Hall, at which home talent was much applauded. Mrs. Cornelia Jordan, poet laureate of the town, a commanding figure in stiff black silk and heavy onyx jewelry, would give a reading from Caudle's Lectures; Mr. Jim Gregory would tell a tale from Uncle Remus in perfect Negro dialect; Mrs. Strother would recite a favorite poem and there would be singing. Once on a very great occasion there was a parody on Pinafore at the old Opera House. It was called The Sarah Jane, after one of the old packet boats. At one of these entertainments the amazing beauty of Otway Owen's voice was discovered. Many of the older residents of Lynchburg feel that nobody ever heard singing who never heard him sing, for truly his was a baritone voice of really great quality.

It was Miss Jeanie Vandergrift who taught the youth of Lynchburg to discard the old square dance in favor of the German. By her energy and enterprise dancing schools were organized, and in spite of the fact that there were still plenty of revivalists of the old school left to threaten the younger generation with eternal damnation, they could not be restrained from this new pleasure.

There were, of course, Fairs each year. These used to be held at what is now called Miller Park, though known in former years as the Fair Grounds. Lynchburg had not felt much need of parks in those days as the town was full of shady lawns and vacant lots for children to play in, and traffic was not as terrifying as it is today. The picnics of that day were held at the Fair Grounds, which was then a really superb grove of oaks. Only a few of the old oaks are still standing and nothing at all is left of the vast growth of heartsease which in spring used to cover the ground with a carpet of royal purple. The Fair, held every fall, was the greatest public event of the year and in those unsophisticated days the whole family of each house would go, and carry with them a great basket full of lunch: fried chicken, ham, beaten biscuit, salads, cakes and pies which had taken days to prepare. Sometimes the governor would be invited to make a speech, and the year that Fitz Lee came the whole town was decorated with his pictures framed in evergreens and flowers, and draped with tattered battle flags. He seemed greatly to enjoy the ovation he received: ladies fluttering their handkerchiefs from front porches and balconies, and the cheering crowds lining the sidewalks. Always the parade consisted of military companies from many towns, a band playing, with our very impressive Fire Department bringing up the rear. The most distinguished citizens were, of course, selected as marshals, being mainly the old Confederate officers, General Munford, Colonel Watts, Major Winfree, Major Halsey, and on very rare occasions old General Jubal Early himself: they were a very knightly company of men.

They rode again in the late spring, when the flowers were in finest bloom and Memorial Day was held. Then their destination was the old Methodist Graveyard, where so many young heroes lie buried. It was the same parade: Band, Firemen, Military, but this time accompanied by all the Garland-Rodes' Camp, in gray suits and veterans' hats, with their crosses of honor, marching out to honor their dead comrades. There came a time when those who were still living could march no longer, and the few that are left now are very old indeed, but they still meet at the Jones' Memorial Library, in the Veterans' Room, with its books about the War, its pictures and portraits, its flags, and a framed letter written by the great "Stonewall" himself.

CHAPTER XVI

LYNCHBURG AWAKENS TO NEW INTERESTS

IT WAS not many years after Surrender before things began to brighten up for Lynchburg. By this time the returned soldiers who had any fight left had found their place in the world of business, many of them to attain marked success. Times were getting easier, and the people relieved from the strain of keeping the wolf from the door were beginning again to enjoy some ease and culture. Miss Lucy Wilson, and her sisters, Miss Margaret and Miss Kate, had for many years taught a private school in their home. This building, the residence of Judge Daniel Wilson, still stands on Federal Street, and for a large portion of Lynchburg's past-middle-aged citizens it holds treasured memories, for here they received their early start in education. But about 1885 these estimable ladies, after many years of untiring activity, were preparing to retire.

Colonel Laurence Marye, who had come to Lynchburg to edit the Virginian, with his wife now opened a school for girls at their home on Court Street, between Sixth and Seventh. Mrs. Marye became greatly beloved here and was a great stimulation to the intellectual life of the people. She aroused in the group she gathered around her a lively interest in the great writers of the day. It soon became old fashioned to quote Thompson's Seasons, or Young's Night Thoughts; and even The War as a subject for conversation was relegated to the past. The greatness of Goethe, introduced for the first time through the mediation of Lewes, George Eliot and her morals, George Sand and her immoralities, Froude and his exposure of the cantankerous side of Carlyle's genius, the unhappy fate of Poe, that lonely, lovely spirit called John Keats, the strange ideas of Shelley, Byron and his vagaries, whether The Egoist or Evan Harrington were the more brilliant performance—these became the prevailing topics of conversation in Mrs. Marye's school room and the various literary societies emanating therefrom. Colonel Marye, a man of culture and great personal attraction, ably assisted his wife in her efforts, and their residence in Lynchburg was a great help to the town, for it came at a time when a revival was greatly needed. After the War, a deadly dullness had settled down. Nothing ever happened. All the younger generation ever heard was the glory of battles already fought, and the delights of a life that was already dead. Small comfort the daughters received from the oft-told tales of their mothers and grandmothers rounds of visiting at gay old Virginia homes and watering-places, of their fine clothes and innumerable conquests, while the young men were forced to listen to tales of glory when glory had departed.

Perhaps the strongest of these revivals of interest in things outside the struggle for daily bread was the awakening of a desire for good music. There were many lovers of music in Lynchburg, among them being Captain Stephen Adams, himself a musician of unusual talent. The Concordia Glee Club and the Mozart Musical Association had been organized, and it was deemed desirable to have a musical director to assist them. Captain Adams had a large acquaintance in musical circles, so to him was assigned the task of securing a suitable musician for director. After some correspondence with Dr. Walter Damrosch, it was decided at his urgent recommendation to offer the office to Professor Louis Schehlmann.

The Professor, as he was affectionately known among the people of Lynchburg for many years to come, was born in the town of Meckenheim, in the Rheinland of Germany, in 1855, the son of Conrad and Frederika Schehlmann. He was educated at Stuttgart, and shortly after leaving school, at the age of eighteen, he came to America. For ten years he lived in Cleveland, Ohio, where he followed the profession of music, and was leader of the principal German Singing Society of that city. Having been reared in the south of Germany, he found the climate of Ohio too severe for him, and for this reason decided to accept the offer to locate in Lynchburg. Among his first activities on reaching the city was the organization of a quartet for instrumental music. In this quartet he himself played the organ, Mr. Neubauer the flute, Mr. Gebhard the violin, and Professor Rubinstein the piano. Frequently they were assisted on the piano by Miss Virginia Burks, the daughter of Colonel Richard Burks. Under the direction of Professor Schehlmann the Mozart Musical Association and the Concordia Glee Club held together a large number of music-lovers, and all who had musical talent revolved around them. Having a complete comprehension of all the technical elements of music, Schehlmann was yet a master in the art of expression, his execution beautiful and colored with deep sympathy and feeling. His own compositions were recognized and valued in every centre of music both in this country and Europe and Sherwood declared him to be the greatest musician he had ever met.

But the Professor's influence was not entirely confined to those who loved and understood music. There was a warmth and geniality, a large and kindly sense of humor in him, that made him especially good company, and greatly endeared him to Virginia people. Although only twenty-eight when he came to Lynchburg, with his mane of black hair, and his black beard, he impressed young people as being much older. Indeed he was looked upon as a sage, but a kindly and a joyous sage, with his rumbling voice and his mighty laugh. He had a profound knowledge and interest in botany, and he possessed a very rare collection of butterflies. In fact, in the whole of life, the Professor had very deep interest and was a charming companion and a courteous gentleman.

November 6th, 1901, he was married to Miss Ruth Harris. Two years later he died very suddenly, and a few months later his wife followed him to the grave at the birth of their only child. Mrs. Schehlmann was herself an accomplished musician. She was a native of Bedford County, the niece of John Goode, member of Congress from Virginia.

CHAPTER XVII
REBUILDING

A MEMORIAL addressed to the Congress of the United States in the year 1875 was written and signed by General Francis H. Smith, Superintendent of the Virginia Military Institute, with the object of obtaining redress for some of the destruction wrought by General Hunter. The South was trying to rebuild and to rise up out of the ashes of defeat. This letter, written in General Smith's hand on eight sheets of ruled legal paper, reads:

"To the Congress of the United States:

This memorial and petition of the Virginia Military Institute respectfully showeth, that

On the 12th day of June, 1864, the buildings, including the cadets' Barracks, Mess Hall, Hospital and Professors' quarters, belonging to the Virginia Military Institute, were set on fire and destroyed by the order of Major General David Hunter, U. S. Army, at that time commanding the forces of the United States, serving in the Valley of Virginia; and by this fire were consumed, together with the Buildings aforesaid, the Library, all the Philosophical and Chemical Apparatus, medical supplies, furniture, provisions, and other stores of the Virginia Military Institute, and also a large amount of private property belonging to the Professors and cadets of said Institute.

The Virginia Military Institute would seek no exemption from any of those evils which are inseparable from a state of War. Its well-disciplined and fully organized corps of cadets were under the command of the Governor of Virginia, and were subject to his orders in defence of the property belonging to the Institution, and committed to their charge by law; and it was intended that they should be used, and they were freely used during the conflict. It does not therefore ask any immunity from any of those rigors of war meted to others. It was to have been expected that the cadets would be pursued by armed force, that they might be killed, captured, or put to flight. The munitions of war were proper objects for capture or destruction. But mod-

Lynchburg in 1875, showing old Covered Bridge.

LYNCHBURG AND ITS NEIGHBORS

ern history is appealed to in vain for such an instance of devastation as that accomplished here by Major General Hunter. The cities of Europe have often been held by hostile armies, and have been given up to sack and pillage; but Institutions of Learning, whether military or not, have been usually protected from the devastation attendant upon the entrance of armies into captured towns. Even in civil wars, *Oxford* and *Cambridge* were held alternately by the contending forces; but their Halls and their Courts, their Libraries and their Archives were preserved, and still remain to show how civilization may ameliorate the rigors of war.

True, the School of Engineers at Mezieres, in which the celebrated *Monge* taught, and that of Artillery at La Fere, in common with all the schools of France, from the University down, were destroyed; but these lawless acts proceeded from the madness of the mob, who, as 'the Republic had no need of chemists' put even *Lavoisier* himself to death. These proceedings of a maddened populace were disavowed by the leaders of the Revolution, and they were made the argument by which *Monge* and *Fourcroy* were enabled to establish the great *Polytechnic School* of France.

Notwithstanding, Major General Hunter, against the remonstrances of some of his General Officers, as we are credibly informed, against the protest of aged citizens who sought to arrest his purpose, and without the justifying excuse of over-ruling military necessity, applied the torch to Libraries, Philosophical Apparatus, Hospital stores, private property and Halls of Science, and left in utter ruin an Institution which had been an ornament and pride of the State and Country."

While the work of rebuilding was going on, Lynchburg was not idle. The tobacco trade had received an immense impetus from the Northern soldiers; they had gained a knowledge of the Lynchburg tobacco during the War, and knew its excellence. The Killickinnick, the Lone Jack, and other brands had grown famous. New business firms of all kinds began to open up. In 1870 Mr. J. P. Bell bought out the publishing house of

Read and Shafftner and began to build up his large enterprise. Throughout the War, Read and Shafftner had engaged in printing and engraving for the Confederate Government, and thus a very valuable collection of historic matter came into the hands of Mr. Bell, which unfortunately was destroyed in a fire that injured the J. P. Bell building some years ago.

The foundations of some large fortunes were laid in Lynchburg during these times. Mr. P. A. Krise had come here a few weeks after the Surrender, bringing with him the few hundred dollars in gold coin with which he started his brokerage business. This precious gold he exhibited, enclosed in a glass fruit jar or so, in the window of Mr. George Davis' hardware store. The people had not seen any gold money for so long that their curiosity was greatly excited by Mr. Krise's store of coin, which he traded in bank paper until legislation for its redemption went into effect. Mr. Krise continued dealing in gold and silver until Congress passed the Act requiring the resumption of specie payments. After that, he continued his business as a banker and broker, and became a very wealthy man.

Mr. George Morgan Jones, a native of Page County, having given four years of faithful service in the Confederate Army, came to Lynchburg in December after the Surrender and formed a partnership with his brothers-in-law, Colonel James W. Watts and Mr. R. T. Watts, in a hardware business. The name of the firm was Jones, Watts and Company, and it became a large and important business in Lynchburg. In 1887 it was sold out to Bell, Barker and Jennings. Having made a great deal of money in this business, Mr. Jones left a portion of his fortune for the endowment of a public library.

Along with these other industries, the Lynchburg Cotton Mill, and the Glamorgan Pipe and Foundry Company were formed, giving renewed vigor to the industrial life of the town. Another business which created much discussion in Lynchburg was the proposed establishment of the Norfolk and Western Railroad Shops in the town. In expectation of this many Norfolk and Western officials came to Lynchburg to make their homes, and among them were: Colonel Huger and his nephew, Alfred Ravanel. Colonel Huger, a son of General Huger, C. S. A., took up his residence in one of the old Murrell homes on Madison Street, the place now owned by Mr. William Hickson. His wife, Miss Julia Treble before her marriage, was the daughter of a former Lynchburg lawyer. They were a charming addition to the social life of the town, and their friends deeply regretted the railroad company's decision to withdraw their offices to Big Lick, a small station near Salem. Many business men felt that Lynchburg was making a great mistake in not allowing the company the necessary concessions to keep its headquarters here. But others, more influential among the citizens, did not care to see the town turned into a manufacturing centre and thus was this opportunity for expansion lost to Lynchburg, which has seen Big Lick, in a short space of time, develop into the large city of Roanoke. Those who are impressed by numbers regret that the community did not show a more hospitable spirit to the Norfolk and Western Railroad Shops, pointing out that Lynchburg might now be a town of a hundred thousand or more.

Some years after the War Mr. James R. Gilliam came from Amherst to make his home in Lynchburg. He became a man of great influence in the community, and there was hardly any field of useful citizenship in which he did not demonstrate his ability. As a merchant, he excelled in handling business. He was soon an important figure in banking circles, and in the organization of companies for mining coal, which was then a new means of realizing on the hidden wealth of the country and out of which great fortunes have since been made. Mr. Gilliam may truly be called a captain of industry, knowing as he did how to take large business in hand and to bend it to successful shape. He was essentially a man of action, and yet a great lover of books and travel. Although he knew the full value of every dollar he had made, yet he had a large mercy for his fellow man and his many gifts to the town were wise and beneficent.

LYNCHBURG AND ITS NEIGHBORS

Another very successful Lynchburg resident was Mr. John D. Langhorne. He was a graduate of Annapolis, and a native of Kentucky, but a kinsman of the other Langhornes in this community. He lived on the outskirts of town in a very handsome home, which had once belonged to the Bococks. He passed his summers here, but his winters were spent in Washington.

After Mr. Langhorne's death, his home became the property of Mr. H. E. McWane, who started the Lynchburg foundry, a great and successful business which has been of exceeding value to the town. Mr. McWane is now dead, but he not only built up a great enterprise, he also exerted a very noble influence in business, as is particularly shown by his just and generous treatment of his employees.

The wholesale shoe business began to expand until Lynchburg became the greatest distributing point for shoes in the South. Mr. John W. Craddock was the leading figure in this commercial business. He and his brother, Mr. A. P. Craddock, came from Halifax Courthouse when they were young men and formed a partnership here with Mr. T. M. Terry under the firm name of Craddock-Terry Company. They acquired a large business, and in spite of various disasters of war and depression have gone forward like a good ship through the storm.

Among her most valued citizens Lynchburg numbers many of German origin. Early in its history the Guggenheimers and the Untermyers made their residence here. Mr. Max Guggenheimer, who fought side by side with our Confederate soldiers in the Home Guard, after the War did all in his power towards re-establishing the business life of the town, giving freely of his time, his encouragement and his money in helping others to get a new start. Soon after the War the Untermyer family moved to New York; Mr. Samuel Untermyer, the head of the family here, having died about the time of the Surrender.

Other Germans have come in the interest of the tobacco export trade; some have remained only a short time, but others have staid to make their homes, and in every case the town has gained largely thereby, for none have made better business men or more public-spirited citizens. Among these the three Suhling brothers, Christian, Johannes and Gerhard, and Mr. Sellman, an associate of theirs in the export tobacco trade, deserve to be remembered with affection for their many good deeds. It is a great pity that the war in Europe caused so many people to feel they owed it to patriotism to treat these good men with suspicion and hostility. In a time of great effort to meet the quota of Lynchburg required by the Red Cross, Mr. Hans Suhling made his gift $10,000. When this gift was received with a needlessly slighting remark, because a little while before he had given the Red Cross in Germany the same amount, he asked: "Can you turn against the cradle that rocked you?" His was a big and generous spirit and of his goodness to the poor and humble a friend of his told a tale which is very characteristic of the man: One Saturday a long string of old Negroes, mainly women, made it a point to file by him as they went out when work was done. "Goodbye, Marse Hans," they said. "Gawd bless you." He was surprised at this unusual demonstration, and asked one of the men, "What are these old darkies telling me goodbye for?" "Mr. Blank has discharged them." He lost no time in seeking out Mr. Blank. "Why did you discharge those old darkies?" he asked. "Those old folks are getting too old to work, Mr. Suhling." "They helped me make everything I've got. They gave me their best years, and I wont turn them out to starve in their old age." "There is no business in that," said this efficiency expert. "If you don't like it you can leave, but they are going to stay." Many other things he said to the expert, which are not exactly printable but which people sometimes say with a great deal of satisfaction to themselves. In no better way than by this story can be illustrated how Hans Suhling accepted, along with his place in Virginia, the best traditions of Virginia citizenship—that sense of obligation to the old colored people which is characteristic of the Virginia gentleman.

CHAPTER XVIII
THE PRESS

THE LYNCHBURG VIRGINIAN, Lynchburg's earliest newspaper, was established in 1808, when the town was still very small. It was first called The Lynchburg Press, but in 1820 it came into the hands of John Hampden Pleasants, one of the most distinguished journalists ever born in Virginia, and at that time the name was changed to the Virginian. Later, when Mr. Pleasants left the Virginian, he made his residence in Richmond, where he founded the Richmond Whig. Mr. Richard Toler succeeded Pleasants as editor of the Virginian, and when he joined the staff of the Richmond Whig some years later, about 1845, William M. Blackford became his successor, in Lynchburg. Upon the retirement of Mr. Blackford, Mr. Abner W. C. Terry was made editor of the Virginian and continued to hold this position until his death in 1851. James McDonald was installed in his place, which he occupied until the beginning of 1857. The paper was next purchased by Charles W. Button, who was its editor until July, 1885, when he was appointed Postmaster of Lynchburg and retired from the editorship in order to assume his new duties. Colonel Laurence S. Marye was then editor until February, 1887, when Mr. Button, having resigned as Postmaster, again resumed the editorship, but held it only one month, as he sold the paper in March to a syndicate of Lynchburg men. The syndicate chose Mr. Alexander McDonald as editor-in-chief, and appointed Mr. W. W. Wysor, a native of Newbern, Pulaski County, assistant to Mr. McDonald.

Mr. McDonald was the last editor of the Lynchburg Virginian, as the paper was sold to Mr. Carter Glass and became merged with the Lynchburg News. This second oldest of Virginia papers had for years wielded a large influence in State and local politics, and was always a warm advocate of the town's best interests. It was in existence for about eighty-five years.

LYNCHBURG AND ITS NEIGHBORS

The Lynchburg News was established on the 15th of January, 1866, by Edward D. Christian, a lawyer of the town, and A. Waddill, a practical and experienced printer. Mr. Waddill subsequently became sole owner of the paper. The first editor of the News was Robert Enoch Withers, who describes his appointment to the office in his Autobiography of an Octogenarian. Colonel Withers had a house and lot in Danville, and soon after the War Between the States he had been looking for a farm to lease or rent. "I argued that we might live on the products of the farm, as I could certainly make bread and meat enough to feed us, and the question of food for my large family was now the dominant one." Hearing that he might be able to rent a good blue grass farm in Southwest Virginia, he started from Danville with this idea in view. But to use his own words:

"As I was passing through Lynchburg I stopped over to visit Mrs. Royall, my wife's mother, and when I again started on my way to the station I met on the street a friend whom I had known from boyhood, Mr. Edward D. Christian, at that time a prominent and prosperous member of the Lynchburg bar, who appeared very glad to see me, and in the course of our conversation, as we walked on together, he said:

'Bob, I have a notion of starting a daily paper here. What do you think of it?'

'I don't think it will pay,' said I. 'Already there are two long established daily papers here, which are as many as this place can support.'

He insisted, however, that his plan was feasible, said that Mr. Waddle, who had been foreman in the Virginian office for more than twenty years was anxious to join in the venture, and would attend to all the practical work of the office, and he could secure the advertising of all the lawyers in the contiguous counties and a large subscription list. Believing that neither he nor Mr. Waddle could edit the paper, I asked:

'Who is to be your editor?'

'I don't know yet,' said he, 'we are thinking of Mr.——,' mentioning a young man of my acquaintance. 'How do you think he would do?'

'Very well if it is to be a literary paper,' said I, 'but if you propose publishing a political paper, he has had no experience in, and I suppose little knowledge of political questions.'

By this time we had reached the street leading to the station, and telling him I had to make the train, I bade him goodbye. As I started off he said:

'Look here, I would rather have you to edit the paper than anyone I know.'

Without pausing in my walk I said: 'Well, you can get me very easily if you pay me enough to support my family.'

'What is your price?' he said.

'Twenty-five hundred a year,' I called back, still without stopping.

'I'll see Waddle and let you know,' he said."

When Colonel Withers reached home after leasing a farm in Russell County, he found a letter and telegrams notifying him that the owners of the News had decided to accept his offer. John G. Perry was the first city editor.

In 1868 Colonel Withers resigned, and then Congressman Thomas Whitehead was made editor-in-chief. Whitehead was succeeded in April, 1880, by Alexander McDonald, and at the same time Carter Glass took the place of city editor. In March, 1887, when Mr. McDonald went to the Virginian, Mr. Glass was given his place as editor-in-chief. In 1888 Mr. Glass bought the paper from Mr. Waddill (or Waddle as it was spelled and pronounced in those days).

The Lynchburg Advance was established on the 5th of May, 1880, by Whitehead, Murrell and Company, who printed daily, semi-weekly and weekly editions, Captain Thomas C. Whitehead being its editor. In May, 1882, was formed a joint stock company which conducted this paper for fifteen months under the business management of W. C. Carrington. In 1883 the company was reorganized, and Mr. T. Davis Evans succeeded Mr. Carrington as business manager. There was a second reorganization in August, 1885, when Major R. H. Glass succeeded Captain Whitehead as editor-in-chief. In 1895 the Advance became the property of the Honorable Carter Glass.

The history of our press can not be completed without further mention of Carter Glass; for while Lynchburg honors him as a statesmen, and as one of the most important figures in the life of our nation, it was through his connection with our local papers that he first attracted public attention. As the years have passed, the newspapers of this town being owned by him and largely operated by his family, the name of Glass in Lynchburg has become synonimous with The Press. The appreciation of Senator Glass which follows was copied from a recent issue of The Christian Science Monitor:

"WATCHING THE WORLD GO BY
By WILLIS J. ABBOT

Carter Glass—Unique, Able, Combative, Unyielding!

Senator Carter Glass, who has been steadily tilting at Mr. Pecora and Senator Couzens during the course of the Morgan investigation, is one of the most unusual and interesting men in the upper house of Congress. By profession a journalist, and the owner of two papers in Lynchburg, Virginia, his career, since he was about forty years of age, has been mainly devoted to politics. He has served in his State Senate, in the House of Representatives, in the United States Senate, and as Secretary of the Treasury during the Wilson Administration. Not a college-bred man, he sports a Phi Beta Kappa key, doubtless conferred upon him as an honorary distinction, as are also his various degrees of LL.D. from Lafayette, Washington and Lee, and the University of North Carolina. Well along in his seventies, the Senator is one of the hardest-working men in the upper chamber, and the natural fires of his intellect, and I might even say of his combativeness, are in no way abated, for Senator Glass is always willing to enter into the most vigorous personal controversies in support of the things he believes to be right.

So ardent, for example, is he in his antagonism to the methods being followed in the inquiry now in progress in Washington into the affairs of the Morgan concern that opponents have bestowed upon him the sneering title of 'chief counsel for the defense.' It just happens that his convictions as to the right of individuals to be protected in their privacy against mere sensational prying on the part of senatorial committees seemed to operate for the protection of the Morgan firm. But no man in public life in the past has advocated more financial reforms antagnostic to the entire Morgan policy than has Carter Glass. He has every right to be aggrieved by the effort of some to make him out as a mere defender of the bankers today, but in all probability is utterly indifferent to what is being said about him. There are few men in public life who care so little for publicity and so little for popular applause or criticism. As a result of this attitude of intellectual indifference, he probably gets more of both than any man in the Senate, unless it be the spectacular Huey Long.

* * *

It was along about 1918, if I remember rightly, that I saw Carter Glass, at that time not very widely known, accomplish the most extraordinary conversion of a hostile audience to his point of view that I have ever witnessed, or could possibly conceive of. It was in the big ballroom of the old Waldorf-Astoria. The occasion was the meeting of the New York Economic Club to discuss the plan of the Federal Reserve, which was then in its earlier stages, and bitterly opposed, as everyone recalls, by the whole banking community of the metropolis. Frank Vanderlip, then at the very height of his success as a banker, led the attack on the Federal Reserve plan. Senator Owen, of Oklahoma, himself a banker, and largely associated with the formulation of the Federal Reserve Act, was to lead in its advocacy, with Glass as an assistant, and decidedly not a 'headliner.'

Senator Carter Glass.

LYNCHBURG AND ITS NEIGHBORS

The audience, one of the most brilliant that I have ever seen gathered on such an occasion, was distinctly hostile to the Federal Reserve plan. It was made up mainly of New York bankers, brokers, Wall Street people, together with their wives and members of their families. The great ballroom was crowded. Vanderlip opening for the attack was cheered to the echo. Senator Owen made, as he always used to make, a most scholarly and convincing speech. It was an admirable plea, adapted, one would say, to reach the consciousness of people trained in the intricacies of high finance. At its close he came into the box where I was sitting and told me that he had been asked to close the debate later.

But then Glass got up. He looked then, as he always does, like a reasonably prosperous farmer, caring little about the fit of his clothes or his personal appearance. He began by questioning his own capacity to instruct or to influence so brilliant a representation of high finance as was before him. He spoke colloquially, in the vernacular, without the slightest effort at oratorical effect. His illustrations were racy of the soil. Anybody could comprehend what he was talking about. I do not think he had spoken ten minutes before he had the audience eagerly listening to every word. In half an hour they were so thoroughly at his command that when his time expired they insisted that he should go on.

At the end of his speech there was practically a unanimous roar of approval and commendation. There was no need for Owen to close. Vanderlip himself admitted that the day was won for the Federal Reserve. Never in the long experience of attendance upon debates of this character have I seen so complete and absolute a victory won by an unpretentious champion and wrested from a hostile and unwilling audience.

* * *

His great success as the formulator and defender of the Federal Reserve Act perhaps created in the mind of the Senator a certain feeling of proprietorship of that admirable piece of legislation. It is he that always construes it, and denounces what he thinks to be the failure of those intrusted with its administration to act thoroughly in accord with its spirit. There is a feeling in the Senate, too, that no measure for banking or currency reform can possibly secure the influential adhesion of Glass unless it originated with him. That feeling, and a certain acidity of comment when dealing with adversaries, have perhaps militated against his popularity in the body of which he has been so long a member. Men revere and admire rather than love him. He defers as little to his constituents as he does to his colleagues. When his keenly analytical mind has blocked out a course of conduct nothing can cause him to diverge from it.

Today his apparent position of defender of the Morgan firm is going to cost him heavily in popularity, but I do not believe he will give a thought to this. His mind is centered upon the course which he believes to be right, and no personal consideration will lead Carter Glass to swerve to one side or the other."

CHAPTER XIX

PUBLIC INSTITUTIONS

MARSHALL LODGE

MARSHALL LODGE was given its charter November 8th, 1793, by John Marshall, who was Grand Master at that time. The station officers were Robert Yancey, Master; James Calloway, Senior Warden, and Samuel Irvine, Junior Warden. The Lodge, first known as Hiram Lodge, was changed to Marshall Lodge, in honor of John Marshall, who in 1801 was made Chief Justice of the United States Supreme Court. The Lodge has an old Bible which contains this interesting memorandum:

"By invitation of the Commandant of the United States forces at New London Military Station, this Lodge attended and conducted the Masonic Ceremonies of Funeral Honors, etc., of our late deceased Brother, General George Washington, on the 22nd day of February, 1800." This Bible at Lynchburg was used on that occasion.

In September, 1794, the Lodge, then called Hiram Lodge, purchased from Philip Payne a lot at the north corner of what is known as Church and Ninth Streets, and upon this lot the first Masons' Hall in Lynchburg was erected. On the 3rd day of December, 1827, Marshall Lodge acquired from William Galt's executors, at the price of $850, a lot described as being on Water and Third Streets, adjoining the Masons' Hall. Water Street is now Ninth, and Third Street is the present Church Street. Though the names of the streets have changed, the home of Marshall Lodge has always been on the spot which it now occupies, at the corner of Church and Ninth Streets. The original Lodge room was in a wooden building that served until 1846. This old building was later removed to Fifth Street, between Main and Church, and there it stood until 1921, when it was pulled down.

LYNCHBURG AND ITS NEIGHBORS

In the early days there were no hospitals. During the War Between the States emergency hospitals were fitted out in various places in town, either in public buildings or private homes, but after Surrender no particular need seems to have urged the people to establish hospitals. When people were ill they were nursed by the members of their own families, and if the illness grew very protracted, the neighbors came in and helped. The only nurses were those employed in cases of childbirth. In 1885 the attention of its members was drawn to the fact that Marshall Lodge's revenues were more than sufficient to meet its own expenses, and the expenses of its charity work, and that the growing surplus might well be applied to some beneficent purpose. It was then decided to adopt a resolution, offered by Dr. A. I. Clark, appointing a committee to find out whether it was practicable to build a hospital in Lynchburg. This was the beginning of the present Memorial Hospital, which for years was known as the Home and Retreat, the first name given this institution.

In April, 1886, the house known as the Harry Langhorne residence, at the corner of Washington and Church Streets, where the home of Mrs. John Witt now stands, was rented for the hospital. Two years later, on the 2nd of October, 1888, the Lodge purchased the home of Mr. Samuel M. McCorkle, who had recently died. This new home of the hospital was a large brick house, with bay windows at each end, occupying the corner of Grace and Fifteenth Streets on Diamond Hill, and was purchased at the price of $6,500 as a permanent place for the institution. During its early years of life, Mrs. Bettie Cole, the daughter of Judge Garland, and a very capable and executive lady, was made matron of the hospital. In the old manner, she was an experienced nurse, and under her management, which lasted for about twelve years, the hospital became firmly established. I have been told that in its early days the hospital seemed a very risky venture and that the Masons practically gave it up, but Mrs. Cole refused to surrender, and carried on at her own expense. After some months, when she had demonstrated that it could be operated with success, the Lodge took up the work again. Now firmly rooted in the community and endowed by gifts from many generous people it has become a solid and substantial part of Lynchburg life.

Epileptic Colony

Mr. T. R. Murkland died from a heart attack on January 24th, 1905, at his home across the river in Madison Heights. A boy carrying newspapers could get no answer to his knock and when the neighbors investigated they found him face downward on the dining-room floor. Apparently he had died just after eating his evening meal. Mr. Murkland was born in British Guiana in 1840, the son of Sidney Smith Murkland, a Scotch Presbyterian missionary. His father, unable to stand the climate of British Guiana, moved to Nova Scotia, and later to Hampden-Sidney, Virginia. Here T. R. Murkland was educated, coming afterwards to Lynchburg, where he was a successful merchant from 1883 until 1898. When he retired he sold his dry goods business to his nephew, Mr. J. A. McGregor. At his death Mr. Murkland was survived by three sons. His brother, Dr. W. N. Murkland, was a noted Presbyterian preacher.

It was found after Mr. Murkland's death that he had left his home on Amherst Heights to establish a hospital for epileptics. Prior to this time the State had made no special provision for epileptics, and the presence of these unfortunates in the asylums was greatly deplored. The gift of Mr. Murkland was gladly accepted, not because in itself it was adequate for such a hospital, but because it called attention to the crying need for an asylum of this nature. It was decided that the Murkland place, on the Amherst Palisades was not suitable for the purpose of the asylum. It was therefore sold and the commission purchased Morrisania, a handsome brick home built many years ago by Mr. Charles Yancey Morris. The estate which had been inherited by the Willis family, descendants of Mr. Morris, included splendid James River bottom land, which it was believed would prove a useful factor in producing food for the patients.

February 16th, 1906, the Senate of Virginia passed the bill which created the Epileptic Colony. It is a branch of the State Hospital at Staunton, and the State provides for its maintenance by an increased appropriation to the Staunton institution. Governor Swanson placed Dr. Priddy at the head of the Epileptic Colony, which he managed with great ability until his death. Dr. J. H. Bell succeeded him in the work.

Lynchburg Female Orphan Home

The history of an institution often begins with the history of an unusual man. Such a man was Samuel Miller: one of the most remarkable men Virginia ever produced, and one of her greatest benefactors. Perhaps he showed a larger beneficence in the bestowal of his fortune than any Virginian has ever yet shown. He was born on the summit of the Ragged Mountains in Albemarle County in the year 1792. The 30th of June is supposed to be the day of his birth, but there is no certainty as to the exact date. His father was a Scotch lawyer, whom the son never knew, and his mother was a mountain woman. She was a weaver, and very poor. Her home was a log cabin with only one room; the floor was of earth, and the window, without sash or glass, had only a batten blind to keep out the weather. Samuel had one full brother named John who was older than he, and these brothers were deeply devoted to each other. What little instruction they received from teachers was given them at the free school at Batesville, a small village about fifteen miles from Charlottesville.

Early in life Samuel was compelled by the extreme poverty of his family to take his part in their struggle for their daily bread. He made his first money by collecting wool off the briars in the pastures where sheep had run. John Miller came to Lynchburg, and by 1814 he was already a successful merchant here. Samuel followed him as soon as he could, and found employment with Benjamin Perkins. By hard work and rigid self-denial he managed to save a little money, and with this he went into business for himself, buying and selling tobacco in a small way. He won the esteem and confidence of the business men of the town.

At some period during this time Samuel became interested in the possibilities of the investment of money in the growing public enterprises of the country. So began his operations in stocks and securities, in which he was to demonstrate such unusual ability. In 1829 his health began to fail; he then retired to a farm he had bought, close to the old Salem Turnpike, in the neighborhood of the Quaker Meeting House, and here he spent the remainder of his years alone except for his servants. In 1841 his brother, John, died, leaving Samuel sole heir to his estate, which was worth $100,000. There is no doubt that these two brothers had planned early in life to build up a large fortune, and to devote this fortune to the education and advancement of the orphaned and destitute youth of Virginia. It is said that they had talked this matter over many times, and after the death of John the remaining brother, throughout his long life, held unswervingly to this noble purpose they had formed together. With the inheritance he had received from John, Samuel was enabled to greatly enlarge the field of his operations, and so his wealth began to increase in leaps and bounds. By the time of the beginning of the War Between the States he was already very wealthy and his riches continued to grow during the War.

There can be no doubt, judging by results alone, that his was a mind of a high order, wise and far-seeing. He lived in the country, his closest touch with the world being a small and remote inland town; he had no information on which to base his calculations except newspaper and magazine quotations, and yet he accumulated a fortune of several millions in stocks and bonds. So unerring was his judgment, so astute his deductions that assuredly he was guided by the purest reason of a profoundly reasoning intellect. He has been accused of being a miser, but he was no miser. On the contrary he was very generous. He never turned a deaf ear to a just appeal for help. Particularly was he willing to assist young men in gaining an education, for far in advance of his time he believed in general education. In all his life he refused to follow the course of the money-lender, or to soil his hands with usury. He also turned a deaf ear to giving loans on homesteads, for he said he would not profit by another man's misfortune.

Somehow he had managed to overcome the disadvantages of his early surroundings, for in no way did Mr. Miller appear lacking among men. It was claimed by all who knew him, intimately or casually, that the impression he created was that of a cultured and remarkably intelligent gentleman. He was of a distinguished presence, tall in stature, and very dignified in manner. Impressed by his personality strangers would often ask what college he had attended, and the answer might well have been given that he had attended the college of George Washington, Sam Houston, Abraham Lincoln, and of Shakespeare. His only college was the school of life, and genius fares very well without any other, particularly was this true in those early days, when opportunity was small, but achievement was great. Mr. Miller did not seek company; he was a reserved man, and he loved solitude. Besides this, he was for years a semi-invalid, and needed to conserve his strength for a great and unselfish purpose, but those who sought him out found him courteous and affable. He made few friends, but he clung to those he did make with great loyalty and devotion.

He was accused of being eccentric, but much of his supposed eccentricity can be explained on perfectly reasonable grounds. For years, in order to get his start in life, he was forced to practice the most rigid restriction on his personal expenditure. Naturally a man like that does not take kindly to extravagant living. He had no health and no desire for eating and drinking and entertaining in that lavish old Virginia manner which is so delightful, but which has wasted many a great fortune. If he had engaged in the princely hospitality fashionable in his day, he might have made himself very popular, and his weaknesses and eccentricities might have been labelled "amusing" and overlooked because of the table he spread for his neighbors. But it is safe to say he would have left no great benefactions and no orphan girls and homeless boys would rise up today to call him blessed. He made no bid for popularity, as he had been lowly himself, he went the way of his sympathies, and made it the high ambition of his life to seek and to save that which was lost.

The home in which he had spent so many years, and figured out his large plans for posterity, is still standing on a farm lying on the old Lynchburg-Richmond Turnpike, and close to its intersection with the Evington Road. It may be that its proximity to the turnpike and access to the stage coaches carrying mail was no small inducement to him in making this place his residence; indeed this location may have had no small part in the success of his plans. From the outer gate of the farm nothing can be seen but a stretch of woods, but about five hundred yards further, situated on an elevation and commanding a fine view, stands an unpretentious frame house which still bears evidence of having once been a substantial and comfortable dwelling. The mantels of this house were marble, and it also boasted a sun parlor. The great trees which surrounded it seventy years ago are now dead; an old oak, nearly six feet in diameter, and a mighty chestnut of a girth of twenty and one-half feet still stand dead in front of the house. The estate, which contained fifteen hundred acres in Mr. Miller's time, was partially sold to Dr. J. J. Terrell, and to other neighbors after his death. The dwelling house and two hundred and twenty-five acres of the land are now owned by Mr. J. L. Tucker and his sisters. Mr. Miller lived almost entirely on the upper floor, where he had his sun parlor built along the whole length of one side of the house. His was the first sun parlor in these parts, and although a sun parlor is now quite acceptable in any home it was then considered but another evidence of his eccentricity.

When Hunter came down from the Valley to destroy Lynchburg Mr. Miller's home lay immediately in the path of his operations. Spies were plentiful in that day when the fortune of the Confederacy was fast waning, and many there were to curry favor with the Union troops by pointing out the Miller home and saying: "There lives one of the richest men in the South.

He is a miser, and he has millions hidden in his house." Mr. Miller prepared himself for this. For days the people had been warned by the smoke from many a burning homestead, and they knew that when Hunter left that neighborhood a crow would have to carry his rations. Mr. Miller went about the work of securing his papers. Many of them he sealed up in metal tubes and buried. Some of these were not dug up until after his death. Feeble and old, he was in his bed when the Union soldiers arrived, but he met them with the courage of true manhood. They threatened and bullied him in their efforts to make him disclose the hiding place of his money and one soldier placed his gun at his breast. Mr. Miller tore open his shirt.

"Shoot," he said, "Shoot! I have at best only a short time to live. I had just as soon go by a bullet. But I will never tell you where I have hidden my money."

Enraged, the man was in the act of firing when another soldier knocked the gun up, and the load intended for Mr. Miller tore a great hole in the ceiling. This would-be murderer actually went off with the false teeth mounted on a gold plate which he took from a glass of water at Mr. Miller's bedside. About $100,000 worth of Government securities were stolen, but these were finally returned from Washington, mainly because Mr. Miller's remarkable memory recalled the number and issue of each bond, and so he had no trouble identifying them. A large number of securities he had tied in bundles, and by removing a board had hidden them in the recess under the staircase. After the close of the War, he had the place opened again, and sent a little Negro boy in to gather them up, but the child came out and said he could find nothing. After repeated searchings in the dark place, he finally reported that he felt something like dried leaves lying around on the floor. These turned out to be the bonds, uninjured. The rats had gnawed away the strings that held them together, but the bonds were intact.

Mr. Miller died March 17th, 1869. Dr. J. J. Terrell, his friend and physician for many years, was with him at the end. He has been many times called Virginia's greatest benefactor. However this may be, he was certainly Lynchburg's greatest benefactor. He left the bulk of his fortune to establish the Miller Manual School of Albemarle, in the county of his birth. To the University of Virginia he bequeathed $100,000 to establish a permanent agricultural department. This has been merged into the Miller Agriculture and Biology Department, of which Dr. Ivy is the present head. For many decades this was the largest single gift made the University. No alumnus of the University of Virginia ever gave as much to his Alma Mater as Samuel Miller, who never received any of her benefits. He gave to Lynchburg the beautiful grove now known as Miller Park, which for many years was used for the Fair Grounds. He also gave to the town the ground for the College Hill Reservoir, and $20,000 in money for enlarging the water system. As the reservoir on Clay Street had long proved inadequate, the city added enough to this sum to build the reservoir on College Hill.

Mr. Miller had a purpose in the naming of the orphanage he gave Lynchburg. He expressly refused to call it after himself because it was his hope that its original endowment would be augmented by other donations. This hope has never been realized in spite of the great need, for there is always a long waiting list for entrance here. But even greater than this is the need for a home for girls such as the Episcopal Church provides for boys in its Boys' Home at Covington, Virginia. There are a great many girls denied admission at the Orphanage because Miss Bowman, very wisely, is afraid to risk having them mix with the children in her care, and yet they are entitled to a home, and to such consideration as may save them from ultimate ruin.

The Lynchburg Female Orphan Asylum was opened January 18th, 1875. Several years before his death Mr. Miller had set aside a beautiful park of forty acres for the establishment of this institution, and he himself had drawn up the charter, constitution and by-laws, along with the plans of the building. He appointed a building committee, and placing his plans in their hands he gave them well-formed ideas of what he wished these buildings to be, which ideas they carried out as far they could. He also appointed a Board of Directors, numbering thirteen. The original members named by him were: Ambrose Rucker, President; John Meem, Vice-President; James O. Williams, Secretary and Treasurer. The other members were Geo. D. Davis, Charles W. Button, David E. Spence, J. F. Slaughter, Dr. J. J. Terrell, Lorenzo Norvell, Don P. Halsey, Wm. A. Miller, T. E. Murrell, and Captain Stephen Adams.

In addition to the grounds and buildings, Mr. Miller's gift to the Asylum was $303,933.78. To this amount has been added the accrued reserve fund of $10,000. It seems strange that no donation has been added to this fund when we think of its noble benefaction to the girls of Lynchburg. Though the cost of living has increased in every way, and the population of the city has increased, this sum has remained the same, and there is always a long list of girls waiting to enter. Even the original building remained the same until about a year ago, when Mr. Wirt H. Miller presented the orphanage with a home for the Nursery Department. The various superintendents have always given the best advantages possible with the income at their disposal. Miss Willie Bowman, the present incumbent, has recently exchanged Asylum for Home in the name of the institution. The children are now exactly like other children in the community, with nothing in dress or rearing to separate them from other children except that they have better advantages than many parents are able to provide. A number of splendid women have gone out from this home.

Old Lynchburg College

The old Lynchburg College, first of the name, opened October 12th, 1852, with a faculty of eleven and almost a hundred students. Major John W. Daniel, Confederate veteran and United States Senator, was an alumnus of this school. The College was really founded by the faculty of Madison College at Uniontown, Pa., and buildings which had recently been put up by Mr. Jesse Hare on Fourth Street (now Court Street)

The old Lynchburg College which used to be on College Hill.

were used until a college building could be erected. The next year a suitable building was made in the square bounded by Floyd, Wise, Fourth and Eleventh Streets. Commencement exercises were held June 25th, 1856, beginning at 10 A. M., at Dudley Hall. A large crowd attended these exercises, and after the benediction was pronounced by Mr. Kinckle, a parade was formed, with music furnished by the College and the Richmond Cornet Band. The parade formed in front of the Methodist Protestant Church, then Wesley Chapel, and its line of march was down Church Street to Tanyard Alley, as Twelfth Street was called, then down Tanyard Alley to Main, then up Main to West Street (now Fifth) and up West Street to its head. From the head of West Street the parade marched to College Hill to attend the ceremonies of laying the cornerstone at four o'clock. But soon after the parade was formed rain came pouring down and spoiled these plans. The next morning at 8:30 the parade formed again, and marched to the College where the crowd had gathered again. There was music by the two bands, a prayer by Rev. Robert B. Thomas and Worshipful Master John Robin McDaniel performed the Masonic ceremony of laying the cornerstone. Rev. Stanley, of the Third Street Methodist Church, offered another prayer after some more music, and then an address was given by Mr. Samuel Garland, Jr. Mr. Garland was then a young lawyer, but later a brigadier-general in the Confederate Army. He was killed at Boonsboro Gap, Maryland. His address was said by Virginians to have been very able and beautiful. The day was excessively warm, and several ladies fainted before the ceremonies were over. It was the fashion to faint then, but in ten years, when face to face with war, these same women showed the strength and fortitude of men.

The College was incorporated in 1856 by the Virginia Legislature. Mr. J. B. Gaddess, a marble worker of this city, had made and presented the College with the cornerstone. The entire cost of the building was $30,000, of which $6,000 was subscribed by Honorable B. S. Bibb, of Alabama; $6,000 by Captain William Harding, of Northumberland County, Virginia, and

$5,000 by Mr. Steele, of Alabama. About $5,000 was raised by the citizens of Lynchburg, mostly through the church, and the College borrowed the sum of $12,260.34. James T. Murfee was architect. Dr. Thomson was its last president. Rev. Alexander Doniphan, who was several times pastor of the local Methodist church, was also connected with the College, which seemed to be under the patronage of the Methodist Protestant Church, and had even been presented to the Virginia Conference at a meeting of the Conference in Abingdon. Eight of the trustees of the College were from this church, being Colonel M. Langhorne, M. S. Langhorne, C. Winfree, D. B. Winfree, L. W. Lambeth, H. Silverthorn, J. S. Blair, and D. B. Rees. It had a flourishing start, but the War Between the States put an end to its career, for the faculty scattered, the students enlisted, and buildings were turned into a hospital for wounded soldiers. Finally the place was sold for a mortgage, probably the $12,260.34, which was borrowed, and portions of some of the buildings were torn down. What was left was eventually made into two homes, which are standing now, one being the residence of Mrs. T. M. Terry and the other of Mrs. Peyton B. Winfree.

Randolph-Macon

Randolph-Macon Womans' College, sometimes called by enthusiastic friends "the Vassar of the South," was established in Lynchburg in 1893. The Randolph-Macon system of Colleges and Academies, of which the parent institution, Randolph-Macon College for young men, is situated at Ashland, Virginia, was chartered in 1830. This name was chosen for the system as a compliment to Nathaniel Macon, of North Carolina, and John Randolph, of Virginia, two of the ablest and most popular men of that day. Lynchburg was selected as the most suitable location for the woman's college because it had good railroad facilities, and was a place of such remarkable beauty. The James River, with the Peaks of Otter, Mount Pleasant, the Sleeping Giant, and all the greater and lesser mountain peaks until the eyes travel around to Candlers Mountain, form a semi-circle about the town. Mr. Chase and other visiting artists have been delighted with the colorful picture our landscape makes with its warmth, vividness and charm of color in the red earth, the green woods and meadows and the blue mountains. The town itself is a lovely sight—a city that sets on a hill and cannot be hid.

Lynchburg was always, from its very beginning, interested in education. In 1815 she had schools of a high grade for boys and girls, and as the town increased in size and well being, it took on an atmosphere of culture. Thomas Jefferson said of Lynchburg that it was the most enterprising spot in the State of Virginia, and that it was entitled to the general patronage for its industry, enterprise and "correct course."

But for more than any other reason Randolph-Macon Woman's College came to Lynchburg because Dr. Smith had decided this was the place for it. He thought as much of Lynchburg as a centre of learning as Jefferson did, and it was only by one vote that the University of Virginia missed being built across the river on Madison Heights instead of at Charlottesville. Randolph-Macon Woman's College then is a monument to its founder, Dr. William Waugh Smith, and owes its existence to the labor of love he put into it. He was greatly aided by the Methodists of Lynchburg.

Dr. Smith had no expectation of being made president of the new College as he was already president of the College for Men at Ashland and chancellor of the Randolph-Macon system. He had decided that Dr. Richard W. Jones, who had built up an institution of learning for women in Mississippi, was the right man for the head of the Lynchburg College. With this end in view Dr. Jones was invited to confer with the trustees, who were in session at that time, and was elected president. After looking over the place, however, he became deeply discouraged. The walls of the main building were about four feet high, and the campus was a field of gullies and red mud. He could not see the future of the College Dr. Smith had enlarged on with so much eloquence and enthusiasm. He felt that building the College in this place was an impossible task, so he immediately resigned.

Dr. Smith tried again. He selected other educators, but like Dr. Jones, when they looked the situation over, they declined with thanks, one and all. Dr. Smith was forced to take the place himself, as no one else would have it, and so he became president of Randolph-Macon Woman's College: its founder and creator. The work grew under his hands, and long before his death, which occurred November 4th, 1919, he was able to enjoy a full measure of his success. He was buried in Hollywood in Richmond, Virginia.

An interesting gift to Randolph-Macon College was the old Saint Paul's Church Bell, with its mellow tone, which was purchased by Mr. P. V. W. Conway and donated to the College. The girls call it Conway.

Sweet Briar

Mrs. Indiana Fletcher Williams founded Sweet Briar College on her family estate of Sweet Briar, five miles from Amherst Courthouse and thirteen miles from Lynchburg. Mrs. Williams was the daughter of Elisha Fletcher, who made a large fortune in Lynchburg.

Elisha Fletcher was born in the North, and came to Virginia as tutor in the family of David Garland. He later taught a private school at New Glasgow. Elisha Fletcher married Miss Crawford, who belonged to a family of wealth and position. After his marriage, he brought his family to Lynchburg and made his home on Elm Avenue, a residential street at that time, which stretched from Twelfth to Pearl Street, and is now Jefferson Street. The Fletcher family became very wealthy and owned much property and their children were given every educational advantage which could be had in that day. One daughter married Mr. Williams, an Episcopal minister. A son, Dr. Fletcher, never married. Another son, Julian, lived in the mountains of Amherst.

The two sisters, Mrs. Mosby and Mrs. Williams, built houses close to each other at Sweet Briar. The buildings were exactly alike, except that one was painted buff and the other gray. An

"Tusculum," the home of the Crawfords in Amherst County, near Clifford. Built the latter part of the 18th century. Kindness of Mrs. John Williams, descendant of the Crawfords, present owners of Tusculum.

English landscape gardener was imported, who planted rare trees and shrubs around both places. These trees, which were gathered from various parts of the world, and planted out with great artistry, with lovely hedges of boxwood, have now reached a very beautiful state of perfection.

There were no children to inherit this fine estate. Mrs. Mosby died childless and Dr. Fletcher never married. Mrs. Williams had only one child, Daisy, who contracted tuberculosis and died when she was a young girl. Mrs. Williams, the last surviving member of the family, left the money and property for Sweet Briar College, which was founded in 1901.

Lynchburg College
Historical Statement

"In February, 1903, the Westover property in West Lynchburg, consisting of about seventy-seven acres of land and one building (the present Westover Hall), was purchased for the founding of Virginia Christian College. The first session opened in September, 1903. Since that date four new buildings have been erected and the campus has been increased to two hundred and fifteen acres. The name of the school was changed to Lynchburg College in 1919. This change was made for several reasons: first, as a member of the National Education Board of the Disciples of Christ the College was assigned definite territory for intensive cultivation. This territory includes Maryland, Delaware, District of Columbia, and Virginia. The members of the Board from the other states felt that the name Virginia Christian College failed to represent the total constituency; second, the Board of Directors desired to eliminate any impression that the work of the College was narrow or sectarian; and third, the service of the College to the local community was increasing and it was felt that the new name would more adequately recognize this increasing relationship between the city and the College.

In December, 1927, the College was admitted to full membership as a standard Liberal Arts College in the Southern Association of Colleges and Secondary Schools. This makes it possible for graduates of the institution to receive full standing and recognition in the graduate and professional schools of the country. The College is also a member of the American Association of Colleges, of the Liberal Arts College Movement, and of the National Education Board of the Disciples of Christ in America.

From the beginning Lynchburg College has been co-educational. It believes that co-education provides the most natural and normal basis of preparation for useful manhood and womanhood.

Purpose

As a Christian college this institution attempts to provide high-grade undergraduate education in an atmosphere which is definitely and wholesomely Christian. It conceives its primary function to be the preparation of Christian citizens, with a passion for truth, equipped to obtain and inspired to embody the truth in their individual conduct and in the life of society.

Buildings and Grounds

A semi-circle of buildings overlook a campus of unusual beauty. Westover Hall, the women's dormitory; the Gymnasium, a gift of the city of Lynchburg; Carnegie Hall, the men's dormitory; and the Administration Building, complete the semi-circle. Norway maples adorn the rolling campus which is a part of extensive grounds largely covered by original forest and decorated by the beauty of a winding stream. The vista extends to the Blue Ridge Mountains, where the Peaks of Otter form a climax to an ever-widening and enchanting landscape.

Student Body

Lynchburg College has no ambition to become a large school, but prefers to maintain the educational advantages which may be secured through a comparatively small student body. At present the enrollment is two hundred and seventy-seven. One hundred and forty-three of these students come from Lynchburg and vicinity. Lynchburg College is receiving approximately as many students from the local high schools as all other colleges and universities combined.

Curriculum

Lynchburg College has a well-organized curriculum leading to the A.B. degree. It also has approved pre-ministerial, pre-medical, pre-dental, pre-pharmacal, and pre-legal courses. Special attention is given to the preparation of high school teachers and, on the basis of the work given in this institution, the student is able to secure the Collegiate Professional Certificate, the highest certificate granted by the State Board of Education in Virginia. The College also offers the following professional courses:

Engineering in co-operation with V. P. I.

Business Administration in co-operation with W. and L.

Courses in Library Science

Home Economics

The Fine Arts Department offers work in music, art, and speech. Lynchburg College might accurately be described as sanely progressive. It does not, without careful consideration, adopt changes and reorganizations of its work, but at the same time it is not tied to educational conservatism or traditionalism.

Faculty

Major attention is given to the selection of those who are to teach in this school. In academic preparation, in teaching ability, and in experience, there are very few, if any, colleges the size of Lynchburg which have superior teaching personnel. The academic work of the College is arranged into five divisions, as follows:

Division of Religion and Philosophy
Division of Language and Literature
Division of Social Science
Division of Education and Psychology
Division of Natural Science

FACULTY PERSONNEL

Dr. J. T. T. Hundley, President of Lynchburg College, holds the A.B. and D.D. degrees, the latter being conferred by Washington and Lee University in 1922. He is president of the National Education Board of the Disciples of Christ in America; a member of the Committee of Nine of the Educational Benevolent and Missionary Agencies of the Disciples of Christ, selected to work out a unified program for all the interests of this Brotherhood; and a member of the Board of Directors of the Christian Board of Publication.

Dr. M. E. Sadler, Dean of the College and Chairman of the Division of Religion and Philosophy, holds the M.A., B.D., and Ph.D. degrees. He served as National Secretary of Religious Education for the Disciples of Christ from 1929 to 1931. In 1928, as a Sterling Research Fellow in the School of Education of Yale University, he made a comparative personnel study of Divinity, Law and Medical Students, which served as a basis for the reorganization of the work in the Yale University School. In 1930-31, under the Institute of Social and Religious Research of New York, he spent ten months in Japan studying the educational work of that country. Dr. Sadler has written the following books and manuals: A Standard Leadership Training Manual, A Manual on Christian Worship, and The Meaning and Importance of Christian Education. At the present time he is serving as president of the Virginia Council of Religious Education and is a member of the Executive Committee of the International Council of Religious Education.

Dr. Robert C. Beale, Chairman of the Division of Language and Literature, holds the A.M. and Ph.D. degrees. He has taught in Southwestern University, Memphis, Tennessee; in George Peabody, Nashville, Tennessee, and the State Teachers College, Fredericksburg, Virginia. He also has been a member of the University of Virginia extension Division Faculty.

Dr. O. J. Grainger, Chairman of the Division of Social Science, holds the A.M. and Ph.D. degrees. For nineteen years he was a missionary in India, and following this service he taught for five years in the College of Missions, a graduate school in Indianapolis, Indiana.

Dr. Richard Clarke Sommerville, Chairman of the Division of Education and Psychology, holds the A.M. and Ph.D. degrees. He has served as president of Greenbrier College, Lewisburg, West Virginia, and of Texas Presbyterian College, Milford, Texas. He has taught in Arkansas College, Batesville, Arkansas; Louisiana College, Ruston, Louisiana; Southwestern College, Memphis, Tennessee; University of the South, Sewanee, Tennessee. Dr. Sommerville is a member of the following societies: American Psychological Association, the American Association for the Advancement of Science, the Tennessee Academy of Science, the Virginia Academy of Science, and Pi Gamma Mu. His publications are as follows: Physical, Motor and Sensory Traits, Archives of Psychology, No. 75, New York, December, 1924.

Prof. Ruskin S. Freer, Chairman of the Division of Natural Science, holds the A.M. degree and is now completing the final requirements for the Ph.D. degree from the University of Virginia. Mr. Freer is a member of the following societies: American Association for the Advancement of Science, Botanical Society of America, Ecological Society of America, American Ornithological Union, Wilson Ornithological Club, Virginia Society of Ornithology (president, 1929—), Virginia Academy of Science, and the Ohio Academy of Science."

Virginia Episcopal School

Virginia Episcopal School is distinctively a church institution conducted under the auspices of the Church, although it is open to boys of all denominations. Its founder was Rev. Robert Carter Jett, who resigned his charge of Emmanuel Church in Staunton, Virginia, where he had served as rector for twenty years, to devote his entire time to raising funds for founding a school for boys. The response was generous, so that he was well able to open the school in 1916-17, when its first session was held. Dr. Jett was rector there for four years, when he was elected bishop of the new diocese of Southwestern Virginia. In the spring of 1920 Rev. William Gibson Pendleton, D.D., became the second rector. He resigned in the spring of 1928, and was succeeded by the present rector, Rev. Oscar de Wolfe Randolph, D.D.

It is not necessary here to enlarge on the excellence of this institution, which has impressed itself already upon our town and upon Virginia, but with mention of the school the people of Lynchburg will recall a tragic episode in the life of this institution when Bishop Jett took a notable stand. In building the road to the school it was necessary for the city to construct a bridge over a deep and dangerous chasm. It was feared from the first that this bridge was inadequate and defective, for although it was but a narrow structure of wood, it received heavy usage. The city had not felt inclined to make a large outlay of money here, and the school did not have the necessary funds for the work. And so the bridge stood for a few years, when the community and State were horrified by the death of Mrs. Pendleton, and the injury of Dr. Pendleton, when their car one night ran over the side railing and into the ravine below. The broken railing on the bridge was mended, and it was pronounced safe for future traffic. A few years later, another car went over the railing of this narrow bridge, killing two ladies, Mrs. Randolph, the mother of the rector, and Mrs. Hugh Worthington, wife of Dr. Hugh Worthington, professor at Sweet Briar College. A young boy with them was desperately injured. The news of this second dreadful accident agonized the city. The matter was taken up by the City Council, and after much deliberation, and examination by experts, it was again decided that the bridge should remain, with a few improvements, to make it safer. When Bishop Jett heard this he made a special visit to Lynchburg and appeared before the Council. He told them that it was not to the honor of the school, or to their honor or to his own honor that this bridge which had proven a death trap, on which the lives of three helpless women had been sacrificed, should be allowed to remain. Without any further comment the City Council reversed its decision. They built a safer and more creditable bridge. Here Bishop Jett, with a fine dignity, asserted the ancient authority of the Church in demanding what was right.

CHAPTER XX

AN EPIC OF AMERICAN INDUSTRY

IN THE spring of 1896 Mr. J. R. McWane, who had been assisting his father, Mr. C. P. McWane, in a small foundry business in Southwestern Virginia, conceived the idea of having his father, who was growing old, sell out his plow patterns and equipment and retire from business.

Following up this plan, Mr. McWane came to Lynchburg and enlisted the co-operation of Mr. H. E. McWane, who at that time was president of the Glamorgan Pipe and Foundry Company. These two gentlemen undertook to form a small company in Lynchburg to take over the patterns and equipment of Mr. C. P. McWane, with the idea of starting a plow foundry. Several well-known business men of Lynchburg became interested, among whom were: N. B. Handy, W. C. Ivey, W. P. Clark, O. B. Barker, B. F. Kirkpatrick, A. P. Craddock, John W. Craddock, R. I. Owen, George P. Watkins, and C. V. Winfree. A charter was secured and the Lynchburg Plow Company was incorporated August 1st, 1896, with a capital of $25,000. Mr. Geo. P. Watkins was chosen as President, and Mr. J. R. McWane, Vice-President and General Manager of the company. The capital was increased from time to time until in 1902 it was $150,000. At this date Mr. H. E. McWane severed his connection with the Glamorgan Pipe and Foundry Company and came with the Lynchburg Plow Company as President and Mr. L. W. Walsh was elected Secretary and Treasurer. About this time, it was thought desirable to build the pipe shop next to the plow foundry.

The infant industry had to struggle against keen competition and only those men who were actively engaged in the management know the many difficulties courageously met and overcome. In the spring of 1905 the company purchased from the Virginia Iron, Coal and Coke Company another pipe plant located at Radford, Virginia, which had originally been built by J. K. Dimmick and Company of Philadelphia. The small company that started out in 1896, making only plow repairs, has grown steadily until it now produces a large tonnage of standard gas and water pipe, flange pipe and fittings, special castings of large size and peculiar design, as well as a large varied line of repair parts for plows, and has built up a large business in its own famous Lynchburg Chilled Plows.

During the World War, the entire facilities of the Lynchburg Foundry Company were placed at the disposal of the War Department for the manufacture of equipment for munition plants and other necessary war operations. The company furnished about five hundred carloads of pipe and fittings for the munition plant at Hopewell, Virginia, and about $1,000,000 worth of material for the "Old Hickory Powder Plant" at Nashville, Tennessee. The "Old Hickory" is the largest powder plant in the world and this contract for the pipe and fittings was one of the largest ever placed in the United States. The company is proud of the fact that all of its war-time contracts were completed on or before schedule dates.

Some idea of the growth of the Lynchburg Foundry Company can be imagined from the fact that its present capital investment is nearly $4,000,000, having grown to this size from the small beginning of $25,000.

Upon the death of Mr. H. E. McWane, his son, Mr. L. H. McWane, succeeded him as President in 1914. Upon the death of Mr. L. H. McWane in 1925, Mr. L. W. Walsh succeeded as President. The present officers are: Mr. L. W. Walsh, President; Mr. Henry E. McWane, Vice-President; Mr. G. R. Johnson, Vice-President; Mr. J. S. Wright, Treasurer; Mr. C. H. Owen, Secretary, and Miss May S. Eanes, Assistant Secretary and Treasurer.

The company employs about five hundred men at the Lynchburg plant and about the same number at the Radford plant.

There is little doubt that the McWane family belonged to

the Scotch clan, McQueen, and probably came over in the Scotch emigration to Virginia in the eighteenth century. For some generations, as was the case with many Virginia settlers, they were occupied with the struggle for adjustment in a new and wild country, and took no part in public life. The first record we have of them is that of James McWane, who lived in Nelson County near Massie's Mills, and was a mechanic of unusual ability. He was a friend and neighbor of Cyrus McCormick and helped him to construct his first grain reaper that approached perfection. Together, in McWane's little log shop in the mountains of Nelson, they toiled to make a practicable piece of machinery, a workable reality, from the dreams of this great mechanical genius. In later years the McCormick family acknowledged this indebtedness and the International Harvester Company sent a representative to Mr. Charles P. McWane, the son of Mr. James McWane, to interview him before his death concerning what he remembered of those events which had transpired in his father's blacksmith shop.

Mr. James McWane married a Ryan, of the same family as Thomas Fortune Ryan. Their son, Charles P. McWane, married Eliza H. Dudley, moved to Wytheville, and there he worked as a millwright and pattern maker. For generations his family had shown remarkable mechanical ability, and he had inherited the same gift; in every community where they lived, they were highly respected for their industry, character and ability, and these qualities he passed on to his son, Henry Edward, born June 16th, 1859.

Henry Edward McWane attended the public school as far as possible, but at that time the places of education had been disrupted, and the people of the South impoverished by the War Between the States. He was not able himself to attend college, but later in life he helped his brothers to obtain the educational advantages which circumstances had denied him. All through his life, however, he continued to educate himself, mind and heart in a very high aspiration towards perfection. In early youth he learned the trade of a moulder, so on reaching manhood he was prepared to enter into his father's business as partner, under the firm name of C. P. McWane and Company, carrying on the general business of founders and machinists. On September 1st, 1882, Henry Edward McWane was married to Miss Blanche Rowell Roberts. Among his attendants at the wedding was Mr. Rolfe Bolling, the brother of Mrs. Woodrow Wilson, who lived in Lynchburg at one time. Mr. Bolling said of Mrs. McWane that she was the most beautiful girl he had ever seen. She was beautiful all her life—from early youth to the time of her death.

In the original shop in Wytheville, one end was for wood, and the other for a smith shop. When iron was to be melted a colored man who owned a mule was called in. It took an hour by this method to melt a thousand pounds of castings. The plows thus manufactured had a ready market, but money was so scarce in those days that the plows were generally paid for in trade; so much flour and so many potatoes being the medium of exchange. These commodities were carefully stored in the second story of the frame building, to be used for winter rations. After a time one moulder was not able to do all the work, so another had to be employed. When Henry Edward McWane became his father's partner the quarters were enlarged, and the machinery increased to one steam engine, three iron turning lathes, one drill press, and one pattern turning lathe. The new partner did the office work and the bookkeeping, and the company now owned a team and employed ten workers! They carried on the general business of founders, machinists, manufacturers of plows and other agricultural implements, and retailed coal and wood as a side line. It was through the coal business that Captain R. H. T. Adams came in contact with the McWane family, recognizing immediately the unusual ability of the youthful partner, H. E. McWane.

In the spring of 1887, due to the influence of Captain Adams, Henry Edward McWane came to Lynchburg to be superintendent of the Glamorgan Company, Founders and Machinists. Here he was notably successful, and began the production of cast iron gas and water pipes, which proved a great advantage to the company. In 1889 he was elected president and general manager, holding this position until 1902. At the time he took charge of the works sixteen men were employed, and the working capital of the company was only $35,000, and when he retired from the Glamorgan Company seven hundred men were in its employment, and the capital was half a million dollars. All this increase took place within thirteen years.

Mr. McWane severed his connection with the Glamorgan in order to purchase the Lynchburg Plow Works, which he did in May, 1902. The capital of the company was increased from $80,000 to $150,000, and the name changed to the Lynchburg Foundry Company. The building was extended by the construction of what is known as the McWane Pipe Works, which is a department of the foundry company. The first year of Mr. McWane's connection with this firm he held the offices of president and treasurer, but after that year he was made president and general manager. In 1906 the Radford Pipe Works was bought, and has since been operated as a department of the Lynchburg Foundry Company.

The early ventures of the firm in making pipe is worthy of mention here. Realizing that the pipe industry had great future possibilities in the South, Mr. McWane and his wife's uncle, Mr. T. W. Roberts, who was associated with him in the Radford plant, decided on a tour of investigation to several New Jersey and Pennsylvania foundries. At that time visitors were not allowed in those plants, but the two young men were not to be daunted. At one place Mr. Roberts tried to get inside by taking a workingman his dinner pail, but the lynx-eyed watchman refused to let him pass. Finally, though, they managed to see the workmen at night, and so to get the desired information. One of the workmen they employed, and later he became one of their foremen. The first pipes they tried to make were watched with intense excitement, but when the flasks were knocked out every single pipe was lost. The next day a good one was made, but it had a hole in it. However, they did not lose heart until they had produced the perfect article.

When the war in Europe began there followed close in its train a season of disaster for the iron and steel business, and especially was this depression felt in the market for cast iron pipes. For a time it seemed that the whole of this trade was in a state of collapse and facing utter destruction. The terrific strain of those months, when the careful building of three generations seemed to be falling to pieces before his eyes, proved too much for Mr. McWane. He broke under the burden and his death came on the 31st of December, 1914.

No man was ever more honored in his community than was Mr. McWane in Lynchburg. The nobility of his character, his strong righteousness, his fine sincerity, the difficulties he had overcome, his regard and friendship for the men he employed, his kindness, Christianity and affection for his family: more high qualities than could possibly be named endeared him to people who knew him personally, and to people who knew him by reputation. It was indeed a fortunate day for Lynchburg when Mr. McWane decided to make his home here. He had done a great part by the community, and the whole town was deeply grieved at his death. Many newspapers and organizations expressed their sorrow at his loss, but perhaps none voiced the general feeling more truly than did Mr. Sydnor Kirkpatrick, when he said, as vice-president and spokesman for the officials of the Foundry Company, that to no man in Lynchburg did the town rest under heavier and more enduring obligation of both a commercial and spiritual nature than to Henry E. McWane.

To his family, his wife and the ten children who survived him, his brothers and sisters and his aged father, his going was a grievous blow. He had been a pillar of his church, and one of the founders of what is now known as the Lynchburg College. As a Prohibition leader, he ranks rather with men like

Philemon Holcombe, whose sympathies went out to women and little children with lives blasted by drunken husbands and fathers, than to the latter-day leaders who used the organization for their own political purposes. It is unbelievable that Mr. McWane would have anything but horror for the trail of blood and murder that followed in the wake of Prohibition enforcement.

In the time of stress following his death, no one doubted the strength of that clan. To the question, "Who will take his place?" the answer was immediate: "Lawrence." Lawrence was the eldest of his four sons. He came forward as chieftain of the clan, and well did he fulfill the trust left him by his father, for under Lawrence McWane's management the foundry marked a new chapter in its development.

Lawrence H. McWane was young for the great responsibility that fell to his lot. It seemed only a short time since he had been digging scrap iron out of the discarded heaps around the plant, and selling it back to the foundry to make his pocket money. Now he was in command, and organizing all the forces of his industry to meet the demands of his country in the great war. He shifted his business to meet these special needs. The foundry might have profited by filling orders for shrapnel, for large contracts were offered, but not having suitable facilities for this work, it was decided to manufacture something for which the plant was better equipped. This happened to be flanged material, for which there grew a great demand, and soon the works were in full blast, turning out new and difficult products. On one occasion some special castings were required to make an installation and delivery was desired in ten days. After much figuring, the customer was advised that it was impossible to deliver the goods in less than two weeks. Lawrence McWane immediately reversed this decision by demanding that they get that word "impossible" out of their vocabulary, for nothing was impossible if the will was there, and the need great enough. The men were told the situation, and *they caught the idea.* They worked at night and on Sunday, and the castings were shipped by express, while still hot, but *within the required time*. This incident was written by Lawrence McWane himself in the Iron Worker, published January 20th, 1919. In the Iron Worker he also told of the importance and magnitude of the work of the foundry during the war. The book is dedicated with this beautiful tribute to "our veteran employees, many of whom for over a quarter of a century have stood loyally by the management of the company, through trials and adversities; whose devotion has been an inspiration, and in whose comradeship are many pleasant memories, this little booklet is affectionately dedicated."

Under the heading of An Appreciation, in this same book, he described how the business management of the foundry had always tried to give labor a square deal; how they wanted their men to be happy and contented, and tried to make them so. "The big family idea" he called it. But remembering that this idea among the McWanes began a long time ago, with the very beginning of the foundry, when such an attitude between capital and labor was an unknown thing, we are brought to the conclusion that it was a part of the old Scotch fealty and clan loyalty transplanted in the new world. And so backed by the loyalty of their men in those days of war, when all the big powder mills and cantonments were clamoring for the delivery of great orders of special kinds of pipes and fittings, the foundry did impossible things—things that seem all but superhuman in these easy-going times of peace.

Having completed the great work of reorganization to meet war-time demands, Lawrence died suddenly on the 25th day of November, 1925, after a swift and fatal attack of pneumonia. At the age of forty-two, a beloved citizen, with years of honor and useful service apparently stretching before him, death came unexpectedly. The words spoken and written in his memory bear a beautiful testimony of his life. Bodies of directors and officials of banks and companies to which he belonged: hardheaded business men they, moved into that realm of poetry which strong emotion and great sincerity will carry men at times, and spoke with beauty, not of his great business ability, but of the youth and charm of him, of the light he had shed on their drab meetings, and of the sweet and genial spirit of this man who had passed out of their lives. As one of them said, Lawrence McWane was "like a ship with shining sails that had put out to sea."

CHAPTER XXI

LYNCHBURG POETS AND WRITERS

LYNCHBURG'S earliest poet, Bransford Vawter, was born in 1815 and died at the age of twenty-three. His family won distinction in the history of this country, and was probably of Huguenot origin. John Vawter, no doubt a near kinsman of the poet, was born in Orange County in 1782. He was a Baptist preacher, but a pioneer and a soldier as well. In 1807 he moved with his father to Indiana, which was a wild country in those days. He settled in Madison, became a citizen of value and importance in that frontier community, was elected colonel of the State troops, and served in the Legislature and Senate as well. He was the founder of the two towns in Indiana, Vernon, the county seat of Jennings County, and Morgantown, in Morgan County.

But the Vawter who was the father of our Lynchburg poet won no such honors. He was a tailor, and very much addicted to drink, but he seems to have been a devoted father to his gifted son. At one time the Vawter family lived on Main Street near the place where the Law Building now stands. Later Vawter built himself what was for that day a very nice home, which is still standing on Polk Street, near the corner of Fifth. The lilacs which still bloom in the yard may have been planted by Mrs. Vawter, who was a Miss Bransford, and died early. Lilacs also bloom in the family square in the old Methodist Graveyard. The lot is enclosed by a brick wall and whitewashed, but there are no stones to mark the graves. The poet is buried here. He attracted the attention of the townspeople, who recognized his talent, and the young men of the day appear to have been deeply attached to him. He is described as having a graceful, slender figure, dark and very brilliant eyes, and well-cut, intellectual features. He was very popular, and a genial, pleasant companion. General David Rodes was a particularly warm friend of Bransford Vawter's, and being clerk of the court he made him his deputy. The elder Vawter, in a fit of despondency, hung himself, and soon after this Bransford Vawter died of tuberculosis. We have left only one poem which we know he wrote. It appeared anonymously in the Southern Literary Messenger, but later it was set to music, and became one of the most popular songs of the day, both in this country and in Europe, where it was translated and sung in many languages. Some of the older people say it was written to Miss Ann Norvell, and others say to Miss Emma Camm, the granddaughter of Parson John Camm of Bruton Church at Williamsburg, who died when quite young. However this may be, it is a lovely lyric and worthy of a place with Ben Johnson's song to Celia and with Lovelace's Song to Lucasta. Lovelace likewise is chiefly remembered for that one song. One perfect song being enough to make men grateful for three hundred years Bransford Vawter also merits our gratitude:

> "I'd offer thee this hand of mine
>   If I could love thee less,
> But hearts so warm, so pure as thine
>   Should never know distress.
> My fortune is too hard for thee,
>   'Twould chill thy dearest joy,
> I'd rather weep to see thee free
>   Than win thee to destroy.
>
> I leave thee in thy happiness
>   As one too dear to love,
> As one I think of but to bless
>   As wretchedly I rove.
> And, oh, when sorrow's cup I drink,
>   All bitter though it be,
> How sweet 'twill be for me to think.
>   It holds no drop for thee.

And now my dreams are sadly o'er,
   Fate bids them all depart,
And I must leave my native shore
   In brokenness of heart.
And oh, dear one, when far from thee
   I ne'er know joy again,
I would not that one thought of me
   Should give thy bosom pain."

Mrs. Cornelia Jane Matthews Jordan was born in Lynchburg, January 11th, 1830. She was the daughter of Edwin Matthews, at one time Mayor here, and was educated at the Academy of the Visitation in Georgetown, District of Columbia. She was married to Francis H. Jordan, of Page County, Virginia, in 1851. In 1863, while visiting in Corinth, Mississippi, where her husband was a staff officer of General Beauregard, she wrote her poem, Corinth. It was published in 1865, but was seized as "objectionable and incendiary" and burned in the Courthouse yard of Lynchburg by order of General Alfred H. Terry, who was provost marshall at the time of the Reconstruction. Several volumes of her poems were published, and Mrs. Jordan occupied the position of Poet Laureate here until she was a very old lady, writing poems for almost every event. All great occasions of the town were celebrated in verse by her. Under the pen name of Hope Dare she conducted a column in the daily paper and was for many years an important figure in the intellectual life of Lynchburg. Mrs. Jordan had one daughter, Theresa, a talented and lovely woman, who married Mr. Saint George Ambler, and left descendants, several of whom are still living here.

Lynchburg may certainly lay some claim to George W. Bagby. His father was a merchant here and he came to live in Lynchburg when he was very young. Old ladies who went to school with George Bagby in the tall brick building at the corner of Eleventh and Church Streets used to love to tell how he would climb at recess to a topmost window, and sit mournfully on the very edge of the sill, with long legs dangling in the air, to scare the little children.

George W. Bagby was born in Buckingham County in 1828. He was educated at Princeton, New Jersey, and at Delaware College. At eighteen he began the study of medicine at the University of Pennsylvania, and after finishing his studies as a doctor, he came to Lynchburg and hung out his sign where the Opera House of Lynchburg later stood; the site which is now in part occupied by the Trenton Theatre. He did not find his work as a physician congenial to his temperament, and soon he began to write for the Virginian. The Virginian had been founded in 1808, and at the time of which we write was edited by James McDonald, afterwards Secretary of the Commonwealth and Adjutant-General of Virginia. Early in the fifties George W. Bagby and George Woodville Latham became jointly connected in the Lynchburg Express, a paper which had been started and conducted by Hudson Garland, who had recently died. This brilliantly edited journal went down in defeat, for the two new literary editors, sad to relate, were more concerned with the literary quality of their paper than with its business management. By this time, however, Bagby's gifted pen had made him a place in the world of letters, for when the War Between the States broke out he was already writing for the Southern Literary Messenger and other journals of this country. His literary work was interrupted while he took up arms for his State, but being too frail in health for active service in the field he was soon given clerical work at headquarters. In 1863 George Bagby was married to Parke Chamberlayne, of Richmond. After the War, he settled in Richmond, where he was made custodian of the State Library, which position he held for many years. He died late in November, 1883. It is the opinion of many writers that Dr. Bagby's writings will one day be resurrected from the neglect of years, and will again receive the recognition they deserve.

Henry Gray Latham, M.D., born March 4th, 1832, was the

second son of Dr. Henry Latham and Rebecca Owen Latham. He received his early education in the private schools of Lynchburg, and attended the University of Virginia, where he took his degree in medicine. As a young man, he was a member of the engineering corps that surveyed the present route of the Norfolk and Western Railroad from Lynchburg to Salem. At the time of John Brown's Raid he was practicing medicine in Lynchburg. He responded to the call of war by organizing, on his own initiative, the artillery company known as Latham's Battery, which took a prominant part in the Battle of Manassas. Dr. Latham was transferred to the medical corps with the rank of major. After the War, he resumed his life as a doctor in Lynchburg. He was much beloved, a man of genial humor, with a charming personality. He had a beautiful baritone voice, was a great lover of music and wrote some very good verse. Dr. Latham died in 1903.

My Castle in the Air
By Dr. Gray Latham

"Though fields are ripe for harvest, and burdened branch and vine
  Yield up their dainty treasures to other hands than mine,
  Though white-clad ships come dancing, wealth-laden, o'er the main,
  While mine went out, hope-freighted, but came not back again,
  Though friends who should be loving deceive me, or grow cold,
  And some, who should be mindful, forget the poor and old,
  The skies are always cloudless, the days are ever fair,
  In Aiden, where I've builded my castle in the air.

  The sunshine and the flowers, the shade in mossy dells,
  The lowing of the cattle, and the tinkling of the bells,
  The swish of circling sickel in the golden-headed grain,
  The murmur of the brooklet, the 'harvest home' refrain,

The whistle of the partridge, the droning of the bees,
The confidential whispering of the leaves upon the trees,
The joyous laugh of children; one face, surpassing fair,
All come to me in Aiden—my castle in the air.

Beloved and grand old castle! God's blessing on the hours
I've passed in peaceful rapture beneath thy sun-bathed towers,
Where fruit turned not to ashes, nor what I touched to dust,
Where hope attained fruition, and love was met by trust;
There envy never enter'd, and falsehood never trod,
And doubt and hate were withered by faith in man and God!
What Kismet is to Mussulman, what, to the Christian, prayer,
Is the refuge in my reverie—my castle in the air."

Mr. Edward S. Gregory was born in Lynchburg in 1843, a brother of Mr. William and James Gregory. He served in the Confederate Army, and after the War for some time edited the Presbyterian Index-Appeal. Later he was ordained a clergyman of the Episcopal Church, and was rector of Epiphany Church, as already recorded in the chapter on the restoration of the Episcopal Church in Lynchburg. He published two volumes of verse, Bonnibell and other Poems, in 1880; Lenore and other Poems, in 1883. Both were published in Lynchburg. He died in 1884, leaving a son and namesake, who lives in Bedford.

"Valete Ac Plaudite

Bread on the waters, bring not back
The floating seaweed on your track,
Nor yet the parasitic seed,
And barnacles in deeps that breed;
Nor yet soaked with salt be found,
What time your cruise is homeward bound;
In fine, be neither less nor worse
Than when you shipped upon your cruise.

Bread on the waters, land at home
The wealth and wonders of the foam:
Let amber, pearl and coral comb
Select their nest within your crumb:
Or land at least with humbled spirit—
Fish, flotsam, spermacite, oil;
And we, to pay the fates their favor,
Will vow to keep on shore forever!

The Caliph of Bagdad

The caliph looked beyond his darkening room
Towards the broken gloried of the west
And pondered many a question in his breast
And still in pondering found but doubt and gloom
Without a star his gropings to illume.
What are the springs of Happiness? he asked
What lifts the hovering shadow from the tomb,
And lends the light in which content hath basked?
May Love with such a heavenly power be tasked—
Can fame or empire real riches give,
Or calm the heart, the heart in outward splenor washed
With hopes that make it glad to wait and live?
But when the caliph's anquish was most deep
The caliph ate and smoked, and went to sleep."

Under the date of April 5th, 1905, the Lynchburg News published a song written "when Martin Hollins and Henry Davis were in the prime and pride of life." This song was sent the News by a friend of Mr. Newman Eubank, who had written what he remembered of it at his friend's request. Mr. Eubank was then in the seventy-ninth year, and said he had an old field education received at the Academy at Spout Springs. He had formerly been a resident of Lynchburg. He wrote from Newport News, where he was then living, as follows:

"Your valued favor of the 29th was duly received, and I comply with your request as well as my impaired vision and trembling hand will permit. To be true to history I must give you the origin and occasion of this song. It was composed by Billy Moon and sung by Joe Sweeney" (Sweeney was General J. E. B. Stuart's famous singer and minstrel) "when he first started out in life. They were contemporaries, born between 1815 and 1820. The first I ever heard of Joe Sweeney was about the year 1837 or '38, when he sang this song accompanied by his banjo, on the race track of Lynchburg, which is now a part of Rivermont. Billy Moon lived just below the Spout Spring in Campbell, near the Appomattox County line. He loaded his ox-cart with sheaf oats and started to Lynchburg by the old stage road. The coaling ground was that district of the county to the right of the road coming this way between Glover's old stand (afterwards owned by Anderson Armistead) and Concord Depot. It had been denuded of all timber to make charcoal for Ross' Iron Works, then located on James River below Robertson's Mill. The Bolling Spring was a tavern kept by a man named Minter. It is now owned by Captain Pettigrew's estate, the father-in-law of Captain L. F. Lucado. Mr. Wright was a wheelwright, and was the father of John P. Wright, who with Edmund Logwood ran a broker's shop in Lynchburg when you and I first went to Lynchburg. After the War, he edited a Republican paper in Lynchburg."

The Coaling Ground

Song as composed by Billy Moon and sung by Joe Sweeney

  As I drove up to Lynchburg town
  I broke my yoke in the coaling ground;
  I drove up to the Bolling Spring
  And tried to mend my yoke and ring.

  Mr. Minter had no augurs to bore the hole;
  Says I, "Mr. Minter, doggone your soul,
  I cut my yoke upon the road,
  And wouldn't have staid if it had been bored."

LYNCHBURG AND ITS NEIGHBORS

I drove on up to Wright's old shop,
I hollered to my driver and told him to stop.
Says I, "Mr. Wright, I haven't long to stay."
So he took up his hammer and knocked away.
He got an old yoke and fixed in the ring.
Says I, "Mr. Wright, do you charge anything?"

"No," says he, "I do not charge
Unless the job is very large.
For little jobs like this, so small,
I do not charge anything at all."

I drove on up to Anthony's Mill,
And there I stalled upon the hill;
And there all night I had to lay
Till ten o'clock the next day.

Says I to my driver, "This wont do,
I will push on, and so must you.
I whipped my steers, and pushed my cart—
I wish I may be dogged, I couldn't make a start!

Against the ground I braced my heel,
I put my shoulder to the wheel,
And then we made a mighty strain;
But all my pushing was in vain.

I sat down ready to cry,
When came a wagoner riding by;
Says I, "Kind sir, some pity take,
And help me up, for conscience's sake."

"Well," says he, "I will help thee."
He took his horses, number three,
I wiped from my eyes the falling tears,
And he hitched in his horses before my steers.

His horses were so big and strong!
Good Lord, how easy he pulled me along!
And I can say to every creed,
"A Friend in need is a Friend indeed."

It was surprising for to see
How the people gathered round me,
To see and to hear what I had to say,
For they heard I had stalled upon the way.

Into Thurman's they did go,
They bought a dozen cakes or more,
And when they told her I had come
Then she drawed a gallon of rum.

My steers stood gently in the yoke,
While to me she kindly spoke.
I ate my cakes and drank my rum—
There stood a man, he wanted some.

"After the narration of his being helped up the hill at Anthony's Mill, I have lost the thread of the tale until he got to Lynchburg. He described in verse Beaver and 'Possum Creek, and even Sandy Hook, where he struck James River again. I can only recall the verse where he got to that point:

'I drove down to the river side
And ventured in to take a ride.'

My memory, like our grandmothers' garrets, is stored with trumpery long since discarded and out of use, such as pots and skillets, looms and spinning wheels, split bottom chairs and old cradles and so on.

I see it erroneously stated that Joe Sweeney was inventor of the banjo. There never was a greater mistake. My father was born in 1777, and I have often heard him say that it was a well-known instrument with the Negroes in the country. My recollection extends back seventy-five years. My father had an old Negro, Davey, who was an expert banjo player. The Negroes used horsehair for strings. I had a banjo myself of my own manufacture seventy years ago. When I was a boy, Henry, a Negro boy and myself, watched every horse that came by my father's home, and if he had a long tail we got a supply of strings. Joe Sweeney was the first banjo-player to use catgut strings, and was the originator of the fifth string, the bass. The banjo and the Negro came to Virginia together.

(Signed) E. NEWMAN EUBANK."

Miss Cornelia Brown, the talented daughter of Mr. and Mrs. Edward S. Brown, has left a record of some lovely poems. This very dear lady had the misfortune to outlive almost all of those nearest and dearest to her. To her parents on their Golden Wedding Day, May 24th, 1895, she composed this poem, which her old friends will read with pleasure:

"She went beside him o'er the hills,
   And all the earth seemed bright,
Adown the hills the little rills
   Were singing with delight.

The flowers blooming by the way,
   With fragrance filled the breeze,
And birds were singing all the day
   Among the leafy trees.

So have the happy days slipped by,
   'Till fifty years have passed,
And rarely has the summer sky
   By clouds been overcast.

Oh, Time, be gentle to them still,
   As in the days gone by,
And ne'er let fear of coming ill
   Within their bosoms lie."

LYNCHBURG AND ITS NEIGHBORS

To Dr. Paxton, who came here for a few years as pastor of the Presbyterian Church but decided to make Lynchburg his permanent home, she wrote:

> "Dear, Parson, since you love to go
> About the country, to and fro,
> A-fishing and a-hunting, too,
> We send this special train to you.
> Pray, Parson, never fly the track,
> But when you go please hurry back.
> Though you send us birds galore,
> And ducks and rabbits by the score,
> We long to have you on the spot
> To give the geese at home a shot!"

Miss Cornelia was decidedly not a gloomy soul, as these rhymes about the groundhog which will show:

> "Groundhog's Day
> 1922

I'm tired to death of wind and rain, and sleet upon the windowpane; and watch the papers every day, for what the weather man will say. We think the weather man right smart; but what he knows, why, bless your heart, is nothing to the groundhog's sense—what *that* pig knows is just immense. If you could see his broad, flat head, his blackish back and stomach red; no neck at all, and whiskers long; you'd think the old-time people wrong, when they declare the groundhog knows the very day the winter goes.

If you could see his swinish eyes, you would not think that he was wise. All winter he has been asleep, with not a clock the time to keep; how can he know the time has come, when he must up and leave his home? But on the minute he's awake, and out to observations take. Now if the blazing sun is out, his shadow falls, without a doubt. Then fast as his stout legs can go he leaves the world to ice and snow. And six long weeks his broad, flat feet stay sheltered in his safe retreat; and we outside will long and long, for budding flowers and springtime song."

Groundhog's Day, which in all countries save our own is known as Candlemas Day, seems always to have been an attractive subject to poets and writers. Even the great Goethe in his writings comments on this day, saying that it was the 2nd of February when he, like bears and all other hibernating animals, must come out of his hole and take a look around.

Mr. and Mrs. Edward Hutter are both Lynchburg writers of note. Mr. Hutter is the son of Mr. and Mrs. Christian S. Hutter. For some years he has written for magazines in this country. His wife, who writes under her maiden name, Grace Adams, is the daughter of Professor and Mrs. William Saunders Adams. She has a doctor's degree in psychology from Cornell, and is author of the book Psychology: Science or Superstition? The American Mercury has published many articles from her pen. The past six months has been a most fruitful period with her, for much of her work has appeared during this time in various publications. The Rise and Fall of Psychology in the Atlantic Monthly attracted widespread commendation. She is preparing another book, to be published in the summer.

Lightfoot Scruggs, son of the late Major Scruggs, and his wife, Virginia Withers Scruggs, is a successful and popular author of magazine articles.

Another Lynchburg writer is Anne Spencer, Librarian of the Negro branch of the Jones' Memorial Library, who writes poems of unusual beauty.

A Journey
By *Murrell Edmunds*

I wandered where the dead men walk,
I listened to the dead men talk,
A hollow spirit laughed at me,
And laughed in impish mockery,
"A lonely fellow, flesh and blood,
Tomorrow he'll be dust—or mud."

I wandered where the dead men play,
I hear a solemn spirit say,
" 'Tis strange to me they never learn
Which ones to crown, and which to burn.
They crown the fools and burn the kings.
Down with poets—silver sings!"

I wandered where the dead men sleep,
I heard a whispered echo, deep,
"Be patient, Poet, I shall show
My groping children where to go."
A flash across the chasm's yawn,
A gleam of light—*the blood red dawn!*

My Mother
By Murrell Edmunds

In baby days you taught me how to pray,
And gave me of a love so full and deep
Its fragrance soothes my heart when shadows creep
Across the burning sands of Life's grim way.
I recked not then the measure of your love,
I only knew the days were long, and sweet,
And sunbeams made for baby's dancing feet,
And you—and angels—came from God above.

Some day I may forget your tender words,
As stumbling through this shadow land I go;
A transient spirit bound, no one may know,
As fleeting as the song of passing birds;
But always I shall feel your spirit nigh,
To calm my soul, to light my failing eye.

A Prayer

By Murrell Edmunds

When I at last am grown content to know
That life is fraught with broken hopes and pain,
That love and joy too often drift again
Into the dark abyss with sin and woe;
When time has taught me the futility
Of seeing life through hope's imperfect eyes,
And casting old delusion's tawdry lies
Against the breast of stark reality;
When I have ceased to curse the luckless soul
Who fails, albeit through no fault of his own,
But fails, perchance, because the gods have sown
A crop of failures—failure was his dole;
I'll beg Thee then, as now, with wistful sigh,
For whom You made this ironic world—and why?

The Path to Thee

By Ellen Douglass Nelson

This path of life
  I tread, dear Lord,
Is dark; I cannot see.
  Is this the path
Dear Lord, to take,
  The one that leads
To Thee?

On and on
  This road I trudge,
My spirit points the way,
  Though hampered
And encumbered by
  This cell of human
Clay.

Send a gleam
   From out the gloom,
Let the truth be known to me;
   Is the way I tread
The one, dear Lord,
   The one that leads
To Thee?

There is a Light,
   It gleams for me!
Through Prayer and Faith,
   Dear Lord, I see
The only path
   That leads
To Thee.

Arabella

By Ellen Douglass Nelson

Merrily—skipping—dancing—
   She rolls her hoop and ball,
While a glint of joyous laughter rings
   Along the churchyard wall.

She does not sense
   The wraith of bones,
Or Death's embrace
   Under fallen stones.

Merrily—skipping—dancing—
   She rolls her hoop and ball,
While a glint of joyous laughter rings
   Along the churchyard wall.

To a Butterfly
By Ellen Douglass Nelson

Would I were
As free as you
In your joyous
World of blue.

Would that I
Had wings as fair,
Little traveller
Of the air.

The following quotations relating to the work of Abe Craddock Edmunds are excerpts from the Peter Quince Radio Book Reviews conducted by the University of Virginia Extension Division in co-operation with the Virginia Quarterly Review. In reviewing The Renaissance, by Abe Edmunds, Mr. Ben Belitt, Assistant in English at the University of Virginia, says:

"The author of Renaissance has a voice and earnestness peculiarly his own. The sweep of his lines are pruned to a personality as rich and profound as that of the finest poets writing today. * * * This much is certain: A more important and penetrating poem than Renaissance has not yet been written in the memory of this generation. * * *

The renaissance deals with aggressive full-blooded men and ideas; the time in which they lived is left to follow in the reader's consciousness as inevitably as the ripple follows the thrown stone. This explains, doubtless, the superiority of Mr. Edmunds' poetic scheme over the longer epic forms that more theatrical and superficial poets have employed on similar occasions—Stephen Vincent Benet, for example in his turgid and disorderly John Brown's Body."

Of Abe Edmunds' Five Men at the Battle of Rheims, Mr. Belitt said:

LYNCHBURG AND ITS NEIGHBORS

"We move on now to the most impressive narrative poem on this evening's list, by Abe Craddock Edmunds, a young Virginian, who in the opinion of this reviewer is producing the soundest work among the Southern poets today.

Five Men is an austere and distinguished achievement. * * * The South has ample reason to honor this poem as its most distinguished achievement in sustained narrative poetry in modern times."

In further discussing Mr. Edmunds' work, Mr. Ben Belitt says that he has "rediscovered values almost entirely lost to poetry since Browning."

By ABE CRADDOCK EDMUNDS

A Herald from a frozen hill
Over the land, ugly and still,
Sent the silver snarl of a horn:
"Glory, men! for winter has gone.

Spring heard the call, and joyfully
Hung her dress in an apple tree
That bent and swayed on the low hill-side.
Her dress was white, as becomes a bride.

For Certain Dowagers

You sit beside a hearth like ermined judges
Passing on issues that a patient god
Would put his finger to his wise lips over.
You venture narrow opinions
On agonies you've never known,
An force your prying wits in sacred places.

I

Your body is a stately theme to be
Chanted by great poets, and my town
And this last age we know are also things
Not to be held in scorn. No ancient kings

LYNCHBURG AND ITS NEIGHBORS

Went bellowing to the wars more arrogantly
Than we have gone. No generals went down
Ways that were gray or starker. Socrates;
Nero; Christ and Judas—my town knows these.
We have our shrines and temples; the bloody sand
Of scarlet Marathon, and a man
To shout of victory and spit blood while he go
To tell the people of it. Down below
The rest of earth, our dungeons. We have all these,
And our Gethsemane and Calvaries.

II

And have our beauty, too. This evening I stood
Upon Beck Bridge, and looked at Wilson's Wood,
Half screened by smoke, and mist about the trees.
The gas house coughed black cinders that a breeze
Took in its hand, and scattered on the air;
Furnaces roared beneath me, and despair
Shrieked, wailing, down the rails.
Tall houses ranged above the bending trees—
Old Southern planters smoking at their ease,
In scorn of all this bustle,—and a great love
Came to me for this city of unrest
And quaint beauty; love of dirt and smoke,
Of screaming whistle and of hammer stroke,
And scornful houses standing in the West.

CHAPTER XXII
NEGRO SONGS AND HYMNS—OTHER OLD SONGS AND BALLADS

NEGRO music, which has contributed so much to the charm of Southern life, is particularly colorful at funerals, wakes and camp-meetings. Perhaps it finds its highest expression in their hymn of the Crucifixion which is sung at Easter. This is a piece of Easter music which they, an unlettered, unlearned race, have evolved of themselves: a spontaneous expression of their own emotions, aroused by the spectacle of Christ's suffering and death, as imaged in their minds by their own preachers. This hymn can be compared with Stainer's Crucifixion without loss of dignity; for it has truth, simplicity and sincerity, and considering its source and origin is probably a much greater achievement. There are many stanzas in this hymn which tells the whole story of our Lord's betrayal, death and resurrection: Judas and his thirty pieces of silver, Peter and his denial of his Master, Pontius Pilate; the soldiers who parted His garments among them and cast lots for them, Thomas the Doubter and the Resurrection—all is there, and it goes like this:

"They crucified my Saviour, and nailed Him to the cross,
They crucified my Saviour, and nailed Him to the cross,
They crucified my Saviour, and nailed Him to the cross,"
Chorus, "And the Lord will bear my spirit home."

Other verses have these first lines:
"And Joseph begged His body, and laid it in his tomb."
"Sister Mary, she came running, a-looking for my Lord."
These lines are repeated three times before the chorus begins.

"The cold grave could not hold Him,
The cold grave could not hold Him,
The cold grave could not hold Him,
Nor Death's cold, iron hand.

>   For angels came from Heaven,
>   For angels came from Heaven,
>   For angels came from Heaven,
>   And rolled the stone away."
>
>   Chorus:
>
> "Jesus rose, Jesus rose,
> Hallelujah, gone to Glory,
> Jesus rose and gone
> To Heaven on the cloud."

A very old hymn among the Negroes, which is typical of their method, is the Old Ship o' Zion:

> First verse: "It is bound for the Land o' Canaan,
> It is bound for the Land o' Canaan,
> It is bound for the Land o' Canaan,
> Git on board, git on board."
>
> Chorus: "The ole Ship o' Zion,
> The old Ship o' Zion,
> The old Ship o' Zion,
> Git on board, git on board."

> Second verse: "Do you think she will be able," etc.
> Third verse: "She has landed many a thousand," etc.
> Fourth verse: "There ain't no danger in the waters," etc.
> Fifth verse: "Jesus Christ, he is the Captain," etc.
> Sixth verse: "She has landed my old mother," etc.
> Seventh verse: "She has landed my old father," etc.

On and on this hymn can go indefinitely, any member of the congregation being at liberty to start a new line in praise of some relative or friend as the preceding line dies out, like this:

> "She has landed Brother Johnson," etc.
> "She has landed Sister Carter," etc.,

until finally all the dead and gone church members have been recalled to memory, to the gratification of their friends and relatives. The hymn being so long-drawn-out is of great assistance in urging mourners up to the "mourners' bench" during a revival, for it is calculated to break down resistance. Many old ladies and gentlemen will recall this hymn with interest and pleasure, heard no doubt, while they attended church with their mammies, as all little white children did in those old times.

I have before me a very worn-out copy of a book of old hymns used by the colored people, with music and words. The front is torn away to the fourth hymn, and the back is gone after page 101, but there are still left 98 hymns, and many of these are gems. The fourth hymn, almost worn away, is the Negro song of freedom, "Free at Last," which goes:

> "Satan is sad and I am glad,
> I thank God I'm free at last."

To show that Negro songs are even today a part of the development of the younger generation, I quote these four lines which I heard for the first time from my little grandson when he was only three years old. He had heard an old colored mammie in Richmond sing them over and over to the child she was nursing, until they were thoroughly impressed upon his youthful memory, and he sang them with that charming lilt which could have been acquired only from a Negro:

> "I wish I had a needle
> As fine as I could sew,
> I'd sew my sweetheart to my side
> And down the road I'd go."

Here is another song that comes from lower Virginia:

> "De hen en chickens went to roos',
> De hawk flew down en bit de goose,
> He bit de ole hen in de back,
> I do believe that am a fact."

Chorus:
> "Oh, Jinny, git yore hoe-cake done, mah dear,
> Oh, Jinny, git yore hoe-cake done."

> "As I was gwine long down de road
> 'Pon a stump dar sat a toad,
> De toad he winked to tadpole's daughter,
> En kicked a big frawg in de water."

Chorus:

> "Oh, Jinny, git yore hoe-cake," etc.

A famous song in its day was The Blue-Tailed Fly:

> "When I was young I used to wait
> On Marster's table en hand de plate,
> I pass de bottle until 'twas dry,
> En breshed erway de blue-tail fly."

Chorus:

> "Jim crack corn, I don' keer,
> Jim crack corn, I don' keer,
> Jim crack corn, I don' keer,
> Ole Marster's gone erway.
> Arter dinner ole Marster sleep,
> En bid dis nigger watch ter keep,
> En when he gwineter shet his eye
> He tell me watch de blue-tail fly."

Chorus:

> "Jim crack corn," etc.

> "When he ride in de arternoon
> I follow wid a hickory broom,
> De pony bein' bery shy
> When bitten by de blue-tail fly."

Chorus:

> "Jim crack corn," etc.

>"One day he ride erroun de farm
> De flies fly roun' him in er swarm,
> Until one bit him on de thigh.
> De pony r'ar, de pony pitch,
> He threw ole Marster in de ditch;
> He die, de jury wonder why,
> De verdict was de blue-tail fly."

Chorus:

>"Jim crack corn," etc.

>"Dey lay him under a simmon tree,
> En writ fur all de worl' ter see,
> Beneath dis stone here I do lie,
> All because of de blue-tail fly."

Chorus:

>"Jim crack corn," etc.

>"Ole Marster gone, now let him rest,
> Dey say all things am fur de best;
> I nebber fergit tel de day I die
> Ole Marster en dat blue-tail fly."

Next to the Blue-Tail Fly in popularity was Ole Zippy Coon:

>"Ole Zippy Coon was a Highland Scholar,
> Ole Zippy Coon was a Highland Scholar,
> Ole Zippy Coon was a Highland Scholar,
> Play upon the banjo day arter tomorrow.

>Raccoon in de gum-stump, coon am in de holler,
> Raccoon in de gum-stump, coon am in de holler,
> Raccoon in de gum-stump, coon am in de holler,
> I'm goin' ter see my sweetheart day arter tomorrow.

Did ye ever see a wild goose sailin' on de ocean?
Did ye ever see a wild goose sailin' on de ocean?
Did ye ever see a wild goose sailin' on de ocean?
Wild goose's motion am a mighty pretty motion."

The soldiers came back from the Mexican War singing this song:

"As I was walkin' de new cut road
I met a tar'pin en a toad,
Ebery time de toad would spring
De tar'pin cut de pigeon wing."

Chorus:
"Picayune Butler, Picayune Butler,
Is she comin' in town?"

The next song is not a Negro song, but it is very old:

IN SPRINGFIELD MOUNTAIN

1

"In Springfield mountain there did dwell,
A love-li youth, I know'd him well;
'Twas Stephen Jones' on-li son,
He just had turned his twen-ti one.
Chorus: "Whack, fal, ral, dal, diddle-da-day."

2

"One Mon-di morning he did go
Out in the meadow for to mow;
He had not mowed half o'er that field
When a wenemous wiper bit him on the heel.

The next verses tell of his sweetheart finding him—then follows:

3

   " 'John, oh John, why did you go
     Out in the meadow for to mow?'
    'Sal, oh Sal, I thought you know'd
    'Twas Dadi's hay and had to be mowed'."
Chorus: "Whack," etc.

4

"At length he did give up the ghost,
   And straightway out of this world did post,
   Crying, crying as he went,
   'Cruel, cruel sar-pri-ent!' "

About a hundred years ago a very young and romantic music-teacher taught music in Lynchburg. He had been engaged to a society belle who discarded him. At a party one night he was asked to sing, and the girl being present he sang in revenge the following lines of his own composition:

"The jig is up, and I've been flung
Sky-high, and worse than that,
The girl whose praises I have sung
With pen, with pencil and with tongue,
Said 'No, no, no,' said 'No, no, no,' said 'No,'
And I fell flat.

Now, like the humble-bee, I'll rove,
Just when and where I please,
Inhaling sweets in every grove,
Humming 'round each flower I love,
And dancing in each breeze, breeze, breeze,
And dancing in each breeze.

Well, thank the fates once more I'm free,
At every shrine I'll bow,
And if again a girl cheats me,
Exceeding sharp I guess she'll be,
I've cut my eye-teeth now, now now,
I've cut my eye-teeth now."

LYNCHBURG AND ITS NEIGHBORS

Perhaps the most beautiful of the river songs is that of the colored boat-men of the South:

> "We pray de Lord He gib us signs
>   Dat some day we be free;
> De norf wind tell hit to de pines,
>   De wild duck to de sea;
> We hab hit when de church bell ring,
>   We dream hit in de dream,
> De rice bird mean hit when he sing,
>   De eagle when he scream."

But for Lynchburgers the song of songs was the old river song of the bateaux, with its plendid swing and rythm:

Song of the Bateaux

> "I hitch up my horse and cyart
>   Bigges' horse behime,
> En when dis nigger cracks his whip
>   You see sich a-pullin' en a-gwine."

Chorus: "Oh, I'm gwine on down
            Ter Lynchburg Town,
            Ter kerry my 'bacca down dar."

> "Squir'l he am a cunnin' bird,
>   He ramble in de dark,
> But how he do git up en git
>   When he hear ole Caesar bark."

Chorus: "Oh, I'm gwine on down," etc.

> "Squir'l he hab a bushy tail,
>   Stump-tail am de hyar;
> Raccoon tail am ringed erroun',
>   'Possum tail go bar'."

Chorus: "Oh, I'm gwine on down," etc.

"De squir'l am a cunnin' thing,
　　He nebber coil his tail,
　He steal all ole Marster's corn
　　En shuck hit on a rail."

Chorus: "Oh, I'm gwine on down," etc.

"Fox, he got a bushy tail,
　　'Possum tail am bar';
　Rabbit got no tail at all,
　　Jes' a little bunch o' har."

Chorus: "Oh, I'm gwine on down," etc.

BOOK II

SOME LYNCHBURG FAMILIES
and
GENEALOGIES

CHAPTER XXIII
SOME LYNCHBURG FAMILIES AND GENEALOGIES

ADAMS

THREE brothers, Duval, Richard and Holcombe Adams, lived at one time on Daniel's Hill, and left many descendants. The Adams family were from Appomattox originally. Their parents were Isaac Adams and Susan Elizabeth DuVal Adams, the daughter of Major William DuVal, an officer in the Revolutionary War. The three Adams brothers had distinguished careers as business men in Lynchburg.

Mrs. DuVal Adams, Jr., who has been for many years associated with the Lynchburg News, was Miss Martha Rivers, of Tennessee, and is an alumnus of Randolph-Macon College.

ADAMS

Captain Stephen Adams was not related to this family, born in New York, he was a graduate of Yale, and came to Lynchburg before the War Between the States. Joining with the South, in the Confederate Army, he was made captain, was seriously wounded, and captured by the Northern soldiers. His wife, Emma Saunders Adams, hearing that he lay near death somewhere behind the Northern lines, went through both Southern and Northern lines to find him. To the hoops under her skirts she had tied little bags containing coffee and sugar and other delicacies for her husband. She finally found him, because of his love of music, for the fame of the Rebel officer lying on his cot playing his violin had spread through the Northern lines. Captain Adams practiced law in Lynchburg for many years. He was judge of the Campbell County Court, and lived in the home now owned by Mr. Ben Hughes.

THE ADDISON FAMILY

The first of the Addison family to come to this country was

Colonel John Addison. He was born in England, and was the brother of Anthony Addison, rector of Abingdon and chaplain to the Duke of Marlborough. He was also brother of Launcelot Addison, Dean of Litchfield, and the uncle of the celebrated Joseph Addison. Colonel John Addison came to Maryland and settled on the banks of the Potomac in 1667. The handsome portrait of him, with curled wig and laced coat, is that of a hale and hearty English gentleman in the prime of manhood. He married Rebecca Dent, the widow of Thomas Dent, in 1676. Her father was the Rev. William Wilkinson, the first member of the English clergy to come to the Province of Maryland. He owned twelve thousand acres of land in Maryland, a large estate even for those days.

In the new country Colonel John Addison immediately began to take a prominent place. He was commissioned colonel by the military authorities on account of the distinguished part he bore in the encounters between the colonists and Indians. In 1692 he was a member of His Majesties' Council, and presiding judge of Charles County. A staunch upholder of the Church of England, he helped establish Broad Creek Church, the oldest Episcopal parish in Maryland, which his grandson, Henry Addison, and his great-great-grandson, Walter Dulany Addison, were to serve as rectors in years to come. He died in 1706 in England, while on a business visit.

At Colonel John Addison's death his son, Thomas, born in 1679, inherited most of his large estate, in this country and in England. Thomas was also a commissioned colonel in the colony. He married Elizabeth Tasker, daughter of Thomas Tasker, April 21st, 1701. By this marriage he had two daughters. After the death of Elizabeth Tasker, he married Eleanor Smith, June 17th, 1709. She was the daughter of Colonel Walter Smith, and the sister of Mrs. Daniel Dulany, whose husband was a prominent citizen of Annapolis. By this marriage Thomas Addison had four sons and one daughter. The sons were sent to Lowther, England, to be educated under the tuition of Mr.

Wilkinson, who was said to be the greatest scholar of the age. The eldest of the four sons, John, married Susannah Wilkinson. Henry, the youngest, married Rachel Dulany, and became rector of Broad Creek Church.

John, born September 16th, 1713, died 1764, married Susannah Wilkinson and had five children. The oldest son, Thomas, was married December 5th, 1767, to Rebecca Dulany. They had five children, Walter Dulany being the oldest. His father died when Walter Dulany Addison was only seven years old. As was the custom in the family, he and his brothers were sent to England to be educated. There they found many friends and relatives, for the Dulanys were Tories, and they had been exiled from the American colony, and their property had been confiscated. The Rev. Henry Addison, who had married Rachel Dulany, was a very learned man, and he was so disgusted at the revolt of the colonies that in his old age he also had gone to England.

After the completion of his education, Walter Dulany Addison returned to Maryland and mingled for a time in Annapolis society, but he soon determined to enter the Episcopal ministry. He married Elizabeth Hesselius on June 5th, 1792. He was now twenty-three, having been born January 1st, 1769. Elizabeth Hesselius was the daughter of John Hesselius (of Swedish parentage), a gifted artist, who had studied under Sir Godfrey Kneller. Mrs. Addison died at the early age of thirty-three, leaving two sons, Edward Brice and Lloyd, and one daughter. Two children had died in infancy.

For years Mr. Addison was rector of old St. John's Church at Broad Creek, the oldest parish in Maryland, which had been established in 1693 with the aid of his ancestor, Colonel John Addison. This church was nearly opposite Mount Vernon and sometimes Washington came there to worship. Mr. Addison was a man of very strong principles, and great power of truth and eloquence. In that day when duelling was a popular way of weeding out one's enemies, he had the courage to call the custom by its true name, *murder,* and to strive, against public opinion and ridicule, to break up this evil. He freed his slaves to his own material disadvantage, and was forced in later life to admit that, with the exception of four, they had proved themselves entirely unfit for freedom. He was the founder of the Theological Seminary at Alexandria, and in his day scarcely a man of his religious convictions had so broad a spirit towards Non-Conformists and Catholics. So great was his love and pity that one year when a cold spell suddenly developed after his sheep had been sheared he sent to Washington for flannel cloth, and had blankets made for the suffering animals. This greatly amused his less humane neighbors, who embellished this incident into a fine tale, and said he dressed his sheep up in red flannel, which frightened the sheep so badly that they ran from each other, and could never be flocked together again. However this good man was never deflected by ridicule from his purpose to do what he conceived to be right. He lived a long and useful life full of honor, but in his later years he suffered great sorrows and losses. By giving freedom to his slaves, and supporting Robert Morris, he parted with a goodly portion of his fortune and having spent most of this world's goods in benevolent deeds he had nothing left for himself. He was forced to give up Oxon Hill, the home of his ancestors which, with Carlisle House, Belvoir and Mt. Vernon, was one of the four great houses near Washington. He lost one of the two sons of his second marriage, Francis Key, named after Francis Scott Key, who was one of Mr. Addison's warmest friends. By Francis Scott Key's influence this lovely boy, child of his father's old age, had just received an appointment to West Point when he died. In the midst of all these misfortunes Mr. Addison lost his eyesight; but he bore life's disasters with invincible fortitude and even learned to be blind with equanimity. He died January 31st, 1848. "Vulnus opemque fero" is the legend of the arms of the Addison House: "I bear a wound and a healing." Never was a motto more perfectly fulfilled than in this man, who found in himself that philosophy which heals all wounds.

Dr. Edmund Brice Addison, eldest son of Walter Dulany Addison, was born at Oxon Hill in 1794 and died in Washington in 1878. He had a fine classical education, and splendid intellectual gifts, and would probably have become a great doctor if he had not preferred country life to the practice of his profession in a city. He married Eliza D. Bowie, of Maryland, who died in 1846 at the early age of thirty-eight. After her death, Dr. Edmund Brice Addison moved to Alexandria, where he lived a very quiet life, devoting himself to his children. He wrote a great deal, and was a delightful companion. It was from his Recollections that his niece, Elizabeth Hesselius Murray, gained much of the information contained in her very interesting book, One Hundred Years Ago. In his later years Dr. Addison suffered the family affliction and became blind, but he bore this trouble with the same fortitude shown by his father.

Edmund Brice, Jr., third son of Dr. Edmund Brice Addison, born in Prince George County, Maryland, May 25th, 1834, began life as a commission merchant in Alexandria, Virginia. In 1861 he located in Richmond, Virginia, and during the War Between the States was attached to the arsenal of the Confederacy. After the War, he entered mercantile life as junior partner of the firm Allison and Addison. In 1895 he became associated with the Virginia-Carolina Chemical Company as first vice-president. He was also connected with many of the largest enterprises in the South, and was a man of prominence and importance in the business world. He was married in Alexandria, October 21st, 1859, to Emily Crockford, of English parentage but born in New Jersey, the daughter of John and Ellen Crockford. Edmund Brice Addison and Emily Crockford Addison had eight children, of whom Walter Edmund Addison, born in Richmond in 1863, and for years editor of the Lynchburg News, was the third.

Walter Edmund Addison

Walter Edmund Addison, editor of the Lynchburg News, was born in Richmond, Virginia, in 1863, and died in Memorial

Hospital on Monday, January 12th, 1925. Senator Carter Glass very justly said of him, "that man has yet to be born who could exceed him in good faith or excel him in concepts of honor."

In his youth Mr. Addison attended Thomas Norwood's school for boys in Richmond, and later went to the Hanover Academy. From 1884 to 1886 he studied law at the University of Virginia. After receiving his degree in 1886, he practiced law in Southwest Virginia until 1901, when he went to Roanoke as editor of the Roanoke World, which is now consolidated with the News under the name of World-News. The following year Mr. Addison became editor of the Roanoke Times, remaining with this paper until he accepted the editorship of the Lynchburg News, which work he entered upon February 1st, 1906.

For the term 1916-1918 Mr. Addison was State Senator from this district. Being urged to run again when this term expired, he declined because the practice was followed by the city and county of alternating in furnishing candidates, although in his special case the county offered to make an exception. In 1917 Washington and Lee University conferred upon him the degree of Doctor of Literature. Mr. Addison was a member of Grace Episcopal Church.

Surviving Mr. Walter E. Addison are his wife, who before her marriage in 1890 was Miss Virginia Harrison, of the University of Virginia; one son, Julien H. Addison, and the following brothers and sisters: W. Meade Addison, James A. Addison, Mrs. R. G. Reynolds, Mrs. John H. Lyons, all of Richmond; Mrs. D. Gray Langhorne, of Pulaski, and John H. Addison, of Great Falls, Montana.

Mr. Addison's earliest ambition was to be an editor. When he was a little boy he got out a weekly newspaper, which shows the natural bent of his mind, but he was thirty-eight before he entered into newspaper work as a profession. Out of deference to his father's desires he put aside his own wishes and studied law, although his greatest urge was to follow the footsteps of his distinguished kinsman, Joseph Addison. By thus forcing himself to be a lawyer, much more than half of his life was gone before he began the career for which he proved himself so eminently fitted. Some of Mr. Addison's editorials reached the very highest peak of literary expression. His farewell to Dr. John Loyd was a noble and touching parting, not for himself alone but for the town where he was much beloved, and in his editorial on the death of his brother-in-law, Beverley Harrison, he spoke with beautiful and poignant perception.

Mr. Walter E. Addison was not a lineal descendant of Joseph Addison, who married the widowed Countess of Warwick, and left no children. Mr. Addison was descended from Joseph Addison's uncle, Colonel John Addison, the first of the name to come to this country. And yet his heritage was very strongly marked and his mind bore the same stamp as that of Joseph Addison. It is easy to imagine the Mr. Addison that Lynchburg knew writing of Sir Roger de Coverley, and the Joseph Addison of 1711 editing some of those noble columns published for nineteen years in the News.

Ambler

Mr. John Jaquelin Ambler, born in Orange County in 1828, was the son of John Jaquelin Ambler, Senior, and Elizabeth Barbour. He married Laura Beverley Davis, of Amherst County. Soon after the close of the War Between the States he came to Lynchburg, where he with Mr. Victor conducted a book and stationery store under the firm name of Victor and Ambler. The children of Mr. John Jaquelin Ambler and his first wife, Laura Beverley Davis, were Laura Beverley, who married Fayette Rodes; Bessie, who was the second wife of Robert C. Gish, and left one child, Beverley Gish; John Jaquelin, Junior, who married Janet Anne Carter, a granddaughter of Colonel Robert Enoch Withers, of Wytheville; Edward C. Ambler, a doctor now practicing in Roanoke, who married Fannie Waller Brown, daughter of Judge John Thompson Brown, of Nelson County. Mr. John Jacquelin Ambler, Senior, was married a second time,

July 16th, 1890, to Miss Sallie Davies, of Bedford County, who survived him with one child, Frankie Preston Ambler. After his retirement from active business, he lived at Saint Moor, a noted country place owned by the Ambler family in Amherst.

The mother of Mr. John J. Nicholas, Miss Lillie Nicholas, Mrs. John L. Caskie, Mr. Harrison T. Nicholas and Mr. Jellis L. Nicholas, all of this city, was Ella Cary Ambler, the sister of Mr. John Jaquelin Ambler.

Mrs. John Camm, the late Mrs. G. Hamilton Wilkins, and Mr. Philip St. George Ambler were also of the Ambler family, and natives of Amherst County, although residents of Lynchburg.

Katherine, Anne Herndon, Philip St. George, Edward Burkadike and John, who never married, were the children of Philip St. George Ambler and Elizabeth Green Ambler. Katherine was married first to Thomas Deane Jellis, a Norfolk and Western Railroad official. Their only child, Elizabeth Ambler, died in infancy. Mrs. Jellis was married a second time, February 7th, 1889, to John Camm, a descendant of the first John Camm, commissioner to Archbishop of Canterbury and head of the Established Church in Virginia. (For Camm, see William and Mary Quarterly, Vol. XIV, No. 2, October, 1905, page 130). The children of Katherine Ambler and John Camm: John Camm, Frank Camm.

Philip St. George Ambler married Maria Theresa Jordan. She died August 3, 1900, leaving Emily Page, who married Wilcox Brown, Philip St. George, Blanche Jordan, Mary Nelson, Theresa Jaquelin, Martha Cary. Edward Burkadike Ambler married Virginia Pascoe and had no children.

Anne Herndon Ambler married Hamilton Wilkins. Children: John Ambler, Gilbert Hamilton, Junior, Cary, and Thomas.

Anthony

Joseph Anthony came from Holland to New Kent County, Virginia. According to a letter which was at one time in the possession of Mr. Robert J. Davis, but is now lost, his adventures on reaching this country were as exciting as those of Captain John Smith. The Anthony family was Italian, and Joseph had nothing when he reached this land, except the genealogy of his descent from Mark Anthony. When he married into a Quaker family his descendants did not think a great deal of this treasure of his long genealogy and finally made a bonfire of it as being an evidence of vanity. He married Elizabeth Clark, daughter of Christopher Clark and his wife, Penelope. He had hired himself to Christopher Clark to pay his passage across the Atlantic. His wife, Elizabeth, was born May 2nd, 1713, and is mentioned in Christopher Clark's will on record now in Louisa Courthouse. His son, Christopher Anthony, married first Judith Moorman. Their children were: Mary, born 1766, Joseph, Elizabeth, Charles, born 1773. His second wife was Mary Jordan, whose only sister married Samuel Harrison. The children of Mary Jordan and Christopher Anthony were: Samuel, Hannah, Sarah, who married Henry Davis, Penelope, Jordan (a banker at Buchanan, who never married), Rachel, Charlotte and Christopher, born 1776, married Anna Couch, a sister of Mrs. Breckenridge, of Grove Hill, near Fincastle. Christopher Anthony, Junior, was a planter and merchant in the Seneca district of Campbell until he reached the age of forty. He then decided to be a lawyer, studied law and met with great success in his practice. At Aaron Burr's request he was impanelled in the jury which tried him in Richmond, because Aaron Burr expressed the sentiment that in Mr. Anthony he would have at least one fair and impartial man to sit on his case. The elder Christopher Anthony, being a staunch Quaker and disapproving of slavery, moved to Cincinnati with his younger unmarried daughters. It is said that by the marriage of two of these daughters he became the ancestor of Senator Pugh and Senator Palmer. In Virginia he left many descendants, among whom are the Breckenridge, the Robertson, the Davis, the Pendleton and the Yancey names.

ARMISTEAD

Mr. Louis Armistead died at Woodstock, Virginia, the home of his son-in-law, Rev. J. A. McMurray, May 2nd, 1918, at the age of eighty-seven. His wife, who died in 1913, was the daughter of Rev. Jacob D. Mitchell, and a half sister of Mrs. George Payne, of Lynchburg. Dr. Jacob M. Armistead, of Agnes Scott College Faculty, Decatur, Georgia, was their son. He survived his parents only a few years.

AUNSPAUGH

Mr. Robert T. Aunspaugh, a native of Bedford, but long a resident of Lynchburg, died at Chase City, November 6th, 1905, aged sixty-eight years. He was a soldier in the Confederate Army. Mr. Aunspaugh's first wife was Anna M. Claytor, of Bedford, who died January 9th, 1891, leaving the following children: Mrs. James R. Kyle, Misses Eugenia, Julia and Annie Aunspaugh, and Claytor and Fred Aunspaugh. Mr. Aunspaugh was married a second time, November 14th, 1900, to Miss Mary M. Owen, of South Boston, where he lived in his later years. While in business in Lynchburg he was a member of the firm of Aunspaugh, Cobbs and Company, the other partners being Mr. John Cobbs and Mr. Charles M. Guggenheimer.

BARKSDALE

The Barksdale family settled in Halifax sometime prior to July 21st, 1786. On this date a will was recorded made by Nathaniel Barksdale, in which he left a goodly estate to his eight children. Among them was Peter Barksdale, who married Elizabeth Worthington, January 11th, 1781. Their son, Nathaniel Barksdale, was married in 1805 to Patsy Hill. Their son, Elisha Barksdale, married Judith A. Barksdale, October 22nd, 1835. They were the parents of William Randolph Barksdale, born 1849, who was made circuit judge in 1874. Judge Barksdale was married to Hattie Bailey Craddock. They had nine children, of these Wm. R. Barksdale, Junior, Elisha B., D. A. Barksdale and John Craddock Barksdale have made their homes in Lynchburg.

William Randolph Barksdale, Junior, married Mary Jane Morgan of an old Lynchburg family. Dr. Elisha Barksdale, a prominent physician here, married Rosa McWane. A. D. Barksdale, a lawyer of note, unmarried. John C. Barksdale married Emma Ivey, of Lynchburg.

Bass

Dr. Ethelbert David Bass married Sarah Judith Leftwich in 1874, and had one daughter, Julia, born 1876, who married Percy Moran Thompson. Dr. Bass was a popular physician in Lynchburg.

Ancestry of Colonel Tavener Beale

1. John Beale died 1399 in Maidstone, Kent, England; had:

2. William Beale, of Maidstone, died 1429, married Katherine; had:

3. John Beale, of Maidstone, died 1461, married Agnes first, Alicia second; had:

4. Robert Beale, of Maidstone, died 1490, married Agnes; had:

5. William Beale, of Maidstone, died 1534, married Johanna; had:

6. Thomas Beale, twice mayor of Maidstone, died February 2, 1593; married first Johanna Cobb; second Alicia Wolgate. Had twenty-one children, according to a monument in All Saints' Church. Maidstone, erected by Gus Sib Thomas, which bears the above pedigree; one of these twenty-one children was:

7. Colonel Thomas Beale, emigrant to Virginia 1645, justice of York County 1652, member of council 1674, died before 1700, married Alice; had:

8. Captain Thomas Beale II, born 1649, died 1679 at Chestnut Hill, home he built on the Rappahannock in Richmond County, where his tomb may still be seen, married in York County in 1671 to Ann Gooch, daughter of Major William Gooch, of Temple Farm, where terms of Yorktown surrender were written.

Major Gooch was member of council and died in 1855. Captain Thomas II had:

9. Thomas Beale III, of Chestnut Hill, died 1729, married Elizabeth Tavener, daughter of Captain John and Elizabeth Tavener; had:

10. Tavener Beale, Senior, removed to the Valley of Virginia, married Frances M. Madison, who married a second time, John Hite. He had:

11. Colonel Tavener Beale, Junior, Lieutenant Eighth Virginia Regiment, Continental Army, built Mount Airy (near New Market), died 1810 near Clifton Forge, where he lived after Selling Mount Airy to his son-in-law, William Steinbergen, married 1764 to Betty Hite, daughter of Jacob Hite by his first wife, Catherine O'Bannon. His children were:

1. John Beale, married Margaret Skillern.
2. Charles Beale, married, first, Eliza Skillern; second, Miss Kyle.
3. Thomas Beale, married Celeste Grand Pierre, of New Orleans.
4. James Madison Hite Beale, married Mary Steinbergen.
5. Katherine Beale, married John Jordan.
6. Elizabeth Beale, married William William Steinbergen.
7. Mary Beale, married Dr. Jacob Williamson.

The Beales intermarried with the Trigg, Radford, Jordan, Steinbergen, Lewis, Moffett, Thompson, Taylor, McChesney, Blackford, and many other prominent families.

John Beale, who married Margaret Skillern, was a merchant and farmer, and had stores at Buchanan, Alexandria and Fincastle. John, and Charles, his brother, built the first bridge at Buchanan over the James River. It was swept away by a freshet and never rebuilt.

Thomas Beale, before going to New Orleans, where he married Celeste Grand Pierre, fought a duel with Mr. Risque, of

LYNCHBURG AND ITS NEIGHBORS

Lynchburg, over Miss Judy Hancock. Mr. Risque was shot in the stomach, but recovered.

Catherine Beale was born September 25, 1765. She married Captain John Jordan. Her daughter, Catherine Jordan, who died November 1858, was married January 17, 1817, to James Paxton, born June 6, 1781, died June 13, 1866, major War 1812. He was the son of William Paxton and Nellie Hay. William was one of the four emigrant brothers from Scotland.

Beale-Hite Line

Jacob, the father of Bettie, the wife of Tavener Beale, was the second son of Yost Hite. He was a man of great energy and aided his father in colonizing the Valley of Virginia, making several voyages to Ireland to secure emigrants. On one of these voyages he met and married Catherine O'Bannon. He built his home in what is now Jefferson County, where he was very prominent. He was dissatisfied with the location of the county seat; he contended for Leetown, but Martinsburg was chosen and he was so incensed over this that he deeded his home to his children and left for South Carolina, where he bought land from an Englishman named Pearis, who had a grant of ten thousand acres. Part of the Pearis grant of land included the present site of Greenville, South Carolina. Here Pearis lived in the midst of Indians, with whom he was on the best of terms, and over whom he had great influence. Hite settled near here about 1773, and he too won the friendship of the Indians.

When the Revolution broke out Hite sided with the colonies, while the Indians, incited by the British agents sent among them, went with the British. Jacob Hite, hearing of the work of these agents, sent his son, Jacob O'Bannon Hite, with presents to the Indian towns, hoping to defeat the efforts of the English. This son had made himself very popular with the Indians, and he and his father were confident of success—too confident, as events proved, for on his way to the Indian towns Jacob O'Bannon Hite met a large party of Indians on the war-path and was instantly murdered.

The murdered man was engaged to the daughter of Pearis, the Englishman. When she heard of his death, and of the Indians' bloody intentions toward the other Hites, braving all dangers, she hurried through the forests to warn her dead lover's people. She reached them in time to warn them to escape to a place of safety, but they were still too confident of the friendship of the Indians. They delayed leaving and the Indians fell upon them and killed Jacob Hite with fiendish tortures. At this time Jacob Hite's sons, John, Thomas and George, were in Virginia. The most plausible tradition among their relatives concerning the fate of the rest of Jacob Hite's family is that they were all murdered with Jacob, except one daughter, Eleanor, and some slaves. On hearing of the massacre, George Hite hurried at once to South Carolina. He found that his sister, Eleanor, had been ransomed by an English officer, who took her to Pensacola, intending to marry her; but the horrors of the massacre were too much for her and she died soon after reaching Florida. George Hite returned to Virginia with one of the slaves that had been captured by the Indians. She had been married to a chief's son and gave birth to a daughter after her return. Besides Eleanor, Mrs. Hite and Frances had totally disappeared. After the Revolution, Colonel Tavener Beale went to South Carolina and engaged Pearis to visit the Indians and ransom the supposed captives, but it is believed that this mission resulted in failure.

The murder of Jacob Hite took place in 1778. George Hite was attending William and Mary College at this time. He served in the latter years of the Revolutionary War in the cavalry and is believed to have been a captain. He married Deborah Rutherford and was the first county clerk of Jefferson County when it was formed from Berkeley. He died in 1817.

The Mrs. Hite of the Indian massacre was the second wife of Jacob Hite. She was Mrs. Frances Madison Beale, widow of Colonel Tavener Beale, Senior. She was born in 1726, the daughter of Ambrose Madison and Frances Taylor, and was descended from Captain Isaac Madison, of Jamestown, 1609, member of the first council in 1624. Frances Taylor, her mother, was the daughter of James Taylor, of Orange County, a Knight of the Golden Horseshoe. James Taylor was the ancestor of five Presidents of the United States: Madison, Taylor, William Henry Harrison, Benjamin Harrison and Tyler. His wife, Martha Thompson, daughter of Colonel William Thompson, of Blackwell's Neck, Hanover County, was a descendant of the Fleming and Douglass families and so came down from Margaret Stuart, and her ancestor, Robert Bruce, King of Scotland.

Beale-Gatewood and Bias Line

Margaret Skillern Beale, third child of Margaret Skillern and John Beale, married Warwick Gatewood, of Mountain Grove, Bath County, Virginia, son of William Gatewood, formerly of Essex County, Virginia, by his second wife, Jane Warwick. His maternal grandfather, Jacob Warwick, gave them the spring property on Elk River. They afterwards bought Belle Vue on Cowpasture River. Their daughter, Mary Catherine, was the second wife of Cesario Bias, his first wife being Mary Jane Gatewood, daughter of Jane Warwick and William Gatewood, who was the widow Kennedy when she married Bias.

Cesario Bias, when he was a small child, was the sole survivor of a wreck on the Atlantic Coast. The ship he was on came from Venice, Italy, and it is said that he was called Bias from the unusual bias cut of the clothes he wore, which were fashioned out of the finest material, causing the belief that he was of gentle birth. In his diary he stated that he first lived in Canada with Colonel Johnson. At the death of Colonel Johnson he was brought by Colonel Robert Nicholas to the Nicholas home in Albemarle County, and sent to school in Warren for six months. He then went to Staunton to join Colonel Nicholas, who was there on a recruiting party, and who placed him in a school for three years. After this term had expired, he went to the Academy. His education being completed, he secured a situation with Mr. Cowan in February, 1816. With Mr. Cowan and his sons Cesario Bias established trading stores, riding on horseback through Mississippi, Georgia, Alabama, Tennessee, and among other places through the Choctaw and Chickasaw Tribes of Indians.

It does not appear that Mr. Bias had any children by his first wife. His children by his second wife were:

1. Warwick Gatewood Bias, married Elizabeth M. Duncan.

2. Margaret Skillern Bias, married Robert Emmet Long, of Lynchburg.

3. Kate Eliza Bias, married Frank Cowan, of Tennessee, Presbyterian missionary to Brazil.

4. James Woods Warwick Bias, Presbyterian minister, died unmarried.

5. Lucy Plunkett Bias, died in childhood.

6. Mary Florence Bias, married Thomas Adams, of Lynchburg.

Cesario Bias bought the Red Sweet Springs, Alleghany County, Virginia. Two years before the close of the War Between the States the Springs were sold and the proceeds invested in Confederate bonds. For awhile the family lived in Fincastle, Virginia, and then bought a farm at Charlotte Courthouse. After the close of the War, they moved to Richmond, where in 1866 Mr. Bias died at the Valentine House, corner Ninth and Capitol Streets. Two years later Mrs. Bias moved from Richmond to Belle Vue, the property on Cowpasture River in Bath County, which she had inherited from her father, Warwick Gatewood. She died at Warwickton in 1874. She and her husband are buried at Warm Springs.

Children of Margaret Skillern Bias and Robert Emmet Long, of Amherst County:

1. Kate Gatewood Long, married Marvin Payne; died without issue, October 25th, 1819.

2. James Melchior Long, married Mary Claire Burton, November 12th, 1927.

3. Bessie Curl Long.
4. Edwin Long.
5. Margaret Cesario Long.

Children of Mary Florence Bias and Thomas Adams, of Lynchburg:

1. John Quincy Adams, married Hazel Kirk Moore.
2. Margaret Gatewood Adams, married Guy Harold Lewis, of Amherst County, Virginia.
3. Mary Catherine Adams, married Wallace Murray Elliot, of Augusta County, Virginia.
4. Rose Virginia Adams, married G. C. Coleman, of Rockbridge County, Virginia.
5. Florence Bias Adams.
6. Frances Cowan Adams.
7. Elizabeth Saunders Adams.
8. Thomas Cesario Adams, married Florence Hughes.

Bell

James Pinkney Bell was born in Caroline County, Virginia, November 18th, 1830. He died in Lynchburg, July 24th, 1911. When he was eighteen he left Caroline County and went into business in Fredericksburg. Later he worked in Baltimore and in Philadelphia, but finally settled in Lynchburg as his permanent place of residence. He lived here more than fifty years, and built up the successful book and printing business known today as the J. P. Bell Company, of which he was the head.

His first work on coming to Lynchburg was in connection with the Richmond Dispatch, the circulation of which was in his charge. During the War Between the States he was war correspondent of the Dispatch, and spent the four years of the War reporting news from the scene of battle to this paper. His letters from the battlefronts were published in the Dispatch, and offer an amazing account of those tragic events as told by an eye-witness. After the close of hostilities, he returned to Lynchburg and resumed his work here. He bought out a publishing house which had worked for the Confederate Government, and became thereby the owner of a very valuable collection of stamps, bonds, and important papers issued by the Confederacy, which some years ago were burned in a fire that destroyed the old place of business.

Mr. Bell was a very progressive and able man of business. Besides running his Lynchburg business he established the publishing house at Roanoke now known as the Stone Printing and Manufacturing Company, the Bell Book and Stationery Company at Richmond, and at one time published a weekly journal. He wrote and edited a book of great importance on the history of the Quakers in Virginia called Our Quaker Friends of Ye Olden Times. He himself came of a Quaker family, and his book is a valuable source of information to the genealogist. It goes back far into the eighteenth century, and gives authentic records and dates of many of the families which took a leading part in settling Lynchburg and the surrounding counties.

Mr. Bell was the son of James Bell and Catherine Terrell Bell, of Caroline County, and his mother was disowned by the Quakers for marrying outside the faith. Mr. Bell married twice, his first wife was Miss Susan Slagle, of Lynchburg, and his second wife was Miss Annie Pope Adams, of Fredericksburg, Virginia. There are three surviving children, Mrs. Lewis G. Bell, Mrs. Charles E. Busey, and Robert Otway Bell.

Bigbie

The Bigbie family came to Lynchburg from Pulaski. The late William Bigbie was the son of Augustine Bigbie and Mary Trevillo Bigbie, who was of Spanish descent.

The Blackford Family

For years Captain and Mrs. Charles Minor Blackford lived in the big brick house at the eastern corner of Pearl and Harrison Streets. Captain Blackford was a prominent and successful lawyer, and Mrs. Blackford, a lady of wit and cleverness, was a dominating figure in the social life of Lynchburg, where for many years she reigned an uncrowned queen. Mrs. Blackford was Susan Leigh Colston, the daughter of Thomas Marshall Colston and Elizabeth Josephine Fisher. Thomas Marshall Colston was the son of Raleigh Colston, of Honey Wood, Berkeley County, Virginia, and Elizabeth Marshall, the sister of Chief Justice John Marshall. The first of the Colstons to come to Virginia was William, a Royalist, the son of a great merchant, who warmly supported the Stuart cause, and was sheriff of Bristol. Mrs. Blackford was close kin to many of the prominent families of Virginia, and an aristocrat of the old school. The Blackford's house was for many years the gathering place of the best minds of Lynchburg. Here many distinguished visitors to the town were entertained and no woman was ever more fitted to fill a large position than Susan Colston Blackford, a woman of sound intellectual gifts, and a warm and generous heart.

The Blackford's sustained a great loss in the death of their only daughter, Nannie Colston, who married Samuel T. Withers, the son of Mr. Phillip Thornton Withers, February 6th, 1883, and died at the birth of her first child, February 8th, 1884. She was much beloved in Lynchburg, and adored by her parents. Charles Minor, Junior, left one son, Charles Minor; R. Colston died unmarried. Captain and Mrs. Blackford were fond of young people; they frequently had Mrs. Blackford's great-nieces, the Camms and the Howards, of Richmond, as their visitors, and finally Miss Gertrude Howard practically made her home with them. Miss Virginia Gildersleeve, another niece, who visited them in later years, won a great position as an educator of women. Miss Howard, who was much admired for her beauty, was married from the Blackford's home to Mr. Olmstead, member of Congress from Pennsylvania. This wedding, which was celebrated at Saint Paul's Church, was an important event in the social life of Lynchburg. Mr. Olmstead has been dead for several years, and his widow is now the wife of Mr. Vance McCormick, of Pennsylvania.

The Blackford family, though long residents of Lynchburg, were not natives of the town. They came first to New Jersey from Scotland, and in the early years were interested in the iron business. They were in Carlyle, Pennsylvania, and in Page County, Virginia, near Luray, where Mr. Benjamin Blackford, born in New Jersey, October 31st, 1767, built the Isabelle and the Caroline Furnaces. He married Isabelle Arthur. They had sons, who built other furnaces.

William Matthews Blackford, born at Catoctin Furnace, Frederick County, Maryland, in 1801, broke away from the family business and studied law. Later he went into newspaper work. After serving in New Granada on a diplomatic mission tendered him by President Tyler, he came to Lynchburg as editor of the Virginian. He became part owner of the paper, which was a Whig organ, and very flourishing. Mr. Blackford was regarded as one of the ablest editors in Virginia. In 1883 he sold out his interest in the paper, and was made cashier of the Exchange Bank, a position he held until his death in 1864, at the age of sixty-three years. He married Mary Berkeley Minor, daughter of Samuel John Minor, of Fredericksburg, October 12th, 1825. The sons of this marriage were: William Willis Blackford, born March 23rd, 1831, who was a brilliant soldier in J. E. B. Stuart's command. It was he who wrote that famous and oft-quoted account of General Lee at the surrender at Appomattox, his farewell to his soldiers, and his departure on Traveller. Charles Minor Blackford, born October 17th, 1833, of whom we have already written, died in Lynchburg, March 10th, 1903. Benjamin Lewis Blackford, born August 5th, 1835, practiced medicine in Lynchburg for many years. He succeeded Dr. Conrad as superintendent of the Asylum for the Insane at Staunton and died at Staunton, September 25th, 1908. Launcelot Minor Blackford, born February 27th, 1837, died at the Episcopal High School, Alexandria, Virginia, May 23rd, 1914. Eugene Blackford, born April 11th, 1839, died February 4th, 1908, in Pikesville, Maryland. Mary Isabella Blackford, born November 27th, 1840, married J. Churchill Cooke.

Bowman

Nathaniel Randolph Bowman died September 17th, 1905, after a long illness. He was born in Prince Edward County, January 16th, 1837, the son of James Taylor Bowman and Tabitha Lovelace. He came to Lynchburg at the age of sixteen, and served with the troops in the Confederate Army. After the close of the War, in 1867, he organized the N. R. Bowman Company to engage in the tobacco business. Mr. Bowman was married twice, his first wife being Miss Matilda Wilkes, of Bedford County. His second wife was Miss Annette Moore, daughter of Mr. Maurice Moore, of Lynchburg. Mrs. Bowman, who survived him, is now dead. His children were Walker Bowman, Mrs. Bransford Younger, Mrs. J. Thomas Gilliam, the late W. L. Bowman, Jr., C. M. Bowman, Miss Nettie Bowman and Miss Louise Bowman. Mr. Bowman's brother, Mr. William Lovelace Bowman, was also a prominent citizen of Lynchburg. He died some time ago. His daughter, Miss Willie Bowman, who was the superintendent of the Lynchburg Orphan Asylum for many years, where she accomplished an important and useful work, died February, 1933. Mr. Earnest Bowman, a son of William L. Bowman, also died several years ago.

Bragassa

The Bragassa family came to Lynchburg in 1858, where Frank Bragassa, and his wife, the pretty Josephine Grovo Bragassa, established a toy shop combined with a bakery and confectionery store. Lynchburg people, for several generations past, well remember Mrs. Bragassa in the store she presided over, at the corner of Twelfth and Court Streets, and her kindliness and patience in dispensing toys and taffy to little children, with now and then an extra stick of candy thrown in for good measure from a kind heart.

Bransford

The Bransfords were an old Lynchburg family, and were intermarried with the Tyree's, who built the famous old house, "Tyreanna." Elizabeth Bransford married Samuel W. Younger, and left a large family, now scattered. Samuel Bransford was killed at the Battle of Seven Pines. Rose Kent Bransford married William G. Gregory, son of James D. and Ann E. Williams Gregory. A member of the Tyree family, who lived in Lynchburg, was Samuel Tyree, for many years a prominent citizen here. He was in the real estate business with Mr. G. H. Wilkins, and the firm of Tyree and Wilkins still bears his name. His wife was Marion Fontaine, a descendant of Patrick Henry.

Breckenridge

Cary Breckenridge, Colonel Second Virginia Cavalry, C. S. A., of Fincastle, Virginia, died on May 11th, 1918. His surviving children are Mrs. John Easley, of Richmond; Miss Emma Cary Breckenridge; Dr. W. N. Breckenridge, of Fincastle; J. T. Breckenridge, of Lake Village, Arkansas; Henry C. Breckenridge, of Chicago; James Breckenridge, of Victoria, Virginia. His daughter, Emma Cary, was in France with the McGuire Unit at the time of his death.

Brown

Mr. Edward Smith Brown, father of Mr. J. Winston Ivey's first wife, and the grandfather of Miss Mary Winston Ivey, was an honored citizen of Lynchburg, and belonged to a very ancient English family. The first of this family of Browns to come to this country was Buckingham Browne, who arrived in Virginia with his wife, daughter, and mother on the 21st day of August, 1703, and settled in Essex County, on a large tract of land granted him by the king. Buckingham Browne was the son of Clement Brown and Mary Glebe Brown. Mary Glebe was the daughter of William Glebe, and was baptized January 4th, 1644. She died February 8th, 1732.

Buckingham Browne was born in England, January 31st, 1671-72, and died February 1st, 1734-35, on his plantation in Essex. He married Elizabeth Mestich on April 21st, 1700, at Radnall Church, Havelstone, England. He had nine children; of these, James, was born in Essex County, Virginia, and was baptized in the Parish Church of Saint Anne by Senor Garzia, October 13th, 1726; he died August 6th, 1814. He married Mary Spearman, the daughter of Job Spearman. She was born November 13th, 1730, and died August 6th, 1823. She had eight children, among them Daniel, who was born May 26th, 1776, and died May 28th, 1863. He was a planter, and lived in Cumberland County at first, but later moved to Powhatan County. He married Nancy Hobson Walton, the daughter of Robert Walton, and Mary Hobson, his wife. Robert Walton was a soldier of the Revolution, and served from the beginning of the war until the end. Daniel and his wife, Nancy, had eight children, the fourth being Edward Smith Brown, who was born in Cumberland County, April 7th, 1818, and died January 3rd, 1908.

The family of Edward Smith Brown belonged to that fine old stock which was really the English landed gentry transplanted to Virginia soil. They were people of strong character, and fine intellectual gifts. Edward Smith Brown assisted in the business of running the farm and went to the best schools Cumberland County afforded. Later he went to Randolph-Macon, and was among the first graduates of that school. He was admitted to the bar in the early forties, practicing his profession in Cumberland and in other counties of Virginia and acquiring a high reputation for legal ability. In 1866 he moved to Lynchburg, and shortly afterwards formed a partnership with Charles L. Mosby, one of the ablest and most accomplished lawyers in the history of the State. Mr. Mosby was in failing health, being much older than Mr. Brown, and during the last ten years of their partnership, which only terminated with the death of Mr. Mosby, he rarely came to the office. This firm, of which William C. Ivey was a partner for a time, stood very high in legal and business circles, and took a leading part in the important litigation of Lynchburg and the surrounding country. Cases in chancery were more congenial to Mr. Brown's particular ability than the contests of the lower courts, and it is said he carried to the Court of Appeals every case he had that was not decided to suit him in the inferior courts. Certainly his cases had great success in that stately forum. In the long and complex legal battles growing out of the will of Samuel Miller, and the settlement of his great estate, the work of this firm was notable.

Mr. Brown spent an enormous amount of labor in the preparation of his cases, not sparing himself day or night. With persistent and tireless effort he would examine every phase of his cause, and every question that would suggest itself to his mind as likely to arise. He would also try to get the opinions rendered in similar cases in Europe and America wherever cases of a like nature had been tried. He would visit Washington and Richmond, and spend days searching the large law libraries for authorities to sustain his contentions. No drudgery of detail, no legal complication, no forbidding array of facts and figures ever turned him aside in his effort to help his client.

His tenacity of purpose was shown in the long, hard struggle he put up in his effort to gain some return from the Federal Government for property he had owned in the State of Kansas which had been confiscated during the War Between the States as belonging to an alien enemy. Knowing that the proceeds of his property had been appropriated by corrupt Federal marshals in collusion with corrupt judges, many of whom still held authority and influence, he went fearlessly to work to prove this in a hostile court, waging for years his unequal contest. Several appeals were taken by him to the Supreme Court of the United States, and through him articles of impeachment were presented by the House of Representatives against a judge of the United States Court in Kansas, charging bribery, corruption, and high misdemeanors in office. Mr. Brown was one of the chief witnesses against this judge, who was forced to resign his office.

Mr. Brown joined the Methodist Church early in life, and was a member of the Court Street Church. He was a devoted student of the Bible, and had a large class which he would never consent to give up, in spite of the feebleness of old age. Almost to the day of his death he was preparing legal documents, and engaging in Biblical research. He was a great student, a profound thinker, and withal the most lovable of men, righteous, charitable and kind. In his last years it was discovered by accident that he was spending some of his spare moments in giving instructions in Latin to a young Catholic who was preparing himself to become a priest. Mr. Edward Smith Brown, from his love of simplicity dropped the *e* from his name, which was originally Browne. He was always helpful and approachable, and there was none of that dry as dust quality of the student and thinker about him, for he was no mere bookworm but a man of warmth and imagination. As an example of the feeling and color of his mind, there is elsewhere quoted in this book his appreciation of the life and character of Samuel Miller, which shows his exquisite understanding and sympathy with a nature so foreign to his own. No man in Lynchburg was more beloved than Edward Smith Brown and he left a blessed memory.

Mr. Brown was married in 1845 to Jane Margaret Winfree, a union of two people of noble qualities entirely suited to each other. In their early married life they lived at Sunnyside, an attractive country seat a few miles below Cumberland Courthouse, which before the War Between the States was one of the most prosperous, and one of the largest slaveholding counties of the State. Their children were:

Cornelia Walton, born April 6th, 1846. She died unmarried in 1926, a few years after the death of her parents. She was a poet, and wrote some lovely verse.

Mary Virginia, born January 9th, 1849, who was married November 5th, 1867, to John Winston Ivey, son of Peter and Sallie Lawson Ivey. Anne, born October 7th, 1856.

Mrs. Brown's mother, Cornelia Myer Tilden, was the second wife of Mr. Christopher Winfree, the son of Valentine and Lucy Cheatham Winfree, of Chesterfield County. Mr. Christopher Winfree's first wife was Miss Polly Warwick, the daughter of Mr. William Warwick, and by this marriage he had three daughters. Mrs. Brown's mother was from Pennsylvania, and descended from the Tildens, the MacCalmonts and the Chambers of that State, and the Pells and the Van Tuyls, of New York. The Van Tuyls belonged to the old Patroons, and were descended from one Van Tuyl, a Dutch ship owner who with his little ship and one brass cannon fought a Spanish privateer with fifteen mounted guns. He sank the great Spanish galleon, and hung all the pirates.

The Tildens were descended from one John Bell Tilden, born in Pennsylvania in 1761, died in 1838, who left Princeton to join the Continental Army about 1779, and was made an ensign. He was present at the surrender of Cornwallis at Yorktown, and his diary, which has been published, gives details of the siege of Yorktown and an account of the hospitality of Westover. He was detailed to receive the arms of the British soldiers as they surrendered. He served until the end of the Revolutionary War, was a member of the Society of Cincinnati, and died in Stephens City, which is a few miles from Winchester, Virginia, in 1838.

It is believed by the writer that Mr. J. Winston Ivey was a near kinsman of William Ivey, a distinguished naval officer in the Revolutionary War. He was born at Sycamore View on Tanner's Creek, Norfolk County, Virginia, which estate he inherited from his father. He was brought up to the sea, and built vessels at his own cost. He suffered much from British depredations; the houses on both his estates were plundered and burned, and his slaves carried away. He joined the Virginia Navy, and September 2nd, 1776, was second lieutenant on the sloop "Scorpion," under Captain Wright Westcott. In this ship he cruised until January, 1777, when he was made first lieutenant of the "Liberty." Later he was promoted to captain, and placed on duty to recruit men for the navy. His last appointment was to the command of the "Liberty," with which he did good service until he died late in 1777, or early in 1778.

Brown

Mrs. Flora A. Brown, age seventy-two years, the widow of Martin L. Brown, Senior, died April 4th, 1918. Mrs. Brown, a native of Amherst, was the daughter of Anderson Higginbotham. She lived in Lynchburg many years, and was survived by the following children: James R. Brown, of Bluefield, West Virginia; William T. Brown, of Richmond; Martin L. Brown, Walter W. Brown, Mrs. J. W. Coleman, and Miss Lottie K. Brown, of Lynchburg, and Mrs. James Spracher, of Graham, West Virginia.

Burks

Colonel Richard Burks was one of those defenders of Lynchburg to whom the City Council voted its appreciation and gratitude after Hunter's efforts to capture the town. Colonel Burks was a large landowner in Rockbridge County. He sold his property and moved to Lynchburg after the War Between the States. He was in appearance the ideal cavalry officer: very tall, with broad shoulders, small waist, flashing black eyes, and face bronzed by out door life. Even as an old man he still retained his striking figure and appearance. He married Sue Yuille, of Campbell County, and of his surviving children Lawrence Burks lives in Lynchburg, Andrew in Birmingham, Alabama, and Jesse in Dothan, Alabama. His daughters: Mrs. Jennie Williams, a musician of rare talent, Mrs. Nina McCorkle and Mrs. Blanche Nowlin, are now dead. Mrs. Nowlin was killed in a recent automobile accident in Houston, Texas. She left two children, J. C. Nowlin, Junior, and Miss Preston Nowlin.

Beverley Burks, son of Richard Burks, Junior, and grandson of Colonel Burks, served overseas in the World War and captured single-handed twelve German soldiers, but as he was marching them in he was surprised and killed by one of the captured Germans, who had a pistol concealed about him.

Burton

The Burton family and their connections in Lynchburg are wide and numerous. The family is descended from the Burtons of Shropshire, England, the present seat of the family being Longnar Hall, near Shrewsbury, County Salop. The name Burton is derived from an old Saxon word, meaning a fortified place, or fort.

    Arms: Per Pale Az. and a cross engralled or between four roses ar.

    Crest: A dexter gauntlet couped at the wrist ppr.

    Motto: Dominus Providebit.

The Burtons trace their line back to Bretagne, where, in the year 1050, one William, son of Roald was Vicount of Nantes. A member of this family came to England with William the Conqueror. Sir Edward Burton, a descendant, was knighted for valor, in 1460, and acquired the estate of Longnar, under Edward IV, of England.

Some of the Burton family came to Virginia as early as 1635. Jesse Burton, ancestor of most of the Burton descendants in Lynchburg, and one of the trustees of the town when it was laid out, was the son of Hutchins Burton and Susannah Allen Burton. He moved to Mecklenburg County from Henrico, where Robert Burton, his father, who married Rachel Hutchins, was constable in 1686. Jesse Burton purchased land in Bedford County from Thomas Jefferson. The land was part of the Forest tract, situated on the border line between Campbell and Bedford Counties, and he called the estate The Oaks. He married Ann Hudson, whose father was a cousin of Henry Clay, and died about 1795, leaving five sons and three daughters. Jesse Burton belonged to the twenty-first generation from the first of the line recorded: one Thomas de Burton, who married Alicia, daughter of Lord Codarcote, in the reign of Henry III, of England.

Many prominent families of Lynchburg and this neighborhood are descended from Jesse Burton and his wife. Their children were:

1. Alexander, married in Bedford; his wife's name unknown to us. Had Jesse, who married and had Gustavus Adolphus, and was the father of Waddy Burton, of Bedford County.

2. William, died unmarried.

3. Robert, lived at Warren in Albemarle County. Was a doctor. Married Mary Elizabeth Powell, daughter of Wyatt and Sally (Floyd) Powell, and the granddaughter of Richard Powell.

4. Jesse, married Elizabeth Norvell.

5. John Hudson, married Margaret Macon.

6. Nancy, married Major (War of 1812) Joel Yancey, of Campbell, later of Bedford.

7. Patsey (Martha), married William Irvine.

8. Sally, married Samuel Jordan Harrison.

The children of Dr. Robert Burton, of Warren, Albemarle County, and Elizabeth (Powell) Burton, were: (a) Addison Burton, (b) Maria Burton. (a) Addison married a Miss Cobbs, of Buckingham County, and had Lucy, who married William Norvell, of Buckingham County; also Ann, Robert and Hudson. (b) Maria married John L. Marye, of Fredericksburg, and had James Braxton, Robert, John L., Lawrence S., Morton, Stewart, Nannie and Evelyn. Her son, Colonel Lawrence S. Marye, lived in Lynchburg for many years. He was a talented writer, and connected with various newspapers. He had no children. His wife conducted a fashionable school for girls on Court Street, as described elsewhere in this book.

John Hudson Burton married Margaret Macon, the daughter of John Macon, of Cumberland County, a descendant of Gideon Macon and a near relation of Martha Washington. John Macon's wife was Grace Cowan, whose other daughter, Elizabeth Macon, was the second wife of Major Joel Yancey, after the death of Nancy Burton Yancey.

The children of John Hudson Burton and Margaret (Peggy) Macon: (a) John, died unmarried. (b) Jesse Alexander, married Damaris Cobbs. (c) Robert Oswald, married Elizabeth Joyner, of North Carolina. (d) Edward Johnson, married Mary Patteson. (e) Grace Ann, married Dr. J. H. Patteson. (f) Virginia, died unmarried. (g) Margaret Macon, died unmarried. (h) Cornelia, married Edward D. Christian. (i) Martha Eliza, married Thomas Poindexter, of Bedford County. (j) Katharine, died unmarried.

Children of Jesse Alexander and Damaris Cobbs Burton, daughter of John Lewis and Susan Hamner Cobbs: Susan Hamner Burton, married James Bowker Nowlin, son of Elizabeth Preston and Matthew Bates Nowlin. They had: Charles Price Nowlin, Virginia Susan Nowlin, John Burton Nowlin and Jesse Graham Nowlin. Dr. John Burton Nowlin, born July 23rd, 1873, married Roberta Ellis Hall, daughter of Thomas and Nannie Ellis Hall, of Buckingham County. Their children are: George Preston Nowlin, who is a doctor, practicing in Lynchburg, and Ellis St. George Tucker Nowlin, who married Mr. Cosby. Jesse Graham Nowlin, unmarried, is a city official in the Chamber of Commerce. Edward Johnson Burton, son of John Hudson Burton, married Mary Patteson. They had: Samuel, Edward Hudson, William Cowan, Lawrence Reveley, Isabel Grace, Margaret Macon, and Gabriella Terrel. Lawrence Reveley Burton married Carrie Rumbough, and had one child, Mary Claire, who married James Melchior Long, November 12th, 1927. (For Long, see Beale ancestry.)

Children of Dr. J. H. Patteson and Grace Ann Burton Patteson: James, married Caroline Brown. Macon B. Patteson, married Ella Frances Corling. Had one daughter, Mary, who married Giles Miller. Samuel Patteson, married, first, Henrietta Rucker; second, Victoria Rucker. Had three children: Lucy, who married Frank West; Henrietta, who married Henry O. White, and Thomas R., unmarried.

The children of James Patteson and Caroline Brown Patteson: Caroline, married Dr. Gilkyson. Mary Grace, married Ashby Perry. Ida Thompson, married Austin E. Bellew. James M. Patteson, Junior, married Helen Woodward. Lewis Randolph Patteson, married Garnett Betty Stafford.

Cornelia Burton, daughter of John Hudson Burton and Peggy Macon Burton, married Edward D. Christian and had the following children: Dudley, died unmarried. Frank Patteson, married Mary Lou Dearing, descendant of John Lynch. Children: Dearing, who married Percy Handy; Lynch, Frank P., Junior, Harrison and Cornelia, who married Claiborne Gooch, Junior.

John H. Christian, married Minnie Hass. Children: Muriel, married Pegram Johnson, of Richmond; Isabel, married Dr. Joseph Hume, of Norfolk; Talfourd, Hallam.

Elizabeth Christian, married Lucian Sneed. No issue.

W. Asbury Christian, minister in the Methodist Church, married Anne McMullen, daughter of Judge McMullen, of Madison, Virginia. Mr. Christian is the author of a most excellent history of Lynchburg.

Martha Ann Burton, daughter of John Hudson Burton, married Thomas Poindexter, of Bedford County. Her daughter, Sallie Ragland Poindexter, married Captain Thomas West, of West's Crossing. Josephine West, married Edward Brockenborough. Dr. Thomas West, married Sallie Ford. Margaret Burton Poindexter, married William Fox Moore. Her son, William Moore, married Alice Preston. Her daughter, Elizabeth, married Frederick Mitchell.

Martha, nicknamed Patsey, the seventh child of Jesse Burton and his wife, married William Ervine, son of William Ervine and Elizabeth Anthony. They lived in Campbell County, and had twelve children, one of these dying in infancy. The children were: William, Jesse, Nancy, Mary, Betsey, Alexander, Edmund, Robert, James, Addison and Juliet.

William Irvine, married Anne Lewis, and had six children: Jesse Irvine, married Clementina Cabell, daughter of Colonel William Cabell, of Union Hill, Nelson County. Their daughter, Mary Eliza, married Phillip D. Christian, of Lynchburg, and had six children. Margaret Frances, married Thomas Rosser, of Campbell, and their daughter, Eliza, married Mr. Faulconer, and had several children. She now lives in Lynchburg with her son, Worthington Faulconer. Mary Irvine, daughter of William and Martha Burton Irvine, married Dr. Paul Cabell, son of Colonel William Cabell. She had four children: Dr. Irvine Cabell, who died unmarried; Anne, Sallie and Paul Carrington. Paul Carrington, married, first, Nannie Rose, of the distinguished Rose family. Their daughter, Rose Cabell, was the first wife of John L. Lee, a quite noted criminal lawyer of Lynchburg. Paul C. Cabell's second wife was Miss Lou Mundy, who had three children: Guy, Mayo and Louise Cabell.

Anne Cabell, married Robert J. Davis, of Lynchburg, son of Henry Davis, and had seven children: Mary, Sallie, Nannie, Paul, Lucy, Robert and William. Of these Mary, Paul and Robert are now dead. William lives in Roanoke. He married Julia Gregory, daughter of Mr. James Gregory of this city, and has one living child, Nell Gregory. Linn Cabell died in infancy.

Sallie Cabell, married Mr. Edgar Whitehead, of Amherst, and had two children, Cabell and Robert. Cabell, married Bena Ayres and is now dead. Robert, married Fannie Vogbaum, and has children.

Dr. Alexander Irvine, son of William Irvine and Martha Burton Irvine, married Lockie Brown, had eight children, seven of these being sons. His oldest son, Dr. William Irvine, married Miss Anna St. Clair, of Charleston, South Carolina, and had eight children. Their son, Dr. St. Clair Irvine, practices medicine at Evington, in Campbell County. He married Evelyn Saunders, daughter of Captain Robert Saunders, C. S. A. They have several children, among them William, recently elected to the Virginia Assembly as representative from Campbell County.

Sarah Hudson Burton, youngest child of Jesse Burton, married Samuel Jordan Harrison. Among their fourteen children was Anne Maria, who married William Wyatt Norvell, of Lynchburg, and had two daughters, Emmeline and Anne. Emmeline Norvell, married James Maurice Langhorne, son of Colonel Maurice Langhorne, and had Anne, who married William Nelson Wellford, and had Emma Norvell, James Langhorne, William Nelson, Francis Corbin and Norvell Warren. Emma, married Jason Dexter Hobbie, and lives in Roanoke.

Ann Norvell, the other daughter of William Wyatt Norvell, married Colonel Winston Radford, C. S. A., of Bedford County. He was killed at the first Battle of Manassas. His children were: Emma, married Mr. Chalmers, and had Emma Norvell, who married Waller G. Wills, of Lynchburg, and had Emma Norvell, Waller and Chalmers. Mrs. Wills died in 1933. Fannie Chalmers, married Waller Jameson, of Roanoke. Wilhemina, daughter of Winston Radford and his wife, Ann Norvell, married Rev. Arthur P. Gray, of Amherst, and left children. Winston, married Lucy Chamberlayne, and left children.

Lucy Harrison, another daughter of Samuel Harrison, married Lorenzo Norvell. She was born in 1813, married in 1831. Her children were: Edward, Robert, Charles, Mary Elizabeth and Lucy Harrison.

Mary Elizabeth, married John M. Miller, of Lynchburg. Their children were: Edgar P. Miller, James Ball Miller, John M. Miller, Junior, Lucy Harrison Miller and Mary Norvell Miller. Of these James Ball died when a young man.

Edgar P. Miller, married Elinor Luke, and has two daughters, Elinor and Lucy Harrison.

John M. Miller, Junior, married Nannie, daughter of Peter J. Otey. Mr. Miller is now a prominent banker of Richmond, and has a large family.

Mary Norvell Miller, married Daniel Allen Payne, and has several children. Of these Elizabeth, married Nelson Carter, and Mary Norvell, married Victor Millner.

Lucy Harrison Norvell, daughter of Lorenzo Norvell and Lucy Harrison, married Frank T. Lee. Her children were: Norvell, Frank T., Junior, Mary and John. Mary, married Arthur Jennings, of Lynchburg.

Jesse Burton, the second child of Sarah and Samuel J. Harrison, became private secretary to Jefferson Davis, President C. S. A. He married Constance Cary, daughter of Archibald Cary and Monimia Fairfax, his wife.

BUSEY

Charles Edgar Busey, D.D.S., M.D., was born in Washington, District of Columbia, October 4th, 1853, and died in Lynchburg, April 5th, 1925. He was the son of Rev. Thomas Henry Busey, of Cumberland County, Maryland, a minister in the Methodist Episcopal Church, who served the churches in Washington for many years. Dr. Busey's mother was Sarah Neely McClannahan Busey, a member of a prominent Roanoke family. Dr. Busey was educated in Baltimore, and studied medicine at the University of Maryland and in New York City. He practiced his profession in Baltimore for some time, but in the early eighties he came to Lynchburg, where he became active in public affairs. Dr. Busey was of great assistance in the organization of the Memorial Hospital, then called the Home and Retreat. He was coroner and city physician for a number of years, and an active promoter in Red Cross work during the World War.

Dr. Busey possessed a cultivated taste for music, and, having a well-trained voice of fine quality, he was deeply interested in the development of higher appreciation of music in Lynchburg. The Mozart Association, and the Concordia Glee Club, of Lynchburg, which were so ably directed by Professor Louis Schehlmann, found in him an ardent and generous supporter. Dr. Busey married Rosa Terrell Bell, daughter of late James Pinkney Bell. Their children are: Mrs. E. Wentworth Thompson, Annapolis, Maryland; Miss Rosa Godey Busey, Lynchburg, Virginia; Mrs. William Wade Hinshaw, Junior, Chicago, Illinois.

CABINESS

Miss Judson Cabiness lived to be an old lady in her home on Court Street. She was little and French in manner and gesture. Even after her hair had turned white, a rose at her throat, or a bright piece of jewelry always attested the Gallic strain in her blood.

LYNCHBURG AND ITS NEIGHBORS

CALHOUN

Captain Charles Alexander Calhoun was born in Franklin County, Virginia, in 1822. He moved to Lynchburg as a young man, and worked for John Davis, later going into the hardware business with Fred Wills. Ten years before the War Between the States he entered into a partnership to purchase Alleghany Springs, and being chosen manager of the Springs he made his residence there. He served in the War with the rank of captain. After surrender, he returned to Alleghany Springs, and in a few years built it up into one of the most popular resorts of the South. The hotel was burned down in 1899, and since then it has only been opened in a small way for the benefit of a few friends and relatives. Mr. Calhoun married Miss Jennie Wills, of Nelson County. He died in February, 1906, being survived by Charles R., William H., E. D. Calhoun, of Christiansburg, and Miss Annie W. Calhoun. A brother, C. A. Calhoun, married Miss Rose Dudley, a daughter of Mr. Peter Dudley, of Lynchburg, and his two sons, Dudley Calhoun and Charles Calhoun, lived here.

CAMM

John Camm, who left descendants now living in Lynchburg and Amherst, was the last colonial president of William and Mary College, the last rector of Bruton Parish Church as the head of Established Church of England, and the last commissioner to Virginia, appointed by the Archbishop of Canterbury. John Camm was the son of Thomas Camm, of Hornsea, on the North Sea, East Riding, Yorkshire, England. He was born at Hornsea in 1718, educated at Beverly, near Hornsea; admitted to Trinity College, Cambridge, June 16, 1738; elected to a scholarship, April 10, 1741, and took his B.A. in 1741-42. Eleven years later he was professor of divinity at William and Mary College in Virginia, having entered this office August 24, 1749, where the records of the Faculty at William and Mary listed him as Master of Arts. From this time he took a leading part in public affairs, particularly those pertaining to the Church. Many of his letters and speeches in the controversy between the clergy and the government over the Two Penny Act have been published. By championing the cause of the clergy in this controversy regarding the payment of their salaries, he made a violent enemy of Governor Faquier.

John Camm married at the age of fifty-one, and lost his professorship on account of a rule in the college that only the president could marry. Later he was made president of William and Mary himself, and head of the Church in Virginia. But Camm was loyal to the English government and an ardent Tory, and when he went up into the pulpit at Bruton Church the students of William and Mary threw rotten eggs at him. He had been made a member of the Council in 1775, and later, in 1777, with the Revolution well under way, he was removed from the presidency. Two years later he died at Half Way House, the property of his wife's people. His wife was Betsy Hansford, whom he had baptized as an infant. She was descended from Captain Charles Hansford, the brother of Colonel Thomas Hansford, who was executed for taking part in Bacon's Rebellion.

The first of the Hansford family who came to Virginia was John Hansford, who was either the son or the nephew of Sir Humphrey Hansford. John Hansford died before Thomas reached his majority and left a goodly estate to his two sons, Charles and Thomas, which included the tavern Half Way House. The widow of John was married a second time to Edward Lockey, one of the wealthiest men in the colony.

The Virginia Historical Collection, Number XI, contains the full history of the Hansford family. According to Campbell's History of Virginia, after Nathaniel Bacon died Colonel Thomas Hansford and some twenty soldiers were captured at the house where Colonel Reade had lived, which appears to have been at or near where Yorktown now stands. Hansford was taken to Accomac, tried, and condemned to be hanged, and was the first native of Virginia that perished in that ignominious form, and in America the first martyr that fell in defending the rights of the people. He was described by Sir William Berkeley as one Hansford, a valiant stout man, and a most resolved rebel. When he came to the place of execution, distant about a mile from the place of confinement, he appeared well resolved to bear his fate, complaining only of the manner of his death. Neither during his trial before the court-martial, nor afterwards, did he supplicate any favor, save that "he might be shot like a soldier and not hanged like a dog"; but he was told that he was condemned not as a soldier but as a rebel. During the short respite allowed him after his sentence, he professed repentence and contrition for all the sins of his past life, but refused to acknowledge what was charged against him as rebellion, to be one of his sins; desiring the people present to take notice that "he died a loyal subject and lover of his country, and that he had never taken up arms but for the destruction of the Indians who had murdered so many Christians." His execution took place on the 13th of November, 1676.

Captain Charles Hansford, the brother of Colonel Thomas Hansford, married Elizabeth, the widow of Josias Moody or Modé. Before her first marriage she was Elizabeth Folliott, daughter of Rev. Edward Folliott, and the granddaughter of Sir John Folliott and his wife, Elizabeth Aylmer, the daughter of John Aylmer, Bishop of London. According to the Encyclopedia Brittanica, John Aylmer was born at Aylmer Hall, Parish of Tilney, Norfolk County, England, in 1521. He was one of the most learned men of this day, and was tutor to Lady Jane Gray. After her execution, and the accession of Mary Tudor to the throne, John Aylmer was obliged to fly to Switzerland, for he staunchly opposed the return of the Catholic religion to England. When Elizabeth became queen he went back to England, and was consecrated Bishop of London in 1576. He died in 1794 at the age of seventy-three.

There were two John Camms in Virginia, one was president of William and Mary, and the other was sheriff of King and

Queen County. In later years there was some confusion among the heirs of the sheriff and of Samuel Garlick, who thought they were descended from John Camm, the president of William and Mary, as related by Mr. Tyler in the William and Mary Quarterly. The matter was finally set right by Mrs. John B. Minor.

John Camm left two daughters and three sons. Eliza Camm married George Blow, of Norfolk. Nancy Camm, married Robert Waller, Clerk of York County. Nancy did not live many years, and Robert Waller was married a second time to the widow Crawford, but his children were the children of Nancy Camm, as his second wife had no children. Thomas Camm was a preacher and married Elizabeth Pescud. Their son, Dr. Edward Camm, married Elizabeth Massenburg, of Hampton. They were the parents of John Camm, who came to Lynchburg and married the widow Jellis, Govan Camm, who married Margaret White, Frank Camm, who was a doctor and practiced medicine here, and Florence Camm, who married Mr. Turpin. Robert Camm was drowned when a youth.

John Camm, Junior, son of President Camm, of William and Mary, was born December 2nd, 1775. He studied law and moved to Amherst, where he was clerk of the court from 1814 until his death in 1818. He married Elizabeth Powell, daughter of Thomas Powell, called "Gentleman Tom," to distinguish him from a shoemaker living in the same town, and Sarah Thomas Powell. Mrs. Camm died January 25th, 1867. She lived near Elon, and her home is still standing. Her daughters were: Nancy, who married Jack Anderson; no children. Sallie, who married Benjamin Donald, of Otterburn; no children. Emma, died unmarried. Elizabeth, married Dr. David Patteson, of Buckingham, and has many descendants, among them Dr. David Patteson Scott, of Lynchburg. Mary Camm, married William Leftwich Saunders, and left many descendants. Robert Camm, or Robin, as he was called, her only son, married Olivia Alexander, of a well-known Campbell County family. They had one son, Robin Camm. He was a distinguished soldier,

Mrs. William Leftwich Saunders
Her maiden name was Mary Camm. The daughter of John Camm, Jr., and the granddaughter of John Camm, president of William and Mary College, and rector of Bruton Church.

and lost an arm in the Confederate service, where he won the rank of lieutenant-colonel. The elder Robin Camm died early, and his wife, Olivia Alexander Camm, was married a second time to Mr. Edward T. Page, of Richmond. Colonel Robin Camm, married Anne Colston, daughter of Colonel Raleigh Colston. They had three children, Robert Camm, Gertrude, and Anne Leigh, who married Mr. Reid Hobson, of Richmond.

The Camm arms, as used in John Camm's book-plate: Or a cross engrailed gu in the first quarter a crescent of the last.

Mary Camm, who married William Leftwich Saunders, son of Colonel David Saunders, of Bedford County, and Lockey Leftwich Saunders, left the following descendants: Mary Elizabeth, married John Quincy Adams; Lelia, married Joseph Winston, of Richmond; Roberta, married Charles Ellis, of Amherst; Pattisonia, never married; Emma, married Captain Stephen Adams, C. S. A.; Atala Waller, married William Jackson (no children); Thomas; William, married Columbia Swann (no children; Robert was killed in the War Between the States; John went West, was a Forty Niner in the gold rush to California and settled near Austin, Texas, and married there.

Children of John: Louise, who married Mr. Bacon; Eugene.

Children of Thomas: Belle, married Major Black, surgeon in the World War; Alma, Charles.

Children of Emma and Captain Stephen Adams: John Adams, lives in Grand Rapids, Michigan; Peter Adams, unmarried; Emma Adams, unmarried; William Saunders Adams, married Grace Kinckle, and has one daughter, Grace, who married Edward Hutter, is the author of distinguished work on psychology.

Children of Roberta and Charles Ellis: William Ellis, married, the first time, Miss Pendleton, and had two children, Charles and William, Junior. Charles, died unmarried; Josias, an Episcopal minister, married Lily Warren, and had children. Mary, married George Payne; no children. Thomas Ellis, married Carrie Barbour. Charles Ellis, died unmarried. Pattie Ellis, married Mr. Jackson, lives in Tazewell, and has children. Lucy Ellis, married Paulus Garland, a lawyer of Amherst; Paul, died unmarried; Felda, married Mr. Wales; Will, is unmarried; Louise, married Dr. Samuel Wilson, of Lynchburg, and has one daughter. Nannie Ellis, married Mr. Hall, of Buckingham; she has several children, among them Roberta Hall, the wife of Dr. Burton Nowlin, of this city; Emma Ellis, married her cousin, Warwick Saunders, and left several children.

Lelia Saunders, the daughter of Mr. and Mrs. William L. Saunders, married Joseph Pendleton Winston, son of Joseph Bickerton Winston and Sarah Madison Pendleton. Lelia Saunders was Mr. Winston's second wife. His first wife, Virginia Bell Pankey, with some of her children, was killed in Richmond, June 19th, 1852, in an uprising of her husband's slaves. Lelia Saunders was born in Lynchburg, December 8th, 1828, and died at Anchorage, Kentucky, February 5th, 1910. Her children were as follows: Donald Winston, born January 29th, 1855, died unmarried. Lelia Winston (called Lily), born in Richmond, October 28th, 1856; died July 29th, 1885; married July 18th, 1877, to Louis Meriwether Griffin, of Richmond. Bernard Winston, born in Richmond, December 19th, 1857; died August 8th, 1894. John Camm Winston, born in Richmond, August 1st, 1861; died August 8th, 1894. Rosalie Winston, married December 12th, 1893, to Arthur Middleton Rutledge II, son of Arthur Middleton Rutledge I and his wife, Gight Underwood, daughter of Judge Joseph Rodgers Underwood, of Kentucky. She lives at Anchorage, Kentucky. Joseph Winston, born in Richmond, married Susan Wilson Dabney. Harry Bickerton Winston died in 1898. Philip O. Winston died in 1891.

Mary Elizabeth Saunders, oldest daughter of Mr. and Mrs. William L. Saunders, married John Quincy Adams, a native of Goochland County. Rosa Adams, married John W. Faulkner, born in Winchester, Virginia. Their children are: William Saunders Faulkner, retired colonel, U. S. A., who married Nancy Welsh, of San Antonio, Texas, and lives in San Antonio. Julia

Frederick Faulkner, married Maximilian I. T. Driver, and has one son, Leopold, who married Anne Wright, of Centreville, Maryland. They have one child, Anne, and live in Philadelphia. John Adams Faulkner, married Marian Tucker Clark, daughter of Dr. A. I. Clark, of Lynchburg, and has three daughters, Anne, Rosalie and Nina. Mary Elizabeth Faulkner, married Alfred Boyd Percy, and has two sons, Alfred, Junior, and John Tucker. Alfred B. Percy, Junior, married Margaret Truehart, of New York. Rosa Adams Faulkner, married Robert Davis Yancey, son of William Tudor Yancey and his wife, Lucy Elizabeth Davis; their children are: Elizabeth Davis Yancey, married Victor Pleasants Abernathy, and died October 13th, 1929, leaving one son, Robert Mastin Abernathy. Rebecca, married Dr. John Bell Williams, of Richmond, Va., son of Judge Samuel Walker Williams, of Wytheville, and has one son, Martin Tudor Hansford Williams. Robert Davis Yancey, Junior, married Elizabeth White, and has three children, Robert White, Nancy Faulkner and Rose Anne Yancey. The fourth child of Robert D. Yancey, Senior, and Rosa Faulkner Yancey, Rosa Adams Yancey, died in infancy. Mary Saunders Yancey, Caroline Anthony Yancey, Henry Davis Yancey are unmarried. Joel Tudor Yancey, graduate of West Point Military Academy, first lieutenant, U. S. A., married Elizabeth Heard, daughter of Alexander Denny Heard, of Jersey City, and has one child, Joel Alexander Yancey. Hamilton Faulkner, youngest child of Mr. and Mrs. J. W. Faulkner, lived in Washington. He married Margaret Campbell. Died June, 1934.

The oldest son of Mr. and Mrs. John Q. Adams, William Saunders Adams, never married. John Q. Adams, Junior, Hubert Preston Adams, Robert Camm Adams, Frank Adams, and Ashby Adams, died unmarried. Thomas Adams, married Florence Bias, and their children are given in the Beale family history, Mrs. Adams being a descendant of Tavener Beale.

The Carrington Family

The Carrington family, prominent in Virginia for many generations, are descended from Paul Carrington, a large shipping merchant of the Barbadoes, who came to Virginia early in the eighteenth century. His son, George, married Anne Mayo, daughter of Major William Mayo. Colonel George Carrington soon rose to prominence in Cumberland County, where he made his home. He was the father of Colonel Edward Carrington, the friend of Washington, and the ancestor of many of Virginia's most valuable and valued citizens. Among his descendants, several of whom have made their home in Lynchburg, is Mr. Randolph Carrington. He came to Lynchburg as a very young man, married and made his home here. He was the son of the Honorable Henry C. Carrington, of Charlotte County. His sister, Mrs. Sidney Stevens, now living in New York, once lived here. His brother, the late Mr. William Carrington, married Miss Carrie Lee Davis, daughter of Mr. Thomas N. Davis, of this city.

Carroll

John Wesley Carroll was born at Staunton, Augusta County, Virginia, March 3rd, 1832, son of Jacob T. and Isabel Layman Carroll. His father was a native of Virginia, a planter by occupation. His mother was a daughter of Daniel Layman, of Carlisle, Pennsylvania. His parents died when he was young, and he came to Lynchburg in 1848 to learn the trade of cabinet-making with Folkes and Winston. At the end of two years he formed a partnership with William Crumpton, a tobacco manufacturer in this city. This partnership lasted for nearly thirteen years. Meantime, in 1859 John Wesley Carroll began the manufacture of granulated smoking tobacco on his own account and soon built up a wide reputation and a vast business. During the War Between the States he continued his business, finding a ready market for his tobacco at $7.00 per pound, Confederate money. When the South was defeated his profits were wiped out, but he continued to work and by 1867 he had so increased his sales that he was able to buy the old Crumpton factory and to double his output. The following year his recently-purchased building was destroyed by fire, but he had it rebuilt on a much larger scale in spite of the serious financial loss he had sustained. This building is still in use. His celebrated brands, which could be purchased the world over, were Lone Jack, Brown Dick and Fabius. He maintained his tobacco products on a consistent high grade of excellence, and received premiums at the Berlin, Vienna, Philadelphia and Paris Expositions.

Mr. Carroll was highly respected in Lynchburg. He was a worthy citizen, upright and public spirited. For thirty-two years he was a member of the City Council and its president for almost this entire term. He was a director of most of the Lynchburg banks and coal companies, president of the Lynchburg National Bank, and president of the Carroll Hotel Company. At his death, February 9th, 1898, he was worth a fortune of nearly a million dollars, of which it was said "there was not a dirty dollar among them." Mr. Carroll was married twice. His first wife was Sarah Elizabeth Crumpton, daughter of William Crumpton, his early business partner. They were married in 1850. She died in 1877, leaving three sons and four daughters, as follows: William G., married Clara B. Miles. Alice M., married James M. Bobbit. Sidney G., married Charles W. Miller. Robert Layman, married Lucy B. Kinnier. Walter Marion, married, first, Martha C. Venner; second, Rebecca Hooper. Mary Isabelle, married John E. Gannaway. Zaida, died July 16th, 1887.

His second wife, whom he married July 31st, 1878, was Sallie F., daughter of Isaac Adams, of Appomattox, and granddaughter of Major William DuVal, who was one of the Committee of Three, including Thomas Jefferson, who moved the Virginia seat of Government from Williamsburg to Richmond. The second Mrs. Carroll had three children: John W., married Madge Layman. I. Holcombe, married Mildred Turner. Sallie, married Chas. A. H. Leys.

The Carson Family

Rev. Dr. Theodore Carson, the son of Judge Joseph F. Carson, was borne in Winchester, Virginia, in 1834, and died in Lynchburg in 1904. He was an M.A. of Dickinson College, Carlisle, Pennsylvania. After his ordination into the ministry, he served the Confederacy for four years as chaplain in the army. After the War, he came to Lynchburg as rector of Saint Paul's Church, remaining here for thirty-three years, until his death at the age of seventy. He was married in 1860 to Victoria Ellen, the daughter of William and Ann (Waters) Allison. Mr. and Mrs. Carson had two children, Joseph Preston Carson, born at "Solitude," the Preston home in Montgomery County, Virginia, August 2nd, 1862, and Maude Lee, born in 1866, who married Professor W. M. Lile, dean of the law department of the University of Virginia.

Mr. Joseph Preston Carson lives at the handsome estate, "Dundee," in Chesterfield County. He was married in Richmond, April 18th, 1900, to Catherine Valentine Montague, born December 17th, 1873, daughter of J. J. Montague, of Princess Anne County. They have three children, Theodore Montague Carson, born February 10th, 1901; Catherine Warren, born May 24th, 1903, and Joseph Preston, Junior, born April 1st, 1905.

Caskie

George E. Caskie, son of John S. and Fannie (Johnson) Caskie, was born in Richmond, March 20th, 1858. He attended Hampden-Sidney College, and then served five years as deputy clerk of the Nelson Court. In 1881 he was admitted to the bar, and formed a partnership with J. Tinsley Coleman. For fifteen years they practiced with great success at Lovingston and surrounding counties. At the end of this time they came to Lynchburg, establishing an office here, where they continued together until 1906. In 1906 Mr. Coleman withdrew to enter into partnership with Judge Horsley, and Mr. Caskie took his eldest son, James R., as his partner, under the firm name of Caskie and Caskie. Mr. Caskie was a citizen of prominence in Lynchburg. Being a great churchman he was an elder in the Presbyterian Church, and superintendent in the Sunday school. He was president of the Presbyterian Orphanage, having to a large extent influenced the Synod in choosing Lynchburg as a site for the Orphanage. Mr. Caskie also served on the school board, of which he became chairman. Able and energetic, he was always alert to secure whatever benefits he could for the town he had adopted as his home.

His marriage to Miss Kimbrough Ligon in 1879 has already been referred to in the sketch of Judge Horsley. At Mr. Caskie's death he left the following children: 1. John, married Nannie Nicholas, of Lynchburg. Son, John S. 2. Martha Virginia, married Clinton DeWitt, Junior. 3. George E., Junior, married Grace Jackson; one daughter, Grace. 4. Fannie J., married Donald G. Moore; one daughter, Betsey. 5. James R., unmarried. 6. William S., unmarried. 7. Maude, married James Owen Watts.

As already recorded, Mrs. Caskie belongs to a famous Nelson family. She was the daughter of Joseph Ligon and Martha Massie Ligon. The Massie family for many generations owned large and valuable estates in Nelson County, and their homes were the centres of noted hospitality.

CLARK

Dr. Abram Irvine Clark was born in Campbell County in the year 1817. His father was Paulette Clark, of English extraction, and his mother was Mary Tucker Irvine, of Scotch-Irish descent. Her family were among the first settlers of Campbell and located on a farm on Falling River in the year 1735. This property is now owned by Dr. J. Paulette Clark. Dr. Abram Irvine Clark determined early in life to study medicine, and stuck to this plan in spite of great impediments. In 1842-43 he attended a course of lectures at the University of Pennsylvania in Philadelphia, and on January, 1843, he received an appointment as assistant to Dr. Buffington at the Fifth Street Dispensary in that city. In 1844-45 he attended lectures at the University of Virginia, where he graduated in July, 1845. He then returned to his native county and settled at the county seat, where he practiced his profession until after the War. In 1864 he married Zulieka Lemmon Withers, a daughter of Colonel Edward B. Withers, of Campbell. She died March 25th, 1882. In 1865 Dr. Clark was elected to the General Assembly of Virginia, which was the first General Assembly held after the War. He served three sessions during that term, one being the special session in the summer of 1867. In January, 1866, Dr. Clark introduced in the Legislature a bill to charter the Lynchburg and Danville Railroad Company, and after a hard-fought battle succeeded in having it passed, although several of his predecessors had failed in getting this bill through the Assembly. When the Reconstruction laws were adopted he was rendered ineligible to hold office, as he had filled the position of justice of the peace under the old regime. In 1873 his disabilities were removed, and he was again elected to the Virginia Legislature. He was re-elected in 1875, and served to the end of the session of 1876-77.

In the summer of 1876 Dr. Clark moved to Lynchburg. He served in the city in many important matters. For a number of years he was president of the Board of Health. It was he who introduced into Marshall Lodge the resolution which caused the establishment of Lynchburg's first hospital, and by his energy was finally installed the Home and Retreat Hospital, later called Memorial Hospital.

Coleman

John Tinsley Coleman was a lawyer of marked ability. He came to Lynchburg from Nelson County, where he was born on August 29th, 1857, the son of Dr. Hawes Nicholas Coleman and Sallie A. E. (Tinsley) Coleman.

The Coleman family had long been distinguished in the annals of Virginia history. Its various branches had flourished in Caroline, Essex, Spottsylvania and Piedmont Counties of Virginia since the first Coleman had come from England in 1640 and settled in the Valley of Rappahannock River. John Tinsley

Christopher Clark Collins

Coleman's grandfather was Richard Hawes, Governor of Kentucky during the War Between the States, who was born in Caroline County, Virginia, February 6th, 1797. He emigrated to Kentucky at the age of thirteen, and secured his education at Transylvania University. In 1862 he was inaugurated at Frankfort, Kentucky, surrounded by the bayonets of General Bragg's Army.

Mr. Coleman's early life was spent in Nelson County. He attended Norwood High School, a Classical and Mathematical Academy on the James River, which was run by Mr. William D. Cabell, and highly esteemed throughout the State. Later Mr. Coleman entered Blacksburg. In 1878 he went to work as clerk in a country store in Nelson County, although at the age of seventeen or eighteen he had felt certain stirrings of ambition to be a lawyer while he listened to the proceedings of a noted case being tried in the local court.

March 26th, 1879, he married Miss Laura Jane Hill, and it was after his marriage that he determined to leave the country store, where that fine mind of his had certainly no rightful place. During the session 1880-81 he studied law at the University of Virginia under Professor John B. Minor and Stephen O. Southall. He graduated from the law department of the University in June, 1881, with the degree of Bachelor of Law. He practiced for a number of years in Nelson County, removing to Lynchburg in 1894, where he achieved signal distinction as a lawyer of learning and ability.

Christopher Clark Collins

Christopher Clark Collins, of a family which has long been respected and well known in Virginia, was born in Lynchburg, December 29th, 1871, being the son of W. J. and Nannie P. (Clark) Collins. He received his education in his native town and at the Virginia Military Institute, where he was graduated in 1892. He then studied medicine, and received his degree at the University of Virginia in 1895. He obtained a place as interne in the United States Marine Hospital in New York, where he served a year and was for another year on the house staff of the Woman's Hospital in New York.

When the Spanish War began agitating the country, and a board of examination for appointment of surgeons in the Army was ordered, Collins, in November, 1898, applied for permission to appear before this board, his application being endorsed by Senator Daniel and Congressman Peter J. Otey, of Lynchburg. He saw his first service at the Army General Hospital in San Juan in January, 1899, and for the next eighteen years served at various stations in this country and in the Philippine Islands. When the World War began he was on the Pacific coast in command of an ambulance company and field hospital, with the rank of major. He was selected to command and to conduct over-seas the Red Cross Base Hospital, Number 12, organized with the Northwestern University Medical School, Chicago, as its parent institution, and Colonel F. A. Besley as its organizing director. They sailed May 19th, 1917, for service with the Expeditionary Forces, Christopher Clark Collins having been made lieutenant-colonel just before his departure. In France he served with the great British General Hospital, Number 18, at Camiers, until the organization of the American Army, when he was transferred as corps surgeon of the Eleventh United States Army Corps commanded by Major-General George W. Read.

Upon Colonel Collins' return from France in 1919 he was assigned to duty with the Militia Bureau in the War Department, was then surgeon of the Third Corps Area until the summer of 1926, when he made his third journey to the Philippines, remaining there two years in command of the Sternberg General Hospital. Returning to this country, he served as instructor at the Headquarters of the Seventy-Eighth Division for a year. Clark Collins' next post was at the Army Medical Center in Washington as assistant commandant of the group of Special Service Schools. This was his last duty, for he was overtaken by sudden death on Sunday, May 11th, 1930, while visiting his relatives in Lynchburg.

In his service with the British, Colonel Collins was mentioned in a dispatch from Field Marshall Sir Douglass Haig, dated November 7th, 1917, "for gallant and distinguished services in the Field." He also received from King George the Decoration of Companion of the Order of Saint Michael and Saint George. For his services with the A. E. F. he received the Distinguished Service Medal with the following citation:

"For exceptionally meritorious and distinguished services. As corps Surgeon, Second Army Corps, from February, 1918, to February, 1919, he displayed professional attainments of a high order in the training of the organizations of the Corps for subsequent operations. During active operations, the efficiency of his organization and arrangements for the care of the sick and wounded and their evacuation contributed in a high degree to the success of the operations of the Corps."

The official reports speak of Colonel Collins always in terms of high commendation and respect, as a conscientious and capable officer, and he held, in addition, the affectionate regard of a host of friends and comrades, both in the Army and in civil life.

Such is the military record contained in the V. M. I. Alumni News of January, 1931. It is the story of a man who won fame and honor by his exceptional merit. Many of us in Lynchburg remember something more of Clark Collins: His beautiful devotion to his aged mother, his love for his old friends, his loyalty to the home and town where he was born. We have a green and gracious memory of the man. In all walks of life, as is said of him on the stone which marks his grave in Presbyterian Cemetery, he was "without fear and without reproach."

CRAIGHILL

The first Craighill to make his home in Lynchburg was Dr. E. A. Craighill. After the War Between the States, Mr. J. William Faulkner had established a drug store here, in which he offered Dr. Craighill a partnership. The firm of Faulkner and Craighill, thus formed endured for twenty-five years. Dr. Craighill married Miss Martha Hobson. They had no children. Colonel Robert Craighill came to Lynchburg later and married Miss Edley Hobson. They left the following children: Colonel Robert Craighill, of the World War, who married Miss Nannie Hutter; Edward A. Craighill; the late Joseph Craighill; Mrs. Harrison Nicholas, Miss Norvell Craighill and Preston Craighill. A third brother, George, married Miss Lillie Langhorne, a daughter of Colonel Maurice Langhorne. His children no longer live here, they were: Elizabeth, who died unmarried; George Peyton, Junior, a minister of the Episcopal Church; Maurice Langhorne, Lloyd and Wistar.

Dabney

The Dabney family was descended from Cornelius d'Aubigne, corrupted by Virginia tongues into de Bony and so to Dabney. They came from a great Huguenot family and were granted a tract of two hundred acres of land in New Kent County in 1664. Cornelius brought a wife with him, but she died soon after reaching Virginia, leaving one son, George. His second wife was Sarah Jennings, who left three sons and four daughters. Lynchburg has descendants from both wives. Mrs. Ernest Heald was Louise, daughter of Rev. Chiswell Dabney, who was the son of John Blair Dabney, of Campbell County. Rev. Chiswell Dabney married Lucy Fontaine. This branch of the Dabney family, as well as the descendants of Chiswell Dabney, in his day a noted lawyer, come from George, the child of the first wife of Cornelius. Mr. Albert Dabney, of Lynchburg, is descended from Sarah Jennings, the second wife of Cornelius Dabney. Mr. Albert Dabney married Miss Jennie Akers, of Lynchburg.

The Davis Family

Samuel, William, Micajah and Evan were the sons of John and Susannah Smithson Davis, of Shropshire, England. After their arrival in Virginia, three of them eventually settled in Bedford County and in Lynchburg. Samuel, the eldest brother,

Henry Davis, who owned most of the Third Ward

born 1740, had married Annis Lipscomb, August 15th, 1769, before coming to this country. With his wife he came to Louisa County, making his home near Green Spring. Later he moved to Bedford, where he died in 1769. His wife lived to be ninety-seven. His children were: Thomas Davis, who married Rachel Dixon in 1798. Their children:

1. Samuel Lipscomb Davis, died young.

2. George Dixon Davis, married Mary Ann Wills. He was born June 10th, 1805, and was married March 4th, 1840. They were the parents of ten children, among these being Mr. Thomas D. Davis, clerk of the court in Lynchburg for many years, who married Miss Lulie Brown, but had no children; Micajah Preston Davis, who married Miss Maude Matthews, and had one son, Fred Davis; Mr. Creed Davis, who married Miss Jennie Lybrook, and Virginia Margaret, who married P. A. Krise.

3. John Thomas Davis, married Margaret Preston, their children being: Mary Elizabeth, married Camillus Christian; their children were Davis, Thomas and Henry. Margaret Preston Davis, never married. Thomas Bowker Davis, a brave Confederate soldier, died in the War. Anne Elizabeth, married Pleasant Preston. Their children were: Samuel D., clerk of the court, who married Texanna Saunders. Their children were: Lottie, who married Withers Clark; Daisy, who married Robert Strother; Texanna, who never married. Thomas S. Preston, married Nannie Preston. Elizabeth, no record. John B. Preston was professor at Bowling Green, Kentucky. Pleasant, married Berta White. Dr. George M. Preston, eminent physician of Lynchburg, died unmarried in 1933.

The second brother, William Davis, Senior, who, being a Quaker, was called Friend Davis, married Mary Gosney. She was the daughter of Henry Gosney, whose wife, Mary Shelton, born 1726, was the daughter of Ralph and Mary Pollard Shelton, of King William County. The children of Mary Gosney and William Davis were:

1. John, married Anne Jennings.

2. Henry, married Sarah Anthony.
3. Susan, died unmarried.
4. Elizabeth, died unmarried.
5. Benjamin, married Catherine Gilbert.
6. Isaac.
7. Mary, married Cornelius Pierce.
8. Nancy, married Peter Dudley.
9. Louisa, died unmarried.
10. Deborah, died unmarried.

John, who married Ann Jennings, had a son, William Minor (Minor is used in this family in the same sense as Junior, meaning a younger member of the family). William Minor, married Nannie Hunter Eubank, and was the father of Thomas Newman Davis, for many years City Collector of Taxes. He married Blanche V. Thompson. His son, Thomas N., is a physician here. His older son, Minor, succeeded him as City Collector.

Nancy Davis, who married Peter Dudley, had the following children: John W. Dudley, married Andalusia Fourqueron; Thomas Stevens Dudley, died unmarried; Mary Elizabeth, married Captain Thomas W. Johns, whose daughter, Miss Deane Johns lives in Appomattox, and many of his grandchildren live in Lynchburg. Fannie Jane, married James F. Payne. Nancy Davis, died in infancy. Peter L. Dudley, Junior, married Bettie Saunders, who had two Dudley children, James and William. She afterwards married Mr. Richard Pollard. Henry Dudley, died unmarried. Louise, died in infancy. Deborah Ann, married Rev. William H. Kinckle, and was his second wife. They had one child, Grace, who married William S. Adams, son of Captain Stephen Adams. They have one child, also named Grace, who married Edward Hutter. She has written a noteworthy book on Psychology, a subject on which she takes rank as an authority in this country. Mr. Hutter is also the author of some distinguished magazine articles and stories. Maria Rose, married J. Edward Calhoun. They were the parents of Dudley and Charles Calhoun, who lived for years in Lynchburg, and left descendants. Robert L. Dudley lived to old age, but died unmarried.

Of special interest to Lynchburg people is the name William Davis, Junior, son of William Davis, Senior, who married Zalinda Lynch, daughter of John Lynch; their son, John Davis, Junior, married Hannah Anthony, daughter of Christopher Anthony, who moved to Cincinnati because as a rigid Quaker he disapproved of slavery. John Davis went with him. His daughter, Ann Maria Davis, married Achilles Pugh, of Cincinnati.

Henry Davis, second child of William Davis, Senior, and Mary Gosney Davis, was a merchant in Lynchburg and a prominent and valuable citizen of the town. On July 10th, 1800, he married Sarah, the daughter of Christopher Anthony, by his second wife, Mary Jordan, and had a large family of children. Mrs. Davis, mentioned several times in Mrs. Cabell's book with admiration and affection, was born in March, 1784, and died in 1824. Her husband survived her over forty years, but never married again. Their children were:

Mary Lou Davis, born January 26th, 1804, married Hobson Johns, of Danville. They had no children.

Samuel, died when a young man; unmarried.

Sarah Ann Davis, born January 9th, 1811, married, first, William Ward Smith; second, Rev. Franklin Genet Smith. Their daughter, by the first marriage, Sallie Ward Smith, married Dr. Frederick William Gustine, a prominent doctor in New Orleans.

Alexander Davis, went West and settled in Galena, Illinois. He married Miss Helen Wann, and had many children, and descendants in the western States. Robert Jordan Davis, born August 13th, 1813, married Anne Carrington Cabell, whose ancestry is given in the Irvine family. Mr. Davis was a member of the Lynchburg bar, a man of high intellectual attainments, and of deep piety. He was greatly honored for the integrity and high Christian virtues exemplified in his life. His children were: Paul, died unmarried; Robert, died unmarried; Mary, died unmarried; Miss Nannie, Miss Sallie and Miss Lucy have each taken a leading part in all matters pertaining to education. William Kinckle Davis, married Julia, the daughter of Mr. James Gregory, a beloved citizen of Lynchburg: one child, Linn Cabell, died in infancy. They have a daughter, Nell Gregory Davis, and live in Roanoke.

Lucy Elizabeth, the youngest child of Mr. Henry Davis, married William Tudor Yancey, son of Major Joel Yancey, of "Rothsay" in Bedford County. She was born in 1820, and died December 20th, 1907. William Tudor Yancey was born November 16th, 1813, and died in the summer of 1889. His father, Major Joel Yancey, mentioned before as the neighbor and friend of Thomas Jefferson, was a near kinsman of Henry Clay, his mother having been Barbara Jennings, a sister of Henry Clay's grandmother. Major Yancey died in 1833, and his family removed to Lynchburg. His second wife, the mother of William Tudor Yancey, was a descendant of Gideon Macon, as related in the Macon family record. Mr. William Tudor Yancey practiced law in Lynchburg with success for many years.

Children of Lucy Elizabeth Davis and William Tudor Yancey:

Mary Lou Yancey, born 1838, died unmarried.

Henry Davis Yancey, born 1840, first lieutenant and color bearer of Second Virginia Regiment of Cavalry, C. S. A., was killed in the Battle of Spottsylvania Courthouse.

Charles Anthony Yancey, died at the age of fourteen.

Caroline Anthony Yancey, married Waller M. Boyd, of Nelson County, Major, C. S. A., Pickett's Division, captured at Gettysburg. Their children were: Henry, died young. Lucy, unmarried. Carrie, unmarried. Alice, died unmarried. Waller M. Boyd, Junior, married, and left children. Thomas Massie Boyd, married Ruby Smith, and has children. Virginia, married Mr. Noel, of Roanoke; has no children. William Tudor Boyd lives in Baltimore, married, and has one child, Waller M. Mary, married Samuel Scott, and has children. Susan Cabell, married Mr. Alex Hollowell; died without children.

William Tudor Yancey, Junior, married, first, Mary Radford, of Radford; no children. His second wife was Eugenia Macon, daughter of Colonel Thomas Littleton Macon, of New Orleans; one son, the late Thomas Macon Yancey.

Three daughters of Mr. and Mrs. W. T. Yancey, Senior, died in childhood. Charles Dabney Yancey, married Blanche Wilkinson, and had the following children: Lucy, married Buller Claiborne, and has one daughter, Eugenia Macon. Carrie Yancey, unmarried. May Miller, married. Alice, unmarried. Lewis, unmarried. Macon, unmarried. Fred, married.

Robert Davis Yancey, born September 15th, 1855, married November 17th, 1892, to Rosa Faulkner, youngest daughter of John William Faulkner and Rosa Adams, his wife.

The children of Robert Davis Yancey and Rosa Faulkner Yancey are:

Elizabeth Davis, born December 20th, 1893; married July, 1913, to Victor Pleasants Abernathy, son of Mr. and Mrs. Maston Abernathy. She died October 13th, 1929, leaving one son, Robert Maston, born November 1st, 1914.

Robert D. Yancey, Junior, married Elizabeth White. Children: Robert White, Ann and Nancy Faulkner Yancey.

Joel William Tudor Yancey, married Elizabeth Heard, and has one son, Joel Alexander Yancey.

Rebecca Yancey, married Dr. John Bell Williams, major World War, son of Judge Samuel Walker Williams and Margaret Grayson Williams; one son, Martin Tudor Hansford Williams, born August 9th, 1924.

Rose Adams Yancey, died in infancy.

Mary Saunders Yancey.

Caroline Athony Yancey.

Henry Davis Yancey.

We have no record of Micajah Davis, third of the brothers who came from Shropshire.

Evan Davis, youngest brother, remained only a short time in Virginia. According to the records of Mr. Alexander Brown, he emigrated to Georgia and settled near Savannah. He lived there until the close of the Revolutionary War, in which he served under Count Pulaski. Evan's son, Samuel, born in Georgia, moved to Kentucky. He married, and was the father of Jefferson Davis, who was born in Christian County, Kentucky, 1808.

The Dillard Family

The Dillard family had its origin in France, the name being spelled d'Illard. In 1514 John Carbonne d'Illard, whose home was at Bagneres-de-Luchon, on the headwaters of the Garonne, appears to have been the head of the family. During the religious persecutions that followed the increase of the power of the house of Guise, many of the Dillards, being Protestants, fled to England to escape persecution. In later years there is an English record that James Stephen Dillard and John Dillard were no longer residents of England, but had gone to the colonies in America.

George Dillard came to Virginia from Wiltshire, England. In 1665 he was credited with two hundred and fifty acres of land for service against the Indians. He was twenty-six when he emigrated to Virginia. In his will he left land to his son, James Stephen Dillard, of James City County, and to his two daughters. James Stephen Dillard married in England and brought his wife to Virginia in 1698. He willed land near Williamsburg to his three sons and to his two daughters, Mary and Sally. One of his sons, James, born in 1704, married Lucy Wise in 1724. Their son, James, married Mary Ann Hunt, July 8th, 1748.

Captain James Dillard and Mary Ann Hunt, his wife, had land in Buckingham County, twenty miles from Lynch's Ferry. Captain Dillard purchased land across from the Ferry, on the Amherst side of the river, and moved his family residence there.

He owned most of the land from Stapleton to Allen's Creek. His wife died August 26th, 1787. Their oldest son, John, who married Sarah Stovall, and lived in Henry County, rendered distinguished service to the American cause in the Revolutionary War, and founded a family whose descendants have been of value to community and State. Another son, James, born October 28th, 1755, was a captain in the Continental troops, and in 1810 received military land warrants for four thousand acres. He married Jane Starke, daughter of Major John Starke and Anne Wyatt Starke, of Hanover County. The oldest son of James and Jane Starke Dillard was Joseph Dillard. He married Polly Bradford, and settled on the Dillard lands in Buckingham. Their third son, Colonel John Dillard, married November 2nd, 1824, Sarah Stovall Christian. Their son, Captain John James Dillard, married April 12th, 1847, Elizabeth Haskins Dillard, daughter of Colonel James Spotswood Dillard and Narcissa Turner.

Dr. John W. Dillard, for many years a prominent physician and surgeon of Lynchburg, was the son of Captain John James Dillard and Elizabeth Haskins Dillard, his wife. He was born in Amherst County, August 12th, 1852, and died May 17th, 1930. His early education was acquired from private tutors. Later he went to Terry's Academy and to the University of Virginia. He finished his medical course at the University in 1875, attended clinics at Bellevue Hospital, and lectures at the University of New York. After this course was finished, he went to London, where he studied at Saint Thomas' Hospital.

In 1800 he married Emma White, daughter of Fannie Ruffner and Dr. Peter White. They had three children: William White Dillard, of Memphis, Tennessee; Fannie White Dillard, who married Dr. Oswald Stuart McCown, of Memphis, Tennessee; John Ruffner Dillard, of Lynchburg, who married Ruth Henderson, daughter of James Henderson, of North Carolina.

Dr. Dillard was a man of unusual personal charm, of great kindness and sympathy, and was much beloved in Lynchburg.

Mr. James Spotswood Dillard, a brother of Dr. Dillard, who

lived on the Forest Road, married Miss Ella Woodruff, of Lynchburg. They had twelve children, many of whom are now living in Lynchburg: John Dillard, married Ruth L. Lavinder; Mary Narcissa, married J. Early St. Clair; James P., married Mabel Carlson; Elizabeth H., married Dr. George J. Tompkins; Margaret W., married Alfred H. Murrell; Ella S., married R. Winston Harvey; Emma S., married Breckenridge Stovall; David Hugh, married Rose van Gelder; Dr. Powell Garland Dillard, married Nannie Sue Hoge; Jean, married Mr. Stanford, and died some years ago; Edwin is dead also.

The handsome brick residence at the corner of Eleventh and Federal Streets, which is now owned by Mrs. D. H. Howard, was the home of Captain John James Dillard. This house was built about the year 1852 by Mr. David Bryce Payne. It was designed by the same architect who planned the home built by William Murrell and later owned by General Munford. The walls were frescoed by an Italian artist. Captain Dillard's daughter, Narcissa, who was the second wife of Rev. Powell Garland, finally fell heir to this residence. Many Lynchburg people living today remember her vivid beauty, with raven-black hair and the complexion of a white camellia.

Judge Dillard, of Amherst, was born at "Edgewood" in Amherst County, August 23rd, 1846. He was the son of General Terisha Washington Dillard and Mary Elizabeth Dillard. He entered Virginia Military Institute August 21st, 1863, and took part in the Battle of New Market, where he was wounded in the leg and head. After the War, he studied law at the University of Virginia. He was made judge of the County Court of Amherst, December 17th, 1879, and held this position with credit for eighteen years. Judge Dillard was witty and cultured, and was considered one of the ablest jurists in the State. He married Mary Evans, of Amherst, and died October 4th, 1898, at his home in Amherst, leaving one child, William Evans Dillard. His wife was the daughter of William M. Evans and Harriet Hubbard McNair Evans, and the sister of Mr. Otto Evans, a well-known attorney of Amherst, who at one time lived in Lynchburg. Mrs. Dillard purchased a home in Lynchburg, 601 Court Street, in 1909. She was the first teacher of domestic science in the public schools, and one of the founders of the Woman's Club of Lynchburg. Her activities in educational lines have been varied and useful. She is a member of the League of Women Voters, the U. D. C., Y. W. C. A., and the D. A. R.

Mrs. Sallie Dillard Larkin, a sister of Judge Dillard, has lived in Lynchburg for many years. She was born at "Edgewood," in Amherst, the home of her grandfather, Colonel William Dillard. She moved later to "Islington," on the James River, another Dillard home, where her girlhood was spent. She received superior advantages in education and musical training. Her marriage to William W. Larkin, a member of the Lynchburg bar, was celebrated at "Islington." Mr. Larkin was born in Prince William County, September, 1837. He lived in Alexandria in his youth and early manhood, and was with the Alexander Rifles when that company was sent against John Brown at Harper's Ferry. He served in the Confederate Army, and had the rank of captain at the time of the surrender. He was wounded in the lung, and although he lived for many years, he finally died from this wound, the weakened lung tissue giving way while he was making a speech in the Courthouse. He died August 25th, 1894. Captain Larkin was descended from Sir Thomas Larkin, who fitted out his own ship and migrated to Maryland. Dr. Parkhurst was a second cousin of Captain Larkin. Captain and Mrs. Larkin had the following children: William W., Junior, and Thomas Dillard, both of Washington, District of Columbia; Mary Dillard and Maude Spotswood Larkin, of Lynchburg.

Dirom

Mrs. Maria Dirom, widow of Mr. Patrick Dirom, age eighty-two years, died in Lynchburg, June 17th, 1918. Mrs. Dirom was born in England, and came to Virginia in 1879. She was a lady of great benevolence, and her whole life was devoted to work among the poor. She left three children, Robert Dirom, Mrs. A. M. Nelson and Miss Ethel Dirom.

Diuguid

The first of the Diuguid family in Lynchburg was Sampson Diuguid. He came from Appomattox in 1817 and here he combined fine cabinet-making with the employment of undertaker. As the town grew larger, the cabinet-making in the establishment was dropped. Sampson Diuguid died in 1852, and was succeeded in the business by George A. Diuguid. George A. Diuguid died in 1887 and his place was taken by the late William D. Diuguid, who made many improvements in the business. The carriage by which caskets are wheeled into church, now used by all undertakers, was an invention of Mr. William D. Duiguid. For three generations in Lynchburg this family have closed the eyes of the dead and have given the bereaved their considerate attention. No men were ever more respected or honored in a community than these three good men. The men of the family are now gone, but the daughter of Mr. William D. Diuguid, with the assistance of Mr. Hudgins, now carries on the firm with the same spirit of dignity that her forerunners observed.

Dunnington

Mr. F. Mallory Dunnington is the representative of a very old family, both in Lynchburg and in Virginia. Going back farther to the Mallory family in England, which in the time of Edward IV produced Sir Thomas Mallory who wrote Morte D'Arthur, we may say with truth that it was an ancient family even in England. The Dunningtons were in Lynchburg in Mrs. Cabell's time, and are distinguished among those who have helped make the history of this town.

DuVal

Mrs. Mary C. DuVal, wife of Edward DuVal, died at the home of her mother, Mrs. Amandus D. Walker, near Forest, June 2nd,

1918. Mrs. DuVal was the daughter of the late Amandus D. Walker, a prominent citizen of Bedford County for many years.

EVANS

John B. Evans was born in Winchester, Virginia, 1828, and died February 26th, 1905. Before coming to Lynchburg he was for forty years a prominent citizen of Staunton. He was in the tobacco business in Lynchburg and was president of the Tobacco Association at one time. Mr. Evans was survived by five daughters and five sons. His sons are: Walter, Robert, Frank, Howard and James.

EDMUNDS

The Edmunds family came from the Eastern Shore of Virginia to Charlotte County, and from Charlotte County to Halifax, where Henry Edmunds established his home at "Elm Hill." His son, John R. Edmunds lived at "Redfield," a very fine estate with a noble colonial mansion. John R. Edmunds married Mildred Coles, daughter of Isaac Coles, Senior, and his wife, Lightfoot Carrington, from Meadsville. Their oldest son, Paul Carrington Edmunds, for many years a M. C. from this district, married Phoebe Ann Easley. These were the parents of Mr. James E. Edmunds and Mr. Paul C. Edmunds, Junior, who came to Lynchburg when very young men, and Mr. Richard Edmunds. The Easleys were an old and aristocratic family of Halifax County, where many of the name still live.

Mr. Richard Edmunds married Willie Murrell, daughter of Mr. Thomas Murrell, a prominent citizen of Lynchburg during his lifetime. Mr. Paul Edmunds married Mallie Otey, daughter of Mr. Hays Otey. Both of these brothers have been dead for some years.

James E. Edmunds, for many years a prominent Lynchburg lawyer, married Hattie Prescott, a niece of the late Mrs. R. G. H. Kean. Their children are: J. Easley Edmunds, married Bertha Dingee. Kate Edmunds, married Dr. Walters. Prescott Edmunds, married his cousin, Celeste Ivey. William Wilson Edmunds is unmarried. Phoebe, married.

FAULKNER

J. William Faulkner was the son of Isaac Hamilton Faulkner and Julia Frederick, his wife, of Winchester, Virginia. Julia Frederick was the daughter of John Frederick, who was born in Saxony, Germany, came to Virginia and married in Winchester. He went to Texas in answer to Sam Houston's call for men from the Shenandoah Valley to fight for Texas, and died from a gun-shot wound received at the Battle of San Jacinto. His wife was a granddaughter of Major Peter Helphenstein, of the Revolutionary War, a well-known figure in the settlement of the Valley of Virginia.

Mr. Isaac Hamilton Faulkner was born at "Easton," on the Eastern Shore of Maryland, the son of James Faulkner, an Englishman, and Rebecca Hamilton, who belonged to a distinguished New York family. Left an orphan at an early age, Mr. Faulkner went to Winchester when he was only thirteen. He was successful in business and became a man of large means before his death in 1894. His son, J. William Faulkner, was born March 17th, 1844. When he was sixteen he marched against John Brown, when the Winchester troops were ordered to Harper's Ferry. When war came he was one of the Stonewall Brigade, and served under General Jackson for two years. His service with the Stonewall Brigade came to an end when he was taken ill with pneumonia. It became known during his illness that he had studied pharmacy and after his recovery he was detailed for hospital duty, as the hospitals had great need of men trained in the knowledge of medicine. Until the close of the War he served in the ambulance corps, where he became acquainted with E. A. Craighill, later his partner in business, who had been detailed to the same duty. At the end of the War Mr. Faulkner decided to locate in Lynchburg, and his father furnished him with the necessary funds to establish himself in the drug business. He opened a drug store on Main Street between Tenth and Eleventh. In 1866 he was married to Rosa, the daughter of Mr. John Q. Adams and Mary Saunders Adams. About this time he invited Dr. Craighill, who was then in Baltimore, to be his partner. This offer being accepted he changed his firm name to Faulkner and Craighill, and for the next twenty-five years, the business operated under that name. Mr. Faulkner retired from the firm about 1891 and one year later went into partnership with J. Owen Hanvey, and located his new business in the Law Building, which at that time had just been built and opened. The firm name was Faulkner and Hanvey. He had only been in the new business a short time when he was stricken with an illness from which he died in the summer of 1894. He left three sons and three daughters, whose names are given in the record of Mrs. Faulkner's family. Mr. Faulkner was survived by several brothers and one sister, all of Winchester. They were: James, Isaac, Walter and Oliver Faulkner, and Virginia, the wife of Dr. Clinton Maynard.

FISHER

F. J. Fisher, the artist, was born in Southwest Virginia, near Wytheville, about the year of 1832. He was a farmer's son, but developed a great talent for drawing. He came to Lynchburg in 1855 from East Tennessee, where his father had moved. He painted many portraits in Lynchburg, and became a leading member of society at the time when Dr. George Bagby, William R. Mosby, the Langhornes, the Meems, and Semple, the editor of the Virginian, were in their prime.

Tuesday, May 9th, 1905, the Washington Post printed this sketch of Fisher: "Flavius J. Fisher, one of the best know portrait painters in the United States, died last night. He leaves a widow and one son, Joseph Albert. Mr. Fisher was born seventy-three years ago at Wytheville, Southwest Virginia. At an early age he displayed talent for painting, and at twelve he was placed in a studio at Philadelphia, where he remained for about five years. He then went abroad and studied in Germany and Paris. He was the first American artist to be admitted to the German

Art Institute at Berlin. For the past twenty-three years he conducted his studio in the Corcoran Building and painted the portraits of many distinguished men, among them Postmaster-General William L. Williams, Ex-Secretary Hoke Smith, Cardinal Gibbons, and the late Albert Pike. During the recent illness, which ended in his death, he completed the portrait of Samuel Miller, a philanthropist of Virginia. This was a remarkable achievement, as Mr. Miller has been dead for many years, and the portrait was painted from memory. Mr. Fisher made several sketches which were submitted to friends of Mr. Miller, who pronounced them excellent likenesses. The picture was painted for the Lynchburg Female Orphan Asylum, in Lynchburg, and is said to be a life-like portrait. The deceased artist had such a keen memory he never required but two sittings from his subject."

Mr. Fisher painted pictures of many Lynchburg people besides Mr. Miller, among whom were Captain John M. Otey and Mr. John W. Carroll. He also made crayon portraits of Ambrose Rucker and William M. Black.

Fleet

The Fleet family is a very old one in Virginia, William Fleet having been a member of the House of Burgesses from Lancaster County in 1652. The family was represented here by Dr. Fleet, for many years a druggist in Lynchburg. Several recipes compounded by him during his lifetime have proved a valuable legacy to his family. His children are as follows: Elsie, married M. D. Morton. Carrie, married Dudley Diggs. Katherine, died unmarried. The late Paul Fleet, who was a valuable and public-spirited citizen, a member of the City Council and Mayor of Lynchburg, died unmarried.

Fleming

The Fleming brothers, who lived in Lynchburg and left descendants, belonged to one of the oldest families in Virginia. Mr. George L. Fleming was married, first, to Miss Murrell, the daughter of Mr. Thomas Murrell. His second wife was Eddie, the daughter of Mr. Holcombe Adams.

FRANKLIN

Mr. James Franklin, Junior, died May 18th, 1906. He and his brother, Major Jacob Franklin, were among several brothers who fought very gallantly for the Confederacy. Mr. James Franklin was wounded seven times. Mr. Franklin was born in Pittsylvania County, May 7, 1839. He came to Lynchburg in 1856. After the War, he was in the tobacco business, and for many years was connected with Murrell, Fleming and Company. Mr. Franklin left one daughter, Mrs. C. C. Waddell, of Norfolk.

FEATHERSTONE

John C. Featherstone was born in Limestone County, Alabama, August 14, 1837. His father, Howell C. Featherstone, was a native of North Carolina, and his mother, Dulaney (Odom) Featherstone, was also born in North Carolina. John C. Featherstone was married January 19th, 1864, to Letitia Preston Floyd, born in Jefferson County, Kentucky, daughter of Nathaniel Wilson Floyd and Eliza W. (Anderson) Floyd. Her grandfather was a pioneer of Kentucky with Daniel Boone, and his brother went with him to Kentucky and was mortally wounded in a fight with the Indians. At the risk of his life he carried his brother's body to a place of safety, so that it might not fall into the hands of the savages.

Captain John C. Featherstone served with the Army of Northern Virginia until a few months before the close of the War. He was wounded at the Battle of Gettysburg and then transferred to Alabama, and was under General Nathan B. Forrest's command until it was cut off by General Sherman and forced to surrender. Captain and Mrs. Featherstone have two children, Nathaniel Floyd, born May 3rd, 1867, and Howell C., born April 27th, 1871. The Featherstones owned a large plantation near Lynchburg, and lived there for many years. Later they moved into the town.

Dr. Floyd, the father of Mrs. Featherstone, had come to Bedford County from Jefferson County, Kentucky, in the first quarter of the nineteenth century. Her brother, Nathaniel B. Floyd, was born in Campbell County, September 19th, 1826. He married Ellen Stith in 1855. They had seven children: Stith, Nathaniel W., Eugene S., Lee B., Charles A., Jesse A., and Ellen S., whose first husband was Robert Pannil. This family owned a large plantation on Salem Turnpike, not far beyond New London Academy.

Floyd

Two members of the Floyd family were Governors of Virginia. John Floyd, born in Jefferson County, April 24th, 1783, was Governor 1830-1834. He died at Sweet Springs, Montgomery County, Virginia, August 15th, 1837. John Buchanan Floyd, born in Blacksburg, Virginia, June 1st, 1806, oldest son of Governor John Floyd and his wife, Letitia Preston, was made Governor of Virginia January 1st, 1849. He became Secretary of War in President Buchanan's Cabinet in 1857. He married his cousin, Sarah Buchanan, but left no children, and died near Abingdon, Virginia, August 26th, 1863. His brother, Benjamin Rush Floyd, the sixth child of Governor John Floyd, married Nancy Matthews, of Wytheville, Virginia. Their daughter, Malvina Floyd, married Major Peter J. Otey, C. S. A., of Lynchburg, and member of Congress from Virginia.

Nickettie, the ninth child of Governor John Floyd, was the mother of the late Dr. George Ben Johnson, of Richmond, Virginia.

Ford

Judge Henry M. Ford, for many years a member of the Lynchburg bar, died October 7th, 1905; age fifty-six years. He had practiced law in Lynchburg since 1889 in the firm of Ford and Ford with his brother and partner, John M. Ford. At one time he was judge of the Circuit Court, which included Henry and Pittsylvania Counties and Danville. He married Miss Hallie Sherman, daughter of the late H. H. Sherman.

Mr. Kiah T. Ford, of another family, who married Annie Howard, the daughter of Mr. Volney Howard, has been in the real estate business here for many years.

Forsberg

Mrs. August Forsberg died March 29th, 1918, in her seventy-ninth year. She was the widow of Colonel August Forsberg, an officer of the Fifty-first Regiment of Virginia Volunteers, C. S. A., who died in 1910. For a number of years he was city engineer here. Mrs. Forsberg herself might have been called a brave soldier in the Confederate service, for she was one of those women who nobly devoted themselves to nursing the wounded and sick in the Ladies' Relief Hospital of Lynchburg. She was twice married. Born Mollie Morgan, her first husband was Captain George Gaston Otey, who left two children, Mrs. Herbert Claiborne Wilkins, of Washington, District of Columbia, and Mrs. Peter Ainslie, of Lynchburg. In 1865 Mollie Morgan Otey married Colonel August Forsberg, who left the following children. Carl S. Forsberg, of Norfolk, Virginia; Rudolph P. Forsberg, of Pittsburgh, Pennsylvania; Fred A. Forsberg, of Columbus, Ohio; Miss Annie Lind Forsberg, and Mrs. John A. Davis, both of this city. Colonel August Forsberg was a native of northern Europe. He served in the Confederate Army and was for over forty-five years a valued and prominent citizen of our town. Mrs. Forsberg was the daughter of James W. and Caroline F. R. Morgan; her grandfather was the brother of General Daniel Morgan, of the Revolutionary War.

Fouard

Mrs. Fouard, a Frenchwoman, who conducted a dye works on Twelfth Street, died April 24th, 1906; aged sixty-five years. She came to this country from Lyons, France. Her death took place at the home of her nephew, Mr. A. Charetie, in Campbell County.

FRANKLIN

The father of the first of the Franklin name to become identified with the business and social life of Lynchburg was Edward Franklin, who was born in Charlotte County, August 4th, 1777. He married Elizabeth Cook in 1803 and moved to Pittsylvania County, where he lived a long and honored life. He was a large land and mill owner, a gentleman justice and an elder in the Presbyterian Church. It is said that both he and his father, Benjamin, served as officers in the old Cub Creek Church. In 1851 he gave land in Pittsylvania County for a church to be used jointly by the Presbyterians, Methodists and Baptists, which was probably one of the early practical efforts towards church union. Edward Franklin was the father of ten children, among whom were James and Edward, Junior, who were prominent merchants in Lynchburg before the War Between the States. Edward died unmarried, and James married Emmeline Leftwich, but had no children. With John M. Miller, Senior, he established a bank which ranked high in the business world of Lynchburg for many years. Another son of Edward, Senior, was Captain John Franklin, of Pittsylvania County, who married Martha Jane Anderson of the family of Captain Charles Calloway and Colonel Jeremiah Early, of the Revolutionary Army. From this union were born six sons and six daughters, the six sons all serving in the C. S. A. One of these sons, Major Jacob H. Franklin, married Eliza Frances, daughter of Colonel Coleman Bennett, whose mother was descended from Major John Ward and Captain Robert Adams, of the Revolution. Major Jacob H. Franklin was a public-spirited man and did much to establish the splendid public school system of Lynchburg, being a member of the Board for thirty years. He was also a trustee of the Miller Orphan Asylum, a director in several banks, and for years a member of the City Council. After the War Between the States he went into business with his brother, Captain James Franklin, He later changed his business to a wholesale trade and was a pioneer wholesale merchant of the city. He died in Lynchburg in 1898.

Three of the six sons of Captain John Franklin and Martha Jane Anderson died unmarried: William E. died during the War Between the States, Thomas C. and Lieutenant Charles Calloway were killed at Chancellorsville. Another son, Captain John A. Franklin, became a successful citizen of Texas. One of his daughters, Emma J., married Joseph L. Lee, of Lynchburg, and another, Nannie K., married Eppa Dennett Guthrie, of Charlotte County. Both are dead and their descendants are prominent and useful citizens of Virginia and other States.

(This paper was prepared by Major John D. Guthrie, of Portland, Oregon and Mrs. Jas. S. Jones, of Chatham, Virginia.)

Gannaway

John E. Gannaway was born at "Edgewood," a noted plantation of Buckingham County, where the Gannaway family lived for many generations, being large land owners and slave owners. He was the son of William E. Gannaway and Katherine Grigg. His grandfather was Colonel John Gannaway, an officer in the Revolutionary Army and a prominent planter in Buckingham, whose home was also at "Edgewood." He had two sons, Richard and William E., both of whom were planters.

William E. was educated at Washington College, which later became Washington and Lee University. When he died in 1910, in his eighty-first year, he was the oldest alumnus of Washington and Lee. His wife died in 1872 at the age of forty. They had three children, John E., Mrs. J. N. Crute, and Richard. Mr. William E. Gannaway was for many years an elder in the Presbyterian Church.

John E. Gannaway was educated in a private school at the home of Colonel Edmund Hubbard, Junior, who lived at Saratoga, and was commonwealth's attorney of Buckingham for many years. Mr. Gannaway left "Edgewood" plantation in 1875, and came to Lynchburg, where for about twenty years he was connected with the hardware firm of Jones and Watts Company. In 1896 he established a business of his own and became a large hardware merchant, his sons, John E., Junior, and Walter C., coming into the business later.

In 1881 Mr. John E. Gannaway married Miss Mary Isabel Carroll, daughter of Mr. John W. Carroll, already mentioned as an early and eminently successful tobacco manufacturer. To them were born seven children:

John E., Junior, married Mary Nelson, the daughter of Thomas Nelson. They have two children, Isabel and Page.

Walter C., who went over-seas with the One Hundred Sixteenth Infantry of the Twenty-ninth Division in the World War, saw active service in the Meuse-Argonne, and was promoted from corporal to lieutenant, married Miss Regis Cassidy.

Mary Bell, married Christian Hoffman.

Zaida, married Dr. Lloyd Sheep, of the United States Army. They have one daughter, Carroll.

Ruth, married James Marshall Taylor, son of Mrs. Mary Champe Winston Taylor, of Ashland. They have one daughter, May Carroll.

Kate, married Clarence Taylor, of Taylorsville, Hanover County.

Sue DuVal, married Leonidas Pope Ward, of Lynchburg.

The Garland Family

The first record of a Garland in Virginia is in Saint Peter's Parish Register: the baptism of Edward, the son of Edward Garland, born May 20th, 1700. From this time the name figures prominently in colonial affairs. Probably the earliest records of the family have been destroyed, as was the case with so many Virginia records, since numbers of the county courthouses were burned during the War Between the States, and at other times. One of the most notable representatives of the Garland family lived in Lynchburg for many years: Judge James Garland, member of Congress during the administration of President Andrew Jackson, and for many years judge of the Corporation Court of this city. He died in 1885 in his ninety-fourth year. He presided over the court with efficiency until his retirement at the age of ninety, being then totally blind. Judge Garland began the practice of law in 1812. Mrs. Aurelius Christian and Mrs. Bettie Cole, two of his daughters, survived him. His granddaughter, Mrs. Sallie Ford (and her children), and his great-grandson, Mr. Boyd Healey (and his children), live in Lynchburg.

Judge Garland is believed to have been descended from the infant, Edward, baptized in 1700 in Saint Peter's Parish. Edward was the father of John, who lived in Hanover County at Garland's Neck, the place now called Blackwell's Neck. His children were: 1. Thomas, who inherited Garland's Neck, and founded the Goochland branch of Garlands; 2. Edward; 3. Robert, founder of the Louisa branch of Garlands; 4. James; 5. John; 6. Lucy; 7. Peter. James married Mary Rice, of Hanover County. He moved to Albemarle, and became rich and prominent. His children were: William, born 1746, married Ann Shepherd; Nannie, born 1748, married Lucas; Nathaniel, born 1750, married Miss Rodes; John, born 1751, died of camp fever in the Revolutionary War; James, born 1753, married Anna Wingfield, whose mother was a Hudson. He was an officer in the Revolutionary War, and was accidentally killed by a sentinel. He left four children: Hudson, Henrietta, Spotswood and James.

Hudson Garland was the father of Judge Garland, of Lynchburg, of whom we have already written. He was the father of Hudson, literary man and poet; of General John Garland, whose daughter married General Longstreet; and of Spotswood Garland. Hudson Garland represented Amherst in the House of Delegates, and held office in Tyler's administration. He was a captain in the War of 1812, and an intimate friend of Andrew Jackson, who gave him a cane made of a fragment of the "Constitution."

Spotswood Garland married Lucinda, daughter of Colonel Hugh Rose and Caroline Jordan, and had Hugh A., who married Ann Powell Burwell; Caroline, who married Maurice H. Garland; Landon Cabell, who married Louisa F. Garland, and Landon C. Garland, L.L.D., who was president of Randolph-Macon College, president of the University of Alabama, and chancellor of Vanderbilt University for a quarter of a century. His sister, Caroline, who married Maurice H. Garland, was the mother of General Samuel Garland, C. S. A., whose life and death have been recorded elsewhere in this book. Hugh A. Garland was author of the life of John Randolph, of Roanoke.

The children of James Garland and Mary Rice were: Sally, born 1754; Edward, born 1756, married Miss Old, and had eight children; Thomas, born 1757, moved to Kentucky and married Miss Fields, and he had eleven children; Mary, born 1760; Betsey, born 1762; Rice, born 1766, married Elizabeth Hamner and lived at Windy Mill, Albemarle County, and had the following children: William, married Nancy Hamner; James, married Mary Clark; Samuel, married Polly Anderson; Rice, married Miss LaStrappe; Betsey, married Mr. White; Mary, married Robert Slaughter; Burr, married Paulina Anderson; Maurice married Carolina Garland; Nicholas, married Miss Phillips.

Rice Garland was a distinguished member of Congress from Virginia, and afterwards judge of the Supreme Court of Louisiana. Robert, born in 1768, and Clifton in 1769, conclude the list of the children of James Garland and his wife, Mary Rice.

William Garland, born 1746, married Ann Shepherd, of Amherst County; issue: David Shepherd Garland; James Garland, who never married; Frances, who married Mr. Pendleton; Mary, who married Mr. Camden. David Shepherd, born 1769, married Jane Henry Meredith, March 4th, 1795. Jane Henry Meredith was the daughter of Colonel Samuel Meredith and Jane Henry, his wife, who was the sister of Patrick Henry. Issue of this marriage: Jane Meredith, who married Dr. John P. Cobbs and moved to Indiana in 1840; Anne Shepherd, who married Dr. Gustavus A. Rose and moved to Indiana in 1840; Sally Armistead, who married Captain William William Waller; Samuel Meredith, who married Mildred Jordan Powell; Mary Rice, who married Colonel Edward A. Cabell; William Henry, who married Frances Eubank; Patrick Henry, who married Miss Floyd; Eliza Virginia, who married George K. Cabell; Louisa Frances, who married Dr. Landon C. Garland; Caroline, died single; Martha Henry, died single.

Samuel Meredith Garland, born November 15th, 1802, married Mildred Jordan Powell, July 8th, 1830. He was a lawyer, and represented Amherst in the Legislature, also a member of the Reform Convention of 1850-51, and the Secession Convention of 1861. In his later years he was clerk of the Amherst Court. His children were: Mildred Irving, who married Colonel John T. Ellis; Martha Henry, who married Colonel Thomas Whitehead; Rev. J. Powell Garland, who married, first, Lucy Braxton, of Fredericksburg, and second, Narcissa Dillard, of Lynchburg, and third, Lucy Lee Richardson, of New Kent County; Ella Rose, who married Henry Wills; Jane Meredith, who married Willis Wills; Sally, died in infancy; David Shepherd, died single; Samuel Meredith, died single; Waller, died in childhood; Paulus Powell, married Lucy Ellis; Bessie Powell, married Rev. Dr. R. T. Wilson.

Of this family several have lived in Lynchburg. Dr. James Powell Garland, D.D., graduated at Emory and Henry College, June 10th, 1857, and was a member of the Methodist ministry for forty-seven years. Much of the time he was stationed in this town, and his children attended the schools and to a large extent were reared here. His son, David Garland, went to Long Island, where he was engaged in editing a Law Encyclopedia. He married in the North, but his daughter, Dorothy, was educated at Sweet Briar, where she met many friends and relatives of her father's people. Mildred Irving Garland, who married Colonel John T. Ellis, was the grandmother of Judge Strode, of the Lynchburg Corporation Court. Judge Strode's mother, Mildred Ellis, a lady of great charm and beauty, married Mr. Strode, who was head of the Kenmore school for boys.

Mrs. Thos. Whitehead also lived here for many years, and her children are well known to all of their day and generation. Her sons, Thomas and Irving Whitehead, lived in Lynchburg, where the latter practiced his profession. Mr. Waller G. Wills, the son of Ella Rose Garland, who married Henry Wills, has long been a leading and honored citizen of Lynchburg, where his mother lived for some years and died. His sister, Miss Donna Wills, is also well known in Lynchburg. The late Sam Wills, a druggist here, was the son of Mr. and Mrs. Willis Wills. Dr. Wilson, well known here a specialist in children's diseases, is the son of Bessie Powell Garland, who married Dr. R. T. Wilson, of Norfolk. Dr. Wilson's wife is Louise Garland, the daughter of Mr. Paulus P. Garland, who married Lucy Ellis.

The home of David Garland is still standing, a prominent feature of New Glasgow, and close by is "Winton," where Patrick Henry's mother lived and is buried. She was so beloved by her son-in-law, Colonel Samuel Meredith, that he asked to be buried at her feet.

James Richard Gilliam

James Richard Gilliam was born in Campbell County, Virginia, October 26th, 1854. His father was James Richard Gilliam, a teacher by profession, and his mother was Annie Slaughter Davenport. He was descended through both parents from people who had helped make Virginia history. Among his father's ancestors were the Bollings and the Wests, including Captain John West, colonial governor. His mother's family produced many eminent men in law, politics, and business. Just before the War Between the States the Davenports in Richmond and Lynchburg were chief owners of the packet line which played such an important part in the Virginia life of that day.

When Mr. Gilliam was only a year old his father died, and when he was six his mother moved to Amherst County. Here he received what education the county schools offered and five months at Mr. Strode's school at Kenmore. Before he was fifteen, and prior to his term at Kenmore, he qualified as deputy sheriff of Amherst. Having lived an outdoor life, he had developed a physique of great strength and endurance, along with a remarkable energy and capacity for exacting labor.

After leaving Kenmore High School, he engaged in mercantile work for six months, and then was once more offered the position of deputy sheriff, which involved duties and responsibilities equal to those of sheriff. So well did he discharge the work of this office that he became known as one of the best county officials in the State.

While holding the position of deputy sheriff James Richard Gilliam acquired a half interest in the Amherst Enterprise, a weekly newspaper of which he was business manager. The little town, however, proved to be too small a field for his activities, and in 1878 Mr. Gilliam came to Lynchburg to live. He left behind him the respect and affection of the entire Amherst community, which viewed his departure with regret.

Mr. Gilliam was married on October 25th, 1887, to Jessie Belfield Johnson, whose father, Fontaine D. Johnson, was a prominent business man of Lynchburg. Mr. and Mrs. Gilliam had four children: Annie (Mrs. Charles E. Conrad), James Richard, Junior, Frank Johnson, and Thomas West. For years Mr. Gilliam lived on Court Street, and later built a home on Madison Street. On locating in Lynchburg Mr. Gilliam first became a partner in a wholesale grocery business, and also in a tobacco commission house. He organized a wholesale and retail furniture company, following that with a profitable venture in wholesale boots and shoes. For ten years he applied himself to this enterprise, but at the end of that time he sold out to his partners in order to turn his attention exclusively to developing coal property and banking interests in which he was interested. From the original development of the coal mining interests in Southwest Virginia and West Virginia he realized the importance of this field, and began to increase his holdings, for he had the nerve and intelligence to act at a time when a lesser man would have been afraid. He was president of the Gilliam, the Arlington, the Shawnee, the Glen Alum, and the Lee Coal and Coke Companies. He also became president of two banks in Lynchburg, and one each in Bedford, Jonesville, Monterey, Clifton Forge, and Lebanon. He was president of the Quinn-Marshall Company, and a special partner in the Lynchburg Shoe Company, both large wholesale houses. In addition to these business activities he discharged his duty to the town with the same ability that he bestowed on his own affairs, being chairman of the Finance Committee of the upper branch of the City Council and president of the Board of Managers of the Home and Retreat (now Memorial) Hospital. He was for many years a member of the Board of Stewards of Court Street Methodist Church.

Mr. Gilliam came to Lynchburg in 1878, when the town was just beginning to recover from the shock of war and Reconstruction. The citizens were then engaged in the brave effort of remaking their town, and to them he added his able assistance and poured new energy and resource into the place at a time when these were vastly needed. His accuracy in judging men and his nerve in taking advantage of opportunities soon brought to the forefront every institution with which he was associated. Many of the enterprises he started then have remained up to the present time. At the time of his death, in 1917, the directors of the Chamber of Commerce voiced the sentiment that "our city as it stands today in the business world is his product more than that of any other one man." He had qualities of goodness and honor that do not always accompany material success, and it was for these qualities that his friends loved him and his fellow citizens respected him. One of his gifts to the community, the chimes he had installed in Court Street Methodist Church, frequently and vividly recall him to the memory of those that knew him: a man who loved the best in literature, who loved to travel, and whose highest aim in life was to help those who could not help themselves.

The life of Mr. Gilliam was remarkable in the fact that he

conquered and won on his own ability alone. He had proved himself a man at an age when most boys are but children, and have yet to face the real struggle of life. He was essentially a captain of industry, but to him clung much of the old order, the ancient Virginia tradition. When he was growing up all rank had been levelled by war, and all the advantages of life which might have been his to count on had been swept away, yet he held always an honorable but modest pride in the knowledge of the greatness of those forbears to which he had so just a claim. His position in the community was one of personal achievement, but achievement resting upon a foundation of the best of Virginia birth and breeding.

Thomas West Gilliam

Mr. Thomas West Gilliam, a successful business man and financier of Lynchburg, was the son of Dr. Glover Davenport Gilliam, of Prince Edward County, who married Elizabeth Bolling Jones. Dr. Gilliam was born in 1800. He lived at Landover on Falling River, near Naruna, and was a large land owner. This branch of the Gilliam family came from Richard Gilliam, son of Epaphroditus and Elizabeth Gilliam. Richard Gilliam married Elizabeth Glover, and was close kin to Glover Davenport, after whom he named his son, Glover Davenport Gilliam.

Mr. T. West Gilliam married Frances Diuguid and had one child, Elsie. Miss Elsie Gilliam was a missionary at one time, but now makes her home in Lynchburg. James Richard Gilliam, a brother of Mr. West Gilliam, married Annie Davenport, and was the father of Mr. James R. Gilliam, who was a prominent and successful citizen of Lynchburg and whose family still live here.

Gilmer

The family of Mr. George Gilmer in Lynchburg represents two noted names in Virginia life and history: Gilmer and Patton. Dr. George Gilmer, a native of Scotland and graduate of the University of Edinburgh, came to Virginia early in the eighteenth century. He settled in Williamsburg, where he successfully combined the vocation of physician, surgeon and druggist for fully fifty years. He died January 15th, 1757, widely loved and honored in the colony. Dr. Gilmer was thrice married, first to the daughter of Dr. Ridgeway, his partner in medicine, and second to Mary Peachey Walker, daughter of Thomas Walker and Susan (Peachey) Walker, of King and Queen County. Dr. Gilmer's second wife was a sister of Dr. Thomas Walker, patriot and early explorer of Kentucky. His third wife was Harrison Blair, daughter of Archibald Blair. The antecedents of Mrs. Gilmer, who was Rita Patton, were also Scotch. The first of the name in Virginia was Robert Patton, who came to Fredericksburg before the Revolutionary War. He married Anna Gordon Mercer, daughter of General Hugh Mercer, who was killed in the Battle of Princeton.

GLASS

Edward Christian Glass was born September 7th, 1852. He was the son of Robert Henry Glass and his first wife, Augusta Christian Glass. He was educated in the private schools of Lynchburg and at Norwood school for boys in Nelson County. He supplemented this by reading and study. When he was eighteen Mr. Glass began his career as a teacher, as one of a corps of twenty teachers in the first public school session in Lynchburg.

Except for two intervals of two years each, Mr. Glass spent his entire life in Lynchburg. Mr. Abram Biggers was Lynchburg's first Superintendent of Public Schools. When he died, William H. Ruffner, State Superintendent of Public Instruction, suggested that his successor should be a practical educator, and Mr. Glass was unanimously recommended by the Lynchburg School Board as having all the necessary qualifications. He was only twenty-six years old when he was notified of his appointment. He was at that time presiding over a corps of twenty-three teachers, and a total enrollment of 1,539 pupils, housed in the present Monroe, Jackson and Polk Street Schools, and the old

Court Street Building (burned since that time), together with several small rented buildings.

This period has been called the darkest period in the history of the public school system in the State. The High School in Lynchburg has been entirely abandoned—voted down in the City Council. The first work of Mr. Glass after his appointment, which was January 9th, 1879, was to restore the High School. In order to do this it was necessary to make a fight on this issue in the election for the City Council. The school issue was forcibly presented to Lynchburg voters and as a result the day was won. The High School was restored, and the entire school system was improved by a new Council, favorably inclined towards general education.

Mr. Glass' next step for improving the schools was to found a system of normal school instruction for those who wished to teach school after graduation. He began this work of training teachers in 1881. By 1889 the summer school methods, which were first held in Lynchburg, had developed into a pioneer institution by which other normal schools were being modeled. This same movement was the forerunner of the present summer school at the University of Virginia. So able were Mr. Glass' views on education, and so useful his work, that he was pressed into service on various educational boards for schools and colleges. He served as co-editor and co-owner of the Virginia Journal of Education, the official publication of the Virginia public school system. He studied the school systems in the United States, in London, Glasgow and Edinburgh, always searching for means by which his own work might be improved. At one time he exchanged teachers from the Buroughmuier High School of Edinburgh, Scotland, securing from its staff a teacher of English for the High School here.

On November 4th, 1879, he married Miss Sue Carter. She died August 28th, 1929, shortly before they were to have celebrated the golden anniversary of their marriage, and from this time his health gradually failed. He died October 26th, 1931.

LYNCHBURG AND ITS NEIGHBORS

Not long before his death the writer was talking with Mr. Glass about the early days of his career, those difficult days in the life of the public schools, when the representative men of Lynchburg voted against continuing the High School. I asked how intelligent men could be so short-sighted. He named over several members of the City Council of that day who had voted against the High School, men whom we both knew to be citizens of value. I was inclined to take a severe view, but Mr. Glass said:

"No, they were not as narrow and illiberal as you think. They were not educated up to the idea in those days. There was much more class distinction than there is now, and many very honest and sincere men believed that it was enough to give the children of the town the simplest education, and let their parents pay for the higher branches if they could afford it. Many in that day did not think it just to tax people to give a high school education to the poor, when they considered a plain grammar school education was enough for the poor anyway." Yet he was entirely without animosity towards those men who did not think his way. This was characteristic of the man. He had that rare quality of being a partisan without bitterness.

A banquet was tendered him by the teachers of the schools on his fiftieth anniversary as Superintendent of the Public Schools of Lynchburg. Many honors were paid him during his life along with honorary degrees, but his friends never thought of him as a learned doctor. To them he was the little red-headed man whose whole life had been torn to pieces by the War, and who somehow had been able to overcome these disadvantages, who had educated himself, and then had set to work to give to others the benefit of what he had won at the cost of so much self-sacrifice.

In our own time few men have done more for Lynchburg than did Edward Christian Glass. His whole life was dedicated to this town, and the school system which he built up were changed from a make-shift program for the education of the poor to an institution of such excellence that private schools soon became a thing of the past in Lynchburg.

The editorial which is quoted here was written by Dr. Douglass Freeman and appeared in the News Leader of Richmond at the time of Mr. Glass' death:

"Ned Glass

High and hideous above Fifth Street stood the old uptown public school of Lynchburg. Boys who climbed up from Main, or came across from Church and Court and Clay had vague ideas that there was another public school somewhere on the side of Diamond Hill, but their curiosity did not extend that far. The last horizon of their educational ken was the high school perched perilously at Eleventh and Court, flanked on one side by Miss Judson Cabiness' house, and fronted across precipitous Court Street by the First Baptist Church. And that high school was synonymous with 'Mr. Glass'—'Ned Glass' as less revering adults called him.

The school system of Lynchburg was Ned Glass. The supreme interest of Ned Glass was the schools. He grew up with them, flourished with them, and saw their reputation spread until a certificate of graduation from that city's high school was as good credentials as a youngster could offer in college. Large service and big honors were his. The 'school of methods,' that has since become the summer school of the University of Virginia, was his dream and his creation. Twenty-five years ago, when education was resurgent in the Old Dominion, the influence of Ned Glass was probably more potent than that of any other man in shaping public school policy. Although he labored for fifty-two years in the public schools of one city, he never grew old. Always there was the same wiry body, the same sure educational vision, the same soft tone, the same unselfish purpose.

Doubtless Lynchburg will memorialize him in a portrait to be hung in the great high school that bears his name. If this is done, let it not be a dressed up portrait with doctoral robes and trappings. Paint him in his workaday clothes, standing under the big tree in the yard of the old high school, ringing the hand bell and watching the youngsters as they troop back into school —watching with those understanding eyes, and with that familiar, gently-wise smile upon his face."

Gooch

The Gooch family of Virginia is descended from Lieutenant-Colonel Henry Gooch, of York County, in Virginia, a member of the same family as Governor Gooch, adherent of Bacon in the uprising known as Bacon's Rebellion. Mr. Claiborne Gooch, of this city, is the son of the late Arthur F. Gooch and his wife, Hannah Este, who died at the home of her son in 1905 in her eighty-second year. She was a native of Trenton, New Jersey, and left two children, Claiborne and Miss Elizabeth E. Gooch. Mr. Claiborne W. Gooch married Virgie, daughter of Mr. John Bell Winfree, an influential citizen of Lynchburg.

The Gordon Family

The Gordons, who settled in Lancaster County about 1738, were of distinguished Scotch ancestry, claiming descent from Rob Roy McGregor and the Scotch kings. James Gordon, from whom the Lynchburg Gordons come, was a colonel of militia and justice of the peace. He was married twice, his first wife being Milicent Conway, his second wife, Mary, was a daughter of Colonel Nathaniel Harrison. James was a pioneer Presbyterian in Eastern Virginia. He died June 2, 1768. Mr. James Newton Gordon, a lawyer, was the first of this family in Lynchburg. He was born May 19th, 1825; his parents were Colonel James Gordon and Agnes Scott, the daughter of Major Samuel Scott. Mr. Gordon married Elvira Moon, of Halifax County, and lived for many years at 1023 Jackson Street, where he died April 15th, 1888. His children were: Imogene Stannard, who married William Minnigerode, of Richmond; Kate Blanks, married Dr. William S. Gordon, of Richmond; Elvira Moon, married Alfred Randolph Carrington, of Charlotte County. The children of Mrs. A. R. Carrington are Elsie, Florence and A. Randolph Carrington, Junior. J. Newton Gordon, son of John Newton Gordon, is a prominent banker and business man in Lynchburg. He was for a long time at the head of the Cooperative Building and Loan Association, and is now in charge of the Federal Loan Banking System in this district.

Gregory

Colonel James B. Gregory, one of Lynchburg's best and most popular citizens, died April 16th, 1906, at his home on Federal Street. He was born in Lynchburg in 1851. His services to the Confederacy were of such value as to be recorded in Stratton's book, War Between the States, although at the beginning of the War Colonel Gregory was only ten years old. He was the son of James D. and Anna Elizabeth Gregory. In 1880 he married Ella Rorer, of Roanoke, who died in a few years, leaving two daughters, Miss Nellie Gregory and Mrs. William K. Davis. He was also survived by three sisters and two brothers, Mrs. Lizzie Jones, Mrs. Thomas C. Miller, Miss Annie Gregory, Mr. D. P. Gregory and Mr. William Gregory.

Gregory

Mr. Patrick Gregory died at his home, Oak Grove, in Campbell County, near this city, October 8th, 1905; aged seventy-eight years. He was born in Limerick, Ireland, and came to this country when very young. During the War Between the States he was a wagon master in Lynchburg in the service of the Confederacy. After this he conducted a dairy business. A man of a genial nature, and in all business relations noted for his integrity, Mr. Gregory was a well-known figure in this section, and esteemed and respected by all who knew him.

Guggenheimer

Among the good citizens of Lynchburg none deserve more honor than the Guggenheimer family, of whom several generations have lived here, and shared the adversity as well as the good fortune of the town. Mr. Charles M. Guggenheimer, who for many years was head of the Guggenheimer business here, was born in Lynchburg, July 24th, 1860. He was the son of Mr. and Mrs. Nathan Guggenheimer. Mr. Nathan Guggenheimer was born in Germany, and came to this country with his brothers when quite a young man. He started in business with the Untermeyer family in 1840. He was a brave Confederate soldier, a man of great benevolence, and he and his brothers were prominent figures in the life of Lynchburg.

Those qualities of mind and heart which brought popularity and prosperity to the elder members of this family were handed down to Charles M. Guggenheimer and his sons. Mr. Charles M. Guggenheimer died April 3rd, 1928, and his oldest son, Charles M. Guggenheimer, Junior, died some months later. Mr. Charles M. Guggenheimer, the elder, married Miss Minnie Rosenbaum, of Richmond. His children now living are Nat S. and Max Guggenheimer, and two daughters, Mrs. Jerome Waterman, of Tampa, Florida, and Mrs. Bertram Nusbaum, of Norfolk. There are six grandchildren in the family.

The Guggenheimers have been living in Lynchburg for nearly a hundred years. Mr. Max Guggenheimer, uncle of the late Charles M. Guggenheimer, was also a valued citizen; generous, public-spirited, enthusiastic and a good man in the very best sense of the word. He, too, shouldered a musket and went to war with the Lynchburg soldiers in the sixties. On his return from the war he married Miss Bertha Rosenbaum. They had one daughter, Cecile, who was noted for her beauty. She died at the early age of twenty-eight, shortly after her marriage to Mr. Milliken.

The Hall Family

Rev. William Thomas Hall, D.D., L.L.D., was born December 5th, 1835, near Reidsville, North Carolina. He died March 17th, 1911, in Presbyterian Hospital, Philadelphia. He was prepared at home for college by his father, graduated at the age of eighteen years from Davidson College, North Carolina, and from Columbia Theological Seminary at twenty-one. At his first pastorate at Lancaster, South Carolina, he was married to Miss Fannie Witherspoon. They had one child, Mary Belle, now Mrs. Ernest Moose. After the death of his first wife, Dr. Hall was a widower for twelve years. He then married Miss Mary Ellen Handy, of Canton, Mississippi, where he had his second charge. His second wife had three children, John Handy, Hannah and Ellen.

Dr. Hall was chaplain in the Thirtieth Mississippi Regiment, under General Bragg, and was known as the "Fighting Parson," because he always went into battle with his regiment. He said, "I could not preach to the men unless I took the same risks they did." For twenty-five years, from 1872 to 1895, he was pastor of the old First Presbyterian Church of Lynchburg, which stood on Main Street. During the last sixteen years of his life he was professor of theology at Columbia Theological Seminary, Columbia, South Carolina, which he had attended in his early manhood.

Dr. Hall was a scholar and student all his life, and a man of deep erudition. It would scarcely be expected that such a man could be popular, in the general sense of the word, his time being spent in study rather than in the company of his fellow man. However, at the time of the first World's Fair in Chicago, when the prize of a journey to the Fair, a round-trip ticket and expenses was offered to the most popular preacher in Lynchburg, it was found that the result of the vote was a tie between Father McGurk, priest of the Catholic Church of the Holy Cross, and Dr. Hall. The matter was settled by giving both of these reverend gentlemen a trip to the Fair.

The second Mrs. Hall was a sister of Mr. Nathan Handy, of Lynchburg. She belonged to an eminent Southern family. John Handy, of Canton, Mississippi, was her father. He was of the firm of Handy and Davis, and handled the affairs of Jefferson

Davis. Her uncle, Judge Handy, a noted jurist, was the associate of Alexander H. Stephens in the troubles of 1860.

Of the son of this couple, John Handy Hall, who met with so untimely a death by motor accident one month after his return from the World War, the War Magazine published the following record: "Lieutenant-Colonel John Handy Hall was born in Lynchburg, Virginia, January 1st, 1874. He was an alumnus of Washington and Lee University and the University of Virginia. He received medals at both of these institutions. He could not say just when he was connected with the organized militia, but had a distinct recollection of attending the Governor's ball at Columbia, South Carolina, in 1895, as a member of the Governor's Guard of the city, wearing epaulettes six inches in diameter, and only a private at that! He became a member of the Virginia militia in 1896, and (undiscouraged) joined the Pennsylvania National Guard in 1904. He was made a major in the One Hundred Eighth Field Artillery. In his leisure moments he practiced law. He served in the Spanish-American War, on the Mexican Border, and in a variety of 'domestic insurrections.' He was a member of the University Club, Southern and Democratic Clubs of Philadelphia and the Army and Navy Club of New York, also a member of the Spanish-American War Veterans, and the Sons of Confederate Veterans." At the close of the World War he held the rank of Lieutenant-Colonel, having served in France and Belgium in the One Hundred Eighth Field Artillery. He was decorated with the Iron Cross by King Albert, of Belgium.

John Handy Hall graduated from the Law School at the University of Virginia in 1895 and later located in Philadelphia, where he practiced law. In 1900 he was connected with the Law Digest, and after this was in the office of William Glasgow. In 1914 he became First Assistant District Attorney with Francis Fisher Kane. In 1918 he was third partner in the firm of Duane and Morris. John Hall married Miss Rebecca Sander Ashcom, and left four children, John Handy, William Thomas,

Nathan Handy and Mary Ellen. His widow married John S. Bleecker, Westchester, Pennsylvania.

Halsey Family

The Halsey family can be traced without a break in England to 1512, during which time they have occupied the Golden Parsonage at Great Gaddesden, in Hertfordshire. There were Halseys, probably the same family, living in Cornwall in 1189, in the reign of Richard I. The manor, Lonsleigh, where they lived was in Cornwall at that time, but although the name is the same, the connection has not been established. It is positively known that John Halsey was living at the Golden Parsonage in 1512. The place was an old church property, taken over by the crown in the fifteenth and sixteenth centuries, and granted to William Halsey, the son of John, by King Henry VIII in a deed dated March 12th, 1548, and ever since that date has remained in the unbroken possession of the Halsey family. It is still standing, until a few years ago the owner and occupant being the Right Honorable Sir Thomas Frederick Halsey, member of Parliament for Herts, a pleasant and cultivated gentleman. The manor and title are now held by his son, Sir Lionel Halsey, an admiral of the British Navy and an intimate friend of the Prince of Wales.

The first of the name in America was Thomas Halsey, who came over, according to the best information we have at hand, in the year 1632, in one of the colonization enterprises of which John Winthrop was the leader. He settled in Lynn, Massachusetts, but later went to Southampton, Long Island, where he became a prominent citizen, dying there in 1679, at the age of ninety. He was a Puritan, but as has been quaintly said, "of a milder type than the settlers of Plymouth Rock." This Thomas Halsey's three sons, Thomas, Isaac and Daniel, and his daughter, Elizabeth, as indicated by his will, were born before 1631. When Southampton was divided into wards in 1644 Halsey is mentioned. Of his sons, one remained in the North, one is known to have left descendants in the West, and the other, Thomas, came to South Carolina. From Thomas Halsey, of South Carolina, the family in Lynchburg is descended.

William Allen Halsey, born at Chowan, North Carolina, before 1773; died in Lynchburg in 1831, and was buried in the Methodist Cemetery, but the site of his grave is unknown. He married Polly Lacy in Goochland County, October 19th, 1793, and was residing in Goochland County in 1792, as shown by certain court proceedings. In 1826 he had a home in Richmond, Virginia, and according to Mrs. Duval, his daughter, he paid poll tax and maintained a residence in Virginia, but carried on his tobacco business in Edenton, North Carolina. His son, Seth Halsey, was born in Goochland County in 1800, but was brought up in Richmond. He married Julia D. B. Peters, whose father was a large land owner in Bedford County. She was a lady of strong character and great worth. Their children were:

Edward Sidney Halsey, born 1832, died 1906; unmarried.

Don Peters Halsey, born September 15th, 1836; died January 1st, 1883, near Tye River in Nelson County. Married March 7th, 1866, to Sarah Warwick Daniel, daughter of Judge Wm. Daniel, Junior, of the Supreme Court.

Alexander Lemuel Halsey, born 1841, killed at the Battle of Smithfield in 1864; Captain Twenty-first Virginia Cavalry, C. S. A.

Stephen Peters Halsey, born in Lynchburg, November 13th, 1843, married Rebecca Emily Holmes, of Maryland, in 1870; no children.

Elmira B. Peters, born 1837, married Dr. Edward Murrell. Her daughter, Julia, married Senator John Warwick Daniel.

Aurelia C., born August, 1845, married August 11th, 1871, to Colonel John G. Meem, C. S. A.

Seth, born 185—, killed by accident while diving in Blackwater Creek; aged thirteen.

Three sons of this family were officers in the War Between

the States and served with distinction. Captain Alexander Lemuel Halsey was killed at the Battle of Smithfield. Major Stephen P. Halsey served from Manassas to Appomattox. Captain Don P. Halsey lost the sight of one eye, and was imprisoned by the enemy. He won a great name for bravery, but gave up his youth and health and a notable career as a lawyer for his State. Just as he was gaining a large success in his profession in Richmond he was compelled to leave and go to the country on account of his failing health. There he died, January 1st, 1883, leaving his wife, who was Miss Sarah Ann Warwick Daniel, and six children. His two daughters followed him to the grave in August. The children were:

Caroline Daniel Halsey, born November 3rd, 1868; died August 18th, 1883.

Don Peters Halsey, born December 29th, 1870, married Miss Mary Michaux Dickinson, of Hampden-Sydney, Virginia.

Julia Olive Halsey, born November 15th, 1873; died August 8th, 1883.

Seth Cabell Halsey, born July 4th, 1876.

John Warwick Daniel Halsey, born January 3rd, 1879.

Edwin Alexander Halsey, born September 4th, 1881.

Major Stephen P. Halsey, a retired tobacconist, still lives in his handsome home on Court Street. Here, during the lifetime of Mrs. Halsey, who was distinguished for her gracious hospitality, much of the social activity of the town centered. Major Halsey has long been a staunch supporter of Saint Paul's Church. Until a few years back he took a leading part in Lynchburg's Memorial Day services, acting as Marshall-in-Chief, and arranging our processions in true military fashion. This, as he humorously said, gave him an opportunity to turn tables on those generals and colonels under whom he had once served and to give orders instead of receiving them.

Close to him on Court Street lives his nephew, Judge Don P. Halsey, of the Circuit Court, who, following in the footsteps of his ancestors, has well served his State and town, as commonwealth's attorney, State senator and judge of the Circuit Court, and has won no small fame as a writer and as an orator of uncommon charm and power. Mrs. Halsey, his wife, belongs to a prominent old Virginia family, which has produced many able men. She numbers among her ancestors the Michaux family, of the Huguenot blood which has added so much glamour and distinction to the South.

Don Peters Halsey: Judge, Circuit Court; born December 29th, 1870, Lynchburg, Virginia; son of Don Peters and Sarah Warwick (Daniel) Halsey; educated in the public schools, Episcopal High School, Hampden-Sydney College, Washington and Lee University; married Mary M. Dickinson, June 11th, 1894, at Hampden-Sydney, Virginia. Commonwealth's Attorney, City of Lynchburg, Virginia, 1895-97; member of Virginia State Senate, 1902-04 and 1908-12; member of Commission presenting statues of Washington and Lee to Statuary Hall, Washington, District of Columbia, 1905; member of Commission presenting copy of Houdon statue of Washington to France (Versailles), 1910; member of Electoral College, 1904; lecturer with Y. M. C. A. (A. E. F.), France, 1918-19; Trustee, Hampden-Sydney College; former member Board of Trustees, Virginia State Normal School at Harrisonburg; Chairman of Commission on proposed Virginia State Liberal Arts College for Women; judge, Sixth Virginia Judicial Circuit, 1925—; author of various articles in legal and other publications. Member: Lynchburg, Virginia, and American Bar Association; Chi Phi; Masons; Elks; K. of P.; I. O. O. F.; Sons of American Revolution; Sons of Confederate Veterans. Club, Westmoreland (Richmond); residence, 720 Court Street; office, Courthouse, Lynchburg, Virginia.

Hamner

The late Edward S. Hamner, who, with C. D. Lumsden, his partner for many years, lived here, was a valuable citizen of Lynchburg. He married Miss White, of Albemarle, and left several children. Miss Sallie Hamner is librarian at Fort Hill Library. Edward S. Hamner, retired naval officer, is in business here. S. Garland Hamner is an attorney-at-law. He married Miss Winchester, of Mississippi. Rawlins Hamner.

The late Mr. and Mrs. Walker Hamner, who lived on Daniel's Hill, left several children. Mr. Roland Hamner is the only son of this family now living in Lynchburg. Mrs. Landon Lowry, who was Ruby Hamner, lives in Bedford. Dell Hamner married E. H. Hancock, and Edith married Harry Shaner, who was City Engineer at the time of their marriage. Several of the grandchildren of Mr. and Mrs. Hamner live here. Until recently Mr. Walker Adams, son of Rosa Hamner and Richard Adams, and Rosalie Morton, daughter of Alpha Hamner Morton, were among their descendants living here. The late Charles D. Hamner was a man of great personal attraction and his death was felt as a distinct loss to this community. His widow, who was Helen Heald, daughter of the late Duncan Heald, of Baltimore, lives here with her two sons. Of this family it may be truly said, that they were distinguished for beauty and charm, and that they have been much beloved in Lynchburg.

HANCOCK

Mr. Ammon Hancock, born April 7th, 1815, died May 4th, 1888, married Charlotte Hewitt in 1851; he was a prominent citizen of Lynchburg. His parents were Justus Hancock, of Bedford County, and Harriet Walden. Mr. Hancock was an early tobacconist here, his sons were also engaged in this business. He was Mayor of Lynchburg, and served the public in many other positions of importance. Many of the Hancock family have taken a leading part in the civic affairs here. The children of Mr. Ammon Hancock were as follows: 1. James, born May 17th, 1852, died January 14th, 1914, married Alice Williams in Lynchburg in 1878. Mr. Hancock and his lovely wife lived during their residence in Lynchburg at the home owned now by Mr. William Hickson, on Madison Street. 2. Ernest Justus Hancock, born November 24th, 1854, died August 1st, 1924, married Julia

E. Kinney, of Coopville, Washington. 3. Edwin Hancock, born April 23rd, 1857, died May 28th, 1910, married Eva Chamblin, of Loudon County, Virginia. 4. Lily Hancock, married Dr. W. B. Thornhill, October 17th, 1889.

John Henry Hancock, a son of Justus and Harriet (Walden) Hancock, married Martha Waller. His children were: Robert Hancock, married Annis Stevens; had one daughter, Annie Roberta, who married William Abbot Henderson. James H. Hancock, married Emma Harris. Emma S. Hancock, married S. N. Burroughs. John Hancock, married, first Matilda Howell; second, Daisy Martin. Ammon Hancock, unmarried. Benjamin Hancock, unmarried. William D. Hancock, unmarried. Samuel E. Hancock, married Alice Hewitt. Richard Hancock, unmarried.

The Handy Family

The name was originally Hendy, or Hands, being of French origin. The family was expelled from France, on account of their religious opinions, and had settled in the County of Essex, England, in the reign of Henry II. Thereafter the name was Handy, the Saxon form, Hendy, being more rarely used.

Samuel Handy, progenitor of this family in Maryland and Virginia, came to America in 1635, and settled at Annamessex, Somerset County, Maryland, which was once claimed by Virginia as a part of Northampton County. Samuel married Mary Sewall, of Annamessex. He died at the age of 101. His descendants have intermarried, for many generations, with some of the most noted families in Virginia and Maryland, among them being the Upshurs and Browns, of Brownville, Northampton County, and the Dashiells and Wilsons and Marins, of Maryland.

There have been many distinguished soldiers, statesmen and lawyers of this name in England, Ireland and America, but perhaps none of them had a more interesting career than Captain George Handy, a Revolutionary soldier. He enlisted at the age of eighteen, under General Smallwood, and immediately went north, taking part in the Battles of Lexington, Bunker Hill, Brandywine, Germantown, and others. Later he served as Captain of Cavalry in Lee's Partisan Legion, and was a member of Lighthorse Harry Lee's staff. Captain Handy was present at the Surrender of Cornwallis, at Yorktown. His exploits are recorded at length in the Memoirs of War in the Southern Department, by Henry Lee, and more recently by Thomas Boyd, in his book, Lighthorse Harry Lee, in which Captain Handy appears often as a gallant courageous soldier. Captain Handy was a warm friend of Alexander Hamilton, with whom he fought in the North, prior to joining Lee's Legion, and for whom he named his son.

Captain George Handy was an original member of the Society of Cincinnati. This honor has descended to his grandson, Nathan Bryant Handy, of Lynchburg, who is probably the youngest living member of the Cincinnati, whose grandfather was a charter member. Captain George Handy was an officer in Lee's Battalion of Light Dragoons. He served with Pulaski's Legion with rank of captain (Heitmanns).

Captain Handy married Elizabeth Wilson, daughter of James and Martha Glasgow Wilson. Two of his sons, John and Alexander Hamilton, moved when quite young from Maryland to Mississippi, where both became noted lawyers. Alexander Hamilton Handy was Chief Justice of the Supreme Court of Mississippi for twenty years.

Mr. Nathan Bryant Handy, of Lynchburg, is the son of John and Hannah Margaret Cox Handy, the grandson of Captain George Handy, the great-grandson of Major Benjamin Handy, who held a major's commission under the colonial government—the great-great-grandson of Ebenezer and Bettie Dashiell Handy, and great-great-great-grandson of the immigrant, Samuel. He was born at Canton, Mississippi, but came to Lynchburg at the age of ten to make his home with his brother-in-law, Rev. W. T. Hall, D.D., L.L.D., for twenty-three years pastor of First Presbyterian Church.

Mr. Handy began his business career in the hardware store of E. L. Bell and Company at the corner Ninth and Main Streets. Four years later he was appointed commercial agent of the Virginia Nail and Iron Works at Reusen, Virginia. In 1891 Mr. Handy organized the N. B. Handy Company. He has served the city in many capacities, on the Police Board, School Board, City Council, chairman of the Democratic Executive Committee, and at present as president of the Associated Charities and vice-president of the Presbyterian Orphans' Home. He is director in several of Lynchburg's financial institutions.

Mr. Handy is an elder in the Presbyterian Church, as have been his progenitors continuously since the establishment of that faith in the United States.

He married Leila Anne, daughter of Isham and Anne Obenchain Percy, of Botetourt County, Virginia. They have two living children. Their son, John Bryant Handy, married Allen, daughter of Hugh and Drucilla Stockley Steele, of Norfolk, Virginia. They have three daughters, Drucilla, Hannah Margaret and Jackallen.

Josephine Percy, daughter of Nathan Bryant and Leila Percy Handy, married James Dearing Christian, son of Judge Frank Patteson Christian, of the Corporation Court of Lynchburg, and his wife, Mary Lou Dearing Christian, daughter of Brigadier-General James Dearing, C. S. A. They have two children, James Dearing Christian, Junior, and Leila Percy Christian.

The children and grandchildren of Mr. and Mrs. Handy have their residence in Lynchburg.

Randolph Harrison

Randolph Harrison, born January 25th, 1858, at West Hill, the home of his parents in Augusta County, near Staunton, died in Lynchburg, February 16th, 1929. He was the son of Henry Harrison, of the James River family of that name, who married Jane St. Clair Cochran. They had fourteen children, of whom twelve lived to maturity. Among these was Judge

George M. Harrison, of the Virginia Supreme Court of Appeals. The parents of Henry Harrison were Carter H. Harrison, of Clifton, who married Janetta Fisher, a niece of Mary Ambler, the wife of Chief Justice John Marshall. While attending school in Richmond, Henry lived in the Chief Justice's house, and sometimes went to market with "Uncle Marshall."

Randolph Harrison was a student at Virginia Polytechnic Institute at Blacksburg; he then taught school in Augusta County for two years. In 1880-81 he studied law at the University of Virginia. In the fall of 1881 he located in Lynchburg, and began the practice of his profession. Several young lawyers came to the bar here at the same time, among them being Roy B. Smith, afterwards judge of the Corporation Court of Roanoke; William Minor Lyle, now dean of the Law School of the University of Virginia; N. C. Manson, Junior, James E. Edmunds, Armistead R. Long, and others. Mr. Harrison and Charles B. Wierman formed a partnership in 1885, which was dissolved in 1886 by Mr. Wierman's departure from Lynchburg for the West. In 1892 Mr. Harrison formed a partnership with Armistead R. Long, which continued until the death of Mr. Harrison, and became one of the best-known law firms in Virginia.

The reputation of Mr. Harrison as an able and successful lawyer was based on his profound knowledge of law, and his well-known probity of mind and character. Perhaps his greatest achievement in his profession was his monumental work on the commission appointed by the Legislature to adjust the State debt. This had been a matter of controversy between Virginia and West Virginia since the time of their partition. The question was finally settled by the Supreme Court of the United States, in a decision which was a decided victory for Virginia, and for Mr. Harrison as well, as he had acted as counsel for the commission.

Aside from the practice of law, Mr. Harrison was a profound student of the War Between the States, its battles and its generals. In Lynchburg he was regarded as an honor to his profession and to the town of his adoption. In all classes of people he aroused a high respect for his fine moral and intellectual qualities, and those closest to him loved him for his worth as a loyal and devoted friend.

Mr. Harrison was married November 17th, 1897, to Miss Julia Halsey Meem, and left three children: Randolph, who is in the United States Consular Service; Aurelia and Julia. A son, his second child, Jacquelin, died in infancy.

HOLCOMBE

The Holcombes of Virginia were descended from Andrew Holcombe, who was transported to the Barbadoes for taking part in the Duke of Monmouth's Rebellion. This family was highly thought of when Lynchburg was still a very small town. James Philemon Holcombe, great-great-great-grandson of Andrew, the Duke's supporter, was born in this city, September 25th, 1820. He conferred a doubtful benefit on the country when he became the leader of the prohibition movement in America. In his wildest dreams, however, he could never have imagined its more recent development of racketeering with hired gunmen. James Philemon Holcombe bought six hundred acres at Bellevue, in Bedford County, in 1863. His first object in buying this estate was to provide a home for a number of valuable slaves his wife had inherited. His wife was Anne Selden Watts, daughter of Colonel Edward Watts and Elizabeth (Breckenridge) Watts. For a time James Philemon Holcombe practiced law at Fincastle, Virginia, near Grove Hill, the famous Breckenridge home, but when he removed to Bellevue he opened a private school for boys, which attracted much attention.

Philemon Holcombe was the oldest of six sons, and as a boy had gone to school to John Carey, a famous teacher of that day. He was commissioner from the Confederate Government to Canada. He died August 26th, 1873, at Capon Springs and is buried at Presbyterian Cemetery in Lynchburg. His monument stands to the right of the main drive, not far from the central gate. Once when it was overturned the whole city turned out to place it in position again, so highly was his memory esteemed. Bellevue was bought by Mr. William Abbot and with his family he continued the school for more than fifty years.

Horsley

Judge John Dunscombe Horsley, lawyer and ex-judge of the Circuit Court, was born at Yorkfield, Nelson County, Virginia, April 30th, 1849. His father was Dr. William Andrew Horsley and his mother was Eliza (Perkins) Horsley, a native of Richmond. One of Judge Horsley's ancestors was a Dunscombe, who followed the cause of Charles Edward, the Pretender, and fought on his side at Culloden. Afterwards he fled to Holland, where he married the daughter of an Amsterdam merchant. Judge Horsley was also descended from Sir William Claiborne, who came to Virginia in 1621.

Judge Horseley went into the War Between the States at the age of fifteen, with the cadets of Virginia Military Institute, which he had recently entered. He served with them until the evacuation of Richmond in April, 1865. After the War, he became a student at Norwood, in Nelson County.

John Dunscombe Horsley was married to Florence M. Tunstall on February 23rd, 1879. She was the widow of John L. Tunstall and the daughter of William Massie, by his fourth wife, Maria Effinger. This was a double wedding and the other couple was Mrs. Horseley's niece, Kimbrough Liggan and George E. Caskie. Both of these couples later left Lovingston, in Nelson County, and became residents of Lynchburg.

In 1866 John Horsley was made judge of the Fifth Circuit. He was re-elected, but after serving four months of his second term he resigned the judgeship to resume the practice of law. He formed a partnership with Captain Charles M. Blackford in 1895 and from this time until his death he made his home in Lynchburg. He purchased the residence which had been owned by Mrs. Seth Halsey, which was on Federal Street, and one of the houses built by the Murrell family. This house now owned by Mr. Fred Harper, whose wife is a descendant of the original owner and builder. At Judge Horseley's death four children survived him, Catherine Dunscombe, Bland Massie, Thomas Staples Martin and Eliza Perkins.

Hutter Family

Robert Cobbs was born in Louisa County in 1754. He was the only son of Mary Lewis and Samuel Cobbs, and the grandson of that Robert Lewis who is known in Virginia genealogy as Robert Lewis, of "Belvoir." Through this line the Cobbs family were descended from Nicholas Martian, the first patentee of Yorktown, and the ancestor of George Washington. Robert Cobbs was the first cousin of Nicholas Hamner Cobbs, beloved and honored bishop of the Episcopal Church. During the Revolutionary War Robert Cobbs fought under his uncle, Charles Lewis, having the rank of captain. At the Battle of Guilford Courthouse he commanded a regiment, and after his death his wife received a pension for his services in the War.

When peace returned his marriage with Anne Gizaage Poindexter took place in Louisa County. In 1795 they moved from Bedford County to their estate, "Plain Dealing," in Campbell County. The fifth child, William Cobbs, was born in Campbell, March 12th, 1792. He married Marian Stannard Scott, of Bedford County, the daughter of Samuel Scott, a major in the Revolutionary War, and Anne Roy, whose home, "Locust Grove," now owned by the Barksdale family, is located west of town on the Forest Road. The Scott family burying ground lies near the gate leading to the old residence, which is a conspicuous building on the road. William Cobbs had only one child, Emma William. In 1828 he bought "Poplar Forest," the Bedford County home of Thomas Jefferson. Francis Eppes, a grandson of Jefferson, had inherited this estate by the will of Jefferson, whose death occurred in 1826, but he sold it two years later, and went to live in Tallahassee, Florida. William Cobbs died in 1852, at the age of sixty years, leaving "Poplar Forest" to his only child, Emma William.

Emma William Cobbs, born in Bedford County in 1822, married Edward Sixtus Hutter, of the United States Navy; the marriage took place in 1840. He was from Easton, Pennsylvania, a son of Colonel C. J. Hutter, of the War of 1812, and a brother of Major George Christian Hutter, who was a veteran of the Mexican and the Indian Wars. As major he paid off the troops at Fort Sumpter under a flag of truce. He remained in the United States Army until Virginia seceded, when he resigned his commission. Major Hutter married Harriet Risque, daughter of Major James Risque, a noted criminal lawyer of Lynchburg's early days. He was the last man of prominence in this section to wear knee breeches and his hair in a queue.

George Christian Hutter was the father of Captain F. C. Hutter, Paymaster of the Confederate Army. The first pay check issued to General Robert E. Lee, as major-general in the Confederate Army, was paid out by Captain Hutter, and is one of the prized possessions of "Poplar Forest." Captain Ferdinand C. Hutter married Mary Lyons, the daughter of Judge James Lyons, of Richmond, Virginia. Another son of Major George Christian Hutter was Major Edward S. Hutter, who raised a regiment of students at the University of Virginia for the Confederate Army. It was he who conceived the idea of building a bridge across the cliffs of Blackwater. He formed a company for this purpose, and for improving and developing the new suburb which was added to the town when the bridge was built. He gave the name Rivermont to that part of the town and called the bridge Rivermont Bridge. He married Nannie Langhorne, daughter of Kitty Dabney and Major Jack Langhorne. Colonel James Risque Hutter, another son of Major G. C. Hutter, served in the Confederate Army with great gallantry. He married his cousin, the daughter of Edward Sixtus Hutter, and lived at the estate "Sandusky," which is one of the old landmarks of Campbell County, and has been elsewhere described in this book. Mrs. Hutter, who was named Lottie, was a lady of unusual beauty. They left several children, some of whom still live at "Sandusky."

William C. Hutter, the oldest son of Edward Sixtus Hutter and Emma W. C. Hutter, was in his fourth year at the United States Naval Academy when Virginia seceded. He resigned and accepted a commission in the Confederate Navy. During the fight between the "Merrimac" and the "Monitor," March 7th, 1862, he lost his life, being a lieutenant at the time, and serving on the gunboat "Raleigh." George E., another son, was graduated at the United States Naval Academy in the Class of 1874.

It is an interesting fact that Edward Sixtus Hutter was on the "Peacock" in the expedition which sailed to the Orient in an early attempt made by this country to formulate treaties for open ports with the Mikado of Japan. This voyage preceded Admiral Perry's expedition by almost a quarter of a century.

Of this family Christian Sixtus Hutter has lived in Lynchburg, and has been a prominent business man for many years. Mr. Hutter is closely identified with civic and church interests. At one time he was a member of the City Council, but of late years his chief contact with the public has been through the church. He has been a vestryman and warden of Saint Paul's for many years, superintendent of the Sunday school at one time, member of the standing committee of this Diocese, and a representative of the Diocese at General Conventions. In his mother's beautiful home at "Poplar Forest," which he now owns," as well as his town residence on Harrison Street, he and his family still maintain the old and gracious traditions of Virginia hospitality.

The following inscription is on a bronze tablet inserted in a moss-covered boulder at the entrance to the box-wood circle at "Poplar Forest," placed there as a marker by the Daughters of the Revolution:

"Poplar Forest in Thomas Jefferson's family 1773 to 1828. While President he designed and built the 'other home'—a retreat for rest and writing. This tablet is placed by Poplar Forest Chapter, D. A. R., Lynchburg, Va., July 4, 1928."

The festival held on the occasion of placing this tablet also celebrated a century of the ownership of "Poplar Forest" by the Hutter family. The estate was first owned by Mr. Wailes, the father of Mrs. Jefferson, who bequeathed it to her at his death. When she died it was inherited by her husband, Thomas Jefferson.

Mr. Christian S. Hutter married Ernestine, youngest daughter of Mr. James M. Booker, a wealthy tobacconist of Lynchburg. Mr. Booker married Caroline Elizabeth Hare, whose first husband was Mr. Selden. She was born in 1822, and died in 1881. Her father, Jesse Hare, a native of Pennsylvania, was one of that remarkable group of business men, who, in the early part of the nineteenth century, transformed Lynchburg from a mere ferry across the James into the greatest tobacco market in the world. Mr. Booker, who married Caroline Elizabeth Hare, then the widow Selden, was of an old family in the annals of Virginia. He was descended from Captain Thomas Purefoy, who came to Virginia in 1621, and was a Burgess from lower Elizabeth City County in 1629-30, and appears at the next session of Burgesses as a member of the Governor's Council. August 1st, 1627, he was in command of a raid made by the colonists on the Chesapeake Indians. Mr. Booker's grandfather, Edward Booker, was a captain in the Revolutionary War, and was at Yorktown with his troops. His parents were Richard Anderson Booker and Eliza (Davis) Booker.

The children of Mr. and Mrs. C. S. Hutter are: Miss Claudine Hutter. Booker Hutter, who married Ella Rodes (see Rodes); they have two children, James and Cary. Christian S. Hutter, Junior, who married Eleanor Buttman, of Charlottesville; they have one child, Peter. Edward, who married Grace Adams. Ernestine, who married Marshall McDonald, of Charles Town, West Virginia; they have one child, Louise. Emily, who married Arthur Pierce Stewart, of Chattanooga, Tennessee. Caroline, who married Cranston Williams; they have two sons, and live in Chattanooga. Beverley Scott Hutter, married Frances Forward, from Urbanna, Ohio; her family were from New

England originally, and prominent in the political life of that section. Quintus Hutter, married Agnes Adams, of Gretna, Virginia; they have one child, Julia Dale. Malcolm Hutter, unmarried.

Isbell

The name Isbell, which is now represented in Lynchburg by Mr. Aubrey Isbell, and his sister, Mrs. Fauntleroy Lambert, is an old name in this neighborhood. Zachary Isbell was one of the trustees of New London when it was made into a town. William J. Isbell owned a ferry, operating from his land in Amherst to Campbell, across the river.

Ivey

The first of the Ivey family to come to Virginia was Thomas Ivey. He was born in 1604 and died in 1653. He married Ann Argent, the daughter of George Argent, gentleman, at Saint Leonard's Parish, Shoreditch, County Middlesex, England. On coming to Virginia he settled near Norfolk some time prior to the year 1641. His name appears on the records of Elizabeth River Parish as church warden in 1641 and until 1648. Elizabeth River Parish included a wide district near Norfolk, Virginia. Descended from Thomas and Ann Ivey was Peter Ivey, born in Prince George County in 1787. Peter Ivey died on August 19th, 1847, in Chesterfield County, where he had moved and become a very successful farmer, having at that time two plantations in Prince George and one in Chesterfield. He served with distinction in the War of 1812. He was married on June 19th, 1817, to Sally Lawson Dance, the daughter of Ezekiel and Esenath Dance, of "Chestnut Level," Chesterfield County. They had thirteen children.

The youngest son of Peter Ivey was John Winston Ivey, the subject of this sketch. He was born at "Chestnut Level," the home of his maternal grandparents, in Chesterfield County, May 18th, 1840. He was educated in the private schools in the county, but his father died when he was only seven, and at the age of fourteen he found himself without any property or means of support. Perhaps this unhappy situation for a boy so young had much to do with that kindness and sympathy for others which graced his character in later years. In spite of his extreme youth, he journeyed from Chesterfield to Lynchburg to be with his older brother, Thaddeus H. Ivey, in the office of the James River and Kanawha Canal Company. The canal was in those days the only means of transportation of either passengers or freight from Lynchburg to Richmond. During the year 1860, when Mr. Ivey was only twenty, he was made a clerk in the Lynchburg National Bank. Except for the absence of one year in the War Between the States, where he displayed a high courage, Mr. Ivey held his position with the Lynchburg National Bank for nine years. At the end of that time he was made teller at the Peoples' Savings Bank of Lynchburg, which institution was later known as the Peoples' National Bank. Four years later he became cashier, and filled this position until 1903, when he was elected to the presidency of the Bank. He remained president of the Peoples' Bank until 1909, when it was his wish to retire, but his friends and associates appointed him vice-president.

At the outbreak of the War Between the States Mr. Ivey enlisted as a private in Company G, Eleventh Virginia Regiment, under the command of General Samuel Garland. He was at the Battle of Manassas, and served with valor until May 2nd, 1862, when in a skirmish before Williamsburg he received very severe wounds, which rendered him unfit for further active service. In 1864, when the armies of the North were at last beginning to take notice of the strategic value of Lynchburg, and were drawing closer to the town, great anxiety was felt for the safety of the funds of the Bank. In those days there were no time locks or bank vaults. Mr. Ivey placed the money in a heavy chest, loaded it on a farm wagon, and with only one companion, a trusted Negro servant, drove to Campbell County, where the chest was buried in a deep hole and covered over with leaves.

When the War was over the chest was dug up and brought back to the Bank with the treasure intact.

Mr. Ivey was an unassuming, home-loving gentleman. Simply and nobly he wore the highest qualities of Christian manhood, and after years of usefulness and honor he died at his home on Court Street, January 8th, 1910. His banking career in Lynchburg extended over a period of forty-nine years, forty of these being spent with one institution. At one time he was a member of the City Council. He was treasurer of the Imperial Colliery Company, and a director of several coal companies. Mr. Ivey loved to hunt and ride and was a member of the Oakwood Club, but his recreations outside his own home were few. He was treasurer of Court Street Methodist Church, South, a member of the Finance Committee, and served on the Board of Stewards for over twenty-five years. Loving the town, and working for its prosperity, he stood for all that was best in this community, and his death was a loss and sorrow to it.

Mr. Ivey's first wife was Mary Virginia Brown, the daughter of Mr. and Mrs. Edward S. Brown. She was born January 9th, 1849, and married to John Winston Ivey, November 5th, 1867. There were three children by this marriage, Otelia Walton, Mary Winston Ivey and Edward Sledd Ivey. Otelia and Edward Sledd died quite young. Miss Mary Winston Ivey is a resident of Lynchburg, living in her father's old home on Court Street. Mrs. Ivey died November 11th, 1887. Mr. Ivey was married the second time to Florence Maitland Jackson, the daughter of William Maitland Jackson, of Chesterfield County. Two children were born of this marriage: John Winston, born August 8th, 1891, and William Maitland, born January, 1894. Mrs. Florence Maitland Jackson Ivey died March 26th, 1896.

J. Winston Ivey was a near kinsman of William Ivey, a distinguished naval officer in the Revolutionary War, who was born at Sycamore View on Tanner's Creek, Norfolk County, Virginia, which estate he inherited from his father. He was brought up to the sea, and built vessels at his own cost. He suffered much from British depredations, the houses on both his estates being plundered and burned, and his slaves carried away. He joined the Virginia Navy, and September 2nd, 1776, was second lieutenant on the sloop "Scorpion," under Captain Wright Westcott. In this ship he cruised until January, 1777, when he was made first lieutenant of the "Liberty," being later promoted to captain, and placed on duty to recruit men for the Navy. Subsequently he was appointed to the command of the "Liberty," giving valuable service until his death late in 1777, or early in 1778.

Jefferson

Among those who have given information for this book is Thomas Jefferson, a well-known and respected colored citizen of the town. His father was brought to Madison from Big Island in 1817 by Mrs. Sallie Taylor, wife of John Taylor. Mrs. Taylor kept a tavern in Madison, where Thomas Jefferson was brought up. He has many recollections of Lynchburg as it was in its earliest days.

Jennings

Mr. T. A. Jennings, a useful and valued citizen here, as was his wife, the late Mrs. Jennings, has three children: Ocie, who married Mr. Stevens; Clyde, who married Miss Tebeau, of an old Texas family, and Dillard. Cecil, a charming and promising young man, died young. Mrs. Jennings was Miss Lena Price before her marriage.

Johnson

Mr. Howard Johnson, whose family owned the home and property which is now known as the Milliken-Guggenheimer Kindergarten, married Rosa Bailey. They lost their oldest son, Howard some years ago. A little later Mr. Johnson died, leaving his widow with one son, Ladd Johnson, who married Alice Suter, daughter of the late John D. Suter. Mrs. Johnson was a well-known and popular business woman of Lynchburg.

JONES

Mr. Charles Jones was in business here for many years and reared a number of children. His wife was Miss McCorkle, of a wealthy and influential Lynchburg family. Mr. Charles Jones' children were Sallie, who married Mr. George M. Moore. She had no children of her own, but raised the young family of her brother, George Jones, who died when his children were quite small. Walter Jones, married Cora, daughter of Mr. John L. Lee (see Lee). They had three children: Corrine, who married John Royall, of Richmond, and now lives in Atlanta; Lee Owen, married Ruth McGann; Agnes, married G. Roberts Neubauer. Alice Jones, married Mr. Edward Montgomery, and lives at Roanoke. Nannie, married Jack Snead, and lives at the old Jones' home at the corner of Church and Washington Streets. Two sons of Mr. Jones met with tragic deaths, one while still a youth accidentally shot himself in the parlor of their home as he was examining a gun, and another was run over and killed while waiting for a train at the depot. Lillian, the youngest child of Charles Jones, married Gus Terry, the son of Mr. Stockton Terry. Her two children are Stockton, who married Helen, the daughter of Mr. Langhorne Lewis, and Gus, who married Thelma Reams. The only daughter of Mrs. Lillian Jones Terry, Lillian, died when she was a small child.

This memorial to a Lynchburg lady, the daughter of the late Mr. Charles Jones, appeared in the Lynchburg News soon after her death:

"Mrs. Sally Jones Moore, a little old lady, died November 8th, 1932, on Diamond Hill, within a stone's throw of the house where she was born. She came from a family of prominence in Lynchburg history, and all her life she walked up and down our hills doing good.

Many years ago she was left a widow in easy circumstances. Each month when her income came she discharged her duties to her household, and to the members of her family with whom she generously shared her benefits; then she put in her pocket one hundred dollars changed into five-dollar bills and went out on the street in search of the poor and needy. Her whole life was full of unselfish purpose. The sum of her days was made up of good deeds to others. She was remarkable for her consideration for the poor, and her sympathy with the distressed and the afflicted, and even more remarkable in that she vaunted none of her benefactions—literally her left hand never knew what her right hand gave. Blessed be her memory."

JORDAN

Samuel Jordan settled on James River at an early date and called his place "Jordan's Journey." He represented the plantation in the first Assembly of 1619, and in the massacre of 1622 he successfully fought off the Indians. He died in 1623. The name Jordan runs through the entire history of Virginia, where they have proven themselves to be people of character and ability.

Colonel John Jordan, in Rockbridge County, was born in Goochland County, June 2nd, 1777. He early provided himself with a heroic mate, for in 1800 he married Lucy Winn, six feet tall, and widely known for her blonde beauty. She was the daughter of Colonel John Winn, of Hanover County. He took her to Lexington, and it was said that no handsomer couple was ever seen in that town. Colonel Jordan was himself six feet three inches tall, with black hair and eyes, and the broad shoulders and narrow hips of an athlete. He served in the War of 1812, using a great sword few men could have handled. When the engineers pronounced it was impossible to build a road over Blue Ridge Mountains near Buena Vista, he said, "Give me the men and I will build the road." Although no engineer, he built the road through Whites Gap into Amherst County, called Jordan's Trail. He also built the road over North Mountain, from Collierstown to Longdale. In fact, he turned out to be quite a builder for he built the Center Building at Washington College, the Annie Smith Academy, now the Virginia Military Institute Hospital. He built the Virginia Military Institute barracks, after the building used as an arsenal in the War of 1812 was torn down, and he constructed the Bateau Canal through the gap in the Blue Ridge Mountains at Balcony Falls. He was president of the Canal Company and helped build the Canal system. Besides this he and his family operated twelve furnaces and a number of forges, having iron works in Rockbridge, Botetourt, Bath, Alleghany, Amherst and Louisa Counties. The furnaces were: Lucy Selina Furnace in Alleghany County, named for his wife; Bath Iron Works near Goshen; Wilson Furnace in Botetourt County; Buena Vista Furnace; California Furnace on Guys Run; Hamilton Furnace, five miles west of Covington; Dolly Ann, three miles east of Jackson River; Low Moore on Jackson River; Victoria Furnace in Louisa County; Stove Coal Furnace near Richmond.

His home was called Jordan's Point, a point of land between North River and Wood's Creek, now known as East Lexington. Here he built his home, "Stono," where Mr. John L. Campbell now lives. It is one of the show places of Lexington. While he was thus engaged his wife was also busy. "During the week her house was like a bee-hive, with the noise of the loom, the buzz of the spinning wheel, the clatter of wool cards, and the glitter of knitting needles. From oldest to youngest, each had a part in the daily work, for all the cloth used by the family was woven by the servants. She sometimes drove in the large family chariot drawn by two fat black horses, Bemey and Jin, but she rarely went anywhere except to church. Grandfather Jordan attended her on horseback dressed in fine blue broadcloth cutaway, with brass buttons. He never road in a carriage. She was a splendid woman, even in old age, dressed in her handsome heavy silks. She loved company and was very hospitable." This account of her was written by her grandson, Captain Charles Francis Jordan, when he was eighty years old.

Colonel John Jordan died July 25th, 1854. His portrait hangs in the Rockbridge County courtroom. His son Samuel took Colonel John's place. Samuel's first wife was Hannah Davis. His second wife was Elizabeth Leibert, a widow, and the first cousin of his first wife. They were both descended from Alex-

Adelaide de Navarro Prescott Kean

ander Mak, who came from Germany and was the founder of the Dunkard religion. William H. Jordan, son of Samuel, by his first wife, Hannah Davis, ran the Amherst Furnace near Snowden. He married Mary Louise Jordan, his cousin. After his death, his family came to Lynchburg. His daughter, Mary, married E. E. Menefee, who died some years ago. Her daughter, Louise, lives in Lynchburg. His son, William Harrison Jordan, Junior, is a lawyer, a member of the Lynchburg bar, and lives with his sister, Miss Katherine Jordan, and his nephew, John Maury Miles, on Grace Street.

Kean

Mr. Robert Garlick Hill Kean was born at Mt. Airy, Caroline County, October 24th, 1828, the son of John Vaughan Kean, of Olney, and Caroline Hill, of the same county. Dr. Andrew Kean, of Cedar Plains, Goochland County, his paternal grandfather, had come to this country from Ireland after completing his education at the University of Dublin. He was a talented and distinguished physician. The mother of Robert Garlick Hill Kean died when he was three years old, and his aunt, Miss Bettie Hill, took her place and became a second mother to him. Mr. Kean, from his youth had the mind of a scholar, eagerly absorbing all knowledge that came his way. He went to the Episcopal High School and then to Concord Academy in Caroline County, where he studied under Frederick Coleman, from whom he received powerful mental stimulus. In 1848 he entered the University of Virginia, and in 1853 settled in Lynchburg. In 1854 he married Jane Randolph, daughter of Colonel Thomas J. Randolph, of "Edgehill," Albemarle County, and granddaughter of Thomas Jefferson. He had formed a partnership with J. O. L. Goggin and was fast building up a marked success at the bar when the clouds of war began to gather. Leaving his wife and family, he entered into that great struggle from which he was to return penniless four years later. He had been compelled to sell his home in order to provide for his family while he was gone to war. In 1866 his wife died. Mr. Kean's ability and knowledge of law were soon recognized, and before many years he was able to provide a handsome home for his family. He was married again in 1874 to Adelaide, daughter of William H. Prescott, of Saint Landry Parish, Louisiana. For some years Mr. Kean had as his law partner Mr. William Minor Lile, but in his capacity as a member of the Board of Visitors he very unselfishly recommended Mr. Lile as assistant to Professor Minor at the University of Virginia, and the recommendation was accepted.

Mr. Kean was known throughout the State for his profound knowledge and scholarly attainment in his chosen profession, and he was especially honored for the help and encouragement he was always willing and ready to give the younger members of the bar. In return he received a peculiarly flattering devotion from these young lawyers, which was something almost akin to worship.

As stated, Mrs. Kean was the daughter of Colonel William Prescott, of St. Landry, Louisiana. Her grandfather, Judge John Moore, of Louisiana, was a member of Congress from 1843 until shortly before the War Between the States. Her great-grandfather was Martin de Navarro, the Spanish Intendente of Louisiana in 1765, and Captain-General of Cuba, who, being a Grandee of Spain, was entitled to sit covered in the presence of royalty. Martin de Navarro had a daughter named Adelaide, and when she had just turned seventeen he decided to marry her to a cousin in Spain. Although this cousin was twice her age, he went to Spain to bring him back along with a trousseau that was worthy of a princess. But Adelaide had fallen in love with a handsome young Frenchman, Louis George Demarett, and with the help of her godmother she was already married to him when her father reached Louisiana with the expectant bridegroom, his father, and the trousseau. Martin de Navarro did not forgive her until her first child was baptized, which was one June 3rd, 1790.

Mrs. Kean's children are scattered and gone from Lynchburg,

but her nieces, whom she helped to rear, live here: Mrs. James Edmunds, Mrs. Edwin Ivey, Mrs. McGavock, and Mrs. Kate Prescott Carter.

Kent

Mr. W. L. Kent, at one time City Electrician, but now retired, is a native of Amherst, where his ancestors were early settlers of the county. For many years he has made his home in Lynchburg, and his mother and sister, the late Mrs. A. M. Campbell, both lived here for many years.

Kinnier

The Kinnier family, and its various branches, have been prominent in the affairs of Lynchburg through a large part of the town's existence. Mr. John Kinnier was a most respected and influential citizen, noted for his high qualities as a man and a Christian. He married Miss Josephine Percy, and left two daughters, Miss Josephine Kinnier and Mrs. Maizie Kinnier Bratton.

Mr. William Kinnier, another honored citizen, was the father of the late Tanner Kinnier, Mayor of Lynchburg and member of the City Council. Misses Mittie and Janie Kinnier and Mrs. Austin Quick are his daughters.

Mr. George Kinnier died February 11th, 1905. He was a Confederate veteran, the father of Mrs. Whittaker, who is the widow of the late Judge Whittaker, of Lynchburg.

The Kirkpatrick Family

Major Thomas Jellis Kirkpatrick, for many years a prominent citizen of Lynchburg, was born July 31st, 1829. He was the son of Rev. John Kirkpatrick, who was born in Mecklenburg, North Carolina, in 1794, and died in February 1842, a minister of the Presbyterian Church at Manchester. He had learned from a Scotchman named Brainard how to teach deaf mutes to speak, and he had a school of these unfortunate people in Manchester. He was a pioneer in this noble work in Virginia and it was said he was successful in teaching all but two in a class of seventeen.

This was about the year 1818. He married Jane M. Brown Jellis, daughter of Captain Thomas Jellis, born in Kent, England, an officer in the English Army. Captain Jellis' wife was Anastasia Deane, whom he met in Ireland. Major Kirkpatricks' godparents were Thomas and Mary (Hutchinson) Kirkpatrick.

Major Thomas Jellis Kirkpatrick was a brave soldier of the Confederacy. He was a captain of the Amherst Artillery, Jackson's Corps, Ewells' Division of the Army of Northern Virginia, was promoted to major and served until the Surrender. In 1866 he formed a law partnership with Captain Charles W. Blackford, a firm which became very successful in succeeding years. Major Kirkpatrick was a very brilliant lawyer, and with Captain Blackford, equally gifted, always charming and agreeable, a strong combination was formed which lasted until 1895. When they parted company it was to go into business with their sons: Major Kirkpatrick with F. Sydnor Kirkpatrick, and Captain Blackford with R. Colston Blackford and Judge John D. Horsley.

Major Kirkpatrick's wife was the daughter of Mr. Fortunatus Sydnor, an honored resident of Lynchburg. Major Kirkpatrick's daughter, Mrs. Sue Speed Kirkpatrick, the widow of Mr. Benjamin F. Kirkpatrick, still lives in the house on Grace Street to which her father brought her mother, a bride, when there were only two other houses on Grace Street. Mrs. Kirkpatrick's only son, Jack, died in France, on the field of honor in the World War.

A sister of Major Kirkpatrick, Katharine, a lady of unusual culture and ability, lived here for many years. Her first husband, Mr. Hobson, died in the War Between the States. She was married again to Major John Henson Flood, born May 15th, 1830, died June 13th, 1899. He was a prominent citizen of Lynchburg, and a very successful tobacconist. By his first wife he had several children, among them were Mary and Bessie Flood. Miss Bessie Flood, married Mr. Jennings, and at her death left two daughters, Esten and Kate Jennings.

LYNCHBURG AND ITS NEIGHBORS

Among the surviving members of Major Kirkpatrick's family are his grandchildren: children of Mr. Sydnor F. Kirkpatrick, Mr. Thomas Kirkpatrick, who married Miss Elizabeth Anderson (the daughter of Dr. Anderson), Misses Margaret and Nellie Kirkpatrick, these three being the children of his first wife, who was Miss McKinley. F. Sydnor, Junior, and Sarah Kirkpatrick are the children of the second Mrs. Sydnor Kirkpatrick, lately deceased. Major Kirkpatrick's two daughters, Misses Lizzie and Janie, died several years ago. They were ladies of charm and culture, representative of all that is best in our Southern life.

KYLE

Dr. Bernard Kyle was born at Buffalo Ridge Springs, Nelson County, Virginia, April 17th, 1887, the son of Joshua Warner Kyle and Ella Catherine (Agee) Kyle. Both his grandfather, Joseph Kyle and Benjamin Agee, were farmers, and both served the Confederacy as loyal soldiers. Dr. Kyle received his early education under a private governess later he was at Virginia Polytechnic Institute for four years, graduating with the degree of Bachelor of Science in 1906. He studied medicine for three years at the University of Virginia, and while attending the University was instructor of chemistry in 1907-08. He graduated from the Medical College of Virginia at Richmond in 1911. After this for eight years he engaged in general practice. He is now orthopedic surgeon and the only specialist of that kind in Lynchburg. He prepared himself for this special work after the World War, in which, as a medical officer, he played a notable part.

He was the first Lynchburg doctor to leave for active service during the War and was assigned to the Twelfth Field Artillery of the Second Division. Dr. Kyle served in every fight in which that famous division took part during 1918, being in the front lines at Verdun, Chateau Thierry, Soissons, Pont-a-Musson, St. Mehiel, Blanc Mont Ridge, Champagne, Somme, Aise Marne and Meuse-Argonne. He advanced with the Army of Occupation to the German border.

On December 5th, 1918, Dr. Kyle was assigned to duty in Base Hospital No. 41 of the University of Virginia, coming home in April, 1919, with the rank of major. During the War he received two citations from the French Government and three from the American, the last being a division citation from Major-General John A. Lejeune, commander of the Marine Corps. His regiment was for some time supporting the marines in their tremendous drives. Dr. Kyle has a Croix de Guerre with Palm and Star.

After leaving the army, he studied orthopedic surgery in Boston, serving on house duty in the Children's Hospital in that city. Ever since his return to Lynchburg he has confined his practice to orthopedic surgery.

Dr. Kyle was married to George Putnam Watkins in 1920. She was born, October 31st, 1899, in Lynchburg, Virginia, and educated at Dana Hall, Wellesley, Massachusetts, in 1914-17. Her parents were George Putnam Watkins, born March 10th, 1852, died September 10th, 1918, and Jimmie Lelia Watts Watkins, born March 14th, 1861, died March 12th, 1922. Mr. Watkins was a prominent business man in Lynchburg and a pioneer of the shoe industry here. Mrs. Watkins was the daughter of Lieutenant-Colonel and Mrs. James Winston Watts. Colonel Watts was a gallant officer of the Second Virginia Cavalry in the Confederate Army. He was born April 19th, 1833, and died December 3rd, 1906.

Dr. and Mrs. Kyle have a daughter, Jimmie Watkins Kyle, born July 27th, 1921.

Dr. Kyle belongs to the Lynchburg and Campbell County Medical Society, the Medical Society of Virginia, the South Piedmont Medical Society, the Southern and American Medical Associations and is a Fellow of the American College of Surgeons. He is a member of Saint Paul's Episcopal Church, in which he has been a vestryman.

KYLE

Mr. James Roland Kyle died November, 1933; age seventy-seven years. Mr. Kyle was born in Prince Edward County, the son of David Washington Kyle and Mary Jane Jones Kyle. Most of his childhood and youth were spent near Forest, in Bedford County. He attended New London Academy and Randolph-Macon College. He had lived in Lynchburg since 1874, except for a few years spent in New York. In 1882 he went into the tobacco business with his brother, the late Thomas L. Kyle. After the death of his brother, Mr. Kyle and Henry A. Allen established the Virginia Laundry Company. Mr. Kyle married Miss Alice James Aunspaugh, October 23rd, 1889. He is survived by his wife and three children, Mrs. S. B. McLaughlin, of Charlotte, North Carolina; Gordon Kyle, of Richmond, and John Holmes Kyle, of Lynchburg.

LANGHORNE

The Langhorne family in Lynchburg came from Henry Scarsbrooke Langhorne, and Colonel Maurice Langhorne, the elder, both of them sons of Major John Scarsbrooke and Elizabeth Langhorne. Mrs. John Payne, of Amherst, is the daughter of Colonel Maurice Langhorne's son, John Archer Langhorne. The Pulaski Langhornes come from this same branch. Mrs. Payne's children now living are: Mrs. Norborne Gatling, of New York, who has one son, Norborne Gatling, Junior; **Daniel Allen Payne,** of Lynchburg, who married Mary Norvell Miller; Mrs. Eliza Payne Eskridge. The widow of the late Spottswood Payne, May Gatling Payne, makes her home at Sweet Briar. Mr. John Meem Payne was for many years a member of the Lynchburg bar, but late in life retired to a home he had purchased at Amherst. He has written a very interesting document concerning his recollections of Lynchburg eighty years ago.

The famous Langhorne sisters are the daughters of Mr. Chiswell Dabney Langhorne, son of John S. Langhorne, "Jack" Langhorne, as he was called here. Chiswell Dabney Langhorne, known as "Shilly" to old friends and comrades in the War, was celebrated as a man "of infinite jest, of most excellent fancy." Mrs. John Lewis, long recognized head of the Woman's Party in Lynchburg; Mrs. Hutter, dead for many years but remembered still for her gifted pen, were the children of Mr. "Jack" Langhorne.

Henry Scarsbrook Langhorne, married Frances Steptoe. His children: John Scarsbrook, married Elizabeth Dabney; Elizabeth, married James Calloway Hunt; Henry Scarsbrook, died unmarried; James Steptoe, married Elizabeth O'Mohundro; William Maurice; Sarah Massie; Thomas Nelson, married Orra Grey; Frances Steptoe, died unmarried.

Henry S. Langhorne was married a second time to Anne Scott, whose father was Charles Alexander Scott. Children: Chas. Scott Langhorne, married Katharine Page Waller; Edward Alexander Langhorne, C. S. A., married Nannie Armistead; Anne Scott, married Colonel Maurice S. Langhorne; Mary Catherine, known as "Mollie," killed in accident, unmarried; George Washington Langhorne, married E. A. Langhorne's widow.

Maurice Scarsbrooke Langhorne was born in Cumberland County, Virginia March 27th, 1823. When he was five years old his father came to Lynchburg with his family, and lived at Judge William Daniel's home, afterwards called the "Point of Honor." Maurice Scarbrooke Langhorne was educated by John Cary. At eighteen years of age he married Martha, the daughter of General David Rodes. In 1851 he married Elizabeth, the only daughter of Casper W. Morris, of Cedar Grove, Philadelphia. Later in life he married his first cousin, Ann Scott Langhorne.

Maurice Scarsbrooke Langhorne was captain of the Rifle Grays, which soon became Company A in the Eleventh Virginia Regiment Volunteers. Brock states that this company was the first military company to offer its services to the cause of the Confederacy. He became major in 1861. His commission as lieutenant-colonel was won before the Battle of Seven Pines, when he received a wound which ended his active service. His commission as colonel was signed 1863, and he was retired to the Invalid Corps in 1864. In December, 1864, when the weather was twenty degrees below zero, he was ordered to gather together the sick and wounded, such as were able to turn out, and to go to Max Meadows to the relief of General Breckenridge. This was Colonel Langhorne's last command and, coming as an order from General Lee, shows the desperation of a dying cause.

Daniel Allen Langhorne was the son of William Langhorne, who married Mary Epes Buckner. He was named for Dr. Langhorne, his father's brother, they being sons of Colonel Maurice Langhorne, the elder. Mr. D. A. Langhorne was a man of great energy and enterprise, and made a large fortune as a railroad contractor. He married Miss Effie Brabbon. His children are Devereux, Daniel Allen, Junior, who died the winter of 1933; Chiswell Dabney, Rita Brabbon and May.

Mr. John DeVal Langhorne, a native of Kentucky and a retired naval officer, moved to Lynchburg and purchased "Westerly," a farm belonging to Frank T. Lee. Mr. Langhorne's first wife was Mary Potter, of Philadelphia. Her children were: Lily, who never married; Mary P., who Mr. Gwathmey, of Norfolk, married; James, who went to San Francisco to live and was a prominent lawyer there, and John. Mr. Langhorne's second wife was Nannie Tayloe, daughter of Mr. George P. Tayloe. Her children were: George, a graduate of West Point and an officer in the United States Army; Cary, Alice and Nannie. The place, "Westerly," which had been used by Mr. John D. Langhorne as a summer home (his family lived in Washington during the winter) was sold to Mr. McWane, and the land surrounding was cut up into lots and is now a part of West Lynchburg.

LEE

Mr. John L. Lee, a native of Bedford, came to Lynchburg at an early age and was a prominent business man here. He was married twice, the only child by his first wife being Cora Lee, who married Walter Jones. His second wife, who was Miss Crockett, had four daughters: Alpha, married Mr. Edward Crump; Lily, married Mr. Richard Carter Stokes; Fannie married Mr. D. Brown Ryland, and Alice was the second wife of Thomas Ryland. Mr. Lee was at one time in business with Mr. W. O. Taylor, another prominent business man of Lynchburg.

Mr. James I. Lee, a brother of John L., was a commission merchant here. He married Miss Anthony. His son, Mr. Garnett Lee, married Jessie Apperson, daughter of Mr. Richard D. Apperson, for many years head of the Traction and Light Company of Lynchburg. Mr. Garnett Lee is in the Apperson-Lee Motor Company.

Lee

John Lynch Lee, a noted criminal lawyer of Lynchburg, was born in New Orleans, July 6th, 1861, the son of John Lynch Lee and Julia G. (Cash) Lee. His father served in the Confederate Army; his mother was of a Philadelphia family. Mr. Lee went to school at Kenmore, in Amherst County, and there he was married, April 26th, 1882, to Rose Cabell, daughter of Paul Carrington Cabell and Nannie (Rose) Cabell, who died a year after their marriage. Mr. Lee studied law and became commonwealth attorney of Amherst. He was married a second time to Mary Elizabeth Walker, daughter of Mr. Branch Walker, of Walkers' Ford. Moving to Lynchburg, he formed a partnership with Mr. Volney Howard. Here he met with brilliant success in criminal law and was connected with many of the most famous cases of Virginia. Mr. Lee died in 1926, being survived by his widow and three children: John L. Lee, Junior, in the Merchant Marine service; Mrs. Richard Wagner, and Mrs. John Abbott, of Lynchburg.

Lucado

The Lucado family were descended from one Jean Loucadou, "et sa Femme," who were among the first refugees of the Huguenots to come to Virginia. (July 31st, 1700, Virginia Historical Collection). Down through the years the baptisms of this family are recorded. In 1744 Pierre Loucadou had been changed to Peter Lookadoo, then named as an inhabitant of Manikintown. Leonard Fretwell Lucado was the son of Thomas Edward Lucado, who married Lucy Walker, both of Buckingham County. Leonard Lucado came to Lynchburg with the old packet boat line and was for many years connected with this enterprise. When the canal was sold to the Richmond and Alleghany Railroad, and the packet boats went out of existence, he entered the wholesale grocery business. Several of Captain Lucado's sisters married in Lynchburg. Mary, married James Mathias; Jeanette, married Powhatan Haynes, and Lucy, married William James. Mr. Lucado's first wife was Ammen Hamner. She left a daughter, who married Mr. Engardt. He was married again to Belle Pettigrew. She had two children, G. Funston and Albert Walker Lucado, who never married and who died about two years ago, being accidentally drowned in James River. G. Funston Lucado was born November 12th, 1861; he died July 24th, 1904. G. Funston Lucado was a graduate of the Virginia Military Institute. He was interested in the coal development of West Virginia, and was very successful in his investments in this industry. He married Margaret Sanford Glass, daughter of Major Robert Henry Glass and Meta Sanford, his second wife. They had one child, Margaret Funston, who married Mr. Goodwillie, of Chicago.

McDowell

Henry Clay McDowell, Federal judge, and later associate judge of this Federal District, died in October, 1933. He was a native of Kentucky and a great-grandson of Henry Clay. Judge McDowell died in Ashland while visiting his sister in the old home of Henry Clay. Judge McDowell was seventy-two years old. He was a graduate of Yale and of the University of Virginia. In 1893 he was married to a distant cousin, Miss Louise Clay, of Rodgersville, Tennessee. He had made his home in

Lynchburg for over thirty years. Judge McDowell was a man of fine intellectual gifts, essentially a student and a thinker.

McKinney

Mr. Samuel H. McKinney was born in Appomattox, but lived in Lynchburg sixty-nine years. He died January 20th, 1910, at the home of his daughter, Mrs. D. M. Penick. His wife was Miss Averett.

McLaughlin

Michael McLaughlin came from County Longford, Ireland, to New York in 1732. After living in New Jersey, Delaware and Maryland, he came to Lynchburg to work on the James River and Kanawha Canal. Later he built the roads which Henry Davis had constructed through the Third Ward, which work was done at Mr. Davis' private expense, since he was owner of almost the entire Third Ward. Mr. McLaughlin retired from active work in 1861, as he was badly crippled from rheumatism contracted from work on the canal. He sent help to Ireland for his other relatives to join him in this country. He died in 1898 at the age of ninety. Mr. McLaughlin married Henrietta Stone, daughter of William Stone and Pamelia Carter, of Prince Edward County. Pamelia Carter was the daughter of Matthew Carter, a soldier in the Revolutionary War.

William H. McLaughlin, son of Michael, was for a long time vice-president of Robinson, Tate and Company, but is now retired from active business. He has a number of children, who have married and make their homes here. Mary, his daughter, married Bernard Y. Calvert, who came from Rockingham, and has been successfully engaged in real estate and insurance business in Lynchburg for a number of years.

Another daughter, Gertrude, is the widow of Herbert Batte, who was a victim of the influenza epidemic in 1918. He left two daughters, Elizabeth and Gertrude. Mr. Batte belonged to a family long distinguished in the annals of Eastern Virginia. The family came from York County, England, and were prominent as soldiers and statesmen in colonial Virginia from our earliest days. (See Colonial Virginia, Its People and Customs, by Mary Newton Stanard).

McNamara

The McNamara family have long been valued citizens of Lynchburg. The late William McNamara, who was connected with the National Mattress Company, left his widow, Mrs. Nora McNamara, and two promising young sons, Maurice and William.

The Macon Family in France

Gideon Macon, of New Kent and Hanover Counties, the first of the name in Virginia, was a Huguenot, and belonged to the family whose record is here given, as found in the Armorial General de la France, Paris, 1738, Vol. I, page 361:

"1. Louis de Macon, Seigneur de Sauzet, diocese de Clermont in Auvergne, was living in 1546. His son:

2. Gabriel de Macon, Seigneur de Sauzet, married the 5th day of February, 1546, Catherine de La Biele, dite De Serre, daughter of Iteron de La Biele dite de Serre and his wife, Anne de Turenne. Their children were: (a) Louis de Macon; (b) Antoine de Macon; (c) Madeleine de Macon; (d) Antoinette de Macon; (e) Gilberte de Macon.

3. Louis de Macon (II du Nom), married February 15th, 1579, Marguerite de Baron, daughter of Jean de Baron and Catherine de Rochfort. Had one child, Jean de Macon.

4. Jean de Macon, married, 1607, Madeleine Becaine, daughter of Etienne Becaine and Francoise de la Chapelle. Jean de Macon died in 1619. Their children were: (a) Louis de Macon (III du Nom); (b) Francois de Macon.

5. Louis de Macon (III du Nom), married, October 20th, 1633, Catherine de Prades, daughter of Annett de Prades and Charlotte de la Salle. Their children were: (a) Emmauel de Macon; (b) Charles de Macon.

6. Emmanuel de Macon, married, July 19th, 1695, Marguerite de la Salle, daughter of Francois de la Salle and Madeleine de Monricaud. Their children were: (a) Joseph de Macon; (b) Charles de Macon; (c) Francois de Macon; (d) another Francois de Macon; (e) Jean de Macon; (f) Isabelle de Macon; (g) Marie de Macon; (h) Anne de Macon; (i) Anne Emmanuel de Macon."

Robert de Macon was mentioned as being at the court of Charles VII in the time of Joan of Arc.

The Macon Family in Virginia

Gideon Macon came from Saone-et-Loire, France, and was a French Huguenot. After fleeing from Catholic persecution in France, he is believed to have remained in England long enough to have become a citizen, because at the time he came, and at the time the records of the births of his children were made, only subjects of the Crown and supporters of the Established Church were allowed in the colony, the Act of Denization not yet having been passed. He came from England to Virginia before 1643, became a large land owner, and also owned a large number of slaves for that time. He was Indian interpreter for the colonial government, and private secretary to the Governor, Sir William Berkeley. He was a vestryman in Bruton Church in 1685, and his name will today be found on one of the pews of that church. Gideon Macon was a member of the House of Burgesses in 1696. He lived at the Island of New Kent County, settling there in 1680, but afterwards moved to Mount Prospect, near Williamsburg, the same home which is now in the possession of Mr. William Hartwell Macon, his grandson in the third degree. Gideon Macon married Martha Woodward, granddaughter of Thomas West, Lord Delaware, governor of the colony. The West name recurs frequently in each generation. Gideon Macon died in 1702 and was buried at Mount Prospect. His tombstone was cut in London, and still marked his grave until 1862, but was destroyed by the Yankees in the Peninsula campaign. The children of

Gideon and Martha Macon were: Gideon (II), born June 20th, 1682, baptized June 22, 1682; Anne, born December 16th, 1685, baptized February 2nd, 1686; William, born November 11th, 1693, died November 1st, 1773; John, born December 17th, 1695; James, born October 28th, 1701, and Martha, who married Orlando Jones, son of the Rev. Rowland Jones, rector of Bruton Church. Martha is buried under the chancel at Bruton Church. Her granddaughter was Martha Dandridge, who, as the widow Custis, married George Washington, and who, through her first husband, John Parke Custis, is the ancestress of the Lee family.

William Macon, of this second generation in America, married Mary, daughter of William Hartwell and Annis, his wife. She was born June 18th, 1700, and died November 19th, 1770. Date of marriage, September 24th, 1719.

The dates given are from Saint Peter's Parish Register, published by the Colonial Dames in 1904, also William Macon's family Bible in possession of William Hartwell Macon corroborates these dates.

Children of William Macon and Mary Hartwell Macon, his wife: Anne, born October 20th, 1720, died November 9th, 1736; Martha, born August 12th, 1722, died April 25th, 1763; Mary, born March 9th, 1723, died January 29th, 1733; William, born January 4th, 1725; Henry, born September 1st, 1727; Elizabeth, born February 15th, 1729; Sarah, born February 21st, 1731; Mary, born April 17th, 1735; Judith, born August 12th, 1737; Hartwell, born June 30th, 1741; Anna, born July 31st, 1747.

In Saint Peter's Parrish Register, William Macon, gentleman, is mentioned as major, and afterwards as colonel of the New Kent militia. He was a member of the House of Burgesses from New Kent County from 1736 to 1740, and a vestryman of Saint Peter's Church. He was the second owner of "Mount Prospect," which was one of the finest homes in that section, and a large land and slave owner. The county records of New Kent were destroyed by fire, but Saint Peter's Register has preserved full particulars of this family, as well as the births, marriages, and deaths of the slaves belonging to Gideon and William. The wills of Gideon Macon were destroyed with the court records.

Henry Macon, fifth child of William and Mary Hartwell, lived in Cumberland County and married twice. His first wife was Rebecca Mayo, born 1732, the daughter of William Mayo, and his second wife, Anne Parratt, married 1731. Rebecca Mayo Macon died before 1762. Henry Macon married the second time Frances Netherland Carlyle, a widow, the daughter of Wade Netherland. She died about 1786, leaving no children, and in her will devising her property to Caty Todd Macon, her step-granddaughter. Henry Macon's children by his first wife were:

William Mayo Macon, married Sally Woodson.

John Macon, married, first, Martha Todd, and second, Grace Cowan.

Henry Macon, also left three daughters, not mentioned in his will, probably having given them their share in his property before his death.

Mary Mayo Macon, married Richard Woodson Michaux, of Powhatan County, son of Captain Joseph Michaux of Powhatan County, and his wife, Judith Woodson. From this couple the late Mrs. Walker Pettyjohn and Mrs. C. A. Sydnor were descended, according to this record.

Sally Woodson Macon, married Mr. Swann.

Rebecca Mayo Macon, married Thomas Redd, of Halifax County.

Henry Macon's will was executed in Cumberland County Courthouse, October 24th, 1785, his two sons being executors with George Carrington, Junior. He had 1,435 acres lying on the south side of Great Guinea Creek, which was willed him by his father, and he in turn left the same to his sons. Henry Macon had other land purchased from Joseph Chatfin, which he left his sons, and at the death of his wife the plantation on which they had lived, including 1,455 acres, thirty head of cattle, thirty head of hogs, etc., slaves, furniture, and so on, was also inherited by his sons. The will of Frances Macon, Henry's wife, was executed on June 26th, 1786; see Will Book No. 2, page 405, Cumberland Circuit Court, Clerk's Office.

John, of the fourth generation from Gideon, first married Catherine Todd, by whom he had two daughters, Caty Todd and Martha. Caty Todd, married Captain Tom Miller; Martha, married Captain John Miller.

Caty Todd Macon and Captain Tom Miller had the following children: Tom, who married Fanny Scott; Margaret, married Mr. Dance; Ann, married George Matthews; Malvina and Sallie, died unmarried.

Martha Macon and Dr. John Miller had the following children: Catherine, who married, first, Edward Cunningham, and second, Stephen Eggleston; Dr. John Miller, who married Miss Morton; William Miller, died unmarried.

Tom Miller and Fanny Scott has one daughter, Grace.

After the death of Catherine Todd, John Macon was married a second time in March, 1788, to Gracy Cowan. She was the daughter of Robert Cowan, of Bedford County, and his wife, Elizabeth Anthony; marriage bond being filed at Powhatan Circuit Court, signed John Macon; witnesses, Jacob Salmons and Abner Crump. His children by Gracy Cowan were: Margaret, married John Hudson Burton; Elizabeth, married Major Joel Yancey, of Bedford County. Robert Cowan Macon, married Lucy Anne Michaux, of Powhatan County; Anna Rebecca, born after her father's death, married Judge Daniel A. Wilson.

John Macon died in 1793. His widow, Gracy Cowan Macon, afterwards married Archibald Freeland. At the time of his death John Macon's home was in Powhatan County, and he owned three large plantations in three different counties.

William and Mary Quarterly for January, 1932, pages 11 and 12, contains a letter contributed by Ellen M. Bagby, which was written by Mrs. Mary Smith Mutter. Mrs. Mutter was the niece of John Augustine Smith, president of William and Mary College, 1814-1825, and the half-sister of Martha Burwell Dabney, who married Dr. Lewis Webb Chamberlayne, and was the mother of Mrs. George W. Bagby. In the letter she writes that the Macon family were French Huguenots, and had an immense property on the Saone River: "There is a city there called Macon. One of the family in 1321 was given a coat of arms for some great act of valor, a French shield (bearing three golden stars surrounded by a gold band) of azure blue; the crest was a sheaf of wheat. My father did not remember the motto. At the revocation of the Ediot of Nantes the family went over to England, and the pioneer to this country, Gideon Macon, came in February, 1642, and was private secretary to Lord Berkeley. He lived about two and a half miles above the White House. My grandfather was of the third generation in Virginia. He lived on the island, and here he entertained General Lafayette on his way to Yorktown at the time of the siege. The American Army encamped on the island, with General Lafayette a guest in the house. Mount Prospect built by my father (Colonel Hartwell Macon, of New Kent, who married Sarah Smith, daughter of Rev. Thomas Smith, of Cople Parish) was a beautiful house. I was raised there."

From papers discovered by Mr. Lyon Tyler in recent years, it appears that Martha, the wife of Gideon Macon, was the daughter of William Woodward. After the death of Gideon, she married a second time, Nathaniel West, believed to have been her cousin. They had one child, Unity West, who married William Dandridge. As is well known, Martha's daughter, Martha, by her first husband, Gideon Macon, married Orlando Jones; her daughter, Frances, married Colonel John Dandridge; their daughter, Martha, married John Parke Custis, and so was an ancestress of the Custis family and the Lee family, and after the death of Mr. Custis she became the wife of George Washington.

Manson

Mr. Nathaniel Clayton Manson, Junior, at one time Mayor of Lynchburg, and later City Attorney, was the son of Nathaniel Clayton Manson and Polly Carey (Wilson) Manson. His father was Nathaniel J. Manson, of Bedford County, who had a large family. Among his children was Mr. Emmett Manson, noted for his piety and high character; Nathaniel J. Manson, married Sally Alexander, born October 18th, 1779, died March 1861, who was the daughter of Robert Alexander, clerk of the court of Campbell. The Alexanders came from the north of Ireland, and emigrated to this country after the siege of Londonderry. Robert Alexander married Ann Austin, daughter of William Austin, a captain in the British Army. The father of Robert, also named Robert, established Liberty Hall Academy, which subsequently became Washington College, and later Washington and Lee University. Mr. Nathaniel Clayton Manson, Junior, of Lynchburg, was married, first, to Lee Field, who died soon afterwards. His second wife was Henrietta Edge Johnston, of Alexandria, who died in the fall of 1892. He married Mary Moore, daughter of Mr. and Mrs. Israel Moore, of Lynchburg, who survives him.

Massie

The first representative of the Massie family is said to have come to Virginia in 1635. Captain Thomas Massie, believed to have been the son of Peter Massie, had large grants in New Kent County, and was a member of the House of Burgesses from New Kent from 1723 to 1726. He married Mary Walker, March 23rd, 1698-99, and died March 2nd, 1731. William Massie was born May 28th, 1718, and died 1749. He married Martha Macon, granddaughter of Gideon Macon. Major Thomas Massie was their son, born August 11th, 1747. He led an eventful life as a soldier of the Revolutionary War, and married Sarah Cocke. Dr. Thomas Massie, son of Major Thomas and his wife, Sarah Cocke Massie, was born October 21st, 1782. In 1803 the family of Major Thomas Massie left Frederick County, where they had been living, and moved to Nelson, then Amherst, where Major Massie had acquired an estate of more than nine thousand acres on Tye River. He died February 2nd, 1834. Dr. Thomas Massie, his son, was brilliantly educated in medicine, finishing his training by four years of study abroad. His first wife was Lucy Waller, and his second wife was Sarah Ann Carrington Cabell. His daughter, Juliet, by his first marriage, married Henry C. Boyd. Their son, Waller Massie Boyd, was in Pickett's Division and was captured at Gettysburg. He was the first planter to cultivate Albemarle Pippins on his land, much against the advice of his neighbors, who predicted that he would ruin his land. He lived to reap a fortune from his orchards. His first wife was Caroline Anthony Yancey, daughter of Mr. William Tudor Yancey, of Lynchburg. Their children were: Henry C. Boyd, who died in his youth; Waller Massie Boyd, William Tudor Boyd, Alice Boyd, Lucy Boyd, Virginia Boyd, Caroline Boyd, Susan C. Boyd, Mary, and Thomas Boyd. His second wife was Mrs. Janet Withers Cook, the daughter of Colonel Robert Enoch Withers, of Wytheville.

Mr. Patrick Cabell Massie, son of Dr. Thomas Massie and Sarah Carrington (Cabell) Massie, was born January 8th, 1829, and died in Lynchburg, September 27th, 1877. He studied law at Yale, but never practiced. He lived at Three Springs, and was married June 18th, 1857, to Susan C. Withers, sister of Colonel Withers, of Wytheville, and daughter of Dr. Robert W. Withers. Robert Withers Massie, their son, a graduate of Virginia Military Institute, came to Lynchburg and engaged in the lumber business. He was married November 11th, 1885, to Mattie W., daughter of Nathaniel Clayton Manson. Their children are: Robert W., Nathaniel M., Catherine D., and Martha Willis Massie.

Miller

There once lived in Lynchburg a family named Miller. And they were a different family of Millers. . . . Miller kept a barroom on Main Street between Ninth and Tenth, and his wife was said to have been an actress. Every afternoon this couple drove out in their buggy, and the children along the route they usually took watched for them eagerly, for they had a little poodle which each day was dyed a new color for the drive. One day the poodle would be baby blue, another pink, and then again a delicate lavender. He would sit upright on the seat between his master and mistress, with a big bow of ribbon around his neck and flap his little paws daintily, much to the watching children.

The general idea was that these people were show people, and as they were a mystery about town, a murder or so and robbery were laid at their door. Some people said "Kip" Miller, as he was called, was the only known burglar who had carried on his robberies for a life-time and yet had never been caught in the act. One tale that was told on him was that he broke into a Lynchburg store one night and robbed it. A man saw him, so the story runs, but was afraid to tell. Sometimes, when this man was drinking he would drop certain hints: "I could tell, if I wanted to, who robbed so-and-so's store." And one morning his dead body was found in an alley. Nobody knew who killed him, but "Kip" Miller was always suspected of the crime. His son, William, Junior, did kill a man named Thomas in a bar-room fight on Ninth Street. William, Junior, was tried and acquitted, for his father secured him the best legal talent. It was also said that "Kip," the father, chartered an engine one night to follow a circus train out of town, and then came back with $15,000, a sum he had stolen from the safe in the circus train.

After a checkered career, this mysterious family of Millers finally died out, one by one, and were buried in a vault in the Presbyterian Cemetery. William Miller, his wife and his two sons, between the years 1886 and 1896, were all gathered together in death in this vault in the cemetery, and if they had relatives, none claimed them. For years any visitor to the cemetery could peer in through the iron bars, for the door of the vault, which was topped by a Masonic emblem, was always kept open.

The caskets were on shelves, and there was a marble top table where reposed a family Bible and some artificial flowers. In some way the rusty chain on the latticed iron door must have pulled apart or broken, for one night not many months ago the coffins were prized open and searched for valuables. The shrouds, with the bones of the dead and broken glass from the caskets were strewn on the floor. The bones were collected and decently buried, and the vault was pulled down. Elizabeth J. Miller died in 1886. William Miller died in 1889. William Miller, Junior, died in 1891. Robert R. Miller died in 1896.

Miller

This letter, written by Mrs. Carter Glass to the Lynchburg News, May 4th, 1932, as an appreciation of Mr. Thomas C. Miller, deserves a place in the records of Lynchburg:

"Thomas C. Miller was a teacher in the public schools of Lynchburg for thirty-nine years, there being one interruption of one year, when the high school was discontinued because of inadequate funds. Prior to his service to his community as a pedague, he had served his State as a soldier during the War Between the States, enlisting in the Confederate Army at the age of eighteen by walking all the way from Lynchburg to Richmond to join the colors. He was seriously wounded and captured at the Battle of Frazier's Farm, near the State capital, and on account of a crippled arm was afterwards unable to take part in field operations, though he served in the reserves and also in the hospital in Charlottesville.

His courage as a wearer of the Gray was often the subject of comment by his comrades in arms, and on one occasion when the late General Holmes Smith was asked who was the bravest private soldier he knew he replied without a moment's hesitation, 'Tom Miller.' After the War, Mr. Miller attended the University of Virginia, where he continued the educational training received in his father's private school, in which not only were the elementary subjects taught, but Latin, Greek, mathematics and moral sciences as well. At the University he studied Latin under both Dr. Gildersleeve and Colonel William E. Peters.

After leaving the University in 1867, Mr. Miller taught school in Bedford County until 1870, when he came to Lynchburg and opened a private school. He conducted this school for a year, giving it up when, after the inauguration of the public school system here in 1871, he was elected principal of one of the schools. John W. Wyatt was elected principal of another school, and these two soon became intimate friends, and combined efforts in trying to persuade Abraham Biggers, School Superintendent, and the School Board to establish a high school.

With the establishment of a high school in 1874, both Mr. Miller and Mr. Wyatt began their careers as teachers in this school, with the latter as principal and the former as associate principal and teacher of Latin. Upon Mr. Wyatt's death in 1891, Mr. Miller became principal. A severe illness in 1904 caused him to resign as principal, but he still continued to teach Latin until 1910, when his failing health forced him to retire.

Such long and faithful service to the youth of this city deserves recognition. As many other educators of this community have been honored for their untiring efforts in the behalf of boys and girls in the public schools, the same tribute should be paid the memory of Thomas C. Miller. Shortly there is to be erected a new elementary school in the West Lynchburg-Fort Hill section. Why not name this school the Thomas C. Miller School?"

This letter, written by Mrs. Glass, brought the memory of Mr. Miller so gratefully before the eyes of the public that the school she mentioned received his name.

MITCHELL

Mr. Daniel Trigg Mitchell, who lived in Lynchburg twenty years, died in Abingdon, his native town, December 14th, 1905. He was cashier of the National Exchange Bank of this city. He married Miss Fannie Loving, a daughter of the late Henry Loving, of Amherst, whose death occurred several years before that of her husband. Two children survived them, Daniel Trigg Mitchell, Junior, and Elizabeth Mitchell.

Montague

Mr. A. P. Montague, of Lynchburg, is an agent for selling machinery—the first business of this particular kind ever established here. His wife, who was Miss Lucy Hundley, is a very accomplished lady and is interested in business clubs and business enterprises among women. At one time she was in the real estate business, and is a prominent member of the Woman's Party in Virginia.

Montgomery

Mr. John Montgomery, one of the oldest and most highly respected citizens of Lynchburg, died August 20th, 1905; aged eighty-one years. For many years he manufactured the well-known Montgomery Wheat Fan. He was born in Waterloo, Pennsylvania, August 4th, 1824. He came to Lynchburg in 1859, and although he was a Northern man he took up arms for the South. He was detailed to work in the caisson shops until late in the War, when he was stationed with a battery on Daniel's Hill, in Lynchburg. A bodily infirmity incapacitated him for more active service. He is survived by two sons, W. Bruce Montgomery, of this city, and J. N. Montgomery, of Rocky Mount.

Moore

George Moore, and John H. Moore, his brother, with their sister, Bettie, made their home here for many years. They were nephews of Mr. Maurice Moore. Mr. George Moore married Miss Sallie Jones. Their only child died when young. Mr. Moore was an important official of the Lynchburg National Bank, and had amassed a fortune when he died. Mr. John H. Moore married Miss Mary O'Brien, a Richmond lady, who survives him. Their children are: Richmond, a doctor practising in New York; George, a member of the Lynchburg Bar; he married Catherine Peters, the granddaughter of Major Stephen Peters, of Bedford County; Misses Mary and Elizabeth Moore, Mrs. Charles Williamson, of Danville, and Mrs. William Moore, of this city.

Joseph Moore was born in Albemarle County, Virginia, April 25th, 1771, and died in Lynchburg, Virginia, July 3rd, 1854. He married Rhoda Harper, November 19th, 1801. The marriage bond is in Albemarle County, Virginia. Their son, Maurice Moore, was born May 21st, 1816, in Fluvanna County, Virginia, and died August 4th, 1887. He was married March 1st, 1837, in Lynchburg, Virginia, to Sarah, the daughter of Israel Sneed, and Nancy (Bondurant) Sneed, of Buckingham County. The Bondurants were a Huguenot family, descendants of Jean Pierre Bondurand, who left France after the Revocation of the Edict of Nantes, and with other French exiles came to America on "Ye Peter and Anthony" ship in September of the year 1700. Israel Sneed was a government inspector of tobacco in Lynchburg, the son of Evans Sneed, of Halifax.

Israel Sneed Moore was born April 16th, 1847, in Lynchburg, Virginia, and died in Lynchburg, March 28th, 1927. He was married December 28th, 1869, to Emily Cornelia Heywood Wise, daughter of David Greiner Wise and Mary Jane (Pitzer) Wise, at the home of the bride's parents, "Bellpre," in Culpepper County, Virginia. Their children were:

Dr. Bernard Wise Moore, married Edith Wane Warfield, and died January 22nd, 1911, at St. Louis, Missouri.

Mary Louisa Moore, married Nathaniel Clayton Manson, Junior.

Maurice Moore, married Mary deCamp Banks. Their only child, Mary deCamp (Polly) died in 1920; aged 18.

Nettie Terrell Moore.

Shirley Cornelia Moore, married Thomas Dickson Torrey, and had one son, Thomas Fuller Torrey, and was married a second time to Johannes Suhling.

Israel Sherwood Moore, married Veronica Mollison. They have two children, Andrew Maurice and Peter.

Donald Graham Moore, married Fannie Johnson Caskie. They have one daughter, Betsy Kimbrough.

Eva Lee Moore.

MOORMAN

The Moorman family intermarried with the Ford family of Lynchburg. Mr. Watkins Leigh Moorman, at one time postmaster here, was born November 7th, 1847. He married, first, Dora Olivia Ford, December 2nd, 1868. Their children were: Herbert Leigh Moorman, who never married, and was connected with the Lynchburg Cotton Mill for many years; Ella Bolling, married Louis Preston Collins; Edna, Olivia Ford and Ottie Culvin Moorman. Mr. Moorman's second wife was Ella F. Ford.

Winnington Leftwich Moorman, born May 28th, 1854, married Otway Ford. They had no children.

MORGAN

In 1901 Dr. Robert Withers Morgan wrote the first dental law ever presented to Congress. It authorized the creation of a Dental Corps in the United States Army and of a commission to examine applicants. Thus he became the father of this important branch of the Service. Major Peter J. Otey, Congressman from Lynchburg at that time, introduced the bill which was passed by Congress in February, 1901. Dr. Morgan later became a member of the commission. He was born in 1844, lived at 1900 Fifth Street in Lynchburg. Dr. Morgan died in 1904, after rearing a large family, among whom is the distinguished artist, Georgia Morgan.

MORGAN

Mrs. Susan Ellen Morgan, widow of George W. Morgan, was the daughter of Mr. Mark Anthony, an old citizen of Lynchburg. She died February 23rd, 1910, leaving three children, Miss Mary Ellen Morgan, George Morgan and Lee Morgan.

LYNCHBURG AND ITS NEIGHBORS

Morris

Dr. Morris, who lived in Lynchburg, married Miss Waller, of Williamsburg, the sister of Mrs. Charles Langhorne, who was Katherine Waller. Dr. Morris' son, Page, married Miss Statham, daughter of Mr. Charles Statham, a wealthy citizen here, and went to live in Duluth, Minnesota, where he became a Federal judge. Lou Bell Morris married Wister Langhorne. He died leaving two daughters, Bessie and Wister. His widow was married again to Mr. Robert Stannard. Mary Morris married Mr. Ben Nowlin, and left three daughters: Miss Chloe, who has been in the Government service for some years; Miss Louise, and the late Mrs. Chauncey Williams, of New Jersey.

Morrison

Dr. James Morrison was born in Lexington, the second son of Dr. Robert Hall Morrison and Margaret White Morrison, who was a granddaughter of Zachariah Johnston, of Washington and Lee. Dr. Morrison was descended from Mary Moore, one of the captives taken from Abb's Valley in an Indian raid, when the Moore family was surprised and almost exterminated. Dr. Morrison's father died when he was very young, and his mother lived only a few years longer. Miss Harriet Morrison, his father's sister and a lady of lovely character, cared for him during childhood and was like a devoted mother to Dr. Morrison.

Dr. Morrison graduated from Hampden-Sydney in 1891. He then took a postgraduate course at the University of Texas, leaving there in 1894. He received his M.D. from the University of Virginia in 1898, graduating at the head of his class. He then went to New York for special work, and came later to Lynchburg, where he established himself in 1900. Along with his high stand as a student, Dr. Morrison took a leading part in college athletics, and was captain of the football team in every university he attended. He has always been an accomplished sportsman, and still retains his love of fishing and hunting.

In June, 1901, he married Elizabeth McCulloch. They have

two children living, Dr. Frederick McC. Morrison and Margaret Morrison. His nephew, Robert Dabney Morrison, has been brought up in his home as his own son. Dr. Morrison has given Lynchburg an eminent service in his profession.

Murrell

William M. Murrell, commonwealth's attorney of Campbell County from 1879 to 1912, and reappointed later to hold this same position, was the son of John Cobbs Murrell. John Cobbs Murrell was a prominent lawyer of his day, and was himself commonwealth's attorney of Campbell County from 1865 until his death, when his son succeeded him. He married Frances Cornelia Smithson. Their son, William M. Murrell, attended Professor Minor's school at Lynchburg. He graduated from Roanoke College in 1874, and then attended the University of Virginia. He married Flora Scott Withers, daughter of Blanche (Payne) and Robert W. Withers. For some years he has lived in Lynchburg.

Another Murrell family in Lynchburg came from Mount Holly, New Jersey, and settled here in the early part of the last century. John and Hardin Murrell were early postmasters in the town. John became a merchant and made a large fortune. His sister married Samuel Claytor, a tobacconist, and their daughter, Rosanna Claytor married Colonel Edmund Steptoe. Dr. Edward Murrell, whose daughter married Senator John W. Daniel, was of this family, also Mr. Murrell, of Tate Springs, the father of Mrs. Fannie Hughes, of this city.

Nelson

Dr. Thos. Hugh Nelson was born in Albemarle County and died in Bedford County in 1861. He married Laura Alexander, of Campbell County. Dr. Thomas Hugh Nelson was the grandson of Thomas Nelson, Junior, of Yorktown, and belonged to one of the great families of Virginia by birth and achievement. Five of Dr. Nelson's sons served in the Confederate Army. John Alexander Nelson gave up his life for Virginia at Raccoon's

Ford, October 11th, 1863. The other children of Thomas Hugh Nelson and Laura Alexander Nelson were Hugh William Steptoe, Thomas and Cleland Kinloch. Dr. Nelson was married a second time, to Mary Anne Matthews, the widow of William Campbell Meem, on October 4th, 1853. The children of this marriage were: Emily Goggin Nelson, married Wm. A. Dabney, October 31st, 1877; Edwin Matthews Nelson, married Meta Dirom, December 8th, 1886. Children: Ethel Nelson, married Mitchell Strother; Phyllis Nelson, married Mr. Byrd. Dr. Frank Walker Nelson, married Kate Hoblitzell, February 13th, 1884, in Baltimore, Maryland. The children of this union were: Frank Page Nelson, Marion Nelson, Bruce Nelson, and Cornelia Page Nelson, who married Charles T. Dabney, December 16th, 1880. Children: Mary Norvell, Page Nelson and Charles Thompson Dabney. Charles K. Nelson, married Rosalie Sayre, of Alabama; no children.

Cleland Kinloch Nelson, whose mother was Laura Alexander Nelson, Dr. Thos. Hugh Nelson's first wife, who died in 1850, was born September 2nd, 1842. He married Ella Clark Scott, born in Wytheville, August 9th, 1852, daughter of Charles and Sarah Anne (Adams) Scott, on November 6th, 1872, at Lynchburg. Her parents were originally from Halifax County. The children of Cleland Kinloch Nelson and Ella Clark Scott Nelson are: Thomas Hugh, Charles Scott, Sallie Scott, Mary Helen, Cleland Kinloch, Frank and Louise.

Nowlin

Mr. Green Nowlin, whose widow and sons still live here, was for many years a man of wealth and prominence in Lynchburg. It is said that he used to proudly tell of the time when, as a boy, he rode on a wagon load of hay to Lynchburg and decided to stay. There are many tales of this kind in the past history of Lynchburg—tales of young men, from families impoverished by the War and other circumstances, who came here to seek their fortunes, and succeeded beyond their largest dreams.

Mr. Nowlin was married twice, first, to Miss Lelia Pendleton, and second, to Miss Lucy Pendleton. He is survived by three sons, Green H., R. Peyton and James Pendleton Nowlin.

OTEY

The Otey family having been written of so extensively in Hopkins and Related Families, it seems hardly necessary to rewrite a complete record in this book. Isaac Otey, born in New Kent County, October 18th, 1765, died near Lynchburg, October 18th, 1839. He was a member of the Legislature from Bedford County, a soldier of the War of 1812, and an honored citizen. He married Elizabeth Mathews, daughter of Captain John Mathews, of Rockingham County. They had twelve children. His third child was John Mathews Otey, who lived in Lynchburg. He was a cashier of the bank here and president of the City Council. John Mathews Otey married Lucy Wilhemina Norvell, December 10th, 1817, and lived in the brick house on the corner of Federal and Eleventh Streets, now owned by Mr. Claiborne Gooch. He had ten children. Seven of his sons fought in the War Between the States with distinguished courage; they were: Dexter Otey, Van Renseelaer Otey, Kirkwood Otey, George Gaston Otey, Walter Hays Otey, John Marshall Warwick Otey and Peter Johnston Otey.

S. Dexter Otey married Mrs. Terry, the widow of A. W. C. Terry, who was killed by James Saunders in a street duel. Dexter Otey was killed in the old Norvell House by Mr. Lyne, as the result of an altercation between these two men.

Kirkwood Otey, who died in 1897, was a colonel of the Eleventh Virginia Regiment, C. S. A.

George Gaston Otey organized and was made captain of the "Otey Battery." He was wounded at Lewisburg, Virginia, May 24th, 1862. His wounds were not considered dangerous by him and against the advice of his doctors he returned to his post of duty. His weakened condition, combined with exposure, caused his death the following October. He was a soldier of remarkable valor. His widow, who in later years married Colonel

August Forsberg, was Mollie Morgan, granddaughter of William, brother of General Morgan, of Revolutionary fame. Captain Otey left two daughters. Caroline Otey, who married Mr. Peter Ainslie, has always lived in Lynchburg.

John Marshall Warwick Otey was on General Beauregard's staff for the duration of the War Between the States. Walter Hays Otey, who married Sallie Elizabeth Wyatt, left one son, the late Dexter Otey, who married Elizabeth Lewis, daughter of Mr. John Lewis, a prominent lawyer, and his wife, Elizabeth Langhorne. Mrs. Henry Sackett, Mrs. Paul Edmunds, Mrs. Henry Adams and Mrs. Clare Handy are the daughters of the late Mr. and Mrs. Hays Otey.

Peter Johnston Otey, major, C. S. A., was president of the Lynchburg and Durham Railroad, and member of Congress from this district. He married Malvina Floyd, daughter of Rush Floyd. They are survived by: Mary Warren Otey, married William Norwood Mitchell, and has one child, Otey Burnham Mitchell. They live in Atlanta, Georgia. Nannie Louis Otey, married John M. Miller, Junior, now living in Richmond, and has eleven children. A son of Major Peter Otey, Floyd, died September 16th, 1888; age sixteen. Natalie Floyd Otey, married Anselm Lynch Ward, May 16th, 1894. Their living children are: Mary, Lynch, Lucy, Floyd, Peter Otey, Dorothea and Virginia. Peter Otey Ward is a graduate of West Point Military Academy and is a lieutenant in the Army. Lynch is married and has one daughter.

Lucy Wilhemina Otey, the only daughter of Mr. and Mrs. John M. Otey, who survived infancy, married John Stuart Walker, of Richmond, who was killed at the Battle of Malvern Hill. Her two sons, John Stuart, Junior, and David Walker, have long been citizens of prominence in Lynchburg. Her only daughter, Loulie, was the first wife of Mr. Edmund Shaeffer.

After the War, Colonel Kirkwood Otey, as commander of the Home Guard and organizer of all of Lynchburg's public functions and parades, helped keep alive the military tradition of the town. Of their four children their oldest daughter, Mina, died in early womanhood. John M. Otey, City Auditor, married Maggie Murrell, daughter of Mr. Thomas Murrell, a prominent citizen here. They have one son, John M. Otey, Junior. Colonel Otey's surviving daughter, Anne Norvell Otey, married James Alexander Scott, born in Richmond, who has for many years been in the insurance business in Lynchburg. They have two sons living, K. Duval and Norvell Scott, and one daughter, Mrs. Lucy Kirkwood Otey Hotchkiss. The youngest son of Colonel Otey, Kirkwood Otey, Junior, no longer lives in Lynchburg.

Lucy Wilhemina, the wife of John M. Otey, and the mother of the seven above mentioned sons, had a notable War record of her own. She organized a hospital in an old hotel which stood at the corner of Sixth and Main Streets on the site now occupied by the Montgomery-Ward Store. The hospital was called the Ladies' Relief Hospital, and the women of Lynchburg were organized into an efficient corps of nurses and assistants to attend the wounded and sick soldiers of the Confederacy as they arrived from the battlefields. Many ladies, among them Mrs. Charles Price, sold their jewels to provide food and comforts for the soldiers.

At one time "Sandusky," built about 1808 by Charles Johnston, already mentioned in these pages, belonged to Mr. John M. Otey. After Mr. Johnston had moved to Botetourt, the place changed hands several times. It was owned by William Radford, Isaac Otey, Edward Watts and Thomas Moore. Eventually it became the property of John M. Otey, who conveyed it to George C. Hutter about 1841. Since that time it has remained in the hands of the Hutter family.

A more distant connection of the Otey family was Octavia Otey, who lived in Lynchburg. Left an orphan at an early age, she was adopted by her kinswoman, Mrs. John Robin McDaniel, and her husband, Mr. McDaniel. She married Mr. Clinton De-Witt, a wealthy and prominent business man, and for many years was a leader in the social and religious life in the city. Her children: Clinton DeWitt, Junior, Mrs. Mary Adams and Mrs. Bessie Packard still live in Lynchburg.

OWEN

Owen Owen and Jane Hughes Owen, his wife, came from Augusta County, near Staunton, and made their home in Lynchburg. They were among the early families of Lynchburg who helped to mould the moral and spiritual life of the town. Dr. William Owen, their son, said that his father and mother brought him here when he was three years old. He died January 22nd, 1876; age eighty-eight years; so his parents must have come to Lynchburg in 1791. Their two sons, Septimus and Benjamin, died young; their daughter, Sarah, who married Mr. Hughes, died in 1820. Dr. William Owen practiced medicine here for sixty years, and was greatly beloved. He was married twice, to Otwayanna Carter, and after her death to Jane Latham, of Culpeper. His sister, Jane Owen, married Dr. Henry Latham, the brother of Dr. Owen's second wife, Jane Latham. Jane Latham Owen had two sons, William Otway and Robert Latham. William Otway Owen was a doctor in Lynchburg for many years. Robert Latham Owen was president of the Norfolk and Western Railroad. He married Narcissa Chisholm. Dr. William Otway Owen married the niece of Narcissa Chisholm, Alice Lynde, and had a large family. His children were: William Otway, Junior, Charles, Owen, Billy, Jane and Alice. Jane, married Charles E. Heald. He was a native of Baltimore, but for many years operated Heald's Bark Mill in Lynchburg. Jane Owen was Mr. Heald's second wife and had no children. Colonel Robert Latham Owen died June 14th, 1873, leaving two sons, William Otway and Robert Latham Owen, Jr. Robert Latham Owen was born February 2nd, 1856. He went to Washington and Lee University in 1877, and began the practice of law in 1880. On December 31st, 1889, he married Miss Daisy Hester. From 1885 to 1889 he was agent for the Five Civilized Tribes of Indians. He organized the First National Bank of Muskogee,

Oklahoma, and was its president from 1890 to 1900. He was interested in banking, real estate and public affairs, and while serving as United States Senator from Oklahoma, which office he held for three terms, 1907-1925, he drafted the Federal Reserve Act and Farm Loan Act.

Page

The family of Ambrose Page is an old one in Lynchburg, being recorded in Mrs. Cabell's Recollections. They were friends and business associates of Bransford Vawter, Lynchburg's earliest poet.

Page

Mr. Edward Trent Page, owner of "Caryswood," in Buckingham, died there after a long illness. Mr. Page graduated with distinction from the University of Virginia. He married Helen Payne, daughter of David Boyce Payne, of Lynchburg, and had one child, Helen, who lived to maturity. She married Angus Echols, of Wilmington, Delaware. Mr. Page was buried at "Caryswood." His Negro servants sang a farewell hymn at his grave. His death took place April, 1906. His wife was killed in an automobile accident, March, 1925.

Dr. Paxton

Rev. Dr. James D. Paxton came here many years ago as pastor of the congregation of the First Presbyterian Church. After fulfilling his mission with honor to himself and to the church he represents and retiring from active service, he decided to make Lynchburg his permanent home. His able and scholarly sermons drew many outside his own flock, and his high qualities as a Christian and a man have endeared him to the people of this community.

The Presbyterian ministers who have lived in Lynchburg have been a fine group of men. Dr. J. M. Rawlings, who preached at the Second Presbyterian Church, gave a devoted service to the people here, and took an active interest in the affairs of the town. Dr. Ramsay was tried and condemned here by the Presbyterian Synod for preaching evolution.

At the beginning of the contest for Local Option in 1886 Dr. W. T. Hall published an open letter, advising that the fight be kept out of the churches, as the church had nothing to do with it, for in the Scriptures we were told to drink wine moderately.

Payne

George Payne, ancestor of the Paynes of Lynchburg, Campbell and neighboring counties, according to Miss Mary Forbes, was brother of Sir William Payne of Tempsford Hall, Bedfordshire, England. Coming to America with another brother, Robert, he settled in Goochland County, while Robert went to Fauquier. George was sheriff of Goochland from 1734-37, preceding Peter Jefferson, the father of Thomas Jefferson. He died in 1744 and was buried in Goochland.

The Paynes trace their descent from royalty through four lines:

1. The Spotswood line—to Robert III, king of Scotland.

2. The wife of Governor Spotswood—to Elizabeth, daughter of Edward I.

3. The Dandridge line—through the Wests—Lords de la Warr.

4. The Reade line—to Alfred the Great.

George Payne married Mary Woodson in 1704 and had four sons, Josias, George, Robert and John.

Josias was a member of the House of Burgesses from Goochland in 1761, 1765, but he afterwards gave his home, "Plymhymmon," to his son, Robert, and moved to Pittsylvania County, where he died. George, son of the first George, was grandfather of General Matthew M. Payne, born January 17, 1784, died 1862, who served forty years in United States Army and received a sword from the State of Virginia as a testimony of distinguished gallantry. Robert has left no issue.

John Payne, a son of Josias, born 1734, married Mary Coles, daughter of Wm. Coles, of Coles Hill, Hanover County. Among their children was Dolly, born May 20th, 1772. Dolly married, first, John Todd, and second, President James Madison. She is celebrated as one of the most gracious of White House mistresses.

John, son of the first George, born December 4th, 1713, in Goochland, married, first, Miss Archer, and second, Mrs. Jane Smith Chichester, of Lancaster County, daughter of Phillip Smith, of Northumberland and granddaughter of Baldwin Mathews, January 23rd, 1757. Colonel John Payne, of "White Hall," as he was widely known, a man of great wealth, lived at "White Hall," Goochland, one of the handsomest Virginia homes of that period. His house was afterwards burned. He was a member of the House of Burgesses from 1752 to 1768, lieutenant-colonel of militia, and member of the Revolutionary Committee of Safety at Goochland. Children of first marriage were: (1) John, married Mary, daughter of John Chichester; (2) Archer, married, first, Martha, daughter of Captain Nathaniel West Dandridge, first cousin of Martha Dandridge, wife of George Washington and sister of Elizabeth Dandridge, wife of Colonel Phillip Payne, of "Airy Mount," and second, Betsy Brooks, and lived at New Market, Goochland; (3) Robert, who died unmarried.

Children of Archer and Martha D. Payne:

1. Anne Spotswood, born April 19th, 1772, married Thomas Mann Fleming.

2. Martha, born November 8th, 1773, married Jeremiah Strother.

3. Archer, Junior, died unmarried.

4. Dorothea Dandridge, born 1777, married Edward Bolling, nephew of Thomas Jefferson, from whom is descended Edith Bolling, second wife of President Woodrow Wilson.

5. Alexander Spotswood, married Charlotte, daughter of Archibald Bryce, of Scotland, who bought seven hundred acres of land on Ivy Creek, Campbell County, where he built a residence called "The Cottage," to which he moved from New Market, in Goochland.

6. Jane, married, first, Robert Bolling; second, James Ferguson.

7. John Robert Dandridge, married Susan Bryce, and lived for years in Lynchburg.

8. Lillias, married Dr. Richard Potter Jones.

9. Catherine, married Archibald Bolling.

Children of Alexander Spotswood and Charlotte Bryce Payne:

1. Dr. Robert Spotswood, born in Goochland, January 15th, 1809, married January 30th, 1840, Frances Russell Meem, daughter of John G. and Eliza R. Meem, of Lynchburg. Moved to Lynchburg in 1831 and practiced medicine until his death, September 28th, 1884. Dr. Payne was the first president of the State Medical Society and first chairman of Lynchburg School Board. Issue: John Meem, married Elizabeth Allen Langhorne; Fanny, died young; Alexander Spotswood, married Elizabeth, daughter of Judge E. C. Burks, of Bedford; Eliza Russell, died unmarried. D. A. Payne, of Lynchburg is John M. Payne's son.

2. David Bryce, married Helen James.

3. James Ferguson, married Frances Dudley, of Lynchburg, daughter of Peter Dudley.

4. William M., married Frances Mitchell.

5. Charlotte E., married John H. Winston.

6. Harriet, married Captain William Steptoe.

The family graveyard at The Cottage has nine graves, marked with the following tombstones: Jefferson Bolling, 1845; Mrs. Catherine Bolling, sister of A. S. Payne, Susan Payne, wife of John R. D. Payne, and sister of Mrs. Alexander S. Payne, Alexander Spotswood Payne, 1858; Josephine Mitchell, daughter of Rev. J. D. Mitchell, Charlotte Payne, wife of Alexander Spotswood Payne, Harriet Steptoe, wife of Captain William Steptoe, Ida, wife of Major William Payne, Kate, sister of Captain William Steptoe.

Children of Colonel John Payne and Mrs. Jane Smith Chichester Payne:

1. Anna, born 1758, married Colonel James Gordon, of Lancaster County.

2. Philip, born 1760, married November 13th, 1783, Elizabeth Dandridge, daughter of Captain Nathaniel West Dandridge, of "Elsing Green," King William County, and Dorothea Spotswood, daughter of Governor Alexander Spotswood. She was sister of Martha Dandridge, wife of Archer Payne and of Dorothea Dandridge, second wife of Patrick Henry. Colonel Philip Payne, militia officer, resided at "Airy Mount," near Marysville, in Campbell County. Part of the house is yet standing and near it is an old rock stable, in good condition. Colonel Payne and his wife, Elizabeth, are buried at "Airy Mount." Colonel Payne's and Patrick Henry's estate adjoined and Payne was an administrator of Henry's estate.

Children of Philip and Elizabeth Dandridge Payne:

1. Jane Smith Payne, born 1784, married Tamerlain Whiting Davies, son of Henry Landon Davies, of Bedford.

2. John Smith, born June 26th, 1786, married Susanna E. Scott. John Smith Payne inherited "Flat Creek Quarter," built a residence, "White Hall," which is still standing and named after his grandfather's place in Goochland.

Children:

1. Robert C., married Sarah Miller.

2. Amanda V., married George Yuille, of Lawyers, from whom are descended: Mrs. J. Paulett Clark, of Lynchburg; Thos. B. Yuille, of New York, and Mrs. Lucy Morris.

3. Mary Clementina, married Frank Scott.

4. Elizabeth, married, first, Robert W. Nowlin; second, Orthodox Creed Clark; issue: Dr. J. Paulett Clark, of Lynchburg.

5. John William.

6. Susan, married Jesse Hargrave, of Chatham.

7. Philip W., born 1821, married Julia Ogden, granddaughter of John M. Gordon. Children: 1. Louisa; 2. J. Gordon; 3. Elias O.; 4. Julia; 5. Dandridge.

John Gordon Payne, born February 6th, 1854, was a leading business man of Lynchburg. At the time of his death, in 1909, he was president of the Adams Brothers-Payne Company, a large coal, wood and lumber concern, and director of a number of corporations. He is buried in Spring Hill Cemetery.

8. Walter Tazewell, born 1826, married Elizabeth K. Ligon. Children: 1. Rosa; 2. Walter; 3. Robert; 4. Susan; 5. Willie.

Rosa Payne, born February 3rd, 1854, married May 3rd, 1875, D. C. Jackson. Children: Elizabeth, married Robert Dirom; Marion, married G. E. Vaughan; Lucy, married B. G. Kerr; Dabney C., married Susan Yuille; Grace, married April 5th, 1906, Geo. E. Caskie, Jr.; Landon; Rosalie, married C. H. Lumsden; Florence, married Dr. G. Blake Harrison; Tazewell P., married Lucy Adams; Alice, married Robert Lee Massie.

9. Ann, married Jack Elliott.

10. Edward S., married Annie Oliver.

11. Martha Harriet, married Marco B. Carter, from whom is descended Mrs. Volney E. Howard, of Lynchburg.

12. Blanche T., married Colonel Robert Withers, clerk of Campbell County.

Children of Philip and Elizabeth Dandridge Payne, continued:

3. Elizabeth Spotswood, born July 1st, 1788, married William Syme Cabell, and moved to Mississippi.

4. Dr. Nathaniel West, born 1790, married 1819, Catherine W., daughter of Robert Alexander.

5. Philip Mathews, born May 29th, 1794, married, first, Eliza

Cobbs; second, Mary E. Mitchell in 1872. Lived at "Oak Grove," Staunton River, Campbell County.

6. Baldwin Matthews, born 1796, married Catherine Coles and lived at his father's residence, "Airy Mount."

7. Ann T., born 1799, married Jeremiah Pannill.

8. Evelina Washington, born 1801, married Edward Ball Withers, of Ivanhoe. Children: 1. Philip T.; 2. Edward; 3. Jeannette; 4. Walter; 5. Alice, died young; 6. Robert Woodson; 7. Zuleika, married Dr. A. I. Clark; children: Withers P. Clark, Miss Alice Clark, Mrs. Cora Clark Mosby, and the late Mrs. John A. Faulkner, of Lynchburg.

9. Camilla West, born 1803, married Samuel Scott, Junior.

10. Louisa Woodson, born 1807, married John Coles.

11. Clarissa Aylett, born 1809, married Robert Wyatt. Children:

    1. Thomas, married Mary Bell.

    2. Nannie, married Philip Yuille.

    3. Sallie, married W. Hayes Otey. Children:

        1. Clare, married Sanderson, of Philadelphia.

        2. Lucy, married Henry P. Adams, of Lynchburg.

        3. Mallie, married Paul C. Edmunds.

        4. Mina, married Henry M. Sackett.

        5. Dexter, married Elizabeth Lewis.

        6. Edith, unmarried.

Children: Philip M. and Elizabeth Cobbs Payne. John Alexander, married Isabella Perrow; Missouri, married Dr. Horace Lemmon.

Children of Philip M. and Mary E. Mitchell Payne:

Catherine, born 1836, married Dr. F. A. Perrow.

Lucretia, V., born 1837, married Captain William E. Johns, of Pittsylvania.

Sarah A., born 1845, married F. C. Perrow. Children: 1. Charles B.; 2. F. Kirk; 3. Dr. Mosby G.

Samuel Garland, born 1847, married Isabella Jones, of Appomattox; son, Dr. Mosby H. Payne, of New York.

Mosby Hale, born May 10th, 1848, married Mary Morris, of Lynchburg.

Helen, born 1857, married A. C. Berryman, of Surry.

Charles R., born 1842, died while in service in the War Between the States.

Mosby Hale Payne was long a resident of Lynchburg and one of its most prominent citizens. He was engaged in the leaf tobacco business and for years was proprietor of Pace's Warehouse, under the firm name of M. H. Payne and Company. Later he moved to Buchanan, Virginia, where he died of typhoid fever. He is buried in Spring Hill Cemetery, Lynchburg. He married Mary Morris and had one son, Samuel Garland Payne, Junior, who died while a student at Hampden-Sydney College, and was also buried in Spring Hill Cemetery.

Payne Family

George Payne, the ancestor of the Payne family in Lynchburg, settled in Goochland County, married Mary Woodson about the year 1704, and died in 1744. He succeeded Peter Jefferson, the father of Thomas Jefferson, as sheriff of Goochland. Two of his sons, John and Josias, were members of the House of Burgesses. The family is said to be descended from Sir Robert Payne, of Bedfordshire, England. Colonel John Payne, of "White Hall," Goochland County, member of the House of Burgesses from 1752 to 1768, was a lieutenant-colonel of militia, and had two sons, Archie and Phillip, who each married a Dandridge, granddaughters of Governor Spotswood, and have descendants living in Lynchburg and Campbell County.

Archie Payne, of New Market, in Goochland County, married Martha Dandridge, oldest child of Nathaniel West Dandridge and Dorothea Spotswood. Nathaniel West Dandridge was the son of Unity West, whose mother was Martha, the widow of Gideon Macon and her second husband, Nathaniel West.

Martha Dandridge, the wife of Archie Payne, daughter of Nathaniel Dandridge, of "Elsing Green," King William County, was third in descent from Unity Croshaw and Honorable Colonel John West, Governor of Virginia and brother of Lord Delaware. Her sister married Phillip Payne, half-brother of Archer.

Alexander Spotswood Payne, the son of Archer, married Charlotte Bryce, of Greenfields, Goochland County, September 6th, 1804. His children were: 1. Dr. Robert Spotswood Payne, who married Fannie Meem, the parents of Mr. John Meem Payne, of Amherst, and of Mr. A. Spotswood Payne and Miss Eliza Payne, now dead. 2. David Bryce Payne, born August, 1812, at Newmarket, Goochland County, died in Lynchburg, November, 1888, married Helen Sophia McComb James, daughter of Dr. Richard Potts James, of Cumberland County. Their children were: Ellen Grattan Payne, who married Dr. George K. Turner; Mary C. Payne; David Bryce Payne, Junior; Richard James Payne; Robert Spotswood Payne; Helen Stockton Payne, who married Mr. Page, and George A. W. Payne, who married Louise, daughter of Mr. Jacob Mitchell, a Presbyterian minister here for many years. 3. James Ferguson Payne. 4. William Michel Payne, married Fannie, daughter of Rev. Jacob Mitchell, Presbyterian minister. 5. Charlotte Payne, married Captain John Winston, who had a military school for boys, called "Westover," on what is now known as the Link Road, near Lynchburg. This school, of which only a chimney now remains, prepared many of the boys of that day for the Virginia Military Institute and for other colleges. 6. Harriet James Payne, married Major William Steptoe, son of Dr. Steptoe, of Bedford County, and half-brother of Colonel Edward Steptoe. She inherited from her father the place now owned by Mr. Stanhope Johnson. At her death this place went to her husband, Major Steptoe, and through him to his sister, Mrs. Eldridge. Alexander Spotswood Payne bought "The Cottage," as it was then known, about the year 1840, having left his home, "White Hall," in Goochland County, in order to be near his children in his old age. He is buried near "The Cottage."

Phillip Payne, son of John Payne, of "White Hall," Goochland County, and half-brother of Archer Payne, married Elizabeth Dandridge, daughter of Colonel Nathaniel West Dandridge. Their children were: 1. Clarissa Elliot Payne, who married Mr. Wyatt. 2. Evelina Washington Payne, married Edward Ball Withers, and was the mother of Zuleika Withers, who married Dr. A. I. Clark, of Lynchburg. Their children were: Miss Alice Clark, Mrs. Cora Clark Mosby, John, who died unmarried; Withers Clark, who married Lottie Preston, and had: Annis, Withers, Charlotte and Nannie, now deceased; Marianne Tucker Clark, married John A. Faulkner, son of Mr. and Mrs. John William Faulkner. Three children survived Marianne Tucker Clark Faulkner at her death, Anne Irvine, Rosalie and Nina. A son of Edward Ball Withers, who left descendants in Lynchburg, was Mr. Phillip Thornton Withers, who married his cousin, Flora Virginia Withers; their daughter, Flora Lee, married Mr. W. O. Smith, and has several children; Janet, married Major Frank Scruggs, who died lately; they had a large family of children, several of whom are now living in Lynchburg.

Other descendants of this family living in Lynchburg are: Mrs. Thomas Page Nelson, and her daughter, Mary C., who is Mrs. John Gannaway; Mrs. Pelham Moorman, and the children and grandchildren of Mrs. Nora Petty, which include Mr. Withers Petty and Mrs. Lawrence Burks.

Phillip W. Payne, married Julia Ogden, granddaughter of John M. Gordon. His children were: Lou, who married E. A. Allen; J. Gordon, who married Nannie Hurt; Elias Ogden, who married Belle S. Walker, daughter of General Lindsay Walker; Julia, never married; Dandridge Payne.

Walter Tazewell Payne, married Elizabeth R. Ligon. Their daughter, Rosa, was the first wife of Mr. D. C. Jackson, and most of their children and grandchildren live here. Walter Tazewell Payne was the son of John Smith Payne, the grandson of Phillip Payne. Among his descendants are: Mrs. Elizabeth Dirom and her children, Guy, Patrick and Robert Dirom, and

Mrs. Elias Richards; Mr. Tazewell Jackson and his children; Mrs. Lucy Kerr and her children; the children of Mr. Garland Vaughan; Mrs. Charles Lumsden and her children; and Mrs. Alice Massie, of Nelson County, and her children.

Peak

The late Malcom Peak, of the Peak Lumber Company, which was once a flourishing business of Lynchburg, left his widow and three children, Lewis, Malcolm and Evelyn. Mrs. Peak has given much good and useful work to the community, being interested in all benevolent enterprises.

Pendleton

Mr. Jacob D. Pendleton, a native of Amherst, and Chief of Police in Lynchburg for many years, died June 17th, 1918.

Phelps

Mr. William Phelps is the representative of a Lynchburg family which was large and influential in the earlier history of the city. As in the case of other old families many of its members are now scattered and gone from Lynchburg. His sister, Miss Norma Phelps, was particularly devoted to good works, and the whole family were noted for their attitude of kindliness towards all mankind.

Percy

Major Alfred Boyd Percy was born in March, 1869, the son of Isham and Anne Obenchain Percy, of Botetourt County, Virginia. His father died when he was twelve years old. At a very early age he entered the law office of Manson and Wilson, and later studied law at the University of Virginia. From the time he began to practice law all who came in contact with Mr. Percy were impressed with his unusual capacity in certain branches of law. He became a successful and useful citizen, but particularly was he valued for his courage, both moral and physical. At no time did he fail to speak the truth as he saw it. He married Mary Elizabeth, daughter of Mr. and Mrs. J. W. Faulkner. Major Percy, who won his majority during the World

War, died in October, 1929. He left two sons, Alfred B. Percy, Junior, and John Tucker Percy. Mrs. Nathan B. Handy, Miss Mary Percy and the late Mrs. John Kinnier were his sisters. His brother, Major Tucker Percy, United States Army, died some years ago.

Perrow

The Perrow family were Huguenots, who after the revocation of the Edict of Nantes in 1685 escaped to England. Thence, with the aid of William, of Orange, they emigrated to America. A colony of these Huguenots settled about the year 1700 at Manakin Town on the south side of James River, twenty miles above Richmond, in what is now Powhatan County. In the list of the heads of families in this settlement, King William Parish appears at the top of the name of Charles Perault. In the registry of baptisms occurs the record in 1728, "Charles Pero, son of Daniel and Marie Pero," and in 1735, "Estiene Pero, son of Daniel and Marie Pero." From Daniel are descended the Perrows of Virginia. The name was variously spelled at that period: Pero, Perro, Peros, Pierro, Perault and Perreau. From Manakin Town numbers of the family migrated to Cumberland County, then to Buckingham, and settled on Slate River, where they owned and operated slate and gold mines. In the latter half of the eighteenth century Stephen Perrow, son of Daniel, and his nephew, Daniel B., sold their holdings in Buckingham and moved to what was then Bedford but is now Campbell County. They settled on adjoining farms along Beaver Creek. The name had by this time been anglicized to "Perrow." Daniel B. Perrow was a man of large means and sporting tendencies. He maintained a stable of thoroughbred horses, and built a track in a field near his home, which is still called "race track field." He was an ensign in the American Army during the Revolutionary War, and later bore the title of "colonel," being probably a colonel of militia. He represented his county in the legislature for eleven terms, a period of twenty-two years. In 1815-16 he was sheriff of the county. No male descendant of Daniel B.

is now living. From Stephen Perrow are descended all those in this vicinity bearing the name. Stephen lived at "Apple Grove," where only the graveyard now remains.

Children of Daniel and Marie Perrow, of King William Parish:

1. Charles, born 1729.
2. Stephen (French Estiene), born 1735.
3. Daniel.
4. Mary G.

Stephen, married May 11th, 1770, Elizabeth Fleming, daughter of David Fleming, of Bedford County. Issue:

1. Mary Ann, married _____ Bailey.
2. Elizabeth, married Neiley Powell, of Amherst.
3. Stephen, married June 9th, 1805, first, Dollie, daughter of Benjamin Cox. Children:
   1. John, married Martha Cowling.
   2. Caroline, married Jack Stevens.
   3. Stephen, married Virginia Hendricks.
   4. William C., married May 17th, 1886, Urania Virginia Cowling.
   5. Dorothea, married Thomas Rucker.
   6. Andrew J., married Nancy McGhee.
   7. Paulina, married _____ Stewart.
   8. James, married Elizabeth Ogden.

Stephen, son of Stephen and Elizabeth Perrow, married, second, Amy Green. Issue:

1. Thomas.
2. Ferdinand A., married Catherine Mitchell Payne.
3. Ann, married Robert Murrell, moved to Missouri.
4. Isabella, married John A. Payne.

Captain William C. Perrow, born 1810, died 1887, was captain of militia during the Civil War. He lived at "Shady Grove," a beautiful old colonial residence still standing near Gladys, built by Patrick Henry. Four of his sons served in the Confederate Army, Alexander D., Stephen C., Fletcher C., and Willis L. Alexander D., married, first, Fannie Brooks, and second, Nettie Spriggs. He lived for years in Lynchburg. Among his children were the late Dr. Ferdinand M. Perrow, graduate of University of Pennsylvania, who practiced in Lynchburg, and Mrs. Robert G. Robertson, now living in Lynchburg. Stephen C. joined an infantry company in Lynchburg commanded by Captain Samuel Preston, of which he was elected lieutenant. In 1864 he resigned to join Mosby's command. After the War, he practiced law at Halifax Courthouse with marked success. Fletcher C., married Sallie A. Payne, daughter of Captain Philip M. Payne, volunteered at the age of sixteen and, joining Company C, Second Virginia Cavalry, engaged in the Battles of Manassas, Fredericksburg, Gettysburg, the Wilderness and Petersburg. His children were the late Chas. B. Perrow, of Altavista; F. Kirk Perrow, Pittsylvania, and Dr. Mosby G. Perrow, of Lynchburg. Willis L. Perrow, married Nellie Brooks, was a courier to General R. E. Lee at the age of sixteen.

Dr. Ferdinand A. Perrow, graduate of several colleges, including the University of Virginia and the University of Pennsylvania, practiced medicine with distinction at Marysville, in Campbell County. Among his children are Robley M. Perrow and the late Charles M. Perrow, both of Lynchburg.

Mosby G. Perrow

Dr. Mosby G. Perrow, Director of Public Welfare in Lynchburg, was born September 20th, 1876, a native of Campbell County and the son of Fletcher and Sallie A. Payne Perrow. He is descended on the Perrow side from the Huguenot, Charles Perault, and on his mother's side from the Virginia Paynes, Dandridges and Spotswoods.

Appointed health officer of Lynchburg when the Health Department began its first really organized work in 1910, Dr.

Perrow has made noteworthy achievement. In his position he has seen the infant mortality rate cut in half, due to increased sewerage, reduction of flies, and the campaigns for public enlightenment carried on by the Bureau of Public Health. He has seen the typhoid rate, the sanitary index of a city, drop from more than one hundred and fifty per thousand population to less than seventy-five per thousand population. This also has been due to sewerage protection, inspection and education of the masses in disease sources, and to the use of typhoid preventive serum.

The tuberculosis rate, another index to efficient health work, has dropped in this city from two hundred and five to less than fifty, as a result of the steady efforts of the Health Department in the maintenance of clinics and in the distribution of milk to undernourished children in the schools.

Important to public health as are the problems of infant mortality, typhoid and tuberculosis, there are countless other details which take up the time of the administrator and his forces in the conduct of the department, such as the direction of various clinics, city nurses, city physicians, work to eliminate insects and animals which are a menace to health, and the superintendence of bacteriological laboratories. The Lynchburg Hospital and City Home are also administered by the Director of the Department of Public Welfare. Dr. Perrow's duties thus are concerned with all matters that pertain to public health.

Dr. Perrow holds his Baccalaureate, Masters and Philosophy degrees from Washington and Lee University. He was Director of Science in the Lynchburg Public Schools from 1902 to 1909, City Chemist and Bacteriologist from 1906 to the present time, has been health officer since 1910 and Director of Public Welfare since 1920. He is a member of the American Association of Science, the American Chemical Society, American Medical Association, the Public Health Association, the American Society of Bacteriologists, the Anti-Tuberculosis League, of which he is a former president; the Virginia Public Health Association, of which he was president in 1913, and the Virginia Academy of Science. He has given special study and has accomplished important work in the fields of chemistry and bacteriology of milk; elimination of insects; distribution of sewage; food preservation; infant mortality, and proper care and filtration of water.

Dr. Perrow was married November 11th, 1902, to Miss Louise Joynes, of Onancock, Albemarle County, and they have two children: Mosby G. Perrow, Junior, who will get his Law degree in June, 1934, from Duke University and has already passed the State bar examination, and Sallie Perrow, who is a student at Farmville State Teachers College.

Peters

William Elisha Peters, LL.D., was born in Bedford County, Virginia, August 18th, 1829. His father was Elisha Peters, a large land owner in Bedford. The father of Elisha Peters was the Rev. William Peters, a minister of the Church of England, who came to this country in 1750, and died in 1773. Elisha Peters, married Cynthia Turner. William Elisha received his early education at New London Academy, where most of the young Virginians of this section were trained for college. He went to Emory and Henry College, and later to the University of Virginia, where he received his M.A. degree. From 1856 to 1858 he attended lectures at the University of Berlin, where he also pursued a special study of Latin. After his graduation at the University of Virginia, he was elected professor of Latin in Emory and Henry College. Here he taught from 1851 to 1861, with the exception of the two years spent in European study. In 1861 Professor William Elisha Peters entered the Confederate Army as a private. He soon gained the rank of captain, and was then lieutenant-colonel, and later colonel. He was known in university circles as "Colonel" Peters. Colonel Peters was a fine soldier, accustomed to giving orders and to carrying out orders, and yet it was he who refused to burn the town of Chambersburg, Pennsylvania, at General Early's command. For General Jubal A. Early had decided on this act of retribution for the countless outrages against civilized warfare which the Northern soldiers had committed in the South. He directed Colonel Peters to give orders to this effect. Colonel Peters refused to do this, saying he would rather be court-martialed than to burn the homes of women and children. The Southern people upheld Colonel Peters, although they realized that General Early had very great provocation.

After the War Between the States, Colonel Peters was elected professor of Latin at the University of Virginia, and this position he filled with great distinction until his death on March 22nd, 1906. As a professor he had few equals and no superiors. He was truly one of the great teachers and a diploma from him qualified a young man to teach Latin in any school or college in the South. Professor Peters was married in 1858 to Margaret Sheffey. His second wife was Mary Sheffey, whom he married in 1873. At his death he was survived by three children, among whom is Dr. Don P. Peters, a well-known Lynchburg surgeon.

Mr. Walker Pettyjohn's Family

Mr. Walker Pettyjohn was born in Amherst County, Virginia, November 2nd, 1870; the son of John P. and Nannie (Ould) Pettyjohn. He was educated in the Lynchburg schools and at Randolph-Macon College. Mr. Walker Pettyjohn, with his father, has for many years had a large contracting business in Lynchburg. He has been Mayor of Lynchburg, member of the City Council, vice-president of the Peoples' National Bank, president of the Y. M. C. A., president of the Chamber of Commerce, member of the Hill City Lodge of Masons and the Rotary Club. Mr. Pettyjohn married Miss Mary Macon Raine, the daughter of Charles Anderson Raine, a prominent tobacconist of Danville, Virginia, and his wife, Elizabeth Caldwell Oliver. Mrs. Pettyjohn was descended from Gideon Macon and Abraham Michaux, two of the early French Huguenot settlers in Virginia; her grandmother having been Bettie Venable

Michaux (the daughter of Mary Mayo Macon and Richard W. Michaux), who married Richard Kendall Raine.

The children of Walker Pettyjohn and Mary Macon Raine Pettyjohn are: Charles Raine Pettyjohn, married Mildred Bruce Hudson, and has two children, Mary Jane and Charles Raine, Junior; Nannie Ould Pettyjohn, married Edward Langhorne Carrington; Macon Michaux Pettyjohn; Mary Macon Pettyjohn, married William Wilbur Winfree, and has one child, William Wilbur, Junior; Walker Pettyjohn, Junior; Clunet Holmes Pettyjohn.

Mr. John P. Pettyjohn, Mr. Walker Pettyjohn, Mr. Charles Raine Pettyjohn, Mr. Macon M. Pettyjohn and Walker Pettyjohn, Junior, represent three generations in the business that Mr. John P. Pettyjohn established in Lynchburg soon after the close of the War Between the States, which soon became the leading firm of contractors and builders in Lynchburg. The company now carries on a progressive business, and has for a long time handled large contracts over an extensive field. They have completed large contracts for the Norfolk and Western Railway Company, the Chesapeake and Ohio Railway Company, the Southern Railway Company, The Viscose Company, Liggett and Myers Tobacco Company, Riverside and Dan River Cotton Mills, Randolph-Macon Woman's College, and other industrial and educational institutions too numerous to mention here.

Priddy

Dr. Albert S. Priddy died at Virginia Baptist Hospital, January 13th, 1925. He is survived by his wife, the former Mrs. Mamie Hardy Mitchell, to whom he was married in Alexandria, October, 1923. Dr. Priddy was born on his father's estate in Lunenburg County, December 7th, 1865, and was the son of Robert W. Priddy and Martha H. (Gaulding) Priddy. He was educated at Keysville, and at the College of Physicians and Surgeons at Baltimore. For some time he practiced his profession at Keysville, Charlotte County. From 1901 to 1909 he was at the Sanitorium of Marion, first as assistant physician and later as superintendent. He was a member of many medical associations, and an active participant in the political life of the State of Virginia. Since the establishment of the State Epileptic Colony on Madison Heights, above Lynchburg, in 1910 he had been its superintendent. He was a psychiatrist, and well known as an authority on mental diseases. He personally superintended the construction, establishment and organization of the Epileptic Colony, which, at the time of his death, was caring for about seven hundred patients.

Radford

Colonel Richard Carlton Walker Radford, the son of William and Elizabeth Moseley Radford, was born in Bedford County in 1822. His father, who was long in the military service of the United States, raised a company of cavalry for the War of 1812, and was the first of the Radford family in Bedford County. Colonel Radford served with honor during the Mexican War, and took part in various Indian affairs on the frontier. For sixteen years he was in the United States Army, and for several years commanded a company in the First United States Dragoons with the work of captain. At the outbreak of the War Between the States he followed the fortunes of Virginia. His first work was the organization of the Second Virginia Cavalry, which he did in a masterly manner, and he ranked as colonel of this regiment during the War. He was married twice, his first wife being Octavia Duval, of Washington. They lived for many years at "Rothsay," near Forest, in Bedford County, which was the original house built by his kinsman, Major Joel Yancey. This was part of the estate owned by Thomas Jefferson. In late years the house was burned down, and another house was built on the old site by Mr. O. Loxley C. Radford, who is now the only surviving son of Colonel R. C. W. Radford. Mr. Duval Radford and Mr. Walker Radford died in recent years.

Colonel Radford's second wife was Fannie C. Steptoe, a granddaughter of James Steptoe, the famed clerk of Bedford Court. Colonel Radford's grandfather, William Radford, with the aid

From "A Quaker Post-Bag." Courtesy of Longmans, Green and Company
Barlborough Hall, Derbyshire—Rodes, Baronets
From Colonial Virginia: Its People and Customs, by Mary Newton Stanard.
Reproduced through courtesy of J. B. Lippincott, Publishers.

of Governor Floyd, in Revolutionary times equipped a number of privateers, and in an engagement with an English fleet both men were captured and confined in the Tower of London. Later, with the help of English friends, they escaped to France, where they were received with great kindness by the French queen, Marie Antoinette, who assisted them to return to America.

Rockenbach

Samuel Dickerson Rockenbach was born in Lynchburg, January 27th, 1869; the son of Frank J. Rockenbach, veteran of the War Between the States. Samuel Rockenbach graduated from the Virginia Military Institute in 1890. He married Emma Baldwin, of Washington, District of Columbia, October 19th, 1898. Samuel Rockenbach was promoted through grades to rank of brigadier-general in the United States regular army, January 23rd, 1924. He was at one time commandant Virginia Military Institute. He served through many wars, with honor, and was awarded distinguished Service Medal, officer of Legion of Honor, Croix de Guerre with Palm by the French and Honorable Companion of the Bath by the British.

Rodes Family

The first Rodes in Virginia was Charles, the son of John Rodes and Elizabeth (Jason) Rodes, of Sturton, England. Charles was the grandson of Sir Francis Rodes, Baronet, of Barleborough Hall, Derbyshire, England, the manor house and estate being still owned and occupied by a descendant of the family. From letters now extant it seems that Charles was a very young man when he came to this country, and that he suffered much adversity here before he finally became established. His grandmother, Lady Rodes (whose maiden name was Martha Thornton) was much troubled about him, but his uncle, Sir John Rodes, seemed quite indifferent to his fate. Charles was married in this country about the year 1695, and his son, John, was born in or near New Kent County, November 6th, 1697. The original New Kent County was cut up into other counties.

John Rodes, the son of Charles, married Mary Crawford, born in 1703, the daughter of David Crawford. Their son, David Rodes, moved from Hanover County, where John and Mary Crawford Rodes had made their home, and coming to Albemarle County, November 19th, 1756, he writes: "Did I, David Rodes, come to the Mountains to live, on Moorman's River, and in May 13th, 1758, I was married to my loving wife, Mary Mills." Mary Mills died April 10th, 1781, and he was married a second time, to Susannah Anderson.

Matthew Rodes was the son of David Rodes by his first wife, Mary Mills. He was born December 9th, 1765, and died April 18th, 1834. He married Anne Blackwell, May 27th, 1794, who was born September 18th, 1774, and died April 29th, 1853. Their son, David Rodes, was born February 27th, 1795, in Albemarle County.

David Rodes, son of Matthew and Anne Blackwell May Rodes, moved to Lynchburg, where for many years he was clerk of the court. His granddaughters have in their possession the various commissions given him by the State of Virginia, beginning with that of ensign, dated September 11th, 1814, up through the different grades of military office and ending with his commission as brigadier-general, dated February 12th, 1834, printed on vellum and signed by Governor John Floyd. General David Rodes was married November 23rd, 1822, to Martha Yancey, daughter of Major Joel Yancey, of Bedford County, who was born in December, 1803. (See Yancey). She had four children: Virginius Hudson Rodes, born January 5th, 1824, died January 13th, 1879, in Mississippi at the home of Mr. Charles Yancey. Virginius Hudson Rodes, never married. Ann Maria Rodes, born April 4th, 1827, was married to Colonel Maurice Langhorne, November 4th, 1843, and died May 18th, 1847. She had one child, Maurice, who died in his youth. Robert Emmett Rodes, born March 30th, 1829, killed at the second Battle of Winchester, September 19th, 1864. He was major-general, C. S. A., and is buried in the Presbyterian Cemetery by the side of his brother, Virginius. He married September 10th, 1857, in Tuscaloosa, Alabama, Virginia Hortense Woodruff and had two children: Robert, who is married, has children and lives in Tuscaloosa, and Belle, who married J. W. Trainor, of Savannah, Georgia. In the historical part of this book is a full account of General Rodes' life and brilliant career as a soldier. The fourth child of General David Rodes and Martha Yancey Rodes was Sallie Harrison Rodes, who married William J. Nelson, of Staunton, Virginia. General David Rodes was married a second time, on May 12th, 1846, to Frances Louisa, daughter of Robert C. Penn, of Bedford County. From this marriage was born, April 11th, 1847, Lucy Steptoe Rodes, who died November 13th, 1894; La Fayette Penn Rodes, born April 2nd, 1848, married July 11th, 1883, to Laura Carter Ambler, the daughter of John Jacqueline Ambler. She died November 8th, 1891, leaving three daughters. General David Rodes had two other children, David and Dabney, by his second wife, who died in infancy.

Mr. La Fayette P. Rodes, who married Laura Carter Ambler, was for many years City Engineer of Lynchburg, where he died May 11th, 1900. His eldest daughter, Laura Beverley Rodes, married J. Dexter Hobbie, Junior, of Roanoke, whose mother belonged to the well-known Wellford family of Lynchburg. Ella Ambler Rodes married J. Booker Hutter, the son of Mr. and Mrs. Christian S. Hutter, whose family history is given elsewhere in this book. Miss Frances Rodes makes her home with her sister, Mrs. Hutter.

Ryland

The Ryland brothers, D. Brown, Thomas and Mosby, came to Lynchburg from King and Queen County when they were very young men. Brown Ryland opened the jewelry store in the Law Building. He married Fannie, daughter of Mr. John L. Lee. His brother, Thomas, married Alice Lee, a sister of Mrs. Brown Ryland. Mosby Ryland never married. Their father, Mr. John N. Ryland, died at the age of ninety-one at "Farmington," his homeplace in King and Queen County. He was survived by ten children.

Sale

Mrs. Bettie B. Sale, daughter of Rev. William V. Wilson and widow of A. J. Sale, died April 28th, 1918, having survived her husband eighteen years. She left the following children: Daniel W. Sale and Miss Grace Sale, of Lynchburg; William G. Sale, of Richmond, and J. Graham Sale, of Welch, West Virginia. She was the sister of William V. Wilson and Miss Grace M. Wilson, of Lynchburg.

Saunders

The family of Dr. James Saunders and Anne Rives Saunders have all either died or are living in other communities. Of three sons Charles was accidentally killed in infancy, another Charles was killed in the War Between the States, and James died in a street duel between Mr. Terry and himself, to avenge what he conceived to be an attack on his father made in an editorial written by Mr. Terry in the Virginian. James Saunders had only been married a few weeks. His wife was Miss Carrie Ludlem, and she afterwards married General James McDonald, who was born in Lynchburg, but later lived in Richmond. Mrs. Otway Allen and Mrs. Beverly Munford, of Richmond, were their daughters. Dr. Saunders had three daughters: Mrs. Fannie Chalmers, whose husband, Dr. James Chalmers, was killed during the War Between the States; Nannie, who married Richard Pollard, and died at the birth of her first child, Nannie; Bettie, who married, first, Peter Dudley, and second, Richard Pollard, her brother-in-law.

The children of Mrs. Chalmers were James S. Chalmers, who never married; Sallie, who died unmarried, and Annie, who married Major William Otway Owen, surgeon, United States Army, a son of Colonel Robert Latham Owen. They had one son.

The daughter of Nannie Saunders, first wife of Richard Pollard, was Nannie, who married Knox Pannill, of Petersburg; no children. The children of Bettie by her first husband, Peter Dudley, were William Saunders Dudley and James Dudley, who married Ellen Younger. No children. He died 1894. Bettie had one child by her second husband, Richard Pollard, Bettie, who was born in 1871, and married John Glass, brother of Senator Carter Glass and son of Major Robert Glass. Mr. and Mrs. John Glass, who are both dead, left two children, Elizabeth, who married Edward Barlow, and Richard, graduate of the United States Naval Academy at Annapolis and now an officer in the Navy.

Schewel

Mr. Elias Schewel, with his wife, who was Miss Bluma Greene, emigrated to this country from Riga, Russia, in the year 1888. At that time there was a great movement of Russian Jews to America, occasioned by the Edict of Segregation issued by Czar Nicholas. On his arrival Mr. Schewel stopped first in Baltimore. He had always associated himself with the orthodox group of his religion, and was educated for spiritual leadership. For this reason he was sent to Lynchburg, to act as rabbi of the orthodox synagogue. Mr. Schewel was a deeply spiritual man, orthodox and pious. The synagogue having just opened here, his remuneration was very small; he had a large family to support and for this reason Mr. Schewel was obliged to enter into business while still serving as rabbi. After a time he resigned his ecclesiastical office and opened a furniture store. He had many difficulties to overcome in the first years of his life in Lynchburg, as his knowledge of the English language was very limited, but in spite of these drawbacks he saw the small business he had formed grow and flourish in its thirty-five years of life before his death. He retired from business about the year 1921, and went to Chicago to live, leaving the management of his store in the hands of his sons, Abe, Ben and Isaac Schewel. In 1923 Mr. Schewel was married a second time, to Miss Sarah Underberg, of Chicago. He had many relatives in Chicago, where he was a member of the Russian Orthodox Congregation. Mr. Schewel was quiet, unassuming, industrious and upright, a high type of Jewish citizen. After a long and useful life, Mr. Schewel died at the age of seventy-four. Eight children survive him, of whom five live in Lynchburg: Messrs. Abe, Ben and Isaac Schewel, Mrs. J. M. Finkel and Mrs. Joseph Oppleman. He was buried in Agudath Sholum Cemetery in Amherst County.

SCOTT

Dr. David Patteson Scott, popularly known in Lynchburg as Dr. "Don" Scott, is a member of the Scott family which originally settled in Caroline County and from which have come a long line of physicians. The first of this family of Scotts in Virginia was James, who came from Aberdeen, Scotland, in 1690. Six of his descendants held commissions under General Washington in the Revolutionary War.

Colonel Thomas Scott was the son of James. His son, William, was born in 1756. Another son of Thomas was Major Samuel Scott, often referred to in this book, who built what is now known as the Barksdale house on the Forest Road, and whose grave is at the gate of this place. William raised a company for service in the Revolutionary War, was made its captain, and was later captured by the British. In 1784 he bought from James Gatewood a tract of land on both sides of the James River containing 1,150 acres, and extending into three counties, Bedford, Campbell and Amherst. William Scott married Anne Jones, the daughter of General and Martha (Waller) Jones, of Spottsylvania. The children of William and Anne Jones Scott were: Gabriel, who never married; Robert, married Miss Price, of Charlottesville; William Waller, lived in Amherst, and married Eliza Pendleton, daughter of Reuben Pendleton and Eliza (Garland) Pendleton; Thomas Hazelwood, lived in Campbell, and married, first, Margaret Parks Burks, and second, Malinda Grigsby; Hugh Roy, lived at the "Grove," and married Elizabeth Burks, and was the father of Samuel Burks Scott, who married Sallie Donald Patteson, daughter of Dr. David Patteson, of Buckingham. Sallie Donald Patteson was the great-granddaughter (through her mother, Elizabeth Camm Patteson) of John Camm, rector of Bruton Church, head of the Established Church in Virginia, and president of William and Mary

College. Hugh Donald Scott, son of Hugh Roy and Sallie Donald (Patteson) Scott, was educated at the Medical College of Virginia, in Richmond. He practiced his profession in Amherst County for thirty-five years, married Evelyn, daughter of Mr. Landon Davies, of Bedford County, and had three children, Stuart Donald, Samuel Burks and David Patteson Scott.

David Patteson Scott, was born in Bedford County, October 30, 1890. He attended Hoge Military Academy, graduated from the Medical College of Virginia in 1911 and was an interne at the Retreat for the Sick and the Johnston-Willis Hospital in Richmond. He practiced his profession in Ashland, West Virginia, until 1915. He then took postgraduate courses in New York, and at Harvard University, and the Massachusetts General Hospital at Boston. From 1917 to 1919 he served in the Medical Department of the United States Army. He then located in Lynchburg, where he has since practiced successfully and with a steadily growing reputation. Dr. Scott specializes in diagnosis. He is a Fellow of the American College of Physicians, a member of the Medical Society of Virginia, and the Lynchburg, Southern Piedmont and American Associations.

Dr. Scott was married February 4th, 1914, to Miss Beulah Davis, born in Charlottesville. They have one child, Judith Donald Scott, born 1922.

Shaner

The Shaner family were natives of Germany. They came to Virginia in the first half of the nineteenth century and have produced some very worthy citizens of Lynchburg. Among these were Mr. Jacob Shaner, who lived on Grace Street for many years and who left several children, and Mr. Lewis Shaner, who had a home on Washington Street and who is also survived by several children. Mr. Randolph Shaner, for many years prominent in business here and a vestryman of Grace Church, having retired, now lives at Coral Gables, Florida.

Shumate

John Rust Shumate, who died February 23rd, 1905, age seventy-two years, was a native of Clark County. He married Miss Lucy Page, of Fauquier County, in 1858. Six daughters and four sons survived him. His sons left Lynchburg some years before their father's death, and are now living in Texas.

SILVERTHORN

Mrs. Clara B. Silverthorn, the widow of William B. Silverthorn, who died at the home of her son, Henry Silverthorn, in Tampa, Florida, September, 1933, at the age of eighty, was a representative of a name once prominent in Lynchburg. The Silverthorn family were silversmiths and for many years had a jewelry store here. The brothers, Henry and William, were well-known figures in the business life of Lynchburg.

SLATTER

John T. Slatter, aged sixty-seven, for twelve years traffic manager for the Lynchburg Chamber of Commerce, died April 3rd, 1930. He was born at Cedar Hill, Tennessee, the son of John Slatter and Hester Ann Simms, whose father was a bishop of the Methodist Church. Mr. Slatter's father was judge of the Circuit Court of Franklin County, and donated the property upon which the University of the South at Sewanee was built. Mr. Slatter graduated from Sewanee in 1889. For a time he worked on a Texas paper, the Austen Statesman. He was later connected with the railroad at Chattanooga, and was employed in traffic management in various towns before coming to Lynchburg. He was married twice, first to Miss Zona Gibbs, of Mississippi, before he was twenty. She died ten years later. In 1907 he married Miss Octavia Lauderdale, of Selma, Alabama, who survived him with one daughter, Mrs. Benjamin Fowlkes, wife of Lieutenant Fowlkes, United States Army. He also left two daughters by his first marriage, Mrs. Giles Bond, of Memphis, Tennessee, and Mrs. Preston Barnes, of Baton Rouge, Louisiana. He was buried in Chattanooga, Tennessee. Mr. Slatter was valued here for his high ideals and strict integrity.

LYNCHBURG AND ITS NEIGHBORS

SLAUGHTER

Dr. Robert Slaughter, Senior, of Lynchburg, had the following children by his second wife, Mary Rice Garland, daughter of Rice Garland and Catherine (Hamner) Garland, of Albemarle County: 1. John Flavel Slaughter, married Mary Harker, Mount Holly, New Jersey; 2. Charles Rice Slaughter, married Catherine M. Garland; 3. Dr. Samuel Slaughter, married Elizabeth Henderson; 4. Austina Slaughter, married Robert Withers Brodnax; 5. Celeste Paulina Slaughter, married Mr. James Madison Cobbs.

1. John Flavel Slaughter, born 18?8, died 1893, and Mary (Harker) Slaughter had the following children: a. Dr. Charles Slaughter, married, first, Mary Duke; second, Hattie Gray. b. John Flavel Slaughter, Junior, never married. c. Robert Slaughter, married Augusta Bannister, of Alabama, and had two sons, Robert and Monroe Bannister Slaughter. d. Dr. Samuel G. Slaughter, married Mamie Richardson and had: Rosalie, Willis and Samuel. Mrs. Slaughter was married a second time, to Judge R. T. W. Duke, of Charlottesville. e. Edith Ridgeway Slaughter was the first wife of Judge R. T. W. Duke, of Charlottesville. They had five children: Mary, R. T. W. Duke, Junior, John S., Eskridge and Helen. f. Dr. Rosalie Slaughter, married Baxter Morton. g. Judge William Austin Slaughter, located at Mount Holly and married Florence Lewis.

2. Charles Rice Slaughter and Catherine M. (Garland) his wife, had the following children: a. Mary E. Slaughter, married J. Singleton Diggs, at one time judge of the Corporation Court of Lynchburg, and had Catherine and Dudley Diggs, who married Carrie Fleet. b. Charles Alex, married Bertha Garland Brown, and had Althea, who married J. M. Vest, of Huntington, West Virginia. c. Catherine Lightfoot.

4. Austina Slaughter, married Robert Withers Brodnax. Their only child, Mary Roberta, married George Cameron, of Petersburg, son of William Cameron, Governor of Virginia.

SMITH

John Holmes Smith, born at "Rothsay," in Bedford, August 12th, 1838, was the son of William T. Smith and Susan Leftwich, his wife. In April, 1861, he joined the Lynchburg Home Guard, which became Company G, Eleventh Virginia Regiment. He advanced through the various grades from third corporal and was commissioned captain in May, 1861. For the greater part of his last eighteen months of service in the Confederate Army he commanded a regiment. He was wounded at Seven Pines and again at Gettysburg. With his regiment he was captured at Sailors' Creek, April 5th, 1865, but was paroled. After the War, he reorganized the Home Guard. He was for many years engaged in the tobacco business in Lynchburg. He married Norvell Hobson, the daughter of Dr. Joseph V. Hobson and Mary E. Bullock, his wife. They had no children.

John Holmes Smith's brother, Woodville G. Smith, was associated with him in the tobacco business, and later was Mayor of Lynchburg. He married Kate Massie Withers, February 8th, 1877. Kate Massie Withers Smith was born October 30th, 1856, the daughter of Colonel Robert Enoch Withers, at one time United States Senator from Virginia. Mr. and Mrs. Smith had one son, Robert Withers, who died before reaching majority, and two daughters, Ethel, who married Townes Gaines, and Kitty.

SPENCER

Dr. Francis Spencer, a native of Maryland, practiced medicine in Lynchburg for a long time. He married Miss Nannie Bailey, well known for her beauty, whose father owned what used to be known as the Spring Warehouse property, situated on those squares surrounding Horseford Road, and now a part of Commerce Street. Here Mr. Bailey conducted a carriage and wagon works. The late Mrs. Harry Snead was a daughter of Dr. and Mrs. Spencer. Mr. Snead, who is now dead, was prominently connected with the Y. M. C. A. work here.

LYNCHBURG AND ITS NEIGHBORS

STABLER

In Alexandria there still stands the old Apothecary Shop where George Washington used to buy his medicine and where Martha had a yearly account. A good deal has been written of late about this drug store, which was saved from destruction by the Association for the Preservation of Virginia Antiquities. It is one hundred and forty years old, and is the second oldest apothecary shop standing in this country. Lynchburg people are interested in this old shop with its funny old scales, and its queer mixers and rare bottles on account of the Stabler family. Edward Stabler, fourth of the name from Edward Stabler, Lord Mayor of York, England, settled in Alexandria in 1729. In that year he established the business which has since been continuously conducted by his family. Mr. Robinson Stabler, a member of this family, lived in Lynchburg for many years, and his son, Robinson Stabler, Junior, is now living here. Harry Stabler, an older son, who died a few years ago, was the author of fascinating stories published for some time in the Saturday Evening Post.

STATHAM

Beaumont Statham died March 11th, 1918, age thirty-three years, at his home on Church Street. He was unmarried and one of the last survivors of a family once prominent and influential in Lynchburg's civil and social life.

STEPTOE

The Steptoe family, of ancient English lineage, is descended from Anthony Steptoe, the third son of Sir Philip Steptoe. He was born in Middlesex County, England, in the year 1653. Anthony Steptoe came to the colony from Cudrig, England, in 1676 and was living in Lancaster County, Virginia in 1697. He had married Lucy Stephen, who died in England. Their children were:

John, born about 1673.

Judith, born about 1675, married Richard Lee, of Westmoreland County, Virginia (see Lee lineage, du Bellet).

John was born in England and was the father of Colonel James Steptoe, of "Harmony Hall," Westmoreland County.

The Honorable James Steptoe, clerk of Bedford and first of the Steptoe family to settle in this section of the State, was the son of Colonel James Steptoe, of "Harmony Hall."

James Steptoe, the clerk of Bedford County, was born in 1750. His older sister, Elizabeth, married Honorable Philip Ludwell Lee, of "Stratford," Westmoreland County.

James Steptoe is described as being the best dressed man in Bedford County and every morning he appeared at court in a suit of fine white broadcloth, imported from London, with black silk hose, silver knee buckles, his hair done in a cue and usually wearing a rose in his button hole. Around Bedford County he has always been held in affectionate remembrance for his generous and lovable nature and the story is told that one day he was riding in his coach to Liberty (now Bedford City) and seeing a crowd around a poor woman's door not far from the road, he ordered his coachman, Ben, to stop and find out the reason. Ben returned, saying, "Marster, de sheriff is selling out ole Mrs. Caffree." Mr. Steptoe got out of his coach, bought all the old woman's possessions and gave them to her. He was especially beloved by his slaves, many of whom he set free after having taught them trades by which they could support themselves.

James Steptoe (clerk of Bedford), married Frances Calloway (see Calloway). Their children were:

1. Elizabeth Prentiss Steptoe, married Charles Johnston. She was his second wife.

2. Frances Calloway Steptoe, married Harry Langhorne.

3. Sally Steptoe, married Thomas Massie.

4. Lucy Steptoe, married Robert Penn.

5. James C. Steptoe, married Miss Mitchell.

6. Dr. William Steptoe, married, first, Miss Brown, and had: Colonel Edward Steptoe, distinguished in the Mexican War,

who married Rosanna Claytor; no issue. Dr. Steptoe's second wife was Miss Dillon, whose children were: a. William Steptoe, married Miss Payne; no issue. b. Mary Catherine, died single. c. Nannie Brown, married Major Eldridge; no issue. d. Elizabeth Steptoe. e. Patrick Dillon Steptoe.

7. George Steptoe; his daughter, Ella, married Mr. Judd.

8. Robert Steptoe, eighth child of James Steptoe (clerk of Bedford), married Miss Leftwich (see Leftwich).

9. Thomas Steptoe, son of the clerk of Bedford, being his ninth child, married Catherine Louise Yancey, the daughter of Major Joel Yancey, of "Rothsay." Their children were: a. Rev. Charles Yancey Steptoe, married Miss Frances Wallace Nalle, whose children were Philip N. Steptoe, Elizabeth and Charles. b. William Tudor Steptoe. c. Thomas Macon Steptoe. d. Bettie Steptoe. e. Fannie Steptoe, who married Colonel Richard Carlton Walker Radford, and had one child, Thomas. (See Radford). f. John Marshall Steptoe. g. Anna Steptoe.

The Steptoe arms: Azure a fleur-de-lys argent.
Crest: Out of a Ducal Coronet or an elk's head sable.
Motto: Spes Mea in Deo.

Stokes

Richard Carter Stokes, son of Josephine Carter and Captain D. R. Stokes, of "Mount Holly," Lunenburg County, is a descendant of one of the oldest and best known families in Virginia. D. R. Stokes was captain of Lunenburg Infantry during the War Between the States and became the first treasurer of that county after the War, which position he held until his death in 1883. Captain Stokes and Josephine Carter Stokes had seven children. Richard Carter Stokes, prominent tobacconist of Lynchburg, was their third child and second son. After the death of Captain Stokes, Mrs. Stokes was married a second time, on November 26th, 1890, to Colonel William J. Neblett, a lawyer and planter, of "Brickhead," in Lunenburg County.

Richard Carter Stokes married Lillian A. Lee, daughter of

Mr. John A. Lee, of Lynchburg. They had one son, Richard Carter Stokes, Junior.

STRATTON

Mrs. Alice B. Stratton, widow of Alexander Stratton, died January, 1910. These were in their time well-known people of Lynchburg.

STRODE

Amherst has had two schools for boys which were largely patronized by the youth of Lynchburg. One of these was Forest Hill, kept by the Wallers at New Glasgow, in ante-bellum days. Another was Kenmore, kept by Mr. Strode, a native of Fredericksburg, who came to Amherst and opened a boys' school, which was successfully maintained for years.

Mr. Strode married Miss Mildred Ellis, of Amherst, and had a large family. He was famous as an educator in the South and accepted a position as president of Clemson College in South Carolina. The work at Clemson proved too heavy for him. In a few years he returned to his home at Kenmore, much broken in health, and died soon after.

Judge Aubrey Strode, recently made judge of the Corporation Court of Lynchburg, is the son of Mr. _____ Strode and Mildred Ellis Strode. Judge Aubrey Strode's first wife was Rebecca Brown, daughter of Judge Thompson Brown, of Nelson. His second wife was Miss Eleanor Hubbard, of Bedford County.

STROTHER

Sidney Strother, youngest son of Dr. William A. Strother, died in Richmond, May 15th, 1918, at the age of fifty-five. He was the last immediate member of this family of Strothers, which is now represented in Lynchburg by Mrs. William Strother, Mrs. Robert Strother and their children.

JOHANNES SUHLING

Johannes Suhling came to Lynchburg in 1886. His brother, Christopher had already been here for two years, having come

Red Hill, Amherst County—The Ellis Home. Courtesy of Kiah T. Ford Company, Realtors.

from Germany in 1884. The youngest brother, Gehart, followed them later. The first name of their business firm was Edmunds, Suhling and Company, Incorporated, which was engaged in the export tobacco trade. This house, formed in 1886, continued in business until 1893, when Mr. Edmunds retired, and the firm Suhling and Company assumed control.

At first all three of the brothers made their homes in Lynchburg, where they had won a well-deserved popularity; but in 1897 Mr. Christopher Suhling, the eldest brother, and his wife, who was a German lady, returned to Germany.

Mr. Suhling's return was for the purpose of establishing in Bremen a selling agency for the Lynchburg business. In this position he was able to learn at first hand the existing conditions abroad, and the business took on new importance in providing for the demands of the tobacco trade throughout the European continent.

In 1915 Mr. Gerhart Suhling died in Lynchburg, and Mr. Christopher Suhling died the next year in Bremen. Thus was broken up this strong union of three brothers, who for many years had been knit together in the very deepest ties of devotion. Johannes Suhling, or "Hans," as he was affectionately known to his friends, was left alone to carry on this highly important industry in Lynchburg and Bremen.

Johannes Suhling was born in Bremen in November, 1866, and was reared and educated in his native city. Suhling and Company was incorporated in 1915, and from that time until his death Johannes Suhling was president of the company, formulating all its policies. He was only twenty when he came to Virginia and established a residence, so the larger part of his life was spent as a citizen of Lynchburg. During the years of their lives he and his brothers had built up a highly important and prosperous business in the export of leaf tobacco. They had extensive operations in Europe, where, after Mr. Christopher Suhling's death, Johannes spent a great deal of his time. On the continent of Europe he was known wherever tobacco was dealt in and his firm enjoys an enviable reputation as tobacco merchants of a high order. His acquaintance among the foreign dealers in tobacco was extensive and intimate, and in this country his company was known throughout the entire dark tobacco belt, as well as the bright tobacco section. Before his death, "Hans" Suhling and his brothers had in operation one of the largest and most important enterprises among the independent dealers of the United States. He died suddenly in New York on his return from Germany in 1923, leaving his wife, Shirley Cornelia, the daughter of Mr. Israel Moore, of Lynchburg.

Taylor

Mr. John J. Taylor, a well-known tobacconist and for many years an honored citizen of Lynchburg, died March 29th, 1918, at the age of eighty-two years. He was visiting in Florida when his death occurred. Mr. Taylor was born in Amherst County, April 3rd, 1836. He was married in 1854 to Miss Sarah Jones, daughter of Rev. Thomas Jones, a Methodist minister. She died in 1910. Mr. Taylor started in the tobacco business at an early age. For many years he was inspector of tobacco at the Liberty Warehouse, and later was connected with Lynch's Warehouse. Mr. Taylor left the following children: Mrs. H. A. Hawkins, of Richmond; Mrs. E. L. Slaughter, of Roanoke; Mrs. S. F. Poindexter, J. O. and D. L. Taylor, of this city, and Oscar H. Taylor, of Rawhide, Nevada.

The Terrell Family

William Terrell was a Quaker. He was persecuted in England because of his faith, and came to this country, where he settled some time between 1665 and 1700. He had three sons, David, Henry and James. From one of these sons descended Dr. John Jay Terrell, who lived near what was in former times known as Rock Castle, but is now called Burton's Creek. The parents of Dr. Terrell were Christopher and his wife, Susan Kennerly, of the Valley of Virginia. Christopher was born in 1798 and died in 1833 at Boonesville, in Missouri, where he had moved with his family.

John Jay Terrell was born in 1829. When his father died he was living in Virginia with his aunt, Miss Judith Terrell. He married Miss Sue Wade, and died in 1919. Judge Alexander Watkins Terrell, of Austin, Texas, at one time Minister to Turkey, and Captain Joseph Christopher Terrell, of Fort Worth, Texas, were his brothers. Dr. Terrell was a much beloved family doctor in Campbell and Bedford. For years he was a familiar figure driving in his buggy along the county roads, and stopping his horse to pass the time with his neighbors. He was a large land owner in both Campbell and Bedford Counties. Three of his children have made their home in Lynchburg: Mrs. Robert Scott, whose son, Dr. Ernest Scott, practices his profession here; Dr. Alex Terrell, for about fifty years a doctor in Lynchburg, and Dr. Thomas Terrell, now in business in this city. Dr. Thomas Terrell has never married. Dr. Alex Terrell married Miss King, daughter of Judge King, of Florida, and has two daughters, Helen and John, and two sons, King and Fred.

Thornhill

Mrs. Judith Hatcher Thornhill died August 9th, 1905; age sixty-four years. She was the wife of S. A. Thornhill and a native of Appomattox, having lived in Lynchburg for fourteen years before her death. She was the mother of Mr. Ben Thornhill, of the Thornhill Wagon Works.

Thurman

The first Thurman came to Lynchburg as inspector of tobacco at Spring Warehouse. The family later went into the saddler business, and established a good trade as honest, upright business men. Senator Allan G. Thurman was born here, but his particular branch of the family moved to Ohio, where he became a famous man. Mr. Alexandar Thurman, for many years head of the First Department and a gallant Confederate soldier, and his brother, Mr. George Thurman, were highly esteemed as citizens of Lynchburg. Mr. Thurman Boyd is a member of this family. He married Lucy Lillian, daughter of the late Edwin

Wills and Bettie (Kinnear Wills), a descendant of John W. Wills, of Lynchburg. Mr. and Mrs. Boyd have a son and a daughter.

Tilden Line

The Tilden family, of which the first wife of Major Winfree was a member, is said to be from England, of great antiquity, and can be traced to a record of William Tylden, of Kent, in the reign of Edward III. The first of this family to come to this country was Captain Richard Tilden, who died in Philadelphia in October, 1762. He married Anna Meyer, who was born in New York, August 31st, 1731. She was the daughter of John Meyer and Elizabeth (Van Pell) Meyer and the granddaughter of William and Elizabeth Van Pell. She had two children, one of whom died in infancy, and the other was named John Bell.

Dr. John Bell Tilden, son of Captain Richard and Anna (Meyer) Tilden, was born in Philadelphia, Pennsylvania, December 9th, 1761, baptized in the Episcopal church, and died in New Town, now Stephen City, Virginia. He went to Princeton College, but left school to join the Continental Army. He was made ensign, May 28th, 1779, in the Second Pennsylvania line, commanded by Colonel Walter Stewart. In 1780 he joined the Pennsylvania line of the Society of Cincinnati. He kept a diary during his service, which is now in the possession of the Pennsylvania Historical Society in Philadelphia. An interesting feature of this diary is his account of the seige of Yorktown and the surrender of General Cornwallis.

Dr. Tilden settled in Frederick County, Virginia, where he practiced medicine until the close of his life. Long before the subject of African slavery took a political shape he manumitted his slaves and sent them to Liberia with one year's outfit. He married Jane Chambers, of York County, Pennsylvania, who was born December 18th, 1776, died May, 1827, the daughter of Joseph and Martha (McCalmont) Chambers, of York, Pennsylvania. Dr. and Mrs. Tilden had eleven children, and two of their daughters married in Lynchburg. Mary Ann Jane, their sixth child, born December 17th, 1795, was married December 9th, 1813, to John Victor, prominent citizen of Lynchburg. Their children were: Tilden, born March 27th, 1815; John Richard, born December 23rd, 1817; Edward William, born September 7th, 1819; Sarah, born May 3rd, 1821; Christopher Winfree, born November, 1826; Marion Jane, born 1828; Robert, born 1831; Henry Clay, born 1833; Octavius, born 1837. The list of children of the seventh child, Cornelia Meyer, who married Christopher Winfree, has already been given in the Winfree line.

TUCKER

No history of Lynchburg is complete without mention of Bishop Tucker, who, with his wife and family, lived here several years. Mrs. Tucker was Maria Washington, the grandniece of General Washington. She was born at Mount Vernon and lived there until she was eight years old. The piety of this good couple, their utter lack of pretense, their hospitality and kindness, made a deep impression upon all who came in contact with them. In Bishop and Mrs. Tucker were seen the perfect example of Virginia's old gentility.

TUCKER

George Tucker was born in the Island of Bermuda, where his people had been socially and politically prominent for generations. In 1818 he came to Lynchburg, at that time a town of three thousand people. Before coming here he had lived in Williamsburg. He was an entertaining writer, and gave an interesting account of a reception in Philadelphia, where he met General Washington. He was greatly impressed by Washington and he describes the imposing figure he presented in black velvet attire. Mr. Tucker was sent to Congress from this district. While he was still in Congress Thomas Jefferson offered him the chair of moral philosophy at the University of Virginia, which he accepted, having already served several terms in Congress. While Mr. Tucker was a resident of Lynchburg he lost his eldest daughter, Rosalie, and in her memory he wrote a small volume, which he circulated among his friends and relatives. Mr. Tucker was the author of many books, but his most important work was A History of United States, published in 1857. This book is in four volumes, and has been pronounced by eminent authorities a valuable addition to our store of historical research. Mr. Tucker was a relative of the well-known family of Virginia Tuckers, who also came from Bermuda. Some of this family had owned land in the Bermuda Islands for two hundred years.

Tunstall

Whitmell Pugh Tunstall, who was born at "Belle Grove," Pittsylvania County, in April, 1810. He came of distinguished people, being the son of Colonel William Tunstall and his wife, Sarah Winifred Barker Tunstall. Through the Barker line he was descended from Sir Owen Glendower. From 1767 until 1836, a Tunstall served as clerk of the Pittsylvania Court. There were three in number, each was named William, and the office went from father to son by regular appointment.

Whitmell Tunstall was a member of the House of Delegates, and it was through his efforts that the charter of the Richmond and Danville Railroad was obtained, of which he became the first president. At an early age Whitmell Tunstall began the practice of law; he soon became an important figure in the State, both as a lawyer and a politician, and a notable future was predicted for him. He was married twice, his first wife being Miss Donaghe, who died early. He was married the second time to Mary Liggatt, the daughter of Alexander Liggatt, of Lynchburg. They had three children:

1. John L. Tunstall, born November 4th, 1845, died March 24th, 1877. John L. Tunstall married Florence Massie, the daughter of William Massie, by his fourth wife, Maria Effinger. John L. Tunstall left two children: W. Massie Tunstall, who married Miss Peebles, and lived at Lovingston, and Corinne, who was married, first, to Holt Terry, of Lynchburg, and second, to W.

Waring, of Washington, District of Columbia. The widow of Mr. Tunstall was married a second time, to John Dunscombe Horsley, judge of the Fifth Circuit of Virginia, whose history is written elsewhere in this book.

2. Alexander Augustus, born in Lynchburg in 1850.

3. Nannie Whitmell, born July 9th, 1853, died November, 1892.

Death put an end to the career of Whitmell P. Tunstall on February 19th, 1854.

Alexander A. Tunstall, son of Whitmell P. and Mary Liggatt Tunstall, was educated in the Lynchburg schools and at Bellevue. In 1869 he entered the law school at the University of Virginia and graduated in the class of 1871. He practiced his profession first in Richmond; but later moved to Lynchburg, where he lived until 1888, when he located permanently in Washington, District of Columbia. He married October 24th, 1876, Ida Gray, who was born October 12th, 1851. Their children were:

1. Benjamin Gray, born November 13th, 1877, who made his home in Norfolk, where he became City Treasurer on October 30th, 1908. Benjamin Gray Tunstall married Mary Franklin Duncan and has a daughter, Lucy Dabney Tunstall, born December 7th, 1910.

2. Sue Reid Tunstall, who was born April 18th, 1879, married December 15th, 1904, Barry MacNutt, and has a son, Alexander Tunstall MacNutt, born September 21st, 1909.

3. Whitmell Pugh Tunstall, born in Lynchburg, Virginia, November 10th, 1880. His early life was spent in Washington, where he attended the public school and graduated. He then entered Lehigh, specialized in engineering and graduated in the class of 1903. Since then he has attained marked success in his chosen profession.

4. Alexander Liggatt, born September 30th, 1883, was mar-

ried February 15th, 1912, to Maude M. Davis and has a daughter, Lorraine Davis, born November 1st, 1914.

Mrs. Whitmell Tunstall, after her husband's death, was married a second time, to Mr. Brooks, who died some years later, leaving her with a son, Emmet. She was very wealthy, and lived for many years on Court Street with her daughter, Nannie, after her older sons had grown up and married. Miss Nannie Tunstall was a figure to be remembered by all who saw her: tall, slender and graceful, with blue eyes and lovely yellow hair, which she wore braided about her fine head, she was very gracious, and her beauty lasted as long as she lived. In Lyon Tyler's Virginia Biography there is a picture of her distinguished father, whom she very closely resembled. She had travelled widely and had seen much more of the world than most women of her day, and she had culture and charm to a very rare degree. She died in 1892, after a brief illness. Her home was a large brick house on the corner of Court and Eighth Streets, used after her death by the Piedmont Club, and later enlarged and turned into an apartment house, which was called the Tunstall Apartments.

The family of Mr. Alexander Tunstall moved to Washington. These were the last lineal descendants of John Lynch. Mrs. Alexander Liggatt, their grandmother, was the daughter of John Lynch, and the only one of his children who lived beyond middle age.

Turner

George W. Turner, who was not related, as far as we know, to any other family of Turners in this part of Virginia, came to Lynchburg and bought the well-known residence at 523 Clay Street over a hundred years ago. He added another half to the original building, and here five generations of his family have lived. George W. Turner was the son of Robert Turner, Junior, who was the son of Robert Turner, Senior, and Mary, his wife. Robert Turner, Senior, was born in 1765 in Eastern Virginia, and came to Amherst between 1791 and 1800. He lived at "Solitude," a home afterwards owned by Lorenzo Norvell, and known later as the Hunt place. It was burned about twenty years ago. Robert Turner, Junior, married Elizabeth Atwell in 1791. He left Amherst about 1812, and went to Kentucky, where he died in Christian County in 1846. His son, George W. Turner, was born at "Solitude" in 1800.

George W. Turner came to Lynchburg before 1831, the date on which he bought the residence at 523 Clay Street. He married Rebecca Catherine Morrell, of Mount Holly, New Jersey. The spelling of this name was changed to Murrell by the members of the family in Lynchburg. The marriage of Mr. Turner and Miss Murrell took place May 20th, 1829, the ceremony being performed by Rev. Francis Genet Smith, of Saint Paul's Church. She was born at Mount Holly in 1812, and died January 28th, 1891, in Lynchburg. She was the daughter of Rebecca Montgomery Hepburn and Harding Murrell, of Mount Holly. Her brother, Harding, was postmaster of Lynchburg at one time.

The children of George W. Turner were:

1. Lucy Murrell Turner, married Gennaro F. B. Bozzaotro, a native of Caserta, Italy, who was banished from his country in one of the many unheavals between Church and State which convulsed Italy at that period of her history. Gennaro Bozzaotro was excommunicated by the Pope. The family still has the Papal Bull of Excommunication. Mr. Bozzaotro was an exotic figure in Lynchburg, where he, an Italian of noble birth, was forced to sustain himself by teaching music. Dr. Sartores, who taught languages at the Lynchburg College, had also been banished from Italy, his property confiscated and his family scattered. He came to Lynchburg because Mr. Bozzaotro lived here. Mr. Bozzaotro was a very accomplished musician and a composer of unusual merit. It is said that the Dead March played at Garfield's funeral was composed by him. His son, Gennaro, died unmarried a few years ago.

2. Annie Elizabeth Turner, born October 16th, 1833, married Dr. Henry Gray Latham, son of Dr. Henry Latham and his wife, Jane Owen. They had Henry Latham, Junior, who married, but

whose children are now dead, and George, who studied medicine, but died unmarried.

3. Ellen Atwell Turner, married Dr. William Hamilton Dulaney, November 22nd, 1864.

4. Maurice Garland Turner, died 1857, unmarried.

5. Dr. George Kempton Turner, born April 22nd, 1840, married Ella Grattan Payne, daughter of David Bryce Payne, of Lynchburg, October 16th, 1866. Their children were: (a) David Payne Turner, born March 16th, 1868, married Penelope Louis Gill, of Tennessee, daughter of Samuel Ward and Mary King Gill. (b) George Maurice Turner, born March 17th, 1871, married October 20th, 1904, to Belle Slaughter, daughter of Samuel Pleasants Slaughter and Nellie Vernon Wheeler Slaughter. (c) Ellen Dulaney Turner, died young. (d) Helen Spotswood Turner, married Andrew T. Henderson, son of Guyne Littleton Henderson.

6. Glenmore M. Turner, born 1843, died November 5th, 1901. Never married. Confederate soldier, Company G, Eleventh Virginia, captured at Gettysburg in Pickett's charge. Held at Fort Delaware and Point Lookout until after close of War.

7. Samuel J. Turner, C. S. A., Company G, Eleventh Virginia.

Dr. George Kempton Turner was educated at Lynchburg College, the University of Virginia, and just before the War Between the States he graduated in medicine at the University of New York, but he was not twenty-one, and could not get his diploma until he became of age. He was in Bellevue Hospital when the War began. Leaving all his possessions in New York, he started South, going through the lines. On reaching Virginia he joined the Eleventh Virginia Regiment as a private. About a year later, when General Joseph E. Johnston was wounded in battle and there was no surgeon near, Dr. Turner was called from the ranks to give him the needed attention. This he did so successfully that he was made assistant surgeon August 16th, 1862, and promoted to surgeon January 12th, 1866.

He saw service in the hospital in Lynchburg, and in North Carolina with General Johnston's command.

Dr. Turner was married October 16th, 1866, to Ella Grattan Payne, daughter of Mr. David Bryce Payne. He moved to Tennessee, where he died, at Morristown, March 26th, 1898. His wife's death had already taken place some years before this time, and they were survived by three children, already mentioned.

Valentine

Miss Carrie Morgan Valentine, the last member of an old Lynchburg family, died at Hurts, in Pittsylvania County, January 12th, 1910. She was the daughter of Mr. George W. Valentine. Her sister, Bettie, died November 22nd, 1909.

Victor

The Victor family came to Lynchburg from Fredericksburg when the first John Victor was a small child. He grew up, learned the trade of silversmith, and was the earliest jeweler in this city. He married Mary Jane Tilden. Mr. Victor had a progressive spirit far in advance of his time, as was evidently felt and appreciated by the people of Lynchburg, for he was made Mayor of the town. It was due to Mr. Victor that the Clay Street reservoir was built. Up to his time the city had an ancient, makeshift water system, the pipes of which were made from bored trunks of trees. Polluted springs were numerous in the city streets, and wells in back yards supplemented the city water supply. Such was the haphazard way in which the people of Lynchburg obtained their water about a hundred years ago, when Mr. Victor determined that the town should have a modern water system. The first city debt of Lynchburg was incurred for this purpose, and the problem of piping water uphill in order to overcome the difficulty presented by its extremely elevated situation, was effectually solved. Mr. John Victor had a son, Henry Victor, who married Jane Tilden McLeod. John Victor, present Mayor of Lynchburg and president of the Peoples' Bank, is the son of Henry, and the grandson of John, who was Mayor a hundred years ago. Mr. Victor has inherited, along with his name, that same ability to cope with civic problems which his grandfather so eminently possessed. He married Miss Mattie Mahood.

The Voorheis Family

Mrs. Rebecca Thompson Voorheis, well known citizen of Amherst, is the daughter of a distinguished family. Her father, Dr. William Thompson, was of Scotch Covenanter stock. Her uncle, Judge Lucas Thompson, born in Amherst, was judge of the Circuit Court of Staunton and later judge of the Supreme Court of Virginia. He taught a law school at his home in Staunton, and it was from the front veranda of this home that Woodrow Wilson accepted his first nomination to the Presidency. Another uncle of Mrs. Voorheis, John, was also a noted lawyer and a man of large fortune. The family home was in Amherst, where Mrs. Beverley Harrison now lives.

Mrs. Voorheis was descended from the Powell and the Lucas families. On the monument in Westminster Abbey to Margaret Lucas, Duchess of Newcastle, is this inscription: "All the men of this name were valiant, and all the women were virtuous." Mrs. Voorheis is the widow of Dr. Field Farrar Voorheis, of Knickerbocker origin, whose people migrated to Tennessee. They had two children: William Thompson Voorheis, a man of brilliant mind and charming personality, at one time professor of Greek and French at the Virginia Military Institute, and for many years before his death district manager of the Southern Bell Telephone Company at Jackson, Mississippi; and Miss Margaret Voorheis, who lives in Amherst.

On the night of January 17th, 1905, Barton Thompson, the only surviving son of George Thompson, a brother of Mrs. Voorheis, was drowned in a vain attempt to save the life of his friend, Ernest Bland, who had broken through the ice while skating in Reservoir Park, Richmond. Thompson had removed his skates and started home, when he heard an outcry made when several men broke through the ice. Thompson turned back and plunged in after Bland, whom he managed to bring to the surface. A rope was thrown him, but he had the unconscious body of Bland in his arms and he could not reach the rope without releasing his hold on his friend: this he would not do, and both sank together. Barton Thompson, though only twenty-five at the time of his death, had had a very eventful life, having served in the Spanish-American War and as a United States marine had been in China during the Boxer trouble. He had also seen service in the Philippines during the insurrection of Aguinaldo.

Dr. William Thompson, the father of Mrs. Voorheis, was a student at Transylvania College, in Kentucky, and during a walking trip with a friend he was a witness to the sale of King Soloman, as described by James Lane Allen in his tale of that name. Dr. Alexander Thompson served with General Forrest in the War Between the States. Dr. John Thompson, another son, was in the Second Virginia Cavalry.

Dr. John Thompson, or "Dr. Jack," as he was known, took his father's place in Amherst and practiced medicine for many years with his brother-in-law, Dr. Voorheis. Amherst Courthouse and the county adjoining was the field of their ministrations.

The Waller Family

The Waller family, which has been prominent in Virginia affairs since the seventeenth century, according to the records, is descended from Alured de Waller, who came from Normandy with William the Conqueror. He settled in the county of Kent, England, and died A. D., 1183. Richard Waller, of this family, distinguished himself at the Battle of Agincourt, and took prisoner the Duke of Orleans, commander-in-chief of the French Army. He received from Henry V of England, in honor of his heroic services, a crest of the arms of France hanging by a label from an oak, with the motto: *Haec Functus Vir-*

LYNCHBURG AND ITS NEIGHBORS

tutis. Benjamin Waller, poet laureate of England, was of this family. The immediate ancestors of the Wallers in Virginia was Edmund Waller, who settled in Spottsylvania County. His son, Benjamin, born 1716, lived in Williamsburg, and was assistant of Thomas Nelson, secretary of the Council of Virginia, judge of the Court of Admiralty, member of the House of Burgesses, and of the patriotic conventions of 1775-76. He married Martha Hall, of North Carolina, and had ten children. From him are descended the family of Mr. John Robertson, of Amherst, the family of Dr. McBryde, who formerly lived in Lexington, the family of Judge Thompson Brown, of Nelson County, the Wallers of Lynchburg and Amherst, the children of the late Mrs. Charles Langhorne, of Lynchburg, and the children of Dr. and Mrs. Morris, of Lynchburg. Among the children of Dr. and Mrs. Morris are Judge Page Morris, Mr. John Morris, Mrs. Lou Belle Stannard, Mrs. Ben Nowlin and her daughters, the late Mrs. Chauncey Williams, Miss Chloe Nowlin and Miss Louise Nowlin.

WALPOLE

Clare Horace Walpole was born in England, a descendant of Sir Robert Walpole, prime minister from 1721 to 1742. Mr. Walpole was a younger brother of the present Earl of Orford and before coming to this country had been a member of the famous English cavalry troop, the Horse Guards. He was wounded in the First Boer War. Coming to Virginia about 1881, Mr. Walpole made his home near Oak Ridge, in Nelson County, but much of his time was spent in Lynchburg with the relatives of his wife. He died May 6th, 1906, from injuries received when he was thrown from his horse. He is survived by his wife, who was Miss Nina Gardner, of Nelson County, and a daughter, Amy Dorothy, who married Hugh Davis, of Norfolk, and has two sons, Walpole and Horace.

WALSH

Misses Lillie and Grace Walsh are descended on the maternal side from Mr. Michael Connell, honored citizen, of Lynchburg, who lived to a great age, as did his sister, Miss Kate Connell. The ladies above mentioned have taught school, both public and private, and are most excellent in this useful work. Miss Grace has written a small but valuable book about Lynchburg, and has compiled interesting and useful data in regard to the Catholic Church here. These two ladies have given a decided impulse to better and higher thinking in this community.

Logan Walter Walsh

Mr. Logan Walter Walsh was born in Kinston, North Carolina. His parents were Dr. John T. Walsh, of Virginia, and Elizabeth J. Green, of North Carolina. Dr. Walsh was both doctor and minister; he taught in a Philadelphia medical college, and was also a pioneer preacher in the Christian Church, where for fifty years he was a prominent figure. Dr. Walsh was the author of several books on Biblical subjects, and editor of several religious papers. Logan Walter Walsh, his son, was educated in private schools, and continued the study of Greek without an instructor. When he was a boy he, with a friend, experimented with telegraphy until he had learned enough to assist the operator in Kinston, and later was offered a position with a railroad there. He left the railroad service to handle Associated Press messages, which work carried him to several different places of residence. He came to Lynchburg in 1889, and became associated with the McWanes in the Christian Church. In 1898 he became general office manager in the Lynchburg Plow Works, the later secretary and treasurer of the Lynchburg Foundry Company, with charge of all purchasing in connection with the plant.

Mr. Walsh married Miss Mollie E. Tuck, daughter of Professor R. M. Tuck, of Danville, Virginia. He has three children, two sons and a daughter. Though unassuming to a marked degree, Mr. Walsh is a most valued citizen of Lynchburg, where he is honored for his ability, and his integrity of character.

LYNCHBURG AND ITS NEIGHBORS

In the fire which destroyed the Lynchburg Foundry some years ago, Mr. Walsh showed the highest order of courage. Against the protest of firemen, and others present at the scene, he went into the burning building and brought out of the office vault the money held there to pay the employees.

WATTS

The Watts brothers, Colonel James Watts and Thomas Watts, after the War Between the States, established a hardware business in Lynchburg with their brother-in-law, Mr. George M. Jones. They were popular among the returned soldiers, who were now turning swords into plowshares. The Watts brothers became very wealthy in the hardware business. Among the children of Mr. Thomas Watts are: R. T. Watts, Junior, who married Miss Gladys Heald, daughter of Mr. Charles E. Heald; R. C. Watts, who married Miss McLaurin, daughter of Senator McLaurin, of Mississippi; Mr. James Owen Watts, who married Maude, daughter of Mr. George Caskie; Dr. Stephen Watts, a noted surgeon at the University of Virginia Hospital, and Mary Watts, who is Mrs. John James. The children of Colonel James Watts were: the late Mrs. George Putnam Watkins, Mrs. Maude Batchelor, Mr. Ashby Watts, who married Miss Fannie Cheatwood, and the late Hubert Watts, who married Miss Ida Hutter.

ANNA PAGE KINCKLE WILLIAMS
(Copied from the Southern Churchman)

"Anna Page Kinckle, born April 20th, 1847, was the daughter of Maria Willis Page, of "Union Hill," Cumberland County, Virginia, and the Rev. William H. Kinckle, of Hagerstown, Maryland. In 1872 she was married to J. Peter Williams, born in Halifax County, the son of Dr. Thomas Jasper Williams and Mary Selden Leigh, and grandson of Judge William Leigh, of Halifax. Mrs. Williams was one of eight children born to the Rev. and Mrs. William H. Kinckle during the twenty-four years he was rector of Saint Paul's Church, at Lynchburg.

When Mrs. Williams was fifteen years of age, her mother died, and she, as the eldest daughter, assumed her place in the home. When she reached the age of twenty, her father's death placed upon her youthful shoulders further responsibilities. This was in the year 1867, when our town, as well as the rest of the South, was desolated by the War. At that time there was no public school in Lynchburg; Saint Paul's Church conducted a Parish School in order to supply some of the educational needs of the town. In this school she taught, and later engaged in the same work at the Parish School organized by Grace Church, which was established under her father's ministry, and made a memorial to him at his death. For the rest of her life she was closely identified with Grace Church, a communicant here, and deeply interested in all branches of its work.

In recent years she was much concerned in the restoration and welfare of Grace Church at Ca Ira in Cumberland County. It was endeared to her by childhood associations, and because her father was the first rector of the church, which was built there in 1840.

In 1893, at the age of forty-six years, Mrs. Williams was left a widow with nine children.

These were the stern materials from which was moulded a character of noblest proportions. She reared her family at the price of rigid self-denial. In her heroic life there was no room for empty show and pretense. She knew the grimness of duty. Never was she deterred by any reason of policy, when the occasion demanded, from expressing with great sincerity her wise and righteous opinions. A woman of charm she was, of culture, of humor, ready and able as few women are, to meet on equal terms with the best minds anywhere; and yet she sought nothing for herself: no pre-eminence of any kind. She was content to shine in her own home, among her own children, an old-time mother, an old-time neighbor and friend, an old-time Christian. When that honored white head was laid low, there entered into eternal rest a great lady of the old South."

Mrs. Williams, at her death, was survived by five daughters: Mrs. Gerhardt Suhling, Mrs. Anne Cummings, Misses Evie, Maria and Hallie Williams, and by four sons: William K., Peter, Thos. J. and Frank Williams.

WILSON

William Venable Wilson, Junior, lawyer, banker, and resident of Lynchburg for over forty years, was a man of substantial attainments. His ancestry runs back in Virginia for two centuries. He was a descendant of James Wilson, who came from the north of England, married Miss Willis, and settled at "Poplar Grove," in Princess Anne County. The third son of James was Samuel, who married Miss Mason, lived in Norfolk, and died in 1710. Willis, son of Samuel, was a sea captain and an instructor in navigation. On a voyage up James River he met and married Miss Goodrich. He left an only son, Benjamin.

Benjamin Wilson, born December 6th, 1733, moved to Cumberland County in 1750, locating on Willis River. He married Anne Gray, daughter of James Gray, a Huguenot. They raised thirteen children, and were married sixty years. Dr. Goodrich Wilson, son of Benjamin and Anne, lived at Farmville, Virginia, and had a large practice as a physician. He married Elizabeth Venable, and they were the grandparents of William Venable Wilson, of Lynchburg. William V. Wilson, Junior, was born in Petersburg, Virginia, April 22nd, 1854, son of Rev. William V. and Grace A. (Wilson) Wilson. His mother was a daughter of Daniel A. Wilson, originally from Cumberland, a prominent lawyer and at one time judge of the Circuit Court.

William V. Wilson, Junior, was raised in Southwest Virginia and studied law in Wythe County under Judge Andrew Fulton. He was admitted to the bar in 1880, having graduated from Emory and Henry College in 1875. For a time he taught school. Being the son of a minister, he early in life became acquainted with self-respecting poverty, and had to look out for his own education and advancement. In 1880 he came to Lynchburg, where he began the practice of law and won great success in his profession. For many years he was president of the Lynchburg National Bank.

THE WINFREE FAMILY

Mr. Christopher Winfree, the first of the name in Lynchburg, settled here in 1803 and engaged in the tobacco business. He was born in Chesterfield County, October 23rd, 1785, and died December 12th, 1858. He was one of the pioneers in the business here, and carried on a large trade in the manufacture of tobacco and in export to Europe. His home was just outside of town, on the Rustburg, or old Campbell Courthouse Road, as it was then known. Mr. Winfree was married twice, his first wife being Polly Warwick, one of the three daughters of William Warwick. His second wife was Cornelia Myer Tilden, by whom he had seven children, as follows: 1. Mary Cornelia, born January 30th, 1819, married Thaddeus Ivey in 1842. William Christopher Ivey was born April 22nd, 1843. He married Emma Walton Moorman, December 20th, 1871, and had two children, Lillian, born September 1st, 1873, died December 22nd, 1881, and Edwin Clark, born December 30th, 1874. Edwin Clark Ivey, married Eleanor Prescott and has Emma, who married John Barksdale; Celeste, married Prescott Edmunds; Edwin C. Ivey, Junior, married Eugenia Goodall, of Staunton. 2. Jane Margaret Winfree, born July 18th, 1821, married Edward S. Brown in May, 1845. (See Brown). 3. Catherine Virginia, born 1824. 4. Christopher Valentine, born November 14th, 1826, died June 18th, 1902, was a prominent citizen of Lynchburg; married twice, first wife being Virginia A. Brown, daughter of Henry J. and Susan A. Hobson Brown. She died in 1884, leaving the following children: Minnie Ivey, born 1862, died young. Henry Lee, born January 16th, 1864, married Elsie Cleveland. Lizzie Kent, married November 16th, 1893, to Walter B. Ryan; her children are: Walter, Christopher W., Philip Henry, Lee W.; Peyton Brown Winfree, born September 10th, 1868, married Mabel Louise Wilbur; children are: Christopher V., Wilbur, Virginia (deceased), Mabel Louise. Walter Russell, born August 3rd, 1875, married Louisa C. Estill; children: Louisa Estill, Sarah Doniphan, Reverly. Major Christopher Winfree's second wife was Miss Sarah C. Doniphan. She had no children. 5. John Bell Tilden Winfree, born May 8th, 1829, married Ann Pennington, December 16th, 1857. He was in his time one of Lynchburg's most outstanding citizens. Mrs. Ben Hughes, Mrs. Claiborne Gooch, and Mr. John Bell Winfree, Junior, his children, live in Lynchburg. The wife of Mr. John Bell Winfree, Junior, was Bella, the daughter of Raymond Fairfax, for many years a resident of Lynchburg, whose brother was Lord Fairfax, of the English nobility.

WINGFIELD

Judge Gustavus Adolphus Wingfield was born in Franklin County, Virginia, October 24th, 1808. He was the son of Lewis and Elizabeth (Parberry) Wingfield. He married Charlotte, the daughter of Samuel and Charlotte (Hook) Griffin. His wife belonged to a Bedford family, was born in Bedford County, January 5th, 1810, and they were married December 14th, 1831. They had nine children, among these being Samuel Griffin Wingfield, who lived in Lynchburg. Judge Wingfield was judge of the Fifth Judicial Circuit, and he was said to have been one of the ablest judges that ever sat on the bench. He died February 18th, 1888. Samuel Griffin Wingfield was born October 17th, 1846, at Bellevue, Bedford County, Virginia. He attended Mt. Laurel Academy in Halifax for two years, and then matriculated at the Virginia Military Institute. He took part in the Battle of New Market. In 1880 he was elected Mayor of Lynchburg, but retired in 1882 to enter the law class at the University of Virginia. After winning his degree as Bachelor of Laws, he had practiced his profession only a short time when he was elected clerk of the Corporation Court of Lynchburg, which position he held until his death, November 12th, 1901. Mr. Wingfield was married October 17th, 1887, to Sallie Lewis Alexander, daughter of John Dabney Alexander, clerk of the Court of Campbell County. They had two children, Samuel Griffin

LYNCHBURG AND ITS NEIGHBORS

Wingfield, Junior, who is with the Curtis Publishing Company of Philadelphia, and Dorothy Wingfield, who married J. K. Irving, Junior of Howardsville, Virginia.

WINGFIELD—LEFTWICH

Mrs. Mary Elizabeth Wingfield died here May 5th, 1918, at 1004 Court Street. She was eighty years old and the widow of Dr. T. H. Wingfield, who died in 1885 at Towson, Maryland. He was a surgeon on the staff of General Robert E. Lee. Mrs. Wingfield was survived by her sister, Mrs. Andrew R. Humes, of New York. Mrs. Wingfield was married here in 1878, and except for Mrs. Humes was the last surviving member of a once large and influential Lynchburg family. She was the daughter of Colonel Augustine Leftwich, of this city. The Leftwich family was descended from the de Vernon family of Left Wich, in Cheshire County, England. Their ancestor, Richard, came to England with William the Conqueror, and was knighted by him, as related in the visitation of Cheshire. In America they furnished many distinguished officers to the Revolutionary War and to the War of 1812. Colonel Leftwich, born in Bedford was a prominent tobacconist here from Lynchburg's earliest days. He was of the twenty-first generation from Richard, the follower of William the Conqueror. The only descendants of Colonel Leftwich left here are Mr. William King, Mr. Gus King, and their sisters, Misses Sallie and Alice King, Mrs. Elizabeth Peck and her daughter, Miss Nancy King Peck.

Lyson's Magna Britannica says: "The Leftwich family descends from a younger branch of the Winnington family, settled at an early period at Leftwich in Davenham, and became extinct in the male line in 1640, when the heiress married Oldfield, now also extinct.

The Leftwich Township is situated one mile from Northwick. The manor, Leftwich Hall, belonged in the reign of William the Conqueror to the Vernons, as part of the Barony of Shipbrook. The Vernon family was descended from Richard de Vernon, one of Hugh Lupus' barons. (As explained in the Visitation of Cheshire, Hugh Lupus was the nephew of William the Conqueror, and was made Earl of Cheshire or Chester, with power to create barons in his own domain.) The de Vernon family became extinct in the elder branch by the death of Warin de Vernon, fifth Baron of Shipbrook, whose wife was Andea, daughter of William de Marlbrook, they having a son, Warin, who died without issue, and three daughters. Margaret, the eldest daughter of Warin and Andea, brought a portion of the de Vernon inheritance to her husband, Richard Willenham, in the thirteenth century. Matilda, also called Maud, daughter of Warin and Andea, married Robert Winnington, who settled at Winnington in 1294, and they had a younger son, Robert or Richard, who married Agnes Leftwich, and assuming his wife's name, Leftwich, was the founder of the Leftwich family, and the ancestor of the Leftwiches who continued to possess the family manor for several generations. When the main line became extinct in the seventeenth century by the failure of male heirs, at the time of the marriage of Elizabeth, daughter of Ralph, to William Oldfield, a younger branch of the Leftwich name from Northwich continued there in 1663. Arms of the family: Fesse, engrailed azure; three garbs. Motto: Ver Non Semper Floret.

(The garbs, which are sheaves of wheat, are from the de Vernon side of the house.)

Ralph Leftwich, first of the name in Virginia, moved to New Kent County, and patented 300 acres in New Kent County, August 10th, 1658. Land was granted him for the transportation of six people into the colony. See Land Office Book in Richmond, Virginia, Book 4, page 272, August 17th, 1663.

Thomas Leftwich, Senior, son of Ralph, was born at some time between 1660 and 1670. He died in 1730 in Caroline County. He married Elizabeth Rosier first. She had no children. She died in 1700 and he married again, his second wife being Mary North, daughter of Augustine North, of Gloucester County. Issue of Thomas and Mary being Mary, Thomas and Augustine.

Augustine Leftwich, Junior, in applying for a pension, states that he was born in Caroline County in February, 1727. Caroline was formed in 1727, from several counties which were originally a part of New Kent. Augustine, Junior, moved to Bedford in 1758. His wife was Mary Turner. Their daughter, Lockey Leftwich, married Colonel David Saunders. William, Thomas and William Leftwich served in the French and Indian War.

SAUNDERS

David Saunders was a native of Louisa County. He moved to Bedford when a boy of thirteen, walking all the way. He bound himself out to make his own living, because his mother, who had been left a widow, had had her entire property destroyed during the raid of Louisa by General Tarleton. At one time David was sheriff of Bedford County. He was colonel of Ninety-first Regiment Virginia Militia in 1804. His son, James Turner Saunders, born July 17th, 1791, died 1864, married Anne Rives, daughter of William C. Rives. For many years Dr. Saunders was in the tobacco business with his brother, William Leftwich Saunders, whose wife was Mary Camm, daughter of John Camm, clerk of Amherst Court, and granddaughter of John Camm, president of William and Mary College. These two men made Lynchburg their home. Dr. Saunders was a prominent figure in politics. He graduated in medicine from the University of Pennsylvania, and served as surgeon in his father's regiment during the War of 1812.

Date of marriage of Lockey Leftwich and David Saunders was September 4th, 1788.

Most of this data came from the Leftwich book, and some was collected by Mrs. Roger A. Pryor, who is also descended from the Leftwich family.

The marriage of Augustine Leftwich and Mary Turner took place February 12th, 1765. Besides Lockey Leftwich, they had other children, among them Peyton Leftwich, and Colonel Thomas Leftwich, who married Jane Stratton, and was the father of Augustine Leftwich, wealthy Lynchburg tobacconist.

Complete list of children of the various members of this family can be obtained from the Leftwich book. Also this book has records of the distinguished service given by members of this family in the French and Indian, Revolutionary Wars, and War of 1812, many of whom attained high rank.

Wooling

Mr. Richard Wooling, one of our oldest citizens, won a host of friends as captain of a packet boat in former times. When this business became obsolete he ran the "Relay House," a hotel in Lynchburg. For many years Captain Wooling has been retired from business. He is an interesting and instructive companion, with a great fund of anecdote, and a broad and kindly wisdom.

Wray

Mr. Jabez Leftwich Wray died here March 8th, 1905, at the age of ninety years. He was the father of four sons, Alonza, Charles H., James W. and John L. Wray.

Wyatt

Colonel John Wyatt, first of the name in Campbell County, was a colonel in the Revolutionary Army. He married Wilhemina Jordan, daughter of Samuel Jordan, and a sister of Mrs. William Cabell and Mrs. John Cabell. Caroline Wyatt, daughter of Colonel John Wyatt, married Edmund Winston; Anne Wyatt married Captain William Norvell. Mrs. Hays Otey was Sallie Elizabeth Wyatt; her father was Robert Wyatt, who married Clarissa Payne, of Seneca Creek neighborhood in Campbell County. Another descendant of this family was Mr. John Wyatt, who taught mathematics in the High School here for many years.

The children of Captain William Norvell and Anne Wyatt were: William Wyatt Norvell, born 1795, married Anne M., daughter of Samuel J. and Sallie Burton Harrison in 1818. Martha Ann Norvell, born 1797, was the first wife of Chiswell Dabney, of Hanover. She died in 1815. Lucy Wilhemina Norvell, born 1801, married John M. Otey, son of Isaac and Elizabeth Otey.

Elizabeth Emmeline Norvell, born 1799, married Edward Trent, of Cumberland County, in 1815, and died in 1819.

Susannah Caroline Norvell, born 1803, married John M. Warwick, son of William and Leanna Dawson Warwick, and grandson of Abraham and Amy Warwick. Mr. and Mrs. John M. Warwick's daughter, Sarah Ann, married Judge William Daniel, Junior, and being his first wife she was the mother of Senator John Warwick Daniel and of Mrs. Don P. Halsey, Senior. Mrs. Warwick died at the age of twenty-four years.

WYSOR

Mr. William Wirt Wysor, who lived in Lynchburg for some years as one of the editors of the Virginian until it was sold in 1893 to Mr. Carter Glass, belonged to a family of prominence in the Southwest. The name was originally spelled Weiser and the family had been magistrates in Gross-Aspatch, Germany, before coming to this country. Mr. Wysor was born in Newburn, Pulaski County, Virginia. His parents were Benjamin F. Wysor, born in 1813, who was a lawyer and for many years commonwealth's attorney of Pulaski County, and Harriet Jane (Jordan) Wysor. Mr. Wysor was appointed vice-consul to Spain under Cleveland's administration and died on the sea while returning to this country.

YODER

Mr. Jacob E. Yoder was born in Burks County, Pennsylvania, February 22nd, 1838. He graduated from the Pennsylvania Normal School during the War Between the States, and came to Lynchburg under the auspices of the Freedmans' Aid Society. He engaged in teaching in Lynchburg, but returned to Pennsylvania for two years, after which he came back, settling permanently here in 1869. When the public school system of Lynchburg was organized in 1871 Mr. Yoder was appointed principal of the Polk Street School. He was afterwards made supervising principal of the colored schools of the city, and held this position as long as the office existed. Teaching was his life work, a labor of great merit, which he only relinquished a few weeks before his death, April 15th, 1905. He was the last of the original teachers who began their work in Lynchburg in 1871, when the public school system was first inaugurated. In addition to his profession as an educator Mr. Yoder was an enthusiastic student and an investigator of various subjects, being one of the best botanists and geologists in the State. He was a well informed and able man, and greatly beloved by those who really knew him, but too modest and unassuming ever to have been estimated at his true worth. In 1871 Mr. Yoder married Miss Anne F. Whitaker, of Connecticut, who at his death survived him with seven children: Miss Eva Yoder, Mrs. Martin L. Brown, Wayland, Adam, Edward, Claude and Rozelle. Mrs. Yoder died the summer of 1933 at the home of her son-in-law, Mr. Martin L. Brown.

Yancey

Charles Yancey, the immediate ancestor of this family in Lynchburg, came to Virginia about the year 1674 with his wife, who was the granddaughter of Alexander Leighton, the famous Scotch divine, whose persecution was one of the greatest scandals of the reign of Charles I. She was also a niece of Robert Leighton, another famous churchman, who was Bishop of Dunblane and later Archbishop of Glasgow. Charles Yancey's name appears on the quit rent roll in 1704 for land in King William County. The will of Robert Yancey, his son, is recorded in 1745 on the first page of the first will book in Louis County Courthouse. Though badly worm-eaten, the name of his wife and of his sons, Charles, Robert, James and Richard can readily be made out.

James Yancey, son of Robert, grandson of the first Charles, was in the Revolutionary War, a major under command of General Green. After the Revolution, he settled in South Carolina, and married Miss Cudworth. He was the grandfather of William Lowndes Yancey, noted orator and statesman of the South. Charles, son of Robert, married Madamoiselle Dumas, daughter of Jeremiah Dumas, of an old French family, who had settled in Louisa County. Charles had several sons, Jeremiah, Archelaus, Charles and Robert. Many of Jeremiah's descendants settled in Albemarle County. Charles, known as Captain Charles, married Mary, daughter of David Crawford, and left descendants in Amherst. Robert married Anne, another daughter of David Crawford. He studied for the ministry, and was ordained in England by the Archbishop of Canterbury. He was rector of Trinity and Tillottson Parishes in Louisa County, and was the first preacher in America to preach universal salvation. (See Cabells and Their Kin). He lived on Little River, in Louisa County, and after his death his wife moved to Buckingham County with their children. Major Charles Yancey was their son. He was known as "the Duke of Buckingham" on account of the princely hospitality which characterized his home and was also called the "wheel horse of Democracy." Many letters written to him by Thomas Jefferson, who was his close friend, have been published. Major Charles was born in 1770, and died in 1857. He married Nancy Spencer. His children were: 1. Mary Chambers, who married Colonel John Horsley, of Nelson County. 2. Francis Westbrooke, who died in 1793. 3. Elizabeth Anne, who was married twice, first to Robert Williams, of New York, and second to Richard Morris, of Gloucester, Virginia. Charles Yancey Morris, who built "Morrisania," opposite Lynchburg, around which mansion the Epileptic Colony was later constructed, was her son. Major Charles Yancey had one sister, Elizabeth Yancey, who married George Miller.

Robert, son of Robert, and grandson of the first Charles mentioned in the Louisa will of 1745, had a son, Joel, who married Barbara Jennings, their marriage bond being in Louisa Courthouse. She was the daughter of Robert Jennings, church warden and prominent citizen of Hanover County, whose will was probated in 1758. He mentions his children by name, Barbara being apparently the youngest. She was a sister of Elizabeth Jennings Hudson, who was the grandmother of Henry Clay. Barbara and Joel had one child, Joel, born in 1773, who was a year old when his father died. The will of the elder Joel is on record in Louisa County.

As a very young man, the second Joel Yancey came to Campbell County. From the county records it appears that he was commissioned by his friends to buy land for them, and some of his operations were in the Seneca Creek District, a popular section in that day. He married Peggy Burton, daughter of Jesse Burton. (See Burton). Her mother was a connection of his mother's family. She died in a few years. Their children, as recorded in his own hand, were:

Robert Jennings Yancey, born November 15th, 1797. Settled in Missouri. Left descendants, several of them being soldiers in the Confederacy.

Harriet Barbara Yancey, born February 2nd, 1800. Died young.

Joel Yancey, born April 7th, 1802. Settled in Missouri.

Martha Anne Yancey, born December, 1803. She married General David Rodes, a native of Albemarle County, but clerk of the Lynchburg Court for many years. (See Rodes). After her death, he married Miss Penn. The children of Martha Ann Yancey Rodes were: Colonel Virginius Rodes, C. S. A. Sally Rodes, who married Mr. Nelson, of Staunton. Martha Rodes, the first wife of Colonel Maurice Langhorne. (See Langhorne). Robert Emmet Rodes, major-general, C. S. A. Charles Rodes was the first ancestor of the Rodes family in Virginia. They were of the English nobility, Charles being of the cadet branch of the house. His uncle, Sir John Rodes, of Barleborough Hall, held the title. Charles worked for his passage to this country, and had a desperate time of it when he reached these shores, as shown by letters recently published. In 1743 the title became extinct in England, as Sir John left no heirs. The descendants of Charles in Virginia were then in direct line of succession, but it does not appear that any of these laid claim to the honor. The Rodes connection in England followed with much pride the career of General Robert E. Rodes, and declared that he was the most eminent member of their family.

After the death of his first wife, Joel Yancey was married to Bettie Macon, October 24th, 1809. (See Macon). She was the daughter of John Macon, of Powhatan, and his second wife, Grace Cowan Macon, daughter of Elizabeth (Anthony) Cowan and Robert Cowan, of Bedford. John Macon was descended from Gideon Macon, and was a near kinsman of Martha Washington. The children of Joel and Elizabeth Macon Yancey were:

John Macon Yancey, born September 11th, 1810, never married, lived in the South.

Catherine Louisa Yancey, born June 16th, 1812, married Thomas Steptoe, son of James Steptoe, clerk of Bedford Court. Left a large family. Lived at "Lesperance," near Lynchburg. (See Steptoe).

William Tudor Yancey, born November 16th, 1813, married Lucy Elizabeth Davis; prominent Lynchburg lawyer; had a large family. (See Davis).

Grace Macon Yancey, born July 6th, 1815, never married.

Charles Dabney Yancey, born May 15th, 1817; moved to New Orleans, where he became a wealthy citizen; married Miss Mallarche; no descendants.

Elizabeth Cowan Yancey, born July 15th, 1819, never married.

Margaret Macon Yancey, born July 14th, 1821, never married.

Mary Barbara Jennings Yancey, born June 30th, 1825. She married Colonel Thomas Littleton Macon. They lived in New Orleans, where she died of yellow fever. Left one child, Elizabeth, who died at the age of thirteen.

Anne Rebecca Mayo Yancey, born January 5th, 1829, never married.

Ellen Graham Yancey, born September 5th, 1831, never married.

Joel Yancey was a major in the War of 1812. He had moved from Campbell to Bedford before his second marriage, where he and his kinsman, Colonel William Radford, together purchased large tracts of land. Their joint estate reached at one time from Forest to Clay. There is no more beautiful stretch of farm land in Bedford than "Rothsay," as Major Yancey named his plantation. He built an imposing brick house in a great grove of oak trees. It stood on the road, a well-known landmark, for over a hundred years. About twenty years ago it was burned down. The owner of the place, Mr. Loxley Radford, rebuilt on the original site, using the same brick. A portion of this land was bought from Thomas Jefferson. Colonel Radford's place stood further from the road and was called "Woodburn." It is now owned by Mr. Alex Mitchell. Major Yancey died in 1833. His wife sold the Bedford place, and moved with her daughters to Lynchburg. She built the house which was used for many years as a Presbyterian Manse, and was resided in by Dr. Paxton. Part of her land she sold as a rectory for Saint Paul's Church. The house she lived in is still standing on Clay Street, and is now owned by Mrs. Thomas Adams. At one time this dwelling contained very beautiful woodwork, but the interior was changed when it was made into a manse. In the original arrangement the house had two very beautiful mantelpieces, one of which was moved by Dr. Paxton to his new home when he retired. It is believed that these mantels were originally in the old house Mrs. Yancey left in Bedford, and were designed by Adam, and that she had them brought from Bedford and placed in her house here.

Major Yancey was a friend of President Jefferson; they were neighbors for over twenty years, and his oldest child, Louisa, later Mrs. Steptoe, had many interesting recollections of Mr. Jefferson. Major Yancey during his lifetime always said that his closest relative living at that time was Major Charles Yancey, of Buckingham. Colonel Robert Leighton Yancey, who was on General Washington's staff, made a codicil to his will, in which he left his sword and epaulettes to his friend and relative, Major

Joel Yancey. These are now in possession of the Missouri branch of the Yancey family. One of the descendants of this branch, Major Sterling Ross Yancey, who had the management of Hoboken Harbor, port of embarkation in the World War, makes his home in New York City.

In the final settlement of the estate of Mary Jennings, as recorded in Will Book 8, Cumberland Courthouse, 1831, Major Joel Yancey received a one-half interest in slaves valued at $5,815 left him; Mary Jennings being his grandmother, the wife of Robert Jennings, whose will has already been mentioned herein.

Robert Davis Yancey

Robert Davis Yancey was born in Lynchburg, Campbell County, Virginia, September 15th, 1855. He died January 3rd, 1931, in the same house and room in which he was born. He was the son of William Tudor Yancey and Lucy Elizabeth Davis Yancey, and a grandson of Major Joel Yancey.

He entered Virginia Military Institute at the age of fifteen and graduated in the class of 1875. He studied law under Professor John B. Minor in the Law School at the University of Virginia, and was admitted to the Virginia bar in 1878. Mr. Yancey then began practice in the law office of Major John Warwick Daniel. From this time he took a lively interest in the political problems of the day, and became an associate in the work of the Democratic Campaign, a newspaper edited in Lynchburg by Captain Page McCarty, a noted Richmond editor. This paper, with its series of remarkably clever cartoons, was famous in its time as an instrument in closing the political career of General Mahone in Virginia.

Mr. Yancey was active in the State Militia, in that period of military ardor which followed the War Between the States, and he was captain in succession of three of the Lynchburg companies. In this capacity he served nineteen years in the Virginia National Guard, and on two occasons was ordered to Pocahontas to quell riots occasioned by strikes in the coal mines, once in General Fitzhugh Lee's administration as Governor of Virginia and again under Governor O'Farrall. He was commanding officer of the Virginia troops each time they were called to Pocahontas, and he executed his duties with tact and success. In the Spanish-American War he was offered a commission as colonel in a personal letter from President McKinley, but his other duties at that time were of such a nature that he felt he could not accept this offer. President McKinley's letter is still in posession of his family.

Mr. Yancey was a member of many fraternal orders, and a charter member of the old Piedmont Club of Lynchburg. He was a lover of dogs and a great sportsman, being a remarkably good bird shot, speedy and accurate in the field. He was a speaker of force and ability, but his friends considered him particularly happy in impromptu address, for which he was well-fitted by a gift of wit and repartee which enlivened any occasion at which he happened to be present.

All his life he was identified with the Democratic Party, to the service of which he gave his best years. He was elected Mayor of Lynchburg in 1890 by a large popular vote, and was re-elected in 1892. He declined a third nomination. In 1894 he was elected Commonwealth's Attorney, an office his father had also held. In 1896 he was defeated for this office by Mr. Don P. Halsey with a majority of thirteen votes. He was elected to the City Council a few months later. In 1898 he defeated Mr. Halsey, and was returned to the office of Commonwealth's Attorney. From this time until 1930 he was re-elected continuously to this office, though opposed in almost every primary, his opponents being some of the strongest lawyers in this community. He served as Commonwealth's Attorney for thirty-four years, until defeated by the infirmities of old age. Though he fought his cases with a fiery vigor characteristic of the man, he was never known to dragoon a suspected criminal into damaging admissions. When asked to take part in the private examination of prisoners before they were haled into court, his invariable answer was: "I am not a detective. I am a court official. It is beneath the dignity of the office to which the people have elected me to interfere in the duties of the police."

He was proud of the well-known fact that his strongest following was among the laboring men of this community; they never had a warmer friend or a stauncher advocate than they had in him. Descended from English, Scotch and Huguenot families of honor and distinction, Mr. Yancey belonged by birth and education, as well as by the strong individualism of his character and his attitude towards life, to the Virginia of the past, and to that old order of Virginians who brought with them from England that supreme gift for unselfish public service.

ACKNOWLEDGEMENTS

In closing the author wishes to acknowledge assistance from the following sources, not hitherto acknowledged:

Mrs. Cabell's Recollections of Lynchburg; Dr. Asbury Christian's Lynchburg and Its People; The Lynchburg Virginian; The Lynchburg News; Dr. Lyon G. Tyler's William and Mary Quarterly, and Virginia Biography; History of the Virginias, by R. A. Brock; Mrs. Charles M. Blackford's Reminiscences; Captain John M. Payne and Mrs. Payne, of Amherst; Mrs. Rebecca Voorheis, of Amherst; Mr. Oakey, of Centenary Methodist Church; J. P. Bell Company; Mr. Martin L. Brown; Miss Ruth Early's books; the late Dr. Henry McIlwaine, of the Virginia State Library; Miss Maude Campbell and Mrs. Lucille Dickerson, of Jones Memorial Library; Major Stephen Halsey; Judge Don Peters Halsey; Dr. and Mrs. John Bell Williams, of Richmond; Mrs. Anna Kinckle Williams, of Lynchburg; Mrs. A. H. Blencowe, and J. W. Fergusson and Sons, Publishers, of Richmond, whose helpful suggestions have made the completion of this work possible.

INDEX

A

Abell, Mr., 131.
Abernathy, R. M., V. P., 295.
Abbot, William, of Bellevue, 337.
Abbot, Willis J., on Senator Glass in Christian Science Monitor, 177.
Abbot, Mrs. John, 358.
Abingdon, 192.
Act of Denization, 361.
Adams, Daniel's Hill Family: DuVal, 241; Holcombe, 241; Capt. C. S. A., R. H. T., 241; 247.
Adams, John Quincy, Family, 279: Ashby, 279; Francis, 279; Hubert Preston, 279; John Q., Jr., 279; Robert Camm, 279; Rosa, 279; Thomas, 279; William Saunders, 279. Family of Thomas: Elizabeth Saunders, 257; Florence Bias, 256, 279; Florence B., 256; Florence Hughes, 257; Frances Cowan, 257; Hazel Kirk Moore, 257; John Q., 257; Mary Catherine, 257; Rose Virginia, 257; Thomas Cesario, 257.
Adams, Stephen, Capt. C. S. A., 241-279.
Addison Family: Anthony, 242; Dr. Edmund Brice, 245; Edward Brice, 243; Elizabeth Hesselius, 243; Eliza D. Bowie, 245; Emily Crockford, 245; Francis Key, 244; Henry, 242; Henry, 243; Rev. Henry, 243-244; James A., 246; Col. John, 243-248; John, 243; John H., 246; Joseph, 242-247; Julian, 246; Launcelot, 242; Lloyd, 243; M e a d e, 246; Rachel Dulany, 243; Rebecca Dulany, 243; Susannah W., 243; Thomas, 243; Walter Dulany, 242-245; Walter Edmund, 245-247. Mrs. Walter Edmund, 246. Arms of Addison family, 244.
Africa, 52, 89.
Agnew, Herman, 125.
Ainslie, Mrs. Peter, born Otey, 307.

Alabama Fifth, Sixth, Twelfth Regiments, 100.
Alabama Troops, 71.
Albemarle County, 67, 143, 184, 189.
Albemarle Pippins, 76.
Alexander, Anne Austin, 367; Robert, 367.
Alexandria, 411.
Algonquin, 58.
Allison & Addison, 245.
American Revolution, 151.
Ambler Family: Anne Herndon, 248; Anne H., 248; Anne Theresa Jordan, 248; Blanche Jordan, 248; Ella Cary, 248; Frankie Preston, 248; Janet Anne Carter, 247; John Jacqueline, 247; J. Jacqueline, Jr., 247; Katharine, 248; Martha Cary, 248; Mary Nelson, 248; Philip St. George, 248; P. St. George, 248; Philip St. G., 248; Sallie Davies, 248; Theresa Jacqueline, 248; Virginia Pascoe, 248.
Amherst County, 67, 131, 139, 194, 247, 248, 257, 272-73.
Anchorage, Ky., 280.
Anderson, Gen. C. S. A., 108.
Annapolis, 242-43.
Anthony Family: Charles, 249; Charlotte, 249; Christopher, 249, 293; Elizabeth, 249; Hannah, 249; Jordan, 249; Joseph, 248, 293; Penelope, 249; Rachel, 249.
Appomattox, 86, 96, 98, 106, 107, 124, 129, 135.
Appomattox River, 98.
Aristotle, 151.
Arlington Hotel, 114.
Armistead, Dr. Jacob Mitchell, 250; Louis, 250.
Arms of Second Virginia Regiment of Cavalry, 67.
Army of Northern Virginia, 68, 98, 111.
Army of the Potomac, 98.
Arrington, Lieut., C. S. A., 109.

INDEX—(*continued*)

Arsenal of the Confederacy, 245.
Ashby, Turner, Gen. C. S. A., 96.
Astor, Lady, 62.
Athens, 151.
Atlantic, 59; Coast, 255; Ocean, 249.
Augusta County, 139, 141, 158, 257.
Aunspaugh Family: Alice, 250; Anna Claytor, 250; Annie, 250; Claytor, 250; Eugenia, 250; Julia, 250; Fred, 250; Robert T., 250; Mary Owen, 250.
Aunspaugh and Cobbs, 250.
Averill's Cavalry, U. S. A., 108-109.
Aylmer, John, Bishop of London, 277; Aylmer Hall, Parish of Tilney, County of Norfolk, England, 277; Elizabeth, 277.

B

Bacon, Eugene, 279.
Bacon's Rebellion, 276.
Bagby, Dr. George Williams, 21, 32, 66, 70, 71, 213, 214.
Bailey, John, 16.
Baldwin, John B., 144-147.
Baltimore & Ohio Railroad, 108.
Baltimore, Md., 155, 257.
Bank Square, 63.
Barbadoes, 282.
Barbour, Carrie, 279.
Barker, O. B., 202.
Barksdale, A. D., 251; Elisha, 250; Elizabeth Worthington, 250; Emma Ivey, 251; John Craddock, 251; Judith, 250; Mary Jane Morgan, 251; Peter, 250; Randolph, 250; Rosa McWane, 251; William R., Jr., 250.
Barlow, Edward, 405; Elizabeth Glass, 405.
Bass, Dr. David Ethelbert, 251; Julia, 251; Sarah Judith Leftwich, 251.
Batesville, 184.
Bath County, 256.
Battle, Gen., C. S. A., 107.
Beale Family: Agnes, 251; Agnes, 251; Alicia, 251; Alicia Wolgate, 251; Alice, 251; Ann Gooch, 251; Betty Hite, 252; Celeste Grand Pierre, 252; Charles, 252; Elizabeth, 252; Elizabeth Taverner, 252; Eliza Skillern, 252; Frances Madison, 252; James Madison Hite, 252; Johanna Cobb, 251; Johanna Thomas, 251; John, 251; John, 251; John, 251; John, 253; Katherine, 251; Katharine, 252; Kyle, 252; Margaret Skillern, 252; Mary, 252; Mary Steinbergen, 252; Robert, 252; Taverner, Sr., 252-254; Col. Taverner, Jr., 252; Thomas, 251; Thomas, 251; Col. Thomas, 251; Capt. Thomas, 251; Thomas III, 252; William, 251.
Bibb, B. S., of Alabama, 191.
Bigbie, Augustine, 258; Mary Trevillo, 258; William, 258.
Biggers, Abram F., 48, 318; Capt. A. F., 48.
Birmingham, 267.
Bishop of North Carolina, 39.
Black, Dr., 279.
Black and Tan Convention, 141.
Blackford, Dr. Benjamin, 260; Chas. Minor, Capt. C. S. A., 85, 86, 129, 132, 133, 258, 260; Charles Minor, Jr., 260; Eugene, 260; Isabelle Arthur, 260; Launcelot Minor, 260; Mary Berkeley Minor, 260; Mary Isabella, 260; Nannie Colston, 129, 259; Raleigh Colston, 259; Susan Leigh Colston, 259; William Matthews, 174, 260; William Willis, 260.
Blackwater Creek, 62.
Blackwell's Neck, 255.
Bleecker, Mrs. John S., 327.
Bluefield, 267.
Blue Ridge Mountains, 28, 29, 58, 84.
Bobbit, James M., 283.
Bolling, George W., 143, 145.
Bolling, Rolfe, 205.
Bolling, 314.
Bolling Spring, 218.
Bond, Mrs. Giles, 408.
Bonn, 117.
Booker, William T., 130.
Boone, Daniel, 25; Jemima, 25.
Boonsborough Gap, 97, 98, 119.
Boonsboro, Ky., 25.

INDEX—(continued)

Boston, 155.
Boston Advertiser, 147.
Boteler, A. R., 90.
Botetourt Artillery, 87, 139.
Botetourt Springs, 27, 30.
Bouldin, E. C., Capt. C. S. A., 88.
Bowie Knife, 68.
Bowman, Nathaniel Randolph, 261; Annette Moore, 261, and Family, 261.
Bowman, Miss Willie, 189, 190, 261.
Boyd, Waller M., Maj. C. S. A.: Caroline Y., 294, 368; Alice, 294, 368; Caroline Anthony Yancey, 294, 368; Henry C., 294, 368; Janet W., 368; Lucy, 294, 368; Mary, 294, 368; Susan C., 295, 368; Thomas, 294, 368; Virginia, 294, 368; Waller M., Jr., 294, 368; William Tudor, 294, 368.
Boys' Home at Covington, 189.
Bozzoatro, F. B. Gennaro, Lucy Murrell Turner, 423; Gennaro, Jr., 423.
Bragg, Gen. C. S. A., 287.
Braggassa, Frank, Josephine Grovo, 261.
Brandy Station, 104.
Bransford, Samuel, 262; Elizabeth, 261; Rosa Kent, 262.
Brazil, 256.
Breckenridge, Cary, Col. Second Virginia Cavalry, C. S. A., 262; Emma Cary, 262; Henry C., of Chicago, 262; James, of Victoria, Va., 262; J. T., of Lake Village, Ark., 262; Dr. W. N., of Fincastle, Va., 262. Mrs. Breckenridge, 249. Grove Hill, home near Fincastle, 336.
Breckenridge, John C., Gen. C. S. A., 83, 86, 92, 91, 121.
Bretagne, France, 268.
British Agents, 253.
British Fleet, 30.
British Guiana, 183.
Bristoe, 110.
Broad Creek Church, Maryland, 242, 243.
Brockenborough, Edward, 271.
Brodnax, Robert Withers, 409; Austina Slaughter, 409; Mary Roberta, 409.

Brooks, Mrs., 422; Emmet, 422.
Brown, Dr. Alexander, 296.
Brown, John Thompson, Col. C. S. A., 417.
Brown, John Thompson, Judge of Nelson County, 414.
Brown, John Thompson, of Ivey Cliff, Campbell County; Wilcox; Perroneaux.
Brown, Martin L., 440; Mrs. Martin L., Family, 266.
Browne or Brown, Edward Smith, 262-265; Anne, 265; Buckingham, 262; Clement, 262; Cornelia Walton, 265; Daniel, 263; Elizabeth Mestich, 262; James, 262; Jane Margaret Winfree, 265; Mary Glebe, 262; Mary Spearman, 263; Mary Virginia, 265; Nancy Hobson Walton, 263.
Brown, John Brown's Raid, 215.
Bruce, Robert, King of Scotland, 255.
Brunswick County, 26.
Bruton Parish, 275.
Buchanan, 59, 65, 78, 82, 252.
Buffalo Lick Plantation, 24.
Buffington, Dr., 285.
Buford's Gap, 28.
Bull Run, 110.
Bunker Hill, 108.
Burgesses, House of, 25.
Burks, Richard, Col. C. S. A., 91, 92, 128, 267. Family, 267.
Burr, Aaron, 249.
Burton, Arms, 268.
Burton, Jesse, 272; Ann Hudson, 268; Sir Edward, 268; Hutchins, 268; Roald, 268; Rachel Hutchins, 268; Susannah Allen, 268; Thomas de, 268; William, 268.
Burton, Addison, 269; Alexander, 268; Ann, 269; Cornelia, 269; Damaris Cobbs, 270; Edward Hudson, 270; Edward Johnson, 269; Elizabeth Joyner, 269; Gabrielle Terrel, 270; Grace Ann, 269; Gustavus Adolphus, 268; Hudson, 269; Isabel Grace, 270; Jesse, 269; Jesse Alexander, 269; Jesse Alexander, 270; John, 269; Katharine, 270; Lawrence Reveley, 270; Lucy, 276; Margaret Macon, 269; Margaret Macon, 269; Margaret Macon, 269;

LYNCHBURG AND ITS NEIGHBORS

INDEX—(continued)

Martha Eliza, 269; Maria, 269; Mary Elizabeth Powell, 269; Mary Patteson, 270; Nancy, 269; Patsey, 269; Dr. Robert, 269; Robert, 269; Robert Oswald, 270; Sally, 269; Samuel, 271; Susan Hamner, 270; Virginia, 270; Waddy, 268; William, 268; William Cowan, 270.
Busey, Dr. Charles Edgar, 274; Rosa Terrell Bell, 274. Family, 274.
Butler, Benj., Gen. U. S. A., 78, 93.
Button, Charles W., 114, 174, 190.

C

Cabell, 250; Mrs. Cabell's Book, 293; Mrs. George, 38.
Cabiness, Miss Judson, 321.
Calhoun, John C., 155.
Calhoun Family, 292, 293.
Calloway, Elizabeth, 25; Elizabeth Prentiss, 26, 27; Frances, 25; James, 181; Col. Richard, 25; Sir William, 25; William, 26.
Calloway County, Ky., 25.
Cameron, William, Readjuster Governor of Virginia, 153, 412; Mary Roberta Brodnax, 409; George, 409.
Camiers, France, 280.
Camm Arms, 279.
Camm, Parson John, President William and Mary College, Rector Bruton Church, Commissioner appointed to represent Archbishop of Canterbury in Virginia, 43, 212, 248; Elizabeth Hansford, 277; Eliza, 278; Elizabeth, 278; Emma, 212, 278; Edward, 278; Florence, 278; Dr. Frank, 278; Govan, 278; John, 278; Mary, 278; Nancy, 278; Sallie, 278; Robin, 278, 279; Dr. Thomas, 278.
Camm, Robin, 278; Olivia Alexander, 278, 279; Annie Leigh Colston, 279; Gertrude, 279; Robert, 279; Robin, Col. C. S. A., 278.
Camm, John, 248; Katharine Ambler Jellis, 248; John, Jr., 248; Frank, 248.
Campbell County, 66, 67, 88, 98, 241.
Canada, 255.
Canal on James River, 77.
Canby, Gen. U. S. A., 148.
Canterbury, Archbishop of, 248.
Capon Springs, 336.
Carlisle, 104, 105, 260, 282, 284, 364.
Carlyle House, 244.
Caroline County, 143, 437.

Carrington, Alfred Randolph, Family, 322, 323; William C., 176.
Carrington, George, 364.
Carrington, Elizabeth Jacqueline Ambler, 54; Col. Edward, 54.
Carrington, Col. Edward, 282, 399; Nannie Ould Pettyjohn, 399.
Carroll, John Wesley, 45, 59; Alice M., 283; Clara Miles, 283; I. Holcombe, 283; Isabel Layman, 282; Jacob T., 282; John W., Jr., M. D., 283; Lucy B., 283; Madge Layman, 283; Martha C., 283; Mary Isabel, 283; Mildred T., 283; Rebecca H., 283; R. Layman, 283; Sallie F., 283; Sallie Frances, 283; Sarah Elizabeth, 283; Sidney G., 283; Walter M., 283; William G., 283; Zaida, 283.
Carson, Theodore M., D.D., Rector St. Paul's Church, 41, 42, 284; Catherine V. M., 284; Catherine Warren, 284; Judge Joseph F., 284; Joseph Preston, 284; J. Preston, 284; Maude Lee, 284. Victoria Ellen Allison, 284.
Carter, Thomas H., 100.
Cary's, John, School for Boys, 336.
Cashtown, 105.
Caskie, George E., 284-285.
Castleman's Ferry, 108.
Catherine's Furnace, 102.
Catholic, 244; Catholic Church, 84.
Catoctin Furnace, 260.
Cavalry, Second Virginia, was called Second when first to be organized, 69, 86.
Cedar Creek, 111.
Cedar Mountain, 110.
Cemetery Ridge, 75.
Central Railroad, 77.
Chalmers' Family: Dr. James, 404; Fannie Saunders, 404; Annie, 404; James, Jr., 404; Sallie, 404.

[452]

INDEX—(continued)

Chancellorsville, 96, 100-103, 111, 118, 119.
Chancery Court, 25.
Charles County, Md., 242.
Charles Edward, the Pretender, 337.
Charlestown, 109.
Charlotte C. H., 256.
Charlotte County, 88, 282.
Charlottesville, 82, 89, 128, 131, 184.
Chase, Mr., 192.
Chatfin, Joseph, 364.
Cherokee, 158.
Chesterfield County, 143, 342.
Chestnut Hill, 251, 252.
Chestnut Level, 342.
Chicago Tribune, 147.
Chickahominy Campaign, 96.
Chickasaw, 256.
Childs, John W., 45; Lucy Brown, 45.
Choctaw, 256.
Christian, Camillus, 291; Mary Elizabeth Davis, 291; Davis, 291; Thomas D., 291; Mrs. Thomas D., 45, 291; Dr. Henry, 291.
Christian, Dr. Asbury, 271; Edward D., 175; Family of, 269-271.
Christian Science Monitor, 177-180.
Church of England, 242.
Cincinnati, Society of, 266.
City Hotel, 99.
Claiborne, Sir William, 337.
Clark County, 89.
Clark, Christopher, 8, 249; Penelope Jordan, 249; Elizabeth, 249.
Clay, Henry, 37, 150, 268, 294.
Clay, Rev. Charles, 36, 37; Gen. Odin, 37.
Clay's Crossing, 30.
Clay Street, 13, 84, 116.
Claytor, Thomas, 13; Rosanna, 376; Samuel, 376; William, 116.
Clement, Adam, 7.
Cobbs, Johanna, 251.
Cobbs' Family, 338, 339; Nicholas Hamner, 37, 38.
Cocke, 13.
Cole, Mrs. Bettie Garland, 182.
Cole, J., 63; S., 63.
Coleman, Frederick, of Caroline County, 349.
Coleman, J. Tinsley, 284-286.
Cold Harbor, 83-100.
College Hill, 191.
College Hill Breastworks, 88.
College Hill Reservoir, 189.
Collier's Weekly, 49.
Collins, Christopher Clark, Col. U. S. A., 287; W. J., 287; Nannie P., 287.
Colonization Society, 66.
Colony of Virginia, 139.
Colston, 129; Raleigh, Gen. C. S. A., 102, 103.
Conservative Party, 136, 139.
Conservative Republican, 145, 146, 148.
Constitutional Convention, first in the world, 137, 139.
Convention Hall, 140.
Cooke, J. Churchill, 260.
Cooper, J. Fenimore, 26.
Corinth, Miss., 213.
Corinth and Other Poems, 136; Burnt in Courthouse Square, 136.
Corcoran Art Gallery, 155.
Corling, Ella Frances, 270.
Cornwallis, Lord, 266.
Cosby, 270.
Couch, Anna, 249.
Courthouse, 11, 40, 44.
Court Street, 269.
Court Street Methodist Church, 45, 264.
Coverley, Sir Roger, 247.
Covesville, 130.
Cowan, 255, 256; Elizabeth Anthony, 365; Gracy, 365; Robert, 365.
Craddock, A. P., 202; John W., 202; Dr. Thomas, 14.
Craddock-Terry Co., 172.
Craighill Family, 289.
Crawford, 194; Col. William, 28.
Creigh, Mr., Hung by Hunter, 78.
Crockett's Gap, 126.
Crook, Gen. U. S .A., 78, 108.
Crumpton, William, 282, 283.
Culloden, 337.
Cumberland County, 39, 263, 269, 430, 431.
Cummings, Mrs. Anne, 432.
Cunningham, Edward, 365; Catherine Miller, 365.
Custer, Gen. U. S. A., Defeat of, 86.
Custis, John Parke, 363.

[453]

INDEX—(continued)

D

Dabney, 290, 377.
Dalzell, 153.
Dance, Esenath, 342; Ezekiel, 342; Lawson, 342; Sally, 342.
Daniel, John Warwick, Maj. C. S. A., U. S. Senator from Virginia, 87, 106, 116, 122, 128, 150-152, 190.
Daniel, Judge William, 63, 122; Sarah Ann Warwick, 122.
Daniel's Hill, 45.
Daniel's North Carolina Brigade.
Danville, 175.
Davies, Nicholas, 30, 31; Judith Randolph, 31.
Davis Family: Evan, Revolutionary Soldier under Pulaski, 296; Samuel, 293, 296; Jefferson, President C. S. A., 273, 296, 326. Samuel, William, Micajah, Evan, brothers from Shropshire, England, their descendants in Lynchburg, 290-296: Anne Elizabeth, 291; Ann Jennings, 291; Anne Maria, 293; Annis Lipscomb, 291; Benjamin, 292; Blanche V. T., 292; Catherine Gilbert, 292; Creed, 291; Deborah, 292; Elizabeth, 291; Evan, 291; Fred, 291; George Dixon, 291; Hannah, Anthony, 293; Henry, 293; W. Minor, 292; Isaac, 292; Jennie Lybrook, 291; John, 291; John, 293; John Thomas, 291; Louisa, 292; Lulie Brown, 291; Margaret Preston, 291; Mary Ann Wills, 291; Mary Elizabeth, 291; Mary Gosney, 291; Maude Mathews, 291; Micajah, 291; Micajah Preston, 291; Minor, 292; Nancy, 292; Nannie Hunter Eubank, 292; Rachel Dixon, 291; Robert Jordan, 249, 293; Samuel, 293; Samuel Lipscomb, 291; Sarah Anthony, 292; Susan, 292; Susannah Smithson, 290; Thomas, 291; Thomas Bowker, 291; Thomas Newton, 282, 292; Dr. Thomas Newton, 292; Virginia Margaret, 291; William Minor, 292; William, Sr., called Friend, 275, 291; William, Jr., 293; Zalinda Lynch, 293.
Davis, Henry, 217, 249, 272.
Davis, Henry, 293; Sarah Anthony, 292; Alexander, 293; Anne Carrington Cabell 293; Helen Wann, 293; Julia Gregory, 294; Linn Cabell, 294; Lucy, 294; Lucy Elizabeth, 294; Mary Lou, 293; Mary, 294; Nannie, 294; Nell Gregory, 294; Paul, 294; Robert, 293; Robert Jordan, 293; Sallie, 294; Sarah, 293; William Kinckle, 294.
Davis, Robert Jordan, and Family, 272.
Davis, William Kinckle, and Family, 272, 294.
Davis, Mrs. George D., 11; John, 275; Mrs. John A., 307.
Davis, Amy Walpole, 431.
Davenport, in Lynchburg and Richmond, 314.
Dearing, James Griffen, Brigadier-Gen. C. S. A., 9, 98, 99, 115.
Decoration Order St. Michael and St. George, 289.
DeJarnette, 143.
Delaware College, 214.
Delaware, Fort, 121.
DeNavarro, Capt.-Gen. of Cuba, Intendente of Louisiana and Florida, 350.
Dennis, Dr., 14.
Denny's Artillery Battalion, 98.
DeWitt, Clinton, 380.
Diamond Hill, 40.
Dickinson College, 284.
Digges, Judge J. Singleton, 409.
Dimmick and Co., 203.
Dinkle and Rumbough, 63.
Dirom, Robert, 300, 387.
Disfranchising Clause, 137.
Dismal Swamp Lottery, 63.
Distinguished Service Medal, 289.
District No. One, 135.
District of Columbia, 138.
Diuguid, 12; Sampson, 300; George A., 300; William D., 300.
Dole's Georgia Brigade, 101.
Donald, Benjamin M., 278.
Doniphan, Rev. Alexander, 192.
Dothan, 267.

[454]

INDEX—(continued)

Douglass, 256; Achilles, 7.
Douthat, Capt. C. S. A., saves Tye River Bridge from destruction, 87.
Driver, M. I. T., 281.
Drought of 1755, 57.
Dudley, Peter L., 48, 292, 404; Nancy Davis, 292; Andalusia Fouqueron, 292; Bettie Saunders, 292; Deborah Ann, 292; Fannie Jane, 292; Henry, 292; James, 292; James, 404; John W., 292; Louise, 292; Maria Rose, 275, 292; Mary Elizabeth, 292; Peter L., 292; Robert L., 293; Thomas Stevens, 292; William, 292, 404.
Dudley, Ellen Younger, 405; Eliza H., 204.
Duke, Judge R. T. W., 409; Edith Ridgeway Slaughter, 409; Eskridge, 409; Helen, 409; John S., 409; Mary, 409; R. T. W., Jr., 409.
Dundee, 284.
Dunnington, Henry, 48; Mallory, 300.
Duval, Mary C., 300.
Duval, Maj. William, 283; Mrs. Duval, 328.

E

Eagle's Eyrie, 30.
Eanes, Miss Mary, 203.
Early, Jubal Anderson, Lieut.-Gen. C. S. A., 110, 111, 112, his home in Lynchburg after the War, 113; his nieces, Miss Mollie and Miss Ruth, 113, 114; his censorship of the town of his adoption, and the people's affection for him, 114-116.
Early, Jeremiah, 308.
Early, Bishop John, 34, 38, 45, 48.
Easley, Mrs. John of Richmond 262.
Echols, Gen., 142; John F., 144, 142.
Edmunds, James Easley, 301, 335; Richard, 301.
Edmunds' Family, 301.
Edmunds, Abe, 227-229; Murrell, 223-225.
Edward IV, 268.
Edwards, William E., D.D., 44.
Eldridge, Maj., 24.
Elk River, 255.
Ellis, Charles, 279; Roberta Saunders, 279; Emma, 280; Rev. Josias, 279; Lucy, 280; Mary, 279; Nannie, 280; Pattie, 279; Thomas, 279; William, 279.
Ellis, Col. John T., 313; Mildred Powell Garland, 313.
Ellison, W. S., Architect, 11, 40.
Elliott, Wallace Murray, 257.
Elon, 278.
Emory and Henry College, 116.
Encyclopedia Brittannica, 277.
England, 138, 242, 243.
Eppes, Francis, 338.
Epileptic Colony, 184.
Epiphany Church, 41.
Episcopal Church during War Between States, 36, 39.
Episcopal High School at Alexandria, 260.
Episcopal Ministry, 243.
Eskridge, 409.
Essex County, 255, 262, 286.
Eubank, Newman, 217-221.
Europe, 117.
Evans Family of Amherst, 298.
Evans, T. Davis, 177. Evans, John B., 301.
Evington, 272; Road, 187.
Exchange Bank, 260.
Express, Lynchburg, 214.

F

Fabius, 283.
Fairfax, Monimia, 273.
Fairfield, 111.
Fair Grounds (Miller Park), 123, 163, 189.
Fairs at old Fair Grounds, 163.
Falling River, 285.
Farmer, 13.
Farmville, 98.
Father of His Country, 157.
Faulconer, 271.
Faulkner, John William, 302-303.
Faulkner, John William, Family of, 289-295.
Fauquier County, 140.
Fauquier, Governor of Virginia, 276.

[455]

INDEX—(continued)

Fauquier Springs, 110.
Featherstone Family, 305.
Federal Force, 24, 77, 101; Government, 28; Gunboats, 91; Typographical Corps, 78, 86, 88.
Federal Reserve Act, 136, 158, 160.
Ferguson, 126, 127.
Fern Moss, 122.
Ferry, Lynch's, 7, 15; Ferry House, 9.
Fifth Alabama Regiment, 100.
Fillmore Millard, President U. S. A., 141.
Fincastle, 249.
First Virginia Regiment, 117, 123.
Five Civilized Tribes, 158.
Five Forks, 96.
Fisher, F. J., Artist and Portrait Painter, 303, 304.
Fisher, Mrs., 54.
Fisher's Hill, 108, 111.
Fitz Lee, Gen. C. S. A., and the Veterans, 163.
Fleet, 304.
Fleming, 255, 304.
Fletcher, 38, 194, 195.
Flood, John Henson, Maj. C. S. A., 352.
Floyd Family 305, 306.
Folkes, 88; Folkes and Winston, 282.
Folliott, Edward, 277.
Ford, Judge Henry M., Family of, 306, 307.
Ford, Sallie, 271.
Ford, The, 8.
Forest Depot, 67, 117.
Forest Road, 87.
Forrest, Nathan Bedford, Gen. C. S. A., 111.
Forsberg, Col. C. S. A., 87, 128.
Fort Morgan, 100.
Forty-niner, 279.
Fowlkes, Mrs. Benjamin, 408.
Fox Hunting, Old Virginia Style, 54.
France, 27, 30.
Frankfort, Ky., 287.
Franklin County, 67, 100.
Franklin, Jacob Maj. C. S. A., 308.
Frederick, Md., 101.
Fredericksburg, 70, 75, 93, 111, 143, 257, 260.
Freedman's Bureau, 135.
Freeland, Archibald, 365; Gracie Cowan Macon, 365.
Freeman, Dr. Douglass; Editorial on "Ned Glass," 321.

G

Gaddess, J. B., 191.
Gaines' Mill, 97.
Galt, William, 181.
Gannaway, John E., Family of, 309, 310.
Garland, Samuel, Gen. C. S. A., 67, 70, 96, 97; Death of, 98, 118, 191, 343.
Garland's Battalion, 70.
Garland, Family of, 34, 111-113, 194, 214, 280, 310, 314.
Garlick, Samuel, 275, 278.
Garrett, Thomas M., Col. C. S. A., 121.
Gatewood, 255.
Gatling, 355.
Gazetteer, 29.
German, 122, 267.
Germanna, 106.
Germany, 117.
Georgetown Convent, 213.
George II, 10; George III, 31.
Georgia, 149, 256, 296.
Gettysburg, 104-106, 119.
Gibbon, Cardinal, 38.
Gibson, Eustace, 139.
Gildersleeve, Virginia, 259.
Giles County, 139.
Gilkyson, Dr., 270.
Gilliam, 261.
Gilliam, A. M., 34.
Gilliam, James Richard, Family of, 314, 317; James Richard, Sr., 314; Annie Slaughter Davenport, 314; Annie, 315; Jessie Belfield Johnson, 315; James Richard, 315; Frank Johnson, 315; Thos. West, 315.
Gilliam, Thomas West, 317; Elizabeth, 317; Elizabeth Bolling Jones, 317; Elizabeth Glover, 317; Elsie, 317; Epaphroditus, 317; Frances

INDEX—(continued)

Diuguid, 317; Dr. Glover, 317; Glover Davenport, 317.
Gish, 247.
Glade Spring, 127.
Glamorgan Pipe & Foundry Co., 202.
Glass, Carter, Senator U. S., 136, 176-180, 246.
Glass, Edward C., Superintendent Public Schools of Lynchburg, 318-322.
Glass, John, 405; Bettie Pollard, Family of, 405.
Glass, Robert H., 177.
Glebe, Family of, 262.
Glen Alton, 47.
Golden Wedding, by Cornelia Brown, 221.
Gooch Family, 47, 322, 434.
Goode's, 37.
Goodwillie, Mrs. Margaret Lucado, 359.
Goose Creek Valley, 28.
Gosney, Henry, 291; Mary, 291.
Gordon Family, 322, 323.
Gordon, John B., Gen. C. S. A., 101, 107.
Gordon's Division, 109.
Grace Episcopal Church, 246.
Graham, 12.

Graham, West Va., 267.
Grand Rapids, 279.
Grant, Gen. U. S., Commander-in-Chief U. S. A., 77, 84-88, 145-149.
Graveyard, Methodist, 13.
Gray, Rev. Arthur P., 273.
Gray, Lady Jane, 277.
Great Falls, Mont., 246.
Great Guinea Creek, 364.
Greek Temple, 22.
Greely, Horace Editor New York Tribune, 144, 145.
Green, Gen. Nathaniel, of Revolutionary War, 27.
Greencastle, Pa., 104.
Greeg, Gen. U. S. A., 132.
Gregory Family, 46, 216, 272, 323; Edward S., 41.
Gregory, Patrick, 323.
Griffin, Lewis Meriwether, 280.
Grove Hill, 249, 336.
Groveton, 110.
Ground Hog's Day, by Cornelia Brown, 222.
Guggenheimer Family, 323, 324.
Guildford Courthouse, Battle of, 338.
Gustine, Dr. Frederick William, 293.
Guthrie, Major John D., 309.
Gwathmey, Mrs. Mary Potter Langhorne, 357.

H

Hagerstown, 101, 104.
Haig, Field Marshall, Sir Douglass, 289.
Halifax County, 26, 143, 250.
Hall of Delegates, 136.
Hall, Rev. William Thomas and Family, 324-327.
Hall, Dr. Isaac, Judge John, Benjamin, 141.
Hall, John Handy, 326.
Halsey, Maj. Stephen and Family, 51, 82, 83, 87, 117, 123-128, 328.
Halsey, Don Peters, Maj. C. S. A., 116-123, 190; Judge Don, 330.
Halsey, Alexander Lemuel, Maj. C. S. A., 117, 124, 328, 329.
Hamilton's Crossing, 101.

Hamner, E. C., 88, and Family, 330, 331.
Hamner, Walker, and Family, 331.
Hampden-Sidney, 183.
Hampden-Sydney, 183.
Hampton, Wade, Gen. C. S. A., 85-86, 92.
Hancock, 331, 332.
Handy, Nathan B., Family of, 202, 325-327.
Handy and Davis, 325.
Hanover Academy, 98.
Harding, Capt. William, of Northumberland County, 191.
Hardwick, W. W., Capt. C. S. A., 91.
Hare, Jesse, 18.
Harper, 47.
Harper's Ferry, 29, 101, 109, 111, 302.

INDEX—(continued)

Harris, W. H. H., 13; Alice, 13.
Harrisburg,
Harrison, Col. Nathaniel, 322.
Horsley, John Dunscombe, Judge, 284; Family of, 336-338.
Hotchkiss, Lucy Kirkwood Otey, 380.
Hotel, Union, 62.
Houdon Statue of Washington, 155.
Houston, Gen. Sam, 186.
Howard, 259.
Howe's History of Virginia, 10.
Hoyle, Charles, 15.
Hubard, William J., Artist, 155.
Hubbard, Col. Edmund, Jr., 309.
Hutter, Christian S., Family of, 23, 28, 223, 339-342.
Hutter Family, 339-342.
Hutter, Edward, Grace Adams, 223, 279, 292.
Huger, Col. C. S. A., 47, 171; Julia Treble, 47, 171.
Hughes, Benjamin, 241; Annabel Winfree, 434.
Huguenot, 290.
Hunnicutt, James W., 139, 140.
Hunter, David, Gen. U. S. A., 78-93, 107, 111, 116, 121, 128, 157, 187, 188.
Hayes, Rutherford B., President U. S. A., 87, 88.
Hays, Harry T., Gen. C. S. A., 88.
Heald, 331, 381.

Henderson, A. T., 424.
Hertfordshire, 327.
Hesselius, 243.
Heth, Stockton, Gen. C. S. A., 103, 105.
Hickson, William, 47, 331.
High Bridge, 98, 99.
Higginbotham, Anderson, 267.
Hill, A. P., Gen. C. S. A., 97; Division, 97, 102-105, 119.
Hill, Miss Bettie, 349.
Hill, D. H., Gen. C. S. A., 83, 88, 92, 101.
Hite, Family, Massacred by Indians, 253-255.
Hoar, Senator U. S., 154.
Hobson, 279.
Hobson, 352.
Hoge, E. J., Col. C. S. A., 92.
Holcombe, 47, 208, Family of, 336.
Holcombe Hall, 117.
Hollins, Martin, 217.
Hollowell, Alexander, 295.
Home and Retreat, or Memorial Hospital, 182.
Home Guard of Lynchburg, 66, 69, 97.
Honeywood, 259.
Hooker, Gen. U. S. A., 102.
Hopewell, 203.
Hopkins, Bishop, of Vermont, 39.
Horseford Branch, 32.
Horseford Road, 16.

I

Imboden, Gen. C. S. A., 86.
Indian Agent, 158.
Indian Massacre, 254.
Indian Relics, 29.
Indian Trail, 28.
Indian Tribes, 9, 15, 25, 27, 28; Powhatan, 15; Manhattan, 15; Algonquin, 15; Monaghan 15; Wyandot, 28; Delaware, 28.
Institute, Virginia Military, 68.
International Harvester Co., 204.
Ireland, 15, 138, 141.
Irish, 15.

Iron Worker, 209.
Irvine Family, 271, 272.
Irvine, Samuel, 181.
Isbell, 342.
Italian, 249.
Ivey, J. Winston, 80, 202, 262, 266; Family of, 342-345.
Ivey, William Christopher, Family of, 263, 265, 266.
Ivy Creek, 87.
Iverson, Alfred, Gen. C. S. A., 119.
Iverson's North Carolina Brigade, 101, 105.

INDEX—(continued)

J

Jackson, Family of, 387-391.
Jackson, Thomas Jonathan, called "Stonewall," Gen. C. S. A., 65, 66, 85, 95, 96, 101-104, 111, 128.
Jackson, William, of Tazewell, 279.
James River, 59, 60, 64, 65, 82, 157, 183, 252; and Kanawha Canal, 59, 129.
Jameson, Waller, 273.
Jamestown, 255.
Japan, Mikado of, 340.
Jefferson County, 253, 254.
Jefferson, Thomas, President U. S., 14, 22, 23, 24, 29, 30, 36, 37, 99, 140, 151, 155-157; his opinion of Lynchburg, 193, 268, 283, 294.
Jefferson, Thomas, respected colored citizen of Lynchburg, 345.
Jeffersonton, 106.
Jellis, 40, 248, 278.
Jennings Co., 211.
Jennings, T. A., 345; Lena Price, 345; Cecil, 345; Mr. and Mrs. Clyde, 345; Dillard, 345; Ocie, 345.
Jennings, Tipton, 46; Mrs. Tipton, 46; Arthur, 273; Ruth, 46.
Jennings, Esten, 352; Kate, 352.
Jennings, Barbara, 294; Sarah, 290.
Johnson, Andrew, President U. S., 135, 145.
Johnson, Col., 255.

Johnson, Howard, 345; Rosa Bailey, 345; Ladd, 345.
Johnson, Edward, Gen. C. S. A., 100, 102, 104.
Johnson, G. R., 203.
Johnston, Charles, 87, 380.
Johnston, Dr. George Ben, 212.
Johnston, Pegram, 271.
Johnston, James, 143, 144.
Johnston, Joseph Eggleston, Gen. C. S. A., 87, 96, 111.
Johnston, R. D., Gen. C. S. A., 118, 121.
Johns, Capt. Thomas W., 292; Mary Elizabeth Dudley, 292.
Jones, Dr. Richard W., of Mississippi, 193.
Jones, Charles, Family of, 346.
Jones, William E., Gen. C. S. A.; Death at Piedmont, 78, 80, 127.
Jones and Watts, Great Hardware Business, 170.
Jordan Family, 249-253, 347-349.
Jordan, Cornelia Jane Matthews, 114, 136, 163, 213.
Joyner, 269.
Judith's Creek, 31.
Justice, Letter of Maj. Stephen P. Halsey, 52.
Justinian Code, 117.

K

Kanawha River, 59.
Kansas, 264.
Kean, Robert Garlick Hill, 349, 350; Adelaide deNavarro Prescott, 350; Family of, 349-351.
Kent, Duchess of, 154.
Kent, England, 251, 352.
Kent, W. L., 351.
Kentucky, 124.
Kernstown, 108, 111.
Kerr, B. Graves, 387; Lucy Jackson, 387.
Key, Francis Scott, 244.
Kinckle, William, Rector of St. Paul's, 39, 40, 191.
King, William, Jr., and Family, 435.
Kinnier Family, 351.

Kirkpatrick Thomas Jellis, Maj. C. S. A.; his Family, 351, 353.
Kirkpatrick, Benjamin F., 202; F. Sydnor, 207.
Kitchens of Old England, 53.
Kneller, Sir Godfrey, 243.
Knight of the Golden Horseshoe, 255.
Kosciusko, Count, Gen. Rev. War, 55.
Kresge Dollar Store, 126.
Krise, Philip A., 291; the beginning of his great fortune, 170.
Ku Klux Clan, 149.
Kyle, Dr. Bernard, 353, 354.
Kyle and Borland, 63.
Kyle, James R., his Family, 250, 355.
Labby, 57.

INDEX—(continued)

L

Ladies' Hospital, 99.
LaFayette, Gen. Rev. War, 27, 155-157.
Lambert, Mrs. Fauntleroy, 342.
Lambeth, L. W., 192.
Langhorne Family, 18, 26, 34, 62, 70, 71, 91, 128, 355, 357.
Langhorne, John DeVal, of Kentucky, 172, 357; Alice, 357; Cary, 357; George, 357; James, 357; John, 357; Lily, 357; Mary P., 357; Mary Potter, 357; Nannie, 357; Nannie Tayloe, 357.
Larkin Family, 299.
Last of the Mohicans, 26.
Latham, George Woodville, 214; Rebecca Owen, 215; Henry, 215.
Latham, Dr. H. Gray, Capt. C. S. A., 72, 214.
Latham's Battery, 71.
Lawton, Heth, 46.
Layman, Daniel, 282; Madge, 283.
Lee, Fitzhugh, Gen. C. S. A., 91, 92, 96, 121.
Lee, Frank T. and Family, 273.
Lee, John Lynch, 272, 358.
Lee, Gen. Robert Edward, Commander-in-Chief C. S. A., 75, 77, 81, 89, 96, 101, 105, 106, 111.
Lee, Family of John Lee, 357, 358.
Leetown, West Va., 253.
Leftwich Arms, 436.
Leftwich, Col. Augustine, 18, 47.
Leftwich Family, 435, 437.
Letcher, Governor of Virginia, 78; Mrs. Letcher, 78.
Letters of a Confederate Soldier, 72, 73, 74, 75.
Lexington, 65; Burnt by Hunter, 78, 88, 99.
Lewis, Mrs. John H., 356.
Lewis, Robert of Belvoir, 338; Charles, 338.
Lewis, 252; Guy Harold, 257.
Lewis, 13; Gen. Andrew, 24, 28; Anne M., 24; Elizabeth M., 25; John, 271; Col. Williams, 24; Col. William J., 24, 25.
Lewisburg, 85.
Leys, C. A. H., 283.
Liberia, 66.
Liberty, 78, 82, 116, 266.

Liggat, Alexander, 48.
Ligon, Kimbrough, 285, 337; Joseph, 285; Martha Massie, 285.
L. M. B., of Bedford, 27.
Lloyd, Dr. John Janney, Elli Hubard, 41, 63.
Locke, 31.
Locke's Mountain, 30.
Lockey, Edward, 276.
Lodge, Senator, 150.
Logwood, 218.
Lone Jack, 59, 169, 283.
Long, 258, 259, 335.
Longnar Hall, 267, 268.
Longstreet, Gen. C. S. A., 69, 118.
Louisa County, 9, 249.
Lovelace, 212.
Lovingston, 284, 337.
Lucado, 358, 359.
Lucullus, 22.
Luke, Elinor, 273.
Lumsden, Charles H., 387.
Lunenburg County, 10, 26.
Luray, 260.
Lyle, William Minor, 284, 335, 350.
Lynch, Anselm, 98; C. E., 62; Chas. H., 7, 98, 99; John, 7, 8, 9, 13, 16, 33; Mary Bowles, 9; Mary Ann, 98; Sarah, 9.
Lynchburg, 77-87, 96, 97, 111-116, 122-134, 150, 158, 189, 190, 257, 260.
Lynchburg, Business Life in 1830, as outlined by Mrs. Royal, 61, 62; as described by Lynchburg Virginian, 62-64; Mills, 62; Toll Bridge, 63. Business rebuilds after War, 168. City Council thanks deliverers of town from Hunter, 91-93. City mentioned, 9-16, 17-19, 28, 29, 34, 35, 211, 213, 257, 258, 260, 261, 267, 269, 270-275, 282, 285-287, 288.
Lynchburg College, First of the Name, 190.
Lynchburg College of Present Day, 193-199.
Lynchburg Fire Company, 32.
Lynchburg News, 49, 245, 246.
Lynchburg-Richmond Turnpike, 187.
Lynchburg Troops, 91, 92.
Lynchburg Virginian, Editor of, 165, 260.

INDEX—(continued)
M

Macon, 294 361, 365.
Macon, Nathaniel, of North Carolina, 192.
Macon, Col. Thomas Littleton, 295.
Magruder, B. H., 143.
MacCalmont, 266.
McGuire Unit, 262.
McCauseland, Gen. C. S. A., 82, 83, 84, 87, 92, 128.
McChesney, 252.
McClellan, Gen. U. S. A., 98, 101.
McCorkle, Samuel M., 182.
McCormick, Vance, 259.
McCown, Dr. Oswald Stuart, 297.
McDaniel, Albon, Mayor of Lynchburg, 34.
McDaniel, John Robin, Master Mason, 191, 380.
McDonald, Alexander, 114, 174, 176; Gen. James, 174, 214.
McDowell, Henry Clay, Federal Judge, 359, 360; Mrs. Louise Clay, 359.
McGregor, J. A., 183.
McGregor, Rob Roy, 322.
McGurk, Father, 38, 41, 325.
McKinley, William, Maj. U. S. A., President U. S., 87, 88.
McKinney, Samuel H., 360.
McLaughlin, Mrs. S. B., 355.
McLaughlin, Michael, 360; William, 360.
McMullen, Judge, 271.
McMurray, Rev. J. A., 250.
McNamara, 361.
McRae, D. K., Col. C. S. A., 119.
McRay, C. C., 142.
McWane and Lynchburg Foundry, 202-210.
Madison, James, President U. S., 151, 255.
Madison Courthouse, 106.
Madison College, 190.
Mahone, William, Gen. C. S. A., 153.
Maidstone, Kent, England, 251.
Maine, 138.
Mak, Alexander, Founder Dunkard Religion, 349.
Malvern Hill, 101, 110.
Manassas, 66; Rout of Union Soldiers, 69, 70, 72, 95, 96, 100, 102, 111, 118, 124, 152.
Manassas Gap, 106.
Manson, 335, 367.
Marie Antoinette, 30.
Marion, Francis, Gen. Rev. War, 54.
Market, City, 59; House, 62.
Marshall, John, Chief Justice of U. S. Supreme Court, 38, 151, 181, 259, 335.
Marshall Lodge, 34, 181; first known as Hiram Lodge, 181-182.
Martian, Nicholas, 338.
Martin, Gen. Joseph, 29.
Martinsburg, 104.
Martinsburg Road, 109.
Martindale, Capt. U. S. A., 89, 90.
Marye, John Lawrence, 137, 143; Lawrence S., Col. C. S. A., 174; Mrs. Marye's School, 165.
Mason, George, 151.
Masonic Fraternity, 34; Hall, 41.
Massie, 49, 337, 367, 368.
Massie's Mills, 49.
Mathews, Edwin, 48.
Matthews, George, 365.
Maury, Matthew Fontaine, 37.
Mayo, Anne, 364; Rebecca, 364; William, 364.
Meade, Gen. U. S. A., 106.
Meem, John Gaw, Col. C. S. A., married Aurelia Halsey, 328; Meem's Garden, 84.
Mecklenburg County, 268.
Memorial Hospital, 245, 246.
Menefee, E. E., 349.
Mercer, Gen. Hugh, 318; Anna Gordon, 318.
Merrimac and Monitor, 340.
Messick, Rev. Frank, 49.
Methodist Church, 44.
Methodist Graveyard, 10, 211.
Methodist Protestant Church, 192.
Michie, Thomas J., 142.
Michaux Family, 364.
Miles, Clara B., 283; John Maury, 349.
Miller, John M., Sr., 308; John M., Jr., 129, 273; Edgar P., 273.
Miller, Samuel, 80, 264, 265, 184-190; threatened by Hunter's soldiers, 188; Miller Agriculture and Biol-

[461]

LYNCHBURG AND ITS NEIGHBORS

INDEX—(continued)

ogy Department, Miller Manual School, 189; Lynchburg Orphanage for Girls, Miller Park, 41.
Miller, Thomas C., 370, 371.
Miller, William A., 190.
Miller, Tom, Dr. John and Family, 365.
Miller, Kip, 368; his wife and family, his dyed poodle dog, 368-370.
Milliken, 324; Cecile Guggenheimer, 324.
Mine Run, 106, 111.
Minnigerode, 322.
Minter, 218.
Minor, Samuel John, 260; Dr. John B., 287.
Mississippi, 149; Twelfth Regiment, 100.
Mississippi River, 18.
Mitchell, Daniel Trigg, 371, 372.
Moffet, 252.
Monocacy, 108, 111.
Montgomery, 100.
Moody, or Mode, 277.
Moon, Billy, 218.
Moore Family, 373, 374.
Moore, Maurice: his relation to the tobacco trade, 58.
Moore, Sallie Jones, Memorial to, 346, 347.
Moore, Thomas, 380.
Moore, Judge John, of Louisiana, 350.
Moorman Family, 374.
Moorman, Marcellus, Col. C. S. A., 69, 91; Micajah, 7.
Morgan, Mrs. Caroline, 48, 307; Gen. Daniel, Rev. War, 307.
Morgan, Dr. Robert Withers, 374; Georgia, 374.
Morgan County, 211; Morgantown, 211.
Morris, Charles Yancey, 183.
Morris, Dr., and Family, 375.
Morris, Robert, 244.

Morrison, Dr. James, 375.
Morton, Alpha Hamner, 331; Rosalie, 331.
Morton's Ford, 121.
Moseley, 30.
Mosby, Gen. C. S. A., 79, 80.
Mosby, Chas. L., 263.
Mountain Grove, Bath County, 255.
Mountains about Lynchburg, 192.
Mount Airy, near Newmarket, 252.
Mount Athos, 24, 25.
Mount Prospect, 363.
Mount Vernon, Life at, 54, 156, 243, 244.
Mount Zion Church, 28.
Mozart Association, 274.
Mundy, Lou, 272.
Munford, Thomas Taylor, Gen. C. S. A., 67, 86, 91, 95, 118, 128, 298, 299.
Munford, Col. George Wythe, 95; Etta Tayloe, 95; Clare, 95; William, 95; Emma Tayloe, 95; Thornton, 95; Glen, 95; George Tayloe, 95.
Murfee, James T., 192.
Murkland, T. R., 183; Sidney Smith, 183; Dr. W. N., 183.
Murrell, David G., 34.
Murrell, Harding, 423; Rebecca Montgomery Hepburn, 423; Dr. Edward, 328.
Murrell, T. E., 190, 305; Murrell, Fleming & Co., 305.
Murrell, 47, 95.
Murrell, 47, 95; William, 298; William M., 376.
Muskogee, 158.
Mutter, Mrs. Mary Smith, 366; describes Mount Prospect, and LaFayette's visit on his way to Yorktown; also the Macon Family in France in 1321, 365, 366.
My Castle in the Air, 215.
Myers, D. W., 26.

N

Narrative, A, of Virginia, 141.
Nashville, Tenn., 203.
National Academy of Design, 155.
Navy of Virginia, 266.
Neeson, James, 144.
Negotiable Instruments, by John W. Daniel, 153.

Negro Cooks, 53.
Negroes, 137, 138, 142.
Negro Songs and Other Old Ballads, 230-238.
Negro Question, 49-52.
Nelson County, 24, 49, 50, 75, 122, 204, 247, 271, 275, 284, 285, 287.

INDEX—(continued)

Nelson, Mrs. A. M., 300.
Nelson, Ellen Douglass, 225-227.
Nelson Family, of Bedford, 376, 377.
Nelson, Peter, 116.
Nelson, Thomas, 140.
Netherland, Frances, 364; Wade, 364.
New England, 57, 157.
New Glasgow, 194.
New Granada, 260.
New Jersey, 260.
New Kent County, 8, 9, 248, 290.
New London, 23, 24, 26, 29, 87, 127, 128.
New London Academy, 23, 29.
New London Military Station, 181.
Newport News, 217.
New Orleans, 18, 252.
Newtown, 79.
New York, 15, 138, 282.
New Yorkers, 137.
New York Times, 147.
New York Tribune, 144, 147.
Ney, Marshall, 28.
Nicholas Family, 248.
Nicholas, Col. Robert, 255.
Nichols, Francis T., Gen. C. S. A., 80; Post Commander at Lynchburg, later Governor of Louisiana, 85, 87, 92.

Non-Conformist, 244.
Norfolk, 145.
Norfolk County, England, 277.
Norfolk County, Va., 266.
Norfolk & Western Railroad, 215; its removal to Big Lick, 171.
North Carolina, 328.
North Carolina Regiments, 97, 98, 119, 121.
North River Canal, 99.
North Sea, 275.
North Western University Medical School, 288.
Norvell Family, 190, 269, 272, 273, 438.
Norwood High School for Boys, 287.
Norwood, Thomas, 246.
Nowlin, Mrs. Ben, 428; Chloe, 428; Louise, 428; Mary, 428.
Nowlin, Blanche, 267; Charles Price, 270; Ellis, 270; Geo. Preston, M.D., 270; Jesse Graham, 270; James Bowker, 270; John Burton, M.D., 270; J. C., Jr., 267; Matthew Bates, 270; Preston, 267; Virginia Susan, 270.
Nowlin, Green, Family, 377.
Nusbaum, Bertram, Mrs., 324.

O

Oaks, The, 268.
Oath of Allegiance, 80.
O'Bannon, 252, 253.
Ogden, 31.
Ohio, 138.
Ohio River, 10, 25, 59, 65.
Oklahoma, 14, 158.
Old Dominion, 135.
Old Hickory Powder Plant, 203.
Old Line Democrat, 136.
Old Line Whig, 136.
Old Lynchburg College, 97.
Old Master and Old Miss, 56.
Olmsted, 259; Mrs. Gertrude Howard, 259.
One Hundred Years Ago, by Elizabeth Hesselius Murray, 245.
Opequon, or Battle of Winchester, 111.
Orange Bridge, 65.
Orange County, 247, 255.
Orange Courthouse and Fredericksburg Turnpike, 102.

Order of St. Michael and St. George, 289.
Otey Family, 47, 69, 128, 273, 288, 378-381, 388.
Otey, Bishop, 38; George Gaston, Capt. C. S. A., 307; John M., 47.
Owen, Owen and Jane Hughes, Family of, 381.
Owen, Robert Latham, Col. C. S. A., Family of, 158, 381.
Owen, Robert Latham, Senator from Oklahoma, Author Federal Reserve Act, 136, 158, 159, 381, 382.
Owen, Dr. William, Family of, 381.
Owen, Dr. William Otway Family of, 381; Otway Owen, his great voice, 163.
Owen, Mrs. R. A., 14, 47; Owen, Mr. R. I., 202.
Ox Hill, 111.
Oxon Hill, 244, 245.
Oxford Furnace, 26.

[463]

INDEX—(continued)

P

Packard, Bessie DeWitt, 381.
Packet Boat, 59.
Page, Ambrose, 382.
Page's Battery, 100.
Page County, 213, 260.
Page, Edward Trent, 382; Helen, 382.
Palmer, Senator, 249.
Pamunkey River, 91.
Pannill, 404.
Pankey, Virginia Bell, 280.
Paris, 27, 155.
Park, Riverside, 14.
Parratt, Anne, 364.
Patteson, Dr. J. H., Family, 12, 270.
Patteson, Dr. David, 278.
Patton, 318.
Patroon, 266.
Paxton, William, 253.
Paxton, Dr. James D., 222.
Payne, Family of, 383-392; Payne, 385-388; John Meem, 385.
Peacock, Voyage to Japan, 340.
Peak, Malcolm, 392.
Peaks of Otter, 37, 60, 78, 83, 85, 116.
Pearis, 253; daughter of Pearis in Hite Massacre, 254.
Peck, Mrs. Elizabeth King, 435.
Pegram, James W., 34.
Pell, 266.
Pendleton, 249, 377; Jacob D., 392.
Pendleton, Maj. C. S. A., 103, 104.
Pendleton, Dr. William Gibson, 290.
Peninsula, 100, 118.
Pennsylvania, 124, 137, 265.
Pennsylvania, Western, 141.
Pennsylvania, University of, 214.
Pensacola, Fla., 100, 254.
Percy, Maj. Alfred Boyd, and Family, 392.
Perkins, Benjamin, 184.

Perrow, 393-397.
Perry, John G., 176.
Pescud, Elizabeth, 278.
Peters, 397, 398.
Peters, William E., Col. C. S. A., and Family, 82, 83, 87, 118, 124, 127.
Petersburg, 98, 141, 143, 145.
Pettigrew, Capt. 218.
Pettyjohn, John P., 45.
Pettyjohn, Walker, Family of, 364, 398, 399.
Peyton, Green, Maj. C. S. A., 110.
Phelps, Capt. R. R., 34; C. and D. B., 62; William, 392.
Philadelphia, 122, 257.
Pickett, 27.
Pickett's Division, 75.
Piedmont, 78, 128.
Piedmont Club, 162.
Piedmont Stage Coach, 63.
Pierce, Cornelius, 292.
Pierpont, Governor of Virginia, 137.
Pikesville, Md., 260.
Pleasants, John Hampden, 174.
Plecker, A. H., Confederate Gunner, Lynchburg Photographer, 87.
Plymouth, Battle of, 98.
Pocahontas, 25.
Poindexter, 416.
Poindexter, 271.
Pollard, Richard, and Family, 404.
Pope, Gen. U. S. A., 101.
Poplar Forest, Home of Jefferson, 14, 22-24, 36, 37, 340.
Port Republic, 111.
Possum Creek, 220.
Potomac River, 104, 106, 109, 242.
Powell, 60, 269.
Powhatan Camp-fires, 53, 116.
Powhatan County, 263.

Q

Quakers, 8, 36, 249, 293.
Quakers in Virginia, 258.
Quaker Meeting House, 9, 84, 87, 150.

Quaker Friends, Our, of Ye Olden Time, by J. P. Bell, 258.
Queen Victoria of England, 76, 154.

R

Raccoon's Ford, 121.
Radford Rangers, 117, 123.
Radford, Richard Carlton Walker, Col. C. S. A., and Family, 380, 400.

Radford, Winston, Col. C. S. A., 67, 68, 69, 118, 273.
Radford, Va., 203.
Radicals, 137.

[464]

INDEX—(continued)

Radnall Church, Havelstone, England, 262.
Ragged Mountains, 184.
Railroad, Lynchburg and Danville, 286.
Ramseur, Gen. C. S. A., 81; his division, 85, 101, 107, 109.
Ramseur's North Carolina Division, 101.
Ramsgate, 154.
Randolph, 151; John, of Roanoke, 192.
Randolph-Macon, 190; Woman's College, 192.
Rapidan, 106.
Rappahannock, Battle of, 111.
Rappahannock River, 106, 251.
Ravanel, Alfred, 171.
Rawson, 63.
Read, Theodore, Gen. U. S. A., 97, 98.
Reade, Col., 276.
Read and Shaftner, 170.
Reconstruction, 213; Laws, 286; Southern States during, 149.
Reconstruction Committee of House, 145, 146, 147.
Restoration of Virginia to the Union, written by Alexander Hugh Holmes Stuart, 148, 149.
Revolution, 253.
Revolutionary War, 57, 68, 254.
Reynolds, Mrs. R. G., 246.
Richmond, 59, 60, 64, 65, 95, 100, 122, 126, 129, 144, 156, 246, 257-259.
Richmond Capital, 154.
Richmond Times, 142; Whig, 142, 174; Dispatch, 27, 137, 141, 257.

Risque, Maj. James, 339.
Rives, 44, 249; Miss Peggy, 130.
Roane, 12.
Roanoke, 247, 294.
Roanoke College, 116, 117.
Roanoke Times, 246; World, 246.
Roberts, 205, 206.
Robertson, Judge John, 25; Bolling, 25; Powhatan, 25.
Robertson's Mill, 218.
Robertson, Wyndham, 144.
Rockbridge, 29, 267.
Rockenbach, Samuel Dickerson, Gen. U. S. A., 401.
Rockfish Gap, 83.
Rocky Mount Races, 63.
Rodes, David, Gen. Virginia Militia, 99; Family, 99, 247.
Rodes, Robert Emmet, Maj.-Gen. C. S. A., 81, 99-106, 107-111.
Rodes' Division, 102, 109. Rodes own Alabama Brigade, 101, 109.
Rodes, Virginius, Col. C. S. A., 110.
Roman Law, 117.
Rose, 272.
Rose Hill, 37.
Ross, Ironworks, 218.
Rosser, Thomas, 271; Eliza, 271.
Rothsay, 294.
Royal, Mrs. Anne, 60, 64, 175.
Rucker, 190, 270.
Ruffin, Frank G., 143, 144.
Rumbough, 270.
Russell County, 176.
Rutherford, 254.
Rutledge, Arthur Middleton, 280.
Ryan, Thomas Fortune, 204.
Ryland Family, 403.

S

St. Anne's Parish, 36.
St. John's Church, 243.
St. Leonard's Church, Shoreditch, County Middlesex, England, 342.
St. Paul's Church, 12, 40, 41, 115, 284.
St. Paul's Church Bell, 194.
St. Peter's Parish Register, 363.
St. Clair, Capt. C. S. A., 82.
San Antonio, 280.
San Juan Army, General Hospital, 288.
Sale, Mrs. Bettie, 404.

Salem, 28, 63.
Salem Church, 111.
Salem Turnpike, 9, 84, 150, 185.
Salop, County, England, 267.
Sandusky, 28, 87; Hunter's Headquarters, 87, 380.
Sandy Hook, 126, 127, 220.
Sandy River, 125.
Sarah Jane, Parody on Pinafore, 163.
Sartoris, Professor, 423.
Saturday Evening Post, 150, 152.
Saunders, Col. David, War of 1812,

INDEX—(continued)

Family of, 279-281, 437. Dr. James Turner and Family, 44, 48, 404; William Leftwich and Family, 279, 280.
Saunders, Evelyn, 272; Maj. Fleming, C. S. A., 272; Capt. Robert, C. S. A., 88.
Saxon, 268.
Scalawag, 140.
Schehlmann, Professor Louis, 166, 167.
Schewel, 405.
Schofield, Gen. U. S. A., 147.
Schoolfield, 12; Benjamin, 63.
Scotch, 204.
Scotch-Irish, 141.
Scotch-Presbyterian Missionary, 183.
Scotch Merchants, 29.
Scotland, 33, 138, 253, 260.
Scott, Agnes College, 250.
Scott, Davis Patteson, M.D., 406-407.
Scott, Samuel, 295; Mary Boyd, 294.
Scott, Charles Alexander, 356.
Scott, Maj. Samuel, 322, 338.
Scott, James Alexander, 380; Norvell Otey, 380; Family of, 380.
Scruggs, Maj. Frank, 223; Virginia Withers, 223; Lightfoot, 223.
Scruggs, Sally, 83.
Scruggs, Benjamin, 48.
Scuffletown, 8, 16.
Seay, Family, 46; Miss Ellie, 46.
Secession, 98, 110, 113, 117, 138, 140.
Second Bristoe, 111.
Second Manassas, 97, 110.
Second Virginia Regiment of Cavalry, 117, 123, 124. Unveiling of Monument to Second Virginia Cavalry, 69, 124, 128.
Seddon, James A., Secretary of War, C. S. A., 124.
Seneca District in Campbell County, 249.
Seven Pines, 97, 100, 118-120, 262.
Senex, 142.
Shaeffer, 379.
Shakespeare, 186.
Shaner, 407.
Sharpsburg, 97, 101, 111, 118, 119.
Sheep, Dr., U. S. A., 310.
Sheffey, Judge Hugh, 142.
Shelton, Ralph, 291; Mary Pollard, 291.

Shenandoah Valley, 88; Campaign in, 108, 121.
Shenandoah River, 108.
Shepherdstown, 89, 111.
Sheridan, Gen. U. S. A., 86-93, 109, 112, 121.
Shoemaker's Battery, 91.
Shrewsbury, England, 267.
Shropshire, England, 267.
Shumate, 407.
Shuget, Dr., 27.
Sickles, Gen. U. S. A., 102.
Sigel, Gen. U. S. A., 79.
Silverthorn, 192, 211.
Simpson, Samuel M., 69.
Skillern, 252.
Slatter, John F., 408, and Family, 408.
Slaughter, John Flavel, 144, 190; Slaughter Family, 409; Mrs. E. L., 416.
Sloop Scorpion, 266.
Smiley, Andrew, 13.
Smith, Eleanor, 242; Col. Walter, 242.
Smith, Gen. Francis, Superintendent Virginia Military Institute, Address to Congress, 168, 169.
Smith, Capt. John, 249.
Smith, Franklin Genet, Rector St. Paul's Church, second husband of Sarah Davis; William Ward Smith her first husband, 38, 63.
Smith, Gen. Holmes, C. S. A., 128, 410; Woodville, Mayor Lynchburg, 410.
Smith, Judge Roy, of Roanoke, 335.
Smith, E. Kirby, Gen. C. S. A., 67.
Smith, Dr. William Waugh, 193, 194.
Smith, John Augustine, President of William and Mary College, 366.
Smithfield, 124.
Sneed, 13.
Soap-stone Quarry, 87.
Soldier of Confederate Army, 125; his endurance, courage and gayety, 125; the horses, 125.
Soldier of the Revolution, 263.
Solitude, 284.
Sommerville Ford, 111.
Song to Celia, 212.
Song to Lucasta, 212.
Southall, 287.
South Boston, 250.

[466]

INDEX—(continued)

South Carolina, 253.
Southern Literary Messenger, 212, 214.
Southern Planter, 57.
South Mountain, or Boonsboro Gap, Battle of, 101.
South River Meeting, 36.
Southside Railroad, 84.
Southwest, 82.
Spanish-American War, 288.
Spearman, Job, 263; Mary, 263.
Speed, John, 46.
Spence, David E., 190.
Spencer, 410; Dr. Frank, Nannie Bailey and Family, 410.
Spout Spring, 217.
Spring Hill Cemetery, 123, 387.
Spring Warehouse, 16.
Spotswood, Governor, 157.
Spotsylvania, 111, 294.
Spotsylvania County, 286.
Spracher, Mrs. James, 267.
Stabler, Robinson, 48, 411.
Stanford, 298.
Stanley, Rev. Dr., 191.
Starke, of Hanover, 297.
Statham, 411.
State Convention, 117.
State's Rights, 66, 93.
State Library, 214.
Staunton, 78, 80, 82, 255, 282.
Stearns, Franklin, 145, 146.
Steele, 192.
Stein, Albert, 33, 34.
Steinbergen, 252.
Stephens City, 266.
Steptoe Family, 411-413.
Sternberg General Hospital, 288.
Stevenson's Depot, 108, 109.
Stevens, Sidney C., 282.
Stokes, Richard Carter, and Family, 413.

Stone Bridge, 69.
Stone Printing and Manufacturing Co., 258.
Stonewall Brigade, 84, 85; when they reached Lynchburg, 85, 116, 153.
Stonewall Creek, 10.
Stowe, Harriet Beecher, 57.
Stratton, 7, 414.
Strode, Judge Aubrey, Family of, 414.
Strother, 291, 414.
Stuart Family, Alexander, 141; Benjamin, 141; Thomas, 141.
James Elwell Brown, or J. E. B. Stuart, Gen. C. S. A., 69, 96, 104, 141, 260.
Stuart, Alexander Hugh Holmes, Member of Cabinet under President Fillmore, leader in movement of Restoration of Virginia to the Union after termination of War Between the States, 141-149.
Suhling Family, 173; Mrs. Gerhardt Suhling, 432; Johannes, 414-416.
Sullivan, 12.
Sumner, Charles, U. S. Senator, 145.
Sumpter, Gen. Rev. War, 54.
Sunnyside, Cumberland County, 265.
Superior Court, 29.
Surrender at Appomattox, 135; described by William W. Blackford, Col. C. S. A., 260.
Suter, John D., 345.
Sutherlin, W. T., 144.
Swann, Columbia, 279; Mrs. Sallie Woodson Mayo, 364.
Sweeny, Joe, 218-220.
Sweetbriar College, 194.
Sweet Springs, 25.
Switzerland, 277.
Sycamore View, 266.
Sydnor, Mrs. C. A., 364.

T

Tait's Mill, 13.
Tan Yard Alley, later Twelfth Street, 191.
Tasker, 242.
Tate, Garland, 62.
Tavern, Indian Queen, 15, 22.
Tayloe, 95, 357.
Taylor, 48, 310.

Taylor, 255; Chancellor Creed, 11.
Taylor, John J., and Family, 416.
Taylor, Mrs. Sallie, of Madison, 345.
Tennessee, 124, 125, 256; Bishop of, 38.
Terrell, Dr. John Jay, and Family, 187, 188, 190, 416.
Terry's Academy, 297.

INDEX—(continued)

Terry, Abner W. C., 174; Stockton, 114.
Terry, 346.
Terry, Mrs. T. M., 192.
Terry, Alfred H., Gen. U. S. A., Commandant District No. 1, 136, 213.
Theatre, Paramount, 17.
The Coaling Ground, 218.
Theological Seminary at Alexandria, 244.
Thomas, Rev. Robert B., 191.
Thompson, Dr. William, of Amherst, 427.
Thompson, Percy Moran, 251.
Thompson, Col. William, 255; Martha, 255.
Thornhill, 332, 417.
Thornton's Gap, 106.
Thurman, 12, 34, 221; Alexander, 88; Allan G., U. S. Senator, 417; George, 417.
Tilden, John Bell, and Family, 418; Capt. Richard, 418.
Tilney, England, 277.
Tinsley, Bugler of Stonewall's Brigade, 84, 85, 116.
Tobacco Trade in Richmond, 57; in Lynchburg, 57-59.
Todd, 25, 364.
Toler, Richard H., 174.
Tompkins, Mrs., 63.
Tories, 243.
Towns, Wm. T., 48.
Tower of London, 30.
Townley House, 154.
Transylvania University, 287.
Traveller, 260.
Tragic Era, The, 139.

Treble, Julia, 47.
Trent, Col. John, 25.
Trenton, 214.
Trevillian's, 85, 91, 128.
Trigg, 252.
Trimble, Gen. C. S. A., 103, 105.
Troubetskoy, Princess, 44.
Trout, Nicholas K., 142.
Truehart, Margaret, 281.
Tuckahoe, 23, 31.
Tucker, Rt. Rev. Beverley Randolph, 419; Maria Washington, 419.
Tucker, George, M. C., Rosalie, 420.
Tudor, Mary, 277.
Tunstall, Whitmell Pugh, 420-422; Mary Liggatt, descendant of John Lynch, and Family, 420-422. Alexander Augustus, 421; Alexander Liggatt, 421; Benjamin Gray, 421; Corinne, 420; Donaghe, 420; Florence Massie, 420; Ida Gray, 421; John Lynch, 422; Lucy Dabney, 421; Lorraine Davis, 422; Mary Franklin Duncan, 421; Maude M. Davis, 422; Nannie Whitmell, 421; Sue Reid, 421; W. Massie, 420, 422.
Turner Family, 422-425. Turner and Kerr, 63.
Tuscaloosa, Ala., 99, 100.
Twenty-first Virginia Cavalry, 127.
Twenty-fourth Virginia Cavalry, 110.
Tye River, 50, 122, 130.
Tyler, President U. S., 255, 260.
Tyler, Dr. Lyon Gardiner, 278.
Tyree, 261; Samuel, 262; Marion Fontaine, 262.
Tyreanna, 261.
Tyro, 49.

U

Underwood, James C., 140, 141.
Underwood Constitution, 142, 146.
Underwood Convention, 137-149.
Union and Confederate Armies compared, 72.
Union Delegates, 117.
Union Hill, 430.
Union Men, 137.
Union Mills, 100.

Uniontown, Ala., 96.
United States Armory at New London, 29.
United States Marine Hospital, New York, 288.
United States Military Academy, West Point, 67.
University of Heidelberg, 117.
University of Virginia, 97, 117, 129, 189, 246, 284, 287, 297.
Untermeyer, Samuel, 159, 160, 161.

INDEX—(continued)

V

Valentine House, 256.
Valentine, 425.
Vandergrift, Miss Jennie, 163.
Van Dorn's Division, 100.
Van Tuyl, 266.
Vaughan, 387.
Vawter, Bransford, Lynchburg's First Poet, 211; John, 211.
Venner, Martha C., 283.
Vermont, 138.
Veracious Chronicler, 152.
Victor, John, and Family, 33-35, 419; Victor and Ambler, 247; School of Miss Maria and Mrs. Victor, 63.
Virginia, 44, 46, 123, 137-139, 148, 150.
Virginia Army, 100.
Virginia Assembly, 7, 8, 272, 286.
Virginia-Carolina Chemical Co., 245.
Virginia Cavalier, A, 152.
Virginia Episcopal School, 199; its founder, Rt. Rev. Robert Carter Jett, his stand on matters of bridge, 200-201.
Virginia Food, 53.
Virginia Fox Hunting, 54.
Virginia Furniture, 53.
Virginia General Assembly, 124, 157.
Virginia Gentry, 54.
Virginia, Greatest Benefactor of, 188.
Virginia Iron, Coal and Coke Co., 202.
Virginia Historical Collection, 276.
Virginia Historical Society, 149.
Virginia, Life in, 52-56.
Virginia Military Cadets, 92.
Virginia Military Institute, 287.
Virginia Military Alumni News, 289.
Virginia Senate, 153.
Virginia and Tennessee Railroad, 77.
Virginian, The Lynchburg, 174, 214, 404, 439.
Virginian Planters, The, 151.
Virginia Quarterly Review, 227.
Virginia State Troops, 67.
Virginia, Vandalism in, 79, 89.
Virginia Women and Their Servants, 54.
Virginia Valley Campaign, 108, 121.
Vogbaum, Fannie, 272.
Voorheis, 426.

W

Wade, James, 33.
Waddill, A. A., 175, 176.
Waddell, Mrs. C. C., 305.
Wagner, Richard, 358.
Wailes, 341.
Walker, James A., Gen. C. S. A., 137.
Walker, Dr., 318.
Walker, Gilbert C., Governor of Virginia, 145.
Walker, Jonas, 145.
Walker, John Stuart, C. S. A., 379; David, 379; John Stuart, Jr., 379; Loulie, 379.
Walker, Jas. A., Gen. C. S. A., 137.
Wallace, Gen. Lew, U. S. A., 108.
Waller Family, 43, 278, 427, 428.
Walpole, Clare Horace, 428.
Walsh, Walter Logan, 429.
Walsh, Misses, 428.
Walton, 263.
Warehouses, Blackwater, 16; Friends, 17; Lynch's, 16; Madison, 16; Martin's, 17; Liberty, 16; Pace's, 59; Planters, 17; Renwicks, 64.
War of Rebellion Records, compiled by U. S. Government, 118.
War Between the States, 50, 57, 66, 77, 95-97, 99, 123, 245-247, 256, 257, 264, 265, 308.
War, French and Indian, 25, 26.
War, Mexican, 24, 46, 110.
War Department, 203.
Ward, Anselm Lynch, and Family, 379; Maj. John, 308.
Ward's Road, 127.
Ward, Leonidas Pope, 310.
Warm Springs, 256.
Warfield, 125.
Warren, 255, 279.
Warrenton Springs, 106.
Warrior's Guard, 100.
Warwick, 12, 47, 48, 122, 255, 439.
Warwick, Countess of, 247.

[469]

INDEX—(continued)

Warwickton, 256.
Washington Artillery of New Orleans, 98.
Washington, George 54, 55, 59, 65, 68. Houdon's Statue of Washington Stolen by Hunter, 78, 155-157, 243. Funeral Honors at New London, 181, 186. Martha Washington, 54, 55, 269.
Washington City, 69, 108, 125, 144, 145, 158, 244, 245.
Washington and Lee University, 78, 153, 158, 246.
Washington Parker's Ford, 111.
Water Committee, 33.
Waterman, Mrs. Jerome, 324.
Watkins, George Putnam, 354, 430.
Watts' Family, 88, 128, 336, 354, 430.
Watts, Col. Edward, 336; Anne Selden, 336; Breckenridge 336; Elizabeth, 336.
Waynesborough, Battle of, 121, 122.
Wellford, 272, 403.
Wells, Governor of Virginia, 146.
Wesley, John, 44.
West, 271.
West Family, 314; West's Crossing, 271.
Westover, 266, 390.
West Point, U. S. Military Academy, 76, 98, 99, 110, 244.
West Street, later called Fifth Street, 191.
West Virginia, 59, 85, 124.
Wharton, Gabriel, Gen. U. S. A., 118, 121.
White, Bishop Howson,
White, Margaret, 278.
White, Dr. Peter, 297.
White Rock Hill, 15.
Whitehead Family, 272; Thomas, Capt. C. S. A., Member of Congress, 176, 177.
Whitehead and Murrell, 176.
White Oak Swamp, 101.
Whitman, Walt, Notes on Virginia after the War, 133.
Whittaker, 351.
Wiermann, Charles B., 335.
Wilderness, Battle of, 107, 111, 152, 153.
Wilkins, G. H., and Family, 248.
Wilkinson, 242, 243.
William and Mary College, 254, 275, 278.
William and Mary Quarterly, 278.
Williams, James O., 190.
Williams, Jennie, 267.
Williams, Dr. John Bell, Maj. World War, 281, 295; Judge Samuel Walker, Attorney-General Va., 281, 295; Martin Hansford, 281; Rebecca, 281, 295.
Williams, Mrs. Indiana Fletcher, Founder of Sweetbriar, 194, 195.
Williams, John S., Gen. C. S. A., 124, 127.
Williams, James T., 46.
Williamsburg, Battle of, 97, 110, 139.
Williamson, Dr. Jacob, 252.
Williamsport, 104, 106.
Williams, Peter, Family of, 430, 431.
Wills, Waller G., Family of, 273, 275.
Wills, John, 11.
Wilson, Woodrow, President, 158.
Wilson Family, 47, 365, 432; Misses Lucy, Margaret and Kate, 47, 165.
Wilson, Dr. Samuel, 280, 314.
Winchester, 108, 109, 111, 121, 266, 280, 284.
Winfree, Family of, 192, 265, 399, 433, 434.
Wingfield, Samuel Griffin, and Family, 434, 435.
Wingfield, Dr. T. H., Mary Elizabeth Leftwich, 435.
Winston, Joseph Pendleton, of Richmond, Lelia Saunders, and Family, 279.
Winston, Judge Edmund, 7, 8, 38.
Witt, Geo. D., 64.
Woodruff, Virginia Hortense, 99.
Woodson, 364.
Woodward, 270, 366.
Wooling, Capt. Richard, 438.
Wray, 438.
Wright, 203.
Wright, 281.
Wyatt, 438, 439; Family, 438, 439.
Wiatt, Samuel, 34.
Wythe County, 139.
Wythe, George, 140, 151.
Wytheville, 125, 126, 204, 247, 281.
Wysor, W. W., Editor Lynchburg Virginian, 114, 439.

INDEX—(continued)
Y

Yancey, Maj. War of 1812, 24, 29, 30, 269; Elizabeth Macon, 365; Family of, 440-445. William Tudor, 24, 281; Lucy Elizabeth Davis, 40, 281. Robert D., 281, 445-447.
Yoder, Jacob E., 439, 440.

Yorkshire, 275.
Yorktown, 110, 251, 276, 333, 338, 341, 418.
York County, 251.
Younger, Mrs. Bransford, 261.
Yuille, 267.

www.ingramcontent.com/pod-product-compliance
Lightning Source LLC
Chambersburg PA
CBHW060347080526
44583CB00012B/210